BEYOND THE BASICS

A TEXT FOR ADVANCED LEGAL WRITING

Second Edition

By

Mary Barnard Ray
University of Wisconsin

Barbara J. Cox
Professor of Law
California Western School of Law

AMERICAN CASEBOOK SERIES®

THOMSON
WEST

Mat # 16944675

American Casebook Series and West Group are trademarks registered in the U.S. Patent and Trademark Office.

ISBN 0–314–24263–5

TEXT IS PRINTED ON 10% POST CONSUMER RECYCLED PAPER

Mary Barnard Ray dedicates this work
to Kathryn, Mark, and Dennis.

Barbara J. Cox dedicates this work
to her family in Lexington, Madison, and San Diego.

*

Preface to the Second Edition

In the decade since the first edition of this book, much has changed. In 1991, we were still teaching students how to cope with Dictaphones, and faxes were not yet demanding instant turnarounds on documents. Plain English was a point of debate, and interrogatories were unlimited. In law schools, advanced writing courses, other than the occasional drafting course, were virtually unknown. Much in the legal writing world has changed, and much of it for the better. And we have also changed, with our professional lives separating us by half a continent and our professional lives taking us both in new, challenging directions.

Yet much has also remained the same. We still teach our students the importance of proofreading, no matter how advanced the computer checkers become. We are still eliminating stubborn bits of legalese, and urging writers to think about their meaning and their readers. Most important, the craft and art of great legal writing still holds challenges for law students. Since we are still friends, still teaching, and still learning more about writing and teaching writing, we offer this new edition to you.

MARY BARNARD RAY
BARBARA J. COX

*

Preface to the First Edition

This book is our attempt to convey to the students of legal writing beyond our classrooms a realization of the breadth, depth, and sheer quantity of knowledge about writing that is available for the learning. We want to help students see the quality that is possible, to invite them to set their horizons beyond adequacy to excellence. In this process, we hope to help the profession as a whole as it moves beyond the status quo to a higher quality of writing.

We hope to expand students' horizons by extending their experience to more forms of legal writing than the office memorandum and appellate brief. These new forms range from jury instructions to letters of retainer. We also hope to expand their view to include a knowledge of writing gleaned from other fields, such as communication science and theory of persuasion. Finally, we hope to expand their repertoire of solutions for more common legal writing situations, such as structuring a memo along any of several large-scale organizational plans.

Yet, with all these dreams, we have tried to keep our feet firmly on the ground by recognizing the real time limitations legal writing instructors face. For that reason, the book includes enough topics to allow the teacher to choose which documents and writing techniques to emphasize, to omit others, and still to have enough material to fill a course. There are enough examples, exercises, and assignments to allow the teacher to assign different ones in different semesters. There are also enough discussable points to provide for lively classes. We want to enable teachers to introduce an advanced legal writing course without facing an impossible workload in the first years or burnout in later years.

There is no way to avoid the fact that both writing and teaching writing are work, but they need not be a grinding chore. We hope that, as you use this book, you as a student or teacher will allow yourself to experiment. Although this approach means you will make more mistakes, it also means you will learn more. We hope it means you can laugh more as well. In keeping with this goal, we hope you develop with your fellow students and teachers a sense of mutual effort, learning, and exploration. Share with each other how a text can be improved, but focus more on the improvement than the initial flaws. Focus on future possibilities more than past failures. Humor, hard work, and hopefulness are the elements of the process upon which you can most rely.

For over a decade, we have enjoyed teaching the course on which this book is based. We hope this book provides you with not just the content of that course, but also some of its intellectual excitement and sense of perennial discovery.

*

Acknowledgements

We have to acknowledge the mutual determination that led us to persist in writing the second edition of this book. When one person's energy lagged, the other was there cajoling, encouraging, prodding, and plodding. For that alternating drive and support, we thank each other.

Thanks also to the many people who provided personal support.

Mary Barnard Ray especially thanks:

her husband and family for managing so well without her when she chained herself (figuratively) to the computer to finish the book;

the 300 or so students who have braved her Advanced Legal Writing course, and the scores of those alums who have shared their subsequent experiences, helping enrich and improve the course;

Barbara Cox who has, one pithy observation at a time, taught her more about working with people than anyone else she has ever known; and

Nori Cross, Mary Ann Polewski, Annie Walljasper, and Barbara Cox for teaching the course with her over the years.

Barbara Cox especially thanks:

Peg Habetler, for sustaining her spirit;

all her friends and family, whose help and support made it possible for her to continue her commitment to this project.

Mary Barnard Ray for teaching her everything she knows about advanced legal writing;

all the legal writing professors at Wisconsin and California Western who have inspired her to renew her commitment to the legal writing field; and

all her Civil Procedure students who have worked through countless "dog-bite" cases to help her refine the materials in chapters 11, 12, and 13 of this edition.

Thanks for technical support go to:

Meredith Madrigal, Mary Ellen Norvell, Donna Vella, and Edna Williamson for administrative support;

Karen Miller and Sandra Moreau for patiently answering countless questions about word processing;

California Western School of Law, for sabbatical release time for Barbara to work on this edition;

the aides and research assistants who have helped over the years with updating the research, photocopying, running to libraries, and doing footnote checks and countless necessary tasks;

the librarians at California Western and Wisconsin who were incredibly helpful and kept their good humor despite many difficult requests and long overdue books, including Bill Bookheim, Barbara Glennan, Mary Jo Koranda, Lilly Li, Amy Moberly, Cheryl O'Connor, Bonnie Shucha, Linda Weathers, and Bobbi Ann Weaver;

Professor Philip Manns for providing substantive review, and Professor Jacquelyn Slotkin for letting us use her legal writing problems; and

Roxanne Birkel, Heidi Hellekson, and the others at West Group who helped us prepare this edition for publication.

Summary of Contents

*

Table of Contents

*

BEYOND THE BASICS

A TEXT FOR ADVANCED
LEGAL WRITING

Second Edition

*

Chapter 1

INTRODUCTION

Like childhood, learning about writing is a process with a beginning, but no clear ending. Or perhaps writing is more like parenthood. You begin the process with feverish enthusiasm, endure through the burgeoning pendency of anticipation, labor long and hard, and finally gaze with wonder at the product. Yet, at that moment, you realize your work has just begun. As you work through this text, we know you will labor hard and advance far in your work, but we also know that you will not finish learning all there is to know about writing.

To help you learn advanced legal writing, this book incorporates information from many areas, such as communication science, psychology, classical rhetoric, and cognitive learning. It blends the academic and the pragmatic, moving between abstract theories and concrete applications and referring to both academic studies and practitioners' observations. It includes techniques for all aspects of writing, such as large-scale organization, sentence structure, word usage, and punctuation. It provides opportunities for practice, reflection, and second attempts. We offer this book to you in the spirit of wonder, humor, sweat, and challenge that occupies us when we ourselves write.

THE NATURE OF WRITING

Writing is probably the most complex mental task any human being undertakes,[1] taxing human capabilities close to their limits, to the extent that "[e]ven slight adjustments in the air we breathe can make our handwriting falter."[2] It does not come naturally.[3]

---

1. "The act of writing must tie together diffusely located parts of the brain, making writing perhaps the most difficult neurological task a human can undertake." Robert Ochsner, *Physical Eloquence and the Biology of Writing* 56 (1990). See also Susan Carey and Rochel Gelman eds., *The Epigenesis of Mind: Essays on Biology and Cognition* (1991).

2. Oscher, *supra* note 1 at 58.

3. H.D. Giles and John M. Wiemann, *Language, Social Comparison, and Power* in *Handbook of Communication Science* 372 (C. Berger and S. Chaffee, eds. 1987) (emphasis omitted).

1

Even when the writer knows clearly what he or she wants to communicate, successful writing still involves (1) transmitting a message from the writer's brain to the hand; (2) funneling that message through the sequential, relatively limited dimension of words on paper;[4] (3) getting the message transmitted from that sequence of words on paper to the reader's brain via the reader's eye; and (4) reconstructing that message (completed by the reader) to fit within the reader's previous knowledge and experience.[5] At any point in this process, the communication can be sabotaged. For example, it can be interrupted by the writer's word choice or even by breakdowns in any of the systems involved, such as spelling or delivery of the mail.[6] As if that were not enough, choosing what to say is also complex.

What is written without effort is in general read without pleasure.[7]

Do not expect yourself to get it exactly right the first time; reconcile yourself to a process of trial and error.

> Once you decide to delete material, for whatever reason, you may find that it is a painful process. It's hard work to get words on paper, and you may not want to cross any of them out.... If you plan a vegetable garden, not everything that grows there will contribute to its beauty or usefulness. You may have to pull out a flower simply because it does not belong.[8]

Yet for all the work, writing is also play, an ability developed gradually through practice.

> You must feel free to take risks ... discovering how many different ways you can view the same experience, trusting in your ability to continually reenvision your thoughts.[9]

Just as athletes and artists begin developing their ability through playing for the joy of it, you can play with writing, learning as you play. You can work hard at writing without losing your sense of fun.

> The most solid advice for a writer is this, I think: Try to learn to breathe deeply, really to taste food when you eat, and when you sleep, really to sleep. Try as much as possible to be wholly alive, with all your might, and when you laugh, laugh like hell, and when you get angry, get good and angry. Try to be alive. You will be dead soon enough.[10]

4. Howard S. Babb, *Prolegomena to the Analysis of Prose Style* in *Essays in Stylistic Analysis* 41 (H. Babb ed. 1972). M.C. Wittrock, *Cognitive Processes of the Brain* in *Education and the Brain: the Seventy-seventh Yearbook of the National Society for The Study of Education, Part II* 61 (Jeanne S. Chall & Allan F. Mirsky eds. 1978).

5. William M. Schutte and Erwin R. Steinberg, *Communication in Business and Industry* 26 (1983).

6. Carl Bereiter and Marlene Scardamalia, *The Psychology of Written Composition* 156 (1987).

7. William Seward, *Anecdotes of Distinguished Persons: Chiefly of the Present and Two Preceding Centuries* 309 (4th ed. 1989) (quoting Samuel Johnson).

8. William Kerrigan, *Writing to the Point: Six Basic Steps* 137 (1983).

9. Lil Brannon, Melinda Knight, and Vara Neverow–Turk, *Writers Writing* 3–4 (1982).

10. William Saroyan, *Preface to the First Edition* in *The Daring Young Man on the Flying Trapeze and Other Stories* 216–18 (1934).

This playful practice allows you not only to develop many mental skills, but also to develop and coordinate habits involving the eye, ear, and hand, which a neuropsychologist has described as three "neurological melodies."[11] You synthesize these physical skills so they work together smoothly; you "subsume all three melodies into one system."[12] Then your mind is free to think and to develop your thoughts as you write.[13] You can take the basics of writing for granted. Just as children master and then synthesize the complex melodies needed for walking, talking, and solving problems through their play, you can master and synthesize the complex melodies of writing through playing with words, structures, and ideas.

THE NATURE OF THIS BOOK

The first half of the book presents many advanced techniques, which you will master as you work through those chapters. The second half, beginning with the chapter on argument, does not introduce new techniques so much as it introduces various uses of those techniques, broadening your understanding as you broaden your experience.

The book is structured around different kinds of legal documents so you can address each topic individually. This organization allows the book to serve as a useful reference. Each chapter contains several elements:

- an explanation of the priorities for that kind of legal writing;
- the relevant strategies and concerns;
- a series of specific how-to points to help you through the task;
- examples, both good and bad;
- exercises for discussion and practice;
- larger writing assignments; and
- a bibliography of sources you may find useful if doing further research on the topic.

When good and bad examples are compared, the good example is in bold face. We have minimized the research required in the exercises and assignments, so you can focus your time on the writing itself.

The order of the chapters arises from the writing concepts that come into focus as we address each legal writing task. In Chapter 3, which covers statutes, you begin grappling with accuracy and clarity in legal writing. Chapter 4, which covers jury instructions, adds understandability, and the contracts chapter addresses consistency and thoroughness.

---

11. "The physiology of writing can be divided into three neurological melodies: kinesthetic, visual, and auditory. Melody results when neurons coalesce into a patterned behavior, that is, when they have 'learned' something as an engram and can repeat it." Ochsner, *supra* note 1, at 55.

12. *Id.* at 57.

13. Writing not only communicates your thoughts to others; it also helps you learn. For a discussion of this, see Janet Emig, *Writing as a Mode of Learning*, 28 College Comp. and Comm. 2 (May 1977), reprinted in Victor Villanueva, Jr., ed., *Cross-Talk in Comp Theory: A Reader* 7 (1997).

Chapter 6, on issues, introduces ways to focus and shade meaning through word choice. The two chapters on statements of fact address the structure of paragraphs and sentences, focusing on clarity in objective statements and on emphasis in persuasive statements. Chapter 9 on discussion sections focuses on patterns and techniques for large-scale organization.

Adapting the core writing concepts covered in chapters 3–9, the remaining chapters of the book apply those concepts to various tasks. Chapter 10 applies organization techniques to persuasive arguments; Chapter 11 applies thoroughness concerns to pleadings. Chapter 12 on orders, notices, and motions again addresses clarity and avoiding legalese in these technical legal documents. Chapter 13 on interrogatories helps you develop skills in thinking through a strategy and implementing it precisely and clearly, reprising the concern from jury instructions (Chapter 4) on writing to lay readers. General correspondence moves you further into strategies for lay readers, basing writing decisions on knowledge of people, rather than solely on the law. The chapter on opinion letters leads you to blend knowledge of people and the law into a document that is deeply concerned with both. Wills and trusts takes this concern and adds to it the drafting demands discussed in earlier chapters. The final chapter on research papers shows you how to present rigorous scholarship in a form that allows something of your personal professional style to emerge.

In summary, by focusing on different aspects of writing and then combining and recombining those concerns in different ways, this book helps you synthesize your skill and knowledge into the unified ability to be a flexible, sophisticated, and broadly skilled writer.

Woven through this book are four general principles:

• consider and respect your reader,

• know what you mean to say,

• adapt the basic techniques you have learned to address the particular circumstances at hand, and

• work step by step rather than attempting to do too much at once.

These principles will guide you as you experiment to improve your writing, helping you evaluate the success of your attempts and synthesize the many bits of information you have learned.

Additionally, three common priorities are woven throughout legal writing: accuracy, accessibility, and appeal. Although the relative importance of these three aspects of writing varies from one legal writing task to another, they remain in all circumstances the general goals of excellent writing. As a reference for you, we have devised the following list of general priorities of legal writing, illustrated with ways each priority exemplifies itself in various aspects of writing.

GENERAL PRIORITIES FOR LEGAL WRITING

Aspect of Writing	#1: Accuracy	#2: Accessibility	#3: Appeal
Overall Organization	• Include all the logical steps needed to support your position. • Group the information to reveal its relevance to your point. • Order the groups in the sequence most relevant to your reader.	• Communicate the overall organization early in the document, and follow it consistently. • When logical, organize to minimize repetition.	• Use headings to convey main substance, rather than form only. • Omit information that adds neither content nor interest.
Paragraph Organization	• State each paragraph's point directly. • Support the point adequately.	• Convey the logical connections between sentences through transitions, parallel structure, or repetition of key terms from one sentence to the next.	• Place main points in emphatic positions at the beginning or end of paragraphs. • Use one-sentence or short paragraphs when useful for transitions or emphasis.
Sentence Structure	• Place the key information in the subject, verb, and object. • Use transitions accurately.	• Delete wordy phrases and passive voice. • Keep subjects and verbs close to each other. • Use phrases before the subject for introductory and transitional information. • Use phrases after the verb or object for explanatory details. • Avoid sentences too long to be read in one breath.	• Use repetition strategically to add emphasis without boredom. • Use short sentences for emphasis. • Vary sentence structure to vary emphasis.
Word Choice	• Choose words that are unambiguous and • sufficiently specific. • Use correct grammar, punctuation, spelling, and citation form.	• Whenever possible, avoid words that are unfamiliar to the reader. • Include definitions when needed. • Maintain a consistent level of formality. • Use tabulation or enumeration for long lists. • Keep headings in parallel form.	• Use words that create the appropriate level of formality. • Use concrete words to increase emphasis or clarity. • Use abstract words to decrease emphasis. • Use apt terms for important points to increase emphasis. • Choose the verb form or auxiliary verb that reveals the correct rela-

Aspect of Writing	#1: Accuracy	#2: Accessibility	#3: Appeal
			tionship between actions.

Another theme of this book is the need for each writer to discover and develop his or her own process for writing. For example, although common wisdom applies in drafting, persuasive writing, and correspondence, each writer will still develop habits of organizing and phrasing that will work together to establish that writer's style. This process does not reduce the thinking aspect of writing, but rather enables you to communicate your thoughts more effectively. We will help you make decisions, rather than reduce the need to make those decisions. The goal of this book is to empower you to write excellent documents consistently; you, the writer, rather than the document itself, are the book's central concern.

Accordingly, the second chapter will deal with the process of writing, one of the most personalized aspects of writing this book covers.

BIBLIOGRAPHY

Ackerman, John M., *Reading, Writing and Knowing: The Role of Disciplinary Knowledge in Comprehension and Composing*, 25 (2) *Research in the Teaching of English* 133 (May 1991).

Babb, Howard S., *Essays in Stylistic Analysis*. New York: Harcourt Brace Javanovich, Inc., 1972.

Bereiter, Carl and Marlene Scardamalia, *The Psychology of Written Composition*. Mahwah, NJ: Lawrence Erlbaum Associates, 1987.

Berger, Charles R. and Steven H. Chaffee, eds., *Handbook of Communication Science*. Beverly Hills: Sage Publications, 1987.

Booth, Wayne C., *Modern Dogma and the Rhetoric of Assent*. South Bend, IN: University of Notre Dame Press, 1974.

Brannon, Lil, Melinda Knight, and Vara Neverow–Turk, *Writers Writing*. Montclair, NJ: Boynton/Cook Publishers, Inc., 1982.

Calleros, Charles R., *Reading, Writing, and Rhythm: A Whimsical, Musical Way of Thinking about Teaching Legal Method and Writing*, 5 J. Legal Writ. Inst. 2 (1999).

Carey, Susan and Rochel Gelman, eds., *The Epigenesis of Mind: Essays on Biology and Cognition*. Mahwah, NJ: L. Erlbaum Associates, 1991.

Chall, Jeanne S. and Allan F. Mirsky, eds., *Education and the Brain: the Seventy-seventh Yearbook of the National Society for The Study of Education, Part II*, 1978.

Flowers, Frank C., *Practical Linguistics for Composition*. New York: Odyssey Press, 1968.

Gregg, L.W. and E.R. Steinberg, eds., *Cognitive Processes in Writing*. Mahwah, NJ: Lawrence Erlbaum Associates, 1980.

Kerrigan, William J., *Writing to the Point: Six Basic Steps*. New York: Harcourt Brace Jovanovich, 3d ed., 1983.

Murphy, James J., ed., *A Short History of Writing Instruction: from Ancient Greece to Modern America*. Mahwah, NJ: Lawrence Erlbaum Associates, 2d ed. 2001.

Oscher, Robert S., *Physical Eloquence and the Biology of Writing*. Albany, NY: State University of New York Press, 1990.

Panetta, Clayann Giliam, ed., *Contrastive Rhetoric Revisited and Redefined*. Mahwah, NJ: Lawrence Erlbaum Associates, 2001.

Pearsall, Thomas E. and Donald H. Cunningham, *How To Write for the World of Work*. Ft. Worth: Harcourt Brace College Publishers, 5th ed. 1994.

Ramsfield, Jill J., *The Law as Architecture: Building Legal Documents*. St. Paul: West Group, 2000.

Saroyan, William, *The Daring Young Men on the Flying Trapeze and Other Stories*. New York: Modern Age Books, 1934.

Schauble, Leona and Robert Glaser, eds., *Innovations in Learning: New Environments for Education*. Mahwah, NJ: Lawrence Erlbaum Associates, 1996.

Schutte, William M. and Erwin R. Steinberg, *Communication in Business and Industry*. Malabar, FL: Krieger Pub. Co., reprint ed., 1991.

Sebeok, Thomas A., ed., *Style in Language*. Cambridge, MA: MIT Press, 1960.

Seward, William, *Anecdotes of Distinguished Persons: Chiefly of the Present and Two Preceding Centuries*. London: Jun and Davies, 4th ed. 1989.

Shannon, Claude E. and Warren Weaver, *The Mathematical Theory of Communication*. Urbana: University of Illinois Press, 1998.

Simons, Herbert W., *Persuasion: Understanding, Practice, and Analysis*. New York: Random House, 2d ed. 1986.

Singer, Isaac Bashevis, *Writing to the Point: Six Basic Steps*. New York: Harcourt Brace Jovanovich, Inc., 1974.

Villanueva, Victor, Jr., ed., *Cross-Talk in Comp Theory: A Reader*. Urbana, IL: National Council of Teachers of English, 1997.

Chapter 2

PROCESS

Whether your reader is an employer, client, or judge, that reader will generally be concerned with your written product: its content, quality, timeliness, and professional appearance. The process by which you produced this document concerns you alone. This does not make the process unimportant; it makes it individual.

Even though the process of writing is secondary to the product, that process is integral to your overall success as a legal writer. Process is critical to such important concerns as avoiding burn-out, completing a task quickly, and coping with challenges such as meeting multiple deadlines, handling a new task, or writing for a difficult reader. Process improves the product. Perhaps most important, a comfortable process helps you enjoy your work, thereby improving the quality of your professional life. However you use your law degree, you will likely spend much of your workday writing. You want to become comfortable with the task that will occupy so many hours of your career.

UNDERSTANDING YOUR PROCESS

Many writing texts address the topic of process,[1] and many of these advocate following the particular general process described in this book. We have found over the years, however, that the variety of workable personal processes defies specific prescription.[2] As a result, this chapter helps you explore, evaluate, and improve your own process of writing. It also discusses some successful processes and summarizes their common qualities. To understand your process, (1) describe your current writing

---

1. *See, e.g.,* Linda Flower, *Collaborative Planning and Community Literacy: A Window on the Logic of Learners* in *Innovations in Learning: New Environments for Education* 25 (Leona Schauble & Robert Glaser eds., 1996); Linda Flower, *Problem-Solving Strategies for Writing in College and Community* (1998); Elizabeth Tebeaux, *Design of Business Communication: The Process* *and the Product* (1990); and Lil Brannon, Melinda Knight, and Vara Nevero–Turk, *Writers Writing* (1982).

2. In each advanced legal writing class we have taught, we have spent time both in class and in conference discussing writing process with students. This chapter is based largely on that experience.

habits, and (2) evaluate how those habits work and whether you need to alter them.

Describing Your Current Writing Habits

The first step in understanding your writing process is seeing what your current writing habits are. This requires a sense of humor and nonjudgmentalness, because you need to look at what you do, rather than what you intend to do but never accomplish. For example, consider the following description.

Process Sample 1

1. Dump all my research note cards on the kitchen table.

2. Stare at the pile, then shuffle through the cards hoping for an inspiration.

3. Get a soda.

4. Sit staring at the pile while I finish my soda.

5. Stack the cards into one neat pile and then read through them, pulling out cards that seem like major points. Feel confused after pulling out about three cards.

6. Get up and walk around the room.

7. Stand staring at the cards and shuffle through them again.

8. Go scrub the bathroom.

9. . . . .

A useful account of your current process also requires specificity. For example, rather than noting only that you outline, look at what you write on the paper. Do you start outlining with a roman numeral "I"? Do you write down a few key terms? Do you write out an opening sentence? To prime your pump, review the three following samples of ways students in our advanced legal writing seminars have described their processes.

Process Sample 2

1. Procrastinate.

2. Arrange all research according to the order the research will be used in the paper.

3. Reread or skim research notes.

4. Attempt to jot down outline for paper.

5. Write out introduction, briefly outlining points to be covered in the paper.

6. Begin arguments.

7. Delete everything and begin again.

8. Repeat # 5, # 6, and maybe # 7.

9. Rework outline, working on making first argument more detailed.

10. Reread specific case language and holdings while writing out the argument.

11. Repeat # 9 and # 10 for other arguments.

12. Break for coffee. (This is the official break because inevitably I would have gotten up earlier.)

13. Reread draft and make corrections.

14. Write conclusion.

15. Print out hard copy.

16. Work on structural changes.

17. Make corrections.

18. If paper isn't due, or is past due, wait a day.

19. Reread and make corrections.

20. Print final copy.

Process Sample 3

When I am sitting down to start a big research project or a paper, the first thing I do is get a large cup of coffee! If I have a memo, I usually will highlight the important parts and place numbers next to things I must do. This way, if there is more than one question, I won't forget it.

When I'm ready to start my research, I will usually go to the library and do all my research before I write anything. I usually start with statutes, then case law. As I do the research, I get a list of cases. Then I will go through the list and find all the cases on point.

When I have a group of cases that I like, I Shepardize those cases, making new lists of cases. I continue this process until I have the best cases that are the most recent I can find. Now I'm ready to write.

I was never good at outlining, so when I started work, I used to write out memos long-hand. Now I am comfortable with a dictaphone and just try to speak through the entire memo. Once I get it back, I can make more serious corrections and rewording.

How I write a specific memo will depend on what I find. In general, I put the strongest cases first. Then I will say how the other side may counter this. I then will summarize with how we can still win in light of all the cases.

When I wrote my law review article, I collected all the research I wanted. I had everything photocopied and organized in a file by topic. I read through each one once, highlighting the articles. Then I wrote out key phrases on index cards and used that to organize my paper. That way I could rearrange the piles and visually see how it would develop. After that, like a memo, I sat down and wrote. I saved later rewrites until I could see the whole project.

Process Sample 4

I start by reading through my notes several times. Next, I write several versions of the problem I want to solve or the conclusions I want to reach, until I find a satisfactory version. After this, I make a list of topics. I usually rearrange the topics several times. I move to my word processor and pull out the provisions of notes according to each topic. Under each topic, I start arranging things into paragraphs. Under each topic, I do several versions until the text flows coherently.

Take the time to review your current writing process, unselfconsciously. This is not a time to be judgmental. Whatever form your process takes, you will find that some elements of the process work well for you and that some need to be improved.

Evaluating and Improving Your Process

After you have reviewed your writing habits, or process, you can begin to evaluate the significance of those habits and determine how your conceptual processes work. Study your process to identify the individual parts that seem ineffective, inefficient, or uncomfortable for you. If you have trouble determining which parts these are, consider at which points you make more mistakes, perhaps even watching for such small things as spelling errors. An increase in the number of these errors can indicate that you, the writer, are under greater stress.[3]

At those points, try substituting a new approach, rather than starting from scratch with a completely new process. This small-scale approach is useful because your writing process is a collection of habits you have built up over time, and these habits, like any others, will not be easy to change. By changing only the parts of the process that do not work, you can avoid unnecessary effort, making changes where they matter most.

As you begin modifying parts of your process to improve it, view the changes you make in the spirit of trial and error, proceeding in stages, gradually moving toward your goal of a streamlined, effective writing process. Give yourself the freedom to experiment. "[A] good plan needs to be detailed enough to test, but *cheap enough to throw away.*"[4]

As you evaluate your current process, you may find the following questions helpful. Ask yourself how you learn,[5] which may be revealed by

---

3. *See* Mina P. Shaughnessy, *Errors and Expectations* (1977).

4. Flower, Problem–Solving Strategies, *supra* note 1, at 91.

5. *See* David A. Kolb, *Learning Style Inventory: Self–Scoring Test and Interpretation Booklet* (1976). Information about this inventory and the theory behind it is avail-

what you remember most readily. For example, when you review a law class, do you find you first remember the fact situations of particular cases? Do you first think of the major headings listed in the table of contents? Or does your memory come as a checklist, listing key legal terms arising in that area of law? The way you remember information is likely to influence how you write; it is particularly likely to influence the central task for all writers: organization.

If you remember specifics first, you might find it helpful to start organizing by writing out a preliminary draft, a draft in which you simply dump words on paper, or write out everything you think you might need to include, with no concern for organization or eloquence. When you are finished, you can read over this draft, listing its valid points, grouping related points together, determining headings for those groupings, and building up from the details to the broad categories that organize your paper.

In contrast, if you remember general points first, you may find it more useful to start organizing by listing the broad issues that arise in the relevant area of law. For each issue, list all of the possible sub-issues, eliminating any that would not apply to the situation at hand. Continue listing and evaluating them until you have divided the major issues into their individual subissues; then apply the law to each sub-issue, determining how to resolve it.

Alternatively, if you find yourself naturally writing out a checklist, proceed with that list until you have written out all the possibilities. Then group the listed items, experimenting with different groupings until you arrive at a grouping that reveals the larger issues. You can then outline your points based on those groupings and sub-issues, filling in support, additional subpoints, and any other points you missed as you wrote out the outline. Start with what you do naturally and well, and use that as the basis from which to move into areas of organization you find more difficult.

Another question to ask yourself is, "Which writing tasks am I most likely to avoid?" Those are likely to be the parts of the writing process you most need to modify. For example, do you work steadily on a writing project until you are ready to write the first draft, but then find yourself too sleepy to work? Do you feel compelled to play video games or clean house before you begin organizing? Do you find it difficult to stop researching, even though you find the same cases and statutes turning up again and again in your research?

If you find the first draft difficult, try reducing your expectations for that draft. Perhaps dictate the draft so you can compose more quickly and with less self-criticism. If you are writing on a computer, cover the screen so you see only the line you are writing. Or write without stopping to include citations. Somehow reduce the tasks you ask yourself to accomplish on that draft so the writing will become manageable.

able in David A. Kolb, *The Learning Style Inventory Technical Manual* (1976).

If you find organizing overwhelming, forego the idea of a traditional outline, at least at this stage of writing. Perhaps you can write a dump draft first. Perhaps you can list points you want to make without labelling them, so you are not yet determining their order or level of generality in the outline. Later you can organize the listed points in relationship to each other in a separate step.

If you find it hard to stop researching, consider whether you are hesitating to take a position because the question could go either way. If so, flip a coin to determine your answer, and write or outline to support that answer for a time. Then write or outline a rough answer on the opposite position. This will provide a more concrete basis for comparison, which may make the decision easier. If you are afraid to stop researching for some other reason, either address the reason honestly and move on, or sidestep it. Whatever the problem that makes you hesitate, identifying the problem alone will be taking a large step toward the problem's solution.

In summary, when you face a writing task that seems to be too much for you,

- try to reduce your expectations to a more attainable level,

- try a different approach to accomplishing the task, or

- identify the problem specifically so you can more readily choose possible solutions.

Each of these techniques allows you to break the challenging task into smaller, more manageable components.

A final question to ask is whether you dwell on any stage. Spending a long time on one stage may signal an area of your writing process that is inefficient, uncomfortable, or distracting for you, which you need to improve. For example, do you tend to rewrite the opening passage again and again, working to get it perfect, until you find yourself left without enough time to do a good job writing the rest of the paper? Or do you find yourself revising the completed draft beyond the deadline when the paper is due?

If you keep rewriting the first passage, consider whether you are expecting too much of the draft.

> In all my writing I have always revised very heavily. I used to hope that as I got better, I would have to revise less, but the opposite seems to be happening .... [6]

Try to accept that the draft will need much revising later; focus now on getting the complete draft written. Your rewriting will be more effective later in your process, when you have already clarified some of the larger-scale questions of the paper.

If you find yourself revising to the point of diminishing returns, as when you miss a deadline, then consider whether you need to clarify in

6. Brannon, *supra* note 1, at 13 (quoting professional writer Kathryn Lance).

your mind what is needed in this revision. Are you revising for eloquence when all the document needs to function is clarity? Are you revising for conciseness when accuracy is the critical issue? Are you revising for perfection, when what you need is adequacy and timeliness? Focusing your revisions on specific qualities can help you make more effective use of the limited revision time you have. To determine your priorities, review the list at the end of Chapter 1. Allot your time so you complete essential tasks before optional ones.

Now that you have described your writing habits, determined what parts of your process could most use improvement, and considered some alternative ways to accomplish those parts of the process, consider your process generally and see how the changes you have in mind fit together.

As you study your process, you may repeat steps, as if you are circling in on your goal rather than marching in a straight line. This is natural, even typical of many writing processes. As you compare your process to others, you will also notice that many different processes still manage to get the job done. One approach to the process of writing is not superior to another, although one may be superior for you, given your own ways of thinking, your strengths, and your weaknesses.

Improving your writing process not only means finding ways to smooth the spots that slow you down. It also means adding new dimensions to your process so you can make improvements in your product that were not possible before. One way to do this is to develop expertise using writing techniques that compensate for any negatives inherent in your current style.

In general, each technique is an asset that brings with it the potential for liability. For example, if you are outstanding at writing concisely, you may find that your letters sound unfriendly because they are so terse. If you are strong in using dramatic short sentences to underscore a point, your fact statements may sound choppy because you overuse the technique. You can compensate for these possible problems by adding an extra step to your process. For example, if you are habitually concise, you can make sure you check all correspondence for tone. If you use short sentences, you can stop to scan your text for too many periods coming too close together.

Often a change in process helps you improve your handling of large- or small-scale writing concerns, especially if you are strong in one of those areas. For example, if you have an excellent eye for detail, so that your citation forms are impeccable, your grammar perfect, and your wording precise, then study large-scale organization techniques to develop similar strengths in that area. If you are quick with broad concepts and can readily develop an overall organization for a document, you may need to develop a detailed checklist for revision to make sure you do not overlook the small but necessary details that will make your presentation of the larger ideas effective. One helpful source of ideas for revising your process is your fellow students or colleagues. With this in mind, we encourage you to discuss your writing problems and solutions with them.

OTHER CIRCUMSTANCES AFFECTING PROCESS

Although you have developed your basic process for writing, you will adapt that process over time as your abilities and knowledge change. Indeed, as you work through this text, you will probably make significant changes in your process. Additionally, you will adjust your process as the circumstances under which your writing changes. The following section discusses some of the more common circumstances and suggests how you may need to adjust your process accordingly.

Working With Other Writers

One challenge is collaborating with other authors on a joint project. Although criticism of writing-by-committee has been common, educators have recently come to see collaborative writing as an effective, if not always efficient, method for learning about writing.[7] Whatever your thoughts are about collaborative writing, attorneys often find themselves working together because a project is too large or too critical for one person to handle. Even when one writer is solely responsible for the document, he or she often submits work to colleagues for extensive commenting.

For these reasons, develop a second general writing process to use when working with other writers. This process will still be influenced by the individual writer, but it will also be influenced by the priorities and style of the working group and of the supervisory staff. Because of this, you may need to make significant changes in your writing process when working with other writers. For example, you may prefer to work late the night before the deadline polishing your writing, but your co-writer may pale at the thought of this last-minute push. You will need to negotiate your processes, compromising and deferring to the plan that promises the best outcome.

Similarly, adjust your writing process when working with a reviewer. For example, you may prefer to leave polishing concerns such as spelling and citation form until the last stages of writing, but these small errors may distract your reviewer. If he or she spends much energy noting criticisms in that area, less energy will be devoted to comments on the things of concern to you. To avoid this frustration, adjust your process to address concerns you know are important to your reviewer. Additionally, submit some specific questions with your text to increase the reviewer's response on those topics. For example, attach a note asking the reviewer to consider whether the organization seems logical, whether the scope is sufficiently broad, or whether a particular image is effective. These questions can make the process more pleasant for you because you get the feedback you need, and for the reviewer because he or she has a focus and can complete the review more readily.

7. Kristin R. Woolever, *Doing Global Business in the Information Age: Rhetorical Contrasts in the Business and Technical Professions*, in *Contrastive Rhetoric Revisited and Redefined* 47 (C. G. Panetta ed., 2001).

If your reviewer prefers to give feedback in meetings, take notes and summarize at the end of the conference to make sure that your understanding of his or her advice is correct. Although you do not want to suggest a lack of trust by taking detailed notes, you do want the points to be clear enough to avoid misunderstanding and to give you a general direction for revision.

Reviewing Another's Writing

Another challenge is editing the work of another writer. Being an editor is difficult. It takes understanding, decisiveness, a lot of courage, and a lot of tact. It takes someone whom the writer can respect but need not fear; someone who can flatter without fawning, encourage with full awareness of the forces that encouragement sets in motion, and squelch where needed, but without rancor. A good editor is someone who can tell the writer that he or she is being pedantic and get away with it.[8]

When you review another's writing, whether as a colleague or a supervisor, remembering a few simple rules can help you be effective without causing resentment. First, focus on the task of preparing this document to do the job that is needed. Look first to accuracy, and then to the other qualities needed for this document. Avoid commenting on aspects of the writing that displease you but do not reduce the effectiveness of the document. For example, unless the writer has asked you to comment on wordiness, let wordiness in a contract pass as long as it does not make the contract less clear or in some other way reduce its effectiveness. In this way, you can distinguish between changes that need to be made in the document and matters of personal style.[9]

Second, when you suggest any significant changes for which the reason is not immediately apparent, explain the reason for the change in positive terms. This explanation may take only a few words, such as "to avoid ambiguity" or "for conciseness." These phrases are much more palatable to the writer than the negative versions: "this was ambiguous" or "wordy." When explaining a problem in the writing, speak in terms of the reader or the document, rather than in terms of the writer or your own opinion. For example, write "The reader may not understand whether this means ...." rather than "You're unclear here" or "I can't understand your meaning here." Although this explanation may take a few more words, the reduction in possible resentment will be worth the time invested.

If you and a colleague work together regularly, coordinate your efforts so you build on each other's strengths. For example, a writer who has a gift for being concise can readily suggest ways to improve your document in those areas. On the other hand, you may be excellent at being thorough and clear, and you can suggest changes in your col-

---

8. "Handholding, fostering, pruning, snipping, squelching, and encouraging have always been the true functions of the editor." Ernst Jacobi, *Writing at Work: Dos, Don'ts, and How Tos* 69 (1979).

9. R. Tortoriello, Stephen J. Blatt, and Sue DeWine, *Communication in the Organization: An Applied Approach* 104 (1978).

league's writing to add those qualities. Similarly, you may find it much more efficient for both of you to proofread each other's work rather than to proofread your own writing. Although this cooperation cannot be forced if colleagues are not willing, it is worth trying when possible. Sharing the revising load can improve the quality of everyone's writing while reducing the fatigue each writer feels, and it can build that pleasant sense of camaraderie and mutual empathy that is a comfort to any writer.

Working With Different Technologies

Another aspect of the writing situation that substantially affects your writing process is the technology you are using to produce your text. Whether you work with a yellow legal pad, a voice recognition system, a word processor, or a system not yet available as we write this text, the way you get words on paper will influence the final product.

Dictation Technologies

If you are working with a technology that allows you to speak and have that dictation converted to written text, you will need to adapt your speaking patterns to produce a successful written document. Contrary to popular wisdom, writing is not like talking on paper, at least not legal writing. Speech is more loosely organized, wordier, and more informal. Speech depends on emphasis and gesture to convey meaning, while writing depends on position and grammatical structure. Speech employs longer introductory phrases; writing begins with the main point.

To adapt speaking to writing, you may decide to speak first and edit later. You may first want to talk freely and naturally, generating your ideas in a rough draft. Then, with your thoughts on paper, you can organize, clarify, and delete. When the information is in place, edit rigorously for wordy phrases and informal language. When you learn what adaptations are needed to convert your speech to writing, you can accomplish this editing quickly.

Alternatively, you may decide to plan before you speak. This planning may be as simple as making a list of your points and then deciding on the best order for those points, or as complex as a detailed outline. For business letters, the simple list often works well. For more complex documents like a brief, a full outline is probably necessary.

At the technical level, take time to clarify your directions whenever someone else is preparing the document. A few basic instructions can greatly improve the quality of the typing you receive. General instructions often include information such as

- how to spell names;
- what format to use (letter, memo, etc.);
- what quality of paper to use (state whether this is a working draft or a final one);
- how many copies to send you;

- whether to store the document on the computer and how to label it for retrieval, if you have an opinion about how that should be done;

- approximately how long the document is, so the typist knows how much time to allow for the project; and

- whether the job is urgent. If you want an urgent request to be met, make sure you make the request as rarely as possible. It may not hurt to take on an apologetic tone, too, when requesting urgent attention.

When dictating the document, remember to do the following.

- If you will not be able to revise the document extensively after it is typed, rely on clear signals of your organization, such as enumeration of points ("first," "second," or "additionally") and transitional phrases ("if . . . then," "therefore," etc.) to help you keep track of your organization as you dictate.

- Stop to think as needed. Many wordy phrases are added to text merely as a sophisticated form of "uh." Stopping to think after every few words has been seen as the mark of a skilled writer, rather than a weakness.[10]

- Speak more slowly and distinctly than you do in normal conversation. It is especially important to enunciate the endings to words.[11]

- When dictating for a typist, use two distinct tones for your voice, one when stating words to be typed and another when you dictate punctuation,[12] spell out a name, or indicate the start of a new paragraph.

With practice, dictation will become more comfortable, and your reader will not have to suffer for your increased convenience.

A final problem to watch for is using inappropriately informal language. Spoken English is generally less formal than written English, so that phrases and words that sound acceptable as you dictate them look inappropriate on the typed page. As with wordiness, periodically edit your dictation and eliminate bad habits that appear.

---

10. Analysis of dictation tapes has shown that writers who can dictate well-composed letters use the stop and revise buttons more frequently than less skillful users of the equipment. Jeanne Halpern, *Effects of Dictation/Word Processing Systems on Teaching Writing* in *Business Communications: Academic and Professional Perspectives* 1–8 (J. Ferrill and S. Moskey eds.,1982).

11. One supervising attorney came to us perplexed with the ungrammatical letters of one of his new attorneys. He knew the writer was able, but the grammatical errors were nevertheless forcing him to consider firing the new attorney. After some investigation, we discovered that the attorney had a slight Southern drawl and weak proofreading skills. As a result, the typist was not hearing the endings of his words and he was not catching the errors when reviewing the documents. With a few practice dictations and a proofreading checklist, the attorney was able to eliminate the problems that threatened his job.

12. Although saying "Dear Mr. Smith, colon, Here is a draft of the contract you requested, period" may seem awkward at first, you will become accustomed to it in time. One doctor who does a great deal of dictating confessed to us that she had been known to say in conversation at a party, "Otherwise, comma"!

Word Processing Technologies

Even though you have already learned to write using word processors, computer-assisted research, and grammar checkers, you will probably adapt your writing process periodically as word processing continues to evolve. For example, systems that formerly highlighted or underlined misspelled words may, in later editions, automatically correct them. Other systems automatically format your content. As word processing becomes more automatic, however, some problems can increase. Spell checkers catch the more obvious errors, tempting the writer to skip the step of proofreading. This omission can have embarrassing results. Word processing systems currently do not tell you that you just addressed the "trail court" or discussed an "important pubic policy." It will not tell you that when you reorganized your brief, you copied a paragraph rather than moving it, so that you now repeat the same paragraph twice in an eight-page brief. Word processors are fast, systematic, and they follow orders without question. They are not intelligent enough, yet, to be trusted to convey your meaning without error. Proofread. It is still a necessary step toward excellence.

Although word processing technology has changed the revision process, it has not made revision unnecessary. For example, word processors have made it easier to generate text, and this has several implications for you as a writer. First, if you generate the words more quickly, you have less time to reflect on the content and sound of those words. This can be an advantage if you tend to revise too much too soon; you may find it much easier to write a dump draft on a computer than with pen and paper. It can be a disadvantage, though, if you neglect revising for clarity. You may generate junk without realizing it. Remember to edit for substance, redundancy, and wordiness.

Word processing can allow other errors to remain undiscovered. The monitor shows the writer only a small portion of the document at a time. This arrangement may be neater than a cluttered desk and an overflowing waste can, but it does not lead to neater organization. When the computer limits your vision to a paragraph or two, you may improve your transitions between paragraphs and sentences but neglect organization between larger parts. You may gradually drift off topic. Your heading format and content may be inconsistent.[13] To prevent this, look at your document page by page to see obvious errors. Then print out your text periodically and proofread the headings; the errors will not be hard to see. They will shout at you from the page, and you can remove them before they shout at your reader.

Finally, word processing can lead a writer to be more concerned about appearance than substance. Word processing software makes desktop publishing possible. The appealing graphics and justified text allows you to prepare a document that looks polished and interesting. This

---

13. The problem of inconsistent format in headings has become much more common since the advent of word processing, appearing in major briefs prepared by firms with impeccable reputations, much to their dismay.

appearance can fool you; the paper may look more organized and finished than it is.

As you enjoy the benefits of word processing technologies, protect the quality of your own thought. No eloquence can hide empty reasoning; no elegant graphics are as impressive as valid thought clearly expressed.

CONCLUSION

In this chapter, you studied your writing process and began adapting it to suit your personal style and the writing situations you face. You will continue adapting as you work through this book. You will adjust your writing process to meet the shifting priorities of each legal writing task, just as you adjust to co-writers and technologies. As you adjust, some elements will remain consistent. These consistencies will indicate how you work as a writer. Build on these strengths, just as you build on your physical abilities, such as eye-hand coordination, as you learn different sports.

Exercise 1

Write out what you do when you sit down to write a project. Be as honest and specific as possible. Then mark your favorite and least favorite parts of the writing process. Consider your favorite parts, and see if they reflect strengths upon which you can build further. Then think about your least favorite parts and consider trying a different approach to those portions of the process.

Exercise 2

Identify the part of your writing process with which you feel most comfortable and explain to the class how you approach that task. Then identify the part with which you feel least comfortable and ask other students how they handle that task.

BIBLIOGRAPHY

Brannon, Lil, Melinda Knight, and Vara Nevero–Turk, *Writers Writing.* Montclair, NJ: Boynton/Cook Publishers, Inc., 1982.

Ehrenberg, Suzanne, *Legal Writing Unplugged: Evaluating the Role of Computer Technology in Legal Writing Pedagogy*, 1 J. Legal Writ. Inst. 1 (1998).

Ferrill, June and Stephen Moskey, eds., *Business Communication: Academic and Professional Perspective.* Houston: The Aetna Institute for Corporate Education, 1982.

Flower, Linda, *Problem-Solving Strategies for Writing in College and Community.* Ft. Worth: Harcourt Brace College Publishers, 1998.

Gruber, Sibylle, ed., *Weaving a Virtual Web: Practical Approaches to New Information Technologies.* Urbana, IL: National Council of Teachers of English, 2000.

Hatch, Richard, *Business Communication: Theory and Technique*. Chicago: Science Research Associates, Inc., 1983.

Jacobi, Ernst, *Writing at Work: Dos, Don'ts, and How Tos*. Rochelle Park, NJ: Hayden Book Co., 1979.

Joram, Elana, Earl Woodruff, Mary Bryson, and Peter H. Lindsay, *The Effects of Revising with a Word Processor on Written Composition*, 26 (2) Research in the Teaching of English 167 (May 1992).

Kolb, David A., *Learning Style Inventory: Self–Scoring Test and Interpretation Booklet*. Boston: McBer and Company, 1976.

Owston, Ronald D., Sharon Murphy, and Herbert H. Wideman, *The Effects of Word Processing on Students' Writing Quality and Revision Strategies*, 26 (3) Research in the Teaching of English 249 (Oct. 1992).

Panetta, Clayann Gilliam, *Contrastive Rhetoric Revisited and Redefined*. Mahwah, NJ: Lawrence Erlbaum Associates, Inc., 2001.

Schauble, Leona and Robert Glaser, eds., *Innovations in Learning: New Environments for Education*. Mahwah, NJ: Lawrence Erlbaum Associates, 1996.

Schumacher, Gary M. and Jane Gradwohl Nash, *Conceptualizing and Measuring Knowledge Change Due to Writing*, 25 (1) Research in the Teaching of English 67 (Feb. 1991).

Sebeok, Thomas A., ed., *Style in Language*. Cambridge, MA: M.I.T. Press, 1960.

Shaughnessy, Mina, *Errors and Expectations*. Oxford: Oxford University Press, 1977.

Smagorinsky, Peter, *The Writer's Knowledge and the Writing Process: A Protocol Analysis*, 25 (3) Research in the Teaching of English 339 (Oct. 1991).

Tebeaux, Elizabeth, *Design of Business Communication: The Process and the Product*. New York: Macmillan Publishing Company, 1990.

Tortoriello, R., Stephen J. Blatt, and Sue DeWine, *Communication in the Organization: An Applied Approach*. New York: McGraw–Hill Book Company, 1978.

Chapter 3

STATUTES, RULES, OR OTHER REGULATIONS

Drafting statutes is challenging because you must draft language that is both comprehensive and specific, handling those problems the statute is intended to resolve and anticipating problems as yet unknown. Either you must fit the statute into an already developed body of law, which requires amending and incorporating by reference, or you must create a new body of law, which requires developing substantive and administrative provisions and handling the numerous details that arise. Although most attorneys do not draft statutes, many are involved in reviewing proposed legislation, drafting or reviewing administrative rules, or developing personnel rules. These rules or regulations function as statutes because they describe, prohibit, or regulate conduct. Drafting them requires focusing on the same considerations that control statute drafting.

Drafting statutes, administrative rules, or other regulations is a useful task with which to begin improving your writing because it requires you to focus on smaller units of text, while still addressing the many issues that occur in other legal writing tasks. In contrast to jury instructions and contracts, which require you to draft larger documents, you will craft statutes, rules, and regulations phrase by phrase, or sentence by sentence. To write even one phrase or sentence in a statute well, you must focus on accuracy and clarity. Although other concerns also arise, the primary ones are stating the content of the statute accurately and making it clear, so those who must use the statute will be able to understand whether and how it applies to them. When drafting, continuously return your focus to accuracy and clarity.[1]

Resolving concerns of accuracy and clarity requires several steps:

1. Both federal and state legislatures have drafting services or commissions that assist drafters in writing statutes. For example, the U.S. Congress is assisted by the Office of Legislative Counsel of the House of Representation and the New York legislature has a Bill Drafting Commission. These offices may publish drafting manuals that can guide you, particularly focusing on that particular legislative body's own rules and procedures. Abner J. Mikva and Eric Lane, *An Introduction to Statutory Interpretation and the Legislative Process* 150 (1997).

- interviewing the clients to determine what their purpose is and researching the existing law, rules, or policies to see how to fit the new language within the old;

- learning the tools that judges use to help them interpret statutes;

- choosing and organizing the possible clauses for inclusion in the statute; and

- drafting and revising the statute to ensure that your language is accurate and clear.

Each step is needed to draft a statute, rule, or regulation that meets your clients' objectives and avoids future problems.

INTERVIEWING YOUR CLIENTS AND RESEARCHING THE LAW

As with any drafting project, whenever you begin drafting a statute or rule, meet with your clients and determine their purpose. Your clients have information you must glean before proceeding because your role is to draft language effectuating that purpose. Determining that purpose can be difficult. When drafting legislation, you will usually work with several sponsors or a committee, and each person may have significantly different purposes for seeking the new statute or amendment. Your clients frequently have only the vaguest sense of what they want. They may know their purpose but may depend on the drafter to suggest possible approaches, including how to accommodate current law. Thus, an initial meeting may not provide you with much assistance, and you may have to complete your research and perhaps develop an initial draft before meeting with your clients again to clarify their desires. Question your clients together to determine what consensus or compromises have been reached and what they as a group believe is the purpose for drafting the statute. This may be a lengthy meeting, and you may need to persevere to enable your clients to state their purpose.

Among the information you must obtain is whether their purpose is to permit, regulate, or prohibit conduct. This information is significant because it affects decisions such as whether to include sanctions and what types of sanctions to include. For example, if your clients want a statute prohibiting the dumping of toxic materials, you must determine whether violations of the statute will result in civil sanctions, such as liability for damage caused, or criminal sanctions, such as fines, or both. Next you must determine whether an administrative department and procedures already exist to implement the statute or whether you need to include a grant of power to create a new department and promulgate administrative regulations. Even the decision to draft new legislation implies a determination that existing law cannot fulfill the purpose, so you may want to begin these meetings by asking "can you address this purpose without drafting a new bill?"[2] After these questions are resolved

2. David A. Marcello, *The Ethics and Politics of Legislative Drafting*, 70 Tul. L.Rev. 2437, 2443 (1996). He raises issues such as federal preemption, state or federal

in as much detail as possible, you will better understand your clients' purpose and be more efficient when drafting language.

In many cases, your clients will be able to tell you whether the statute, rule, or regulation expresses their purpose only after you have created a draft and explained the choices you made when drafting. "Only in the drafting is the proponent's intent developed."[3] Thus, you must accept that your clients are likely to propose extensive revisions to harmonize their purpose with your draft. Do not take this personally.

While you must hold discussions and conferences with your clients, try to discourage them from joining you in the drafting process. It is preferable, and quicker, to have in-depth conferences with your clients throughout the drafting process than to have them actually participate in drafting. In an ideal situation, you would be able to check with your clients throughout the drafting process to ensure that all the policy choices you have to make while writing comport with their intentions; in the demanding reality of legislative sessions, it is less likely you will have many opportunities to determine your clients' intentions.[4] Always remember that the lawyer's ethical duty to keep your clients informed exists throughout the drafting process. While it is more difficult to do during the press of committee meetings or floor debates, you should take reasonable steps to clarify the policy and substantive choices they want you to make, especially when drafting amendments to the bill.[5]

When you begin drafting, consider how this new statute or rule fits within the existing regulatory scheme. If it will regulate an area never before regulated, then you need to complete different research than if you are amending or adding to an area already regulated. You must consider how this addition may alter other areas of the regulatory scheme, and you may want to research how others have handled this problem. Thus, if you are adding a new rule to your company's personnel policies regulating domestic partner benefits, which had never been provided before, you may want to contact other corporations to see how they have handled the issue and to review their policies for possible use. You may also consider how the domestic partner policy affects other policies concerning disability leave, sick leave, and insurance coverage.

If you are drafting a statute that amends or adds to an already regulated area, then you must consider how to fit this change into the existing scheme. Your research should include:

constitutional restrictions that may prohibit the proposed law, sufficient coverage by current statutes so that only new administrative regulations may be needed, and other reasons why drafting may be unnecessary. *Id*. at 2443–44.

3. *Id*. at 2440.

4. *Id*. at 2441. Be careful not to use these difficulties in connecting with your clients as permission to make policy choices of your own. "The drafter who less frequently inquires about the client's desires will have greater latitude to exercise discretion and accordingly can play more of an 'advocacy' role in shaping the legislation." *Id*. at 2446. When you find yourself making policy decisions while drafting, be sure to raise them with your clients to make sure your decisions express their intentions.

5. *Id*. at 2458–59, citing Model Rules of Professional Conduct 1.2(a) which establishes the client as the ultimate decision maker, and Rule 1.4(B) which requires the lawyer to explain matters sufficient to permit the client to make informed decisions.

(1) analyzing the existing statute,

(2) studying the administrative practices under that statute,

(3) studying court decisions interpreting the existing statute,

(4) considering the regulatory experience of other states with similar statutes, and

(5) considering what other areas in the statutes will be affected and how to change or amend them to fit the altered situation.[6]

Placement of the statute may affect its subsequent interpretation because courts frequently interpret statutes in light of the surrounding statutes. "The decision to locate a new enactment within an existing body of law rather than in a separate section or to locate it within one body of law rather than another can carry with it significant jurisprudential baggage not readily apparent on the face of the draft."[7]

Researching and working with your clients may take the bulk of your time. Professor Frank Cooper relates the experience of Professor Harry Jones in drafting an amendment to a state statute on which the committee members had reached "complete agreement." Jones' time sheet for the project, which resulted in a four and one-half page proposal, was research time (58 hours), conference time (18 hours), and writing time (4 hours).[8] Much of the conference time resulted after he completed his research, which unearthed policy questions about which the committee members completely disagreed. While your drafting may take you longer than it took Professor Jones, it will entail a relatively small portion of the total time expended. In part, this is because drafting is made more efficient by the time spent gaining an understanding of what your clients want and researching the area of law in which the statute will operate.

JUDICIAL INTERPRETATION OF STATUTES

After you interview your clients and research the law, take the time to understand the tools that judges use when interpreting statutes.[9] Understanding the way judges interpret statutes is essential to effective drafting. Keep in mind that they may use legislative history, canons of statutory construction, and other tools to help them interpret your statute and determine whether it applies to a given fact situation.

When interpreting statutes, judges start by reading the statute to determine whether, under its plain meaning, it controls the factual

6. Frank Cooper, *Writing in Law Practice* 304 (2d ed. 1963).

7. Marcello, *supra* note 2, at 2448. He also notes that this decision on where to place the statute is often one made by the drafter alone, "frequently not even given a second thought by the vast majority of clients." *Id.*

8. Cooper, *supra* note 6, at 304. "[T]hat only four hours were taken to write a four-page statute indicates that the committee was not permitted to participate in the actual drafting. Had this been the case, the 'actual writing time' would surely have been at least forty hours." *Id.*

9. These considerations are not as important when drafting personnel rules, but they are important when drafting administrative rules because they undergo the same interpretation process as statutes.

situation facing the court. If the court cannot determine whether the legislature intended the statute to apply, the judge's next step has recently been subject to serious debate. For most of the 20th century, judges would turn to the statute's legislative history seeking to find whether the legislature's purpose when passing the statute included regulation of situations such as the one facing the court.[10] Legislative history is best documented at the federal level, where the resources are available to compile this information throughout the drafting and political process. In contrast, most states do not have these resources and thus state court judges use legislative history much more rarely.[11]

By the end of the 20th century, some scholars and judges argued that the legislature's purpose was impossible to discern either because of the complexity of the legislative process and the number of individuals involved or because the resulting statute was simply reflective of procedural maneuvers or unrepresentative committee reports.[12] These judges (most notably 7th Circuit Judge Frank Easterbrook and Supreme Court Justice Antonin Scalia) believe judges should consider the ordinary meaning of the statutory text, often supplied by dictionaries,[13] and then turn to canons of statutory construction, grammatical implications, and the rest of the statutory code, instead of legislative history, if the statute's purpose is unclear.[14]

10. John F. Manning, *Legal Realism and the Canons' Revival*, 5 Green Bag 2d 283, 287–89 (2002). This increasing use of legislative history was evidenced by the fact that the Supreme Court cited legislative history 19 times in 1938 and 336 times in 1978. *Id.* at 287 n.21. The Court used legislative history in virtually all statutory construction cases in 1981, in 75% of cases in 1988, in only 18% in 1992, and in 49% in 1996. Jane S. Schacter, *The Confounding Common Law Originalism in Recent Supreme Court Statutory Interpretation: Implications for the Legislative History Debate and Beyond*, 51 Stan.L.Rev. 1, 9–10,15 (1998)(citing studies by Judge Patricia Wald on the 1981 and 1988 Terms and by Professor Thomas Merill of the 1992 Term, as well as her own study of the 1996 Term).

11. Philip P. Frickey, *Revisiting the Revival of Theory in Statutory Interpretation: A Lecture in Honor of Irving Younger*, 84 Minn.L.Rev. 199, 203 (1999). Many state courts do not consider legislative history to be a valid step for interpreting statutes, and use it only to support or detract from what the canons of statutory construction say. *See also* Russell Holder, *Comment: Say What You Mean and Mean What You Say: The Resurrection of Plain Meaning in California Courts*, 30 U.C. Davis L.Rev. 569 (1997) and Philip A. Talmadge, *A New Approach to Statutory Interpretation in Washington*, 25 Seattle Univ.L.Rev. 179 (2001).

12. Manning, *supra* note 10, at 290. Since intent was indiscernible, only the rules actually enacted into law should be used. *Id.* For a list of articles by Easterbrook and Scalia, *see* Charles Tiefer, *The Reconceptualization of Legislative History in the Supreme Court*, 2000 Wis.L.Rev. 205, 208 nn.10–11.

13. For an interesting critique of the Court's increasing use of dictionaries, *see Looking It Up: Dictionaries and Statutory Interpretation*, 107 Harv.L.Rev.1437 (1994)(showing an increase in usage from an average of 5 times per term between 1958 and 1983 to not fewer than 15 times per term between 1987 and 1992, and thirty-two references in the 1992 term). *Id.* at 1438; *see also* Schacter, *supra* note 10, at 18, finding dictionary use in 18% of majority opinions of statutory cases in 1996.

14. Frickey, *supra* note 11, at 205 and Tiefer, *supra* note 12, at 209. These theories influenced judges in the lower federal courts and fit well with practice in state courts. Frickey, *supra* note 11, at 203. In fact, Justice Scalia's article, *The Rule of Law as a Law of Rules*, 56 U.Chi.L.Rev. 1175 (1989) was the third most cited article in cases involving statutory construction from 1988–1997. Gregory Scott Crespi, *The Influence of a Decade of Statutory Interpretation Scholarship on Judicial Rulings: An Empirical Analysis*, 53 S.M.U.L.Rev. 9 (2000).

But other judges choose to retain the use of legislative history to aid in interpreting the statutes before them, and its use found a resurgence on the Supreme Court in the late 1990s.[15] While acknowledging the difficulty of discerning the purpose of the Congress that enacted the statute, these judges use committee and conference committee reports to help understand drafting choices and changes in a bill's language, as well as limited use of speeches by floor managers or committee chairs.[16]

Although this particular debate may be resolved before you start drafting statutes or rules, similar debates will arise in the future and you need to be aware of how they may impact your drafting. Even with the care you take in drafting, you may find your statute at issue in a lawsuit, with a judge given the responsibility of interpreting that statute's language. By understanding the different ways that judges read statutes, you will be better able to

- make your language as accurate and unambiguous as possible;

- organize the draft to increase its clarity, both large-scale and small-scale;

- choose words that precisely convey the intended meaning; and

- use punctuation that clarifies, not confuses.

If the court cannot determine the legislative intent from the statute's plain meaning or from its legislative history, then the court may turn to standard canons of statutory construction to interpret the statute's meaning.[17] The problem with using statutory canons is that different ones lead to contradictory interpretations. Consider the following examples. "A statute cannot go beyond its text" is countered with "to effectuate its purpose a statute may be implemented beyond its text."[18] "Titles do not control meaning; preambles do not expand scope; section headings do not change language" or "The title may be consulted as a guide when there is doubt or obscurity in the body; preambles may be consulted to determine rationale, and thus the true construction of terms; section headings may be looked upon as part of the statute itself."[19]

Because of these contradictions, some commentators believe that these canons may be irrelevant when drafting statutes. They believe that, although courts use the canons to resolve inconsistencies or to supply omissions, the drafter "who tries to write a healthy instrument does not and should not pay attention to the principles that the court

---

15. Tiefer, *supra* note 12, at 207–09. These judges do not rely on "the old-fashioned use of legislative history, in which congressional majorities are presumed to share the same general purpose in enacting a statute." *Id.* at 207.

16. *Id.* at 209 and 233–40.

17. An excellent list of these canons of construction can be found in Karl Llewellyn, *Remarks on the Theory of Appellate Decision and The Rules or Canons About How Statutes Are To Be Construed*, 3 Vand. L.Rev. 395 (1950).

18. *Id.* at 401–06.

19. *Id.* at 403–04.

will apply if [the drafter] fails. [The drafter] simply does his [or her] best, leaving it to the courts to accomplish what [the drafter] did not."[20]

Nevertheless, you may want to become acquainted with some of the basic canons of construction that most courts use when interpreting statutes.[21] Your knowledge of these canons will help you anticipate how courts would approach interpreting your statute and allow you to clarify your language or organization so interpretation may be unnecessary.

Drafters can use these canons to clarify statutory language. For example, Professor Pratt discusses the canon of "last antecedent," which "provides that a qualifying phrase modifies the immediately preceding word or phrase and not words or phrases that are more remote."[22] She illustrates this canon using the following statutory excerpt.

> (3) "Conditions of ordinary visibility" means daylight and, where applicable, nighttime in nonprecipitating weather.[23]

A court using the last antecedent canon would interpret the phrase "nonprecipitating weather" as referring to nighttime alone and not to daylight, although the legislature probably intended it to refer to both options.[24] If you were aware of this canon when drafting a similar statute, then you would be able to anticipate the problem and revise the definition. Thus, you can use your knowledge of canons to avoid ambiguities or errors that would force a court to interpret the statute. You may also want to spend some time researching which statutory canons of construction are used frequently by the courts in your jurisdiction. Read cases where the courts have used these canons and anticipate the occasions when their use may be required. This knowledge will enable you to alter your drafting to avoid those problems.

In addition to these canons, remember that federal and some state statutes have interpretation acts that define specific words used in those statutes. Although no past legislature can tie the hands of future legislatures,[25] determine whether interpretation acts exist in your jurisdiction and decide whether to use the definitions contained in them or to change them. If you use those definitions, clarify that you are incorporating them in the statute you are drafting. One way to do this is to say "In addition to the definitions in sections 1–7 of Title 1, the following definitions apply to this title."[26]

---

20. Reed Dickerson, *The Fundamentals of Legal Drafting* § 3.9 (1986).

21. For an excellent discussion of textual, substantive, and other canons of construction, *see* William N. Eskridge, Jr., Philip P. Frickey, and Elizabeth Garrett, *Legislation and Statutory Interpretation* 249–87, 329–74, and Appendix A (2000).

22. Diana V. Pratt, *Legal Writing: A Systematic Approach* 15 (3d ed. 1999).

23. *Id.* quoting the Colorado Ski Safety and Liability Act, Colo.Rev.Stat. § 33–44–103(3) (1984).

24. *Id.*

25. Dickerson, *supra* note 20, at § 13.7.

26. *Id.* Sections 1–7 of Title 1 are part of the federal counterpart to state interpretation acts. 1 U.S.C. §§ 1–7 (2002). Section 4, for example, states "The word 'vehicle' includes every description of carriage or other artificial contrivance used, or capable of being used, as a means of transportation on land." 1 U.S.C. § 4 (2002). Thus if you knew of the existence of this section, and incorporated it into your statute, you would not need to define "vehicle" again and would not invite the possible inconsisten-

In summary, understanding the roles of legislative history, canons of statutory construction, and interpretation acts in judicial interpretation of statutes can help you clarify the statutory language you draft. Having this broader knowledge will help you in the next step, choosing the clauses to include and determining their organization.

CHOOSING AND ORGANIZING STANDARD CLAUSES

When choosing what clauses to include, consider the purpose of the statute you are drafting, because the clauses you will need to include will depend on the purpose and comprehensiveness of the statute. Comprehensive statutes usually include most of the following standard clauses.

- Official Title (or long title)
- Enacting Clause
- Short Title
- Purpose (in lieu of preamble)
- Definitions
- Substantive Clauses
- Administrative Clauses
- Miscellaneous Clauses
  - Amendments
  - Incorporation Clause
  - Exceptions
  - Severability Clause
  - Savings Clause
  - Effective Date

If you are simply amending a statute to add a particular provision, you will not have to create all these clauses.

The following subsections discuss the specific drafting concerns for some of these standard clauses found in most comprehensive statutes.

Official Title

All statutes begin with an official, or long, title which precedes the enacting clause and states the content of the statute.

To amend the Alaska Native Claims Settlement Act to provide Alaska Natives with certain options for continued ownership of lands and corporate shares pursuant to the Act, and for other purposes.[27]

No standards are prescribed for the titles of federal statutes, and drafting the official title is left to the drafter.[28] Most states, however, do

cies that may result from having two definitions in the Code.

27. P.L. 100–241, 101 Stat. 1788 (1988).

28. Dickerson, *supra* note 20, at § 13.6, at 282.

expressly regulate the titles of their statutes, with the regulation most frequently being located in the state's constitution.[29] Some states have drafting rules that also control titles.[30]

Given these restrictions on official titles, consider waiting to draft this clause until after you have drafted the statute. This will best ensure that the title includes all the subjects that are covered in the bill and the statute will not fall prey to challenges due to conflicts between the title and the subject matter.[31] Additionally, when drafting, remember the political attractiveness of statutes whose titles include terms such as "Reform Act" or "Public Protection Act." Your clients may want you to include these terms in the title of your statute to make it easier to pass.

Also consider how the use of certain keywords in the title or elsewhere in the statute may affect which legislative committee has jurisdiction over the bill. This, in turn, may significantly affect whether it will be adopted. "The drafter can influence a bill's committee assignment by the artful avoidance or deliberate selection of certain keywords that would be sure to commit the bill to a particular committee."[32] Your clients have the best understanding of how these committee assignments will affect the passage of the bill and you should consult them about this important political question.

Enacting Clause and Short Title

The enacting clause is the technical beginning of the statute.[33] The form of federal statutes' enacting clauses is fixed by statute.[34]

Be it enacted by the Senate and House of Representatives of the United States of America in Congress assembled:

Immediately following the enacting clause is the short title. The short title allows for easy reference to the statute and helps both the legislature and the public understand the act by stating its subject matter. As noted earlier, the long title cannot allow for this easy

---

29. For example, article 4, section 17 of the Minnesota Constitution states: "No law shall embrace more than one subject, which shall be expressed in its [long] title." William N. Eskridge, Jr., Philip P. Frickey, and Elizabeth Garrett, *Cases and Materials on Legislation: Statutes and the Creation of Public Policy* 412 (3d ed. 2001). All states except North Carolina and the New England states have a one-subject provision in their constitutions. Charles Bernard Nutting, *Legislation: Cases and Materials* 686 (1978).

30. For example, Minnesota's joint legislative rules state that "the title of each bill shall clearly state its subject and briefly state its purpose" and "that when a bill amends or repeals an existing act, the title shall refer to the chapter, section, or subdivision." Eskridge, *supra* note 29, at 412.

31. *See* for example, the cases cited in Horace Emerson Read, *Materials on Legislation* 152–57 (1982).

32. Marcello, *supra* note 2, at 2451. Marcello describes how use of the keywords, "Civil Procedure–Venue" instead of "Health and Welfare," permitted assignment of a bill on where cases would be heard following denial of welfare benefits to a committee chaired by the sponsor of the bill, rather than another committee which may have been less supportive of it. *Id.* at 2451–52.

33. Some states require the enacting clause to be the first section of the act. Norman J. Singer, 1A *Sutherland Statutory Construction* § 20.6 (6th ed. 2002). In those states without such a requirement, consider placing the enacting clause after the official title. *Id.*

34. 1 U.S.C. § 101.

reference because of the constitutional requirement that everything included in the act be noted in the long title. For example, the long title, the enacting clause, and the short title may look as follows.

[Long Title]

To amend part E of title IV of the Social Security Act to provide States with more funding and greater flexibility in carrying out programs designed to help children make the transition from foster care to self-sufficiency, and for other purposes.

[Enacting Clause]

Be it enacted by the Senate and House of Representatives of the United States of America in Congress assembled,

[Short Title]

SECTION 1. SHORT TITLE

This Act may be cited as the "Foster Care Independence Act of 1999."[35]

Purpose or Policy Clause

The purpose or policy section can be important when "the effectiveness of the statute is dependent upon a proper appreciation of the legislative intent . . . ."[36] Whether you need to include a purpose or policy clause depends on several factors. First, include a purpose clause when the statute you are drafting is regulating a new area and the statute's scope or purpose are unknown.[37] Second, include a purpose clause if it helps the reader interpret the statute in light of any uncertainty that remains even after you have tried to remove it by clarifying the statute's specific provisions.[38] Third, include a purpose clause when the legislature wants to permit discretion in the statute's application to provide guidance for administrators implementing the statute.[39] Finally, do not include this clause solely to compensate for mistakes or imprecision in drafting. Instead, focus on making the statutory language clear.

Because clauses preceding the enacting clause are not considered part of the statute, place the purpose or policy clause within the statute rather than placing it in a preamble, which precedes the enacting clause.[40] If you include a purpose or policy clause, eliminate the legalese so often found in older statutes.

Whereas, there are pending before the Legislature of the State of Minnesota, certain bills, which, if enacted into law, would materially decrease the amount of income for said School District for the ensuing years, and . . . .

---

35. Pub. L. No. 106–169, 113 Stat. 1822 (1999).

36. Singer, *supra* note 33, at § 20.12.

37. *Id.* at § 20.5.

38. Dickerson, *supra* note 20, at § 13.5.

39. *Id.*

40. Singer, *supra* note 33, at § 20.5. The majority of American jurisdictions follow the rule that, because the preamble precedes the enacting clause, it was not enacted by the legislature and thus is an extrinsic aid to interpretation. Read, *supra* note 31, at 158.

Whereas, the said School Board wish in fairness to all of their employees who come under the provisions of said Teachers Tenure Act to make no adjustments in salaries which are unwarranted by the final circumstances which will be determined on the basis of whether or not the aforementioned bills become laws;

Now, therefore, be it resolved . . . . [41]

The purpose of this clause is to clarify the scope or meaning of the statute. To accomplish this, make its language as clear as possible.

Definitions

Use a definition section when you need to clarify terms or to indicate that a defined term will have the same meaning throughout the statute. But use definitions sparingly. If you are using a word in its ordinary meaning, do not define it.[42] If, however, you are adding or subtracting something from its ordinary meaning, define it. When you include a definition, the courts will follow that definition, even if it is challenged. For example, in *Commonwealth v. Massini,* the defendant was convicted of violating § 941 of the Pennsylvania Penal Code for shooting and killing his neighbor's cat.[43] Section 941 made it a misdemeanor to "wilfully and maliciously kill ... any domestic animal of another person" and defined "domestic animal" as "any equine animal, bovine animal, sheep, goat or pig."[44] The trial court submitted the question of whether the cat was a domestic animal to the jury, thus ignoring the statutory definition of domestic animal, which clearly excluded cat. On appeal, the court stated the following:

> When the legislature defines the words it uses in a statute, neither the jury nor the court may define them otherwise.... The legislature may create its own dictionary, and its definitions may be different from ordinary usage. When it does define the words used in a statute, the courts need not refer to the technical meaning and deviation of those words as given in dictionaries, but must accept the statutory definitions.[45]

The appellate court noted that the legislature's definition, which omitted "cat," was not simply an oversight but was based on common law.[46] The legislature could make it a violation of § 941 to kill a cat but that "decision must be theirs and not ours."[47] When the legislature defines its language, those definitions are binding on the courts interpreting the

---

41. *Id*. at 162, quoting from *Downing v. Independent School Dist. No. 9,* 291 N.W. 613, 614 (Minn.1940).

42. Mikva and Lane, *supra* note 1, at 166. Defining common language may raise doubts about other ordinary language used in the bill. *Id*. citing Lawrence E. Filson, *The Legislative Drafter's Desk Reference* 120 (1992).

43. 188 A.2d 816 (Pa.1963).

44. *Id*. at 817.

45. *Id*.

46. *Id*. at 818. Cats could not be subject to larceny at common law because they had no intrinsic value. Thus the legislature had seemingly incorporated the common law into its definition of domestic animal.

47. *Id*.

statutes, unless the definitions are arbitrary or uncertain.[48] Therefore, when you define terms, do so carefully.

Using a definition section may allow you to increase the readability of the statute by defining classes within the statute. The statute can then refer to these classes by name throughout, thus shortening each provision and keeping definitions out of the substantive provisions. For example, if you are drafting a statute concerning the powers of cities and those powers vary depending on size, you might want to use the following definitions.

> Class I cities have populations of 20,000 or less. Class II cities have populations of more than 20,000 and less than 100,000. Class III cities have populations of 100,000 or more and less than 500,000. Class IV cities have populations of 500,000 or more.

Then throughout the statute, when referring to each type of city, simply refer to the class.

> **All Class II cities must have a city manager elected by the residents of the city.**

rather than

> All cities having populations of more than 20,000 and less than 100,000 must have a city manager elected by the residents of the city.

When deciding what definitions to include, review the definitions already included in the interpretation act for the relevant statutes. If a term is defined in the interpretation act and you want a different meaning in your statute, then add a definition of the term or state that the interpretation act's definition should not be followed. The following sentence is one way to do this.

> No legislative enactment shall control the meaning or interpretation of any word or phrase used in this statute, unless the enactment specifically refers to this chapter or is specifically referred to in this chapter.

When defining terms, be sure to explain your intended meaning clearly and then use the defined term consistently throughout the statute. These definitions must be clear, because your audience will not be able to conform their behavior to comply with the statute if they cannot understand it. If you use legal terms of art given meaning through judicial usage, be sure to define those terms whenever your intended meaning is different from the traditional usage. For example, you would define terms such as "negligence" or "strict liability" if you do not want a court to impute a common law meaning to those terms.

Place the definition section after the introductory sections (the enacting clause, the short title, and the purpose clause). But place it before the substantive and administrative sections, so the reader will understand the terms that are used throughout the remainder of the

---

48. Singer, *supra* note 33, at § 20.8.

statute. This placement is contrary to the practice of putting this section at the end of the statute.[49] Putting the definition section at the end results in confusion and misunderstanding because the reader would have to infer how terms are used while reading the statute.

Substantive and Administrative Clauses

These two sets of clauses comprise the heart of most statutes, especially those that are comprehensive rather than amendments to existing legislation The substantive clauses set forth the rights and duties of those affected by the statute, as well as defenses and exceptions to the statute. The administrative clauses identify the agencies responsible for creating and enforcing the regulations needed to implement the substantive clauses of the statute.

Each section should contain only one point, with a subsection used for each subpoint. This organization will increase clarity. Also use clear headings to help the reader work through the statute.

When drafting substantive clauses, consider your audience, and then organize the statute so it proceeds logically for that audience. Start with those sections that regulate or proscribe conduct; then move to enforcement and sanctions. When drafting the clauses controlling conduct, balance the need for generality against the need for specificity. "[I]f the standards of conduct are too general the act may be invalidated for uncertainty and if they are too exact they may violate constitutional requirements of equality and due process."[50] The sanction clauses are vital parts of the statute and frequently the parts most subject to debate.[51] When drafting these clauses, consider the types of sanctions available (criminal, civil, or administrative) and determine how your clients' policy considerations fit with their choice of sanctions.

When drafting administrative clauses, continue making only one point per section. This is particularly important with these clauses because they tend to be revised frequently and limiting the subject matter for each section allows for easy amendment.[52] The usual organization of these sections is to start by creating the department, selecting the officers, and stating the length of their terms. Then list the powers and duties of the department.[53] When stating these powers and duties, move from the general to the specific so the reader will be able to understand the breadth of the department's powers and duties from the beginning.[54]

---

49. *Id.* at § 20.9.

50. *Id.* at § 20.16, at 101.

51. Mikva and Lane, *supra* note 1, at 166. For example, whether to include provisions for federal enforcement of the Voting Rights Act of 1965, instead of simply providing that race or color should not deny or abridge the right to vote, was one of the focal points of Congressional debate. *Id.* at 166–67.

52. Singer, *supra* note 33, at § 20.15.

53. *Id.*

54. Singer provides a detailed sample of administrative provisions covering the officers, powers and duties, organization, salaries, and personnel matters. *Id.*

Miscellaneous Clauses

After drafting most of the statute, you must determine whether any clauses need to be added to fit the new statute into the existing statutory framework and into the affairs of the people whose conduct will be affected by it. For example, you may need to add clauses that amend or repeal other statutes, incorporate provisions from other statutes, permit exceptions, or address severability if some part of the statute is declared unconstitutional. You may also need to add clauses to preserve rights, remedies, and privileges currently in effect that would otherwise be destroyed by the statute's enactment. Finally, you must declare when the statute will take effect.

Amendments

When drafting amendments to prior legislation, two options are available. You can use the strike-and-insert method, where you note specific words that are deleted and others that are inserted.[55] This method works well if you need only a few changes in other statutes to make them consistent. If, however, your statute requires major changes in other statutes, amend those statutes by drafting clauses that substitute new sections (with the necessary changes) for the old sections.

Section 211. Annual Report on Amounts Necessary to Combat Fraud

(a) In General–Section 704(b)(1) of the Social Security Act (42 U.S.C. 904(b)(1)) is amended–

    (1) by inserting "(A)" after "(b)(1)"; and

    (2) by adding at the end the following new subparagraph:

        "(B) The Commission shall include in the annual budget prepared pursuant to subparagraph (A) an itemization of the amount of funds required by the Social Security Administration for the fiscal year covered by the budget to support efforts to combat fraud committed by applicants and beneficiaries."[56]

Incorporating Provision

When drafting clauses that incorporate language or concepts from other statutes by reference, be careful not to destroy the clarity you worked so hard to attain. For example, extensive references to other statutory sections make it difficult to understand what the current statute means. Consider the following example, which is virtually incomprehensible.

Section 202(p) of the Social Security Act (1956)

(P) In any case in which there is a failure—

55. Some states prohibit the strike-and-insert method of amending and require that amended sections be set out in their entirety. Eskridge, *supra* note 29, at 413.

56. "Foster Care Independence Act of 1999," Pub. L. No. 106–169, § 211, 113 Stat. 1822 (1999).

(1) To file proof of support under subparagraph (D) of subsection (c)(1), clause (i) or (ii) of subparagraph (E) of subsection (f)(1), or subparagraph (B) of subsection (h)(1), or under clause (B) of subsection (f)(1) of this section as in effect prior to the Social Security Amendments of 1950 within the period prescribed by each subparagraph or clause....[57]

As this example shows, care must be taken so cross-references do not get out of hand. For example, the following provision is much easier to understand.

Section 212(a) of the Revenue Act of 1918

That in the case of an individual the term "net income" means the gross income as defined in Section 213, less the deductions allowed by Section 214.

This cross-reference shows how you can incorporate by reference without losing the ability to present information so the reader can understand it.

Exceptions

When drafting clauses that limit the general terms of the statute, include them in a separate "Exceptions" section. Do not use a proviso, which is a clause added to a section establishing a general rule and which begins "provided, however ...." The proviso structure is problematic because it often leaves the reader unclear whether the limitation is general to the entire act or specific to the section in which it is included.[58] Be sure to list all the intended exceptions; courts usually cannot add exceptions or qualifiers to statutes.[59] For example, 15 U.S.C. § 45 lists unlawful methods of unfair competition and then states:

(5) Exemption from Liability

No order of the Commission or judgment of court ... shall ... relieve or absolve an person, partnership, or corporation from any liability under the Antitrust Acts.

Severability Clause

When drafting severability clauses, your purpose is to allow for enforcement of those sections of the statute that remain constitutional, despite the unconstitutionality of a particular section.[60] Although courts presume the constitutionality of statutes, severability clauses clarify what is to happen if the courts find part of a statute unconstitutional. The clause indicates that, although some applications of the statute may be invalid, the legislature intends for the statute to apply to those situations where it remains valid. The following example shows this.

If any provision of this Act is invalid, then all valid provisions that are severable from the invalid provision remain in effect. If a

---

57. James Peacock, *Notes on Legislative Drafting* 28 (1961).

58. Singer, *supra* note 33, at § 20.22.

59. *Id.*

60. *Id.* at § 20.27.

provision of this Act is invalid in one or more of its applications, then the provision remains in effect for all applications that are severable from the invalid applications.

Savings Clause

A savings clause indicates that the statute applies prospectively and preserves the rights and duties existing at the time the statute takes effect. This clause softens the effect of a new law or the amendment or repeal of an old law by not disrupting transactions already in progress under the old law.

This Act does not affect rights and duties that matured, penalties that were incurred, and proceedings that were begun before its effective date.

Effective Date

Usually, a statute will take effect according to the standard law of your jurisdiction. For example, federal acts take effect when they are signed by the President, unless stated otherwise.[61] In over forty states, the effective dates of state statutes are regulated by their constitutions.[62] If you want to set a different effective date, include a clause stating when the statute takes effect. For example, you can write

The amendments made by subsection (a) shall take effect on October 1, 20___.

Most comprehensive statutes include these standard clauses, and reviewing them will help you decide which clauses to include in the statute you are drafting. This review allows you to be more thorough when you start to draft because you can focus on drafting, not on choosing which clauses to include.

DRAFTING CONSIDERATIONS FOR STATUTES

Having determined the clients' intent and completed your research, and having determined which clauses to include in your statute, rule, or regulation, you now begin drafting. The work you have done in the preceding steps should have enabled you to choose the content. Accuracy and clarity are now your main focus.

Accuracy

Accuracy is especially important when drafting statutes. The reader is trying to determine exactly what the statute permits, requires, or prohibits. Your task is to ensure that the statute communicates that correctly. Accuracy is also important because concerns about constitutional due process attach to statutes, with the Supreme Court noting that statutes can be unconstitutional when they are vague, ambiguous, or unclear.[63] Four ways to increase accuracy in statutes are to

---

61. Nutting, *supra* note 29, at 725.

62. For example, *see* Ind. Const. art. IV, § 28; Ore. Const. art. IV, § 28.

63. For a discussion of the void-for-vagueness theories applied by the Supreme

- choose words that communicate your meaning;
- organize content of the chapter logically, putting all related information together;
- use sentence structure that reflects the logical structure of the content; and
- use correct punctuation.

Choose Words That Communicate Your Meaning

Making statutory language clear is often surprisingly difficult. Statutes must communicate to many readers, and the language that seemed clear to one may present different meanings to others. For example, if you review your state's statutes, you would probably find examples of lack of clarity like the following.

A person more than twenty-one years old . . . .

Does this mean twenty-two and over or twenty-one and one day? Clarify the meaning here, and of any time in general, by identifying the point in time precisely.

A person who is twenty-one years old or older . . . .

Rather than

After the Administrator appoints an Assistant, he or she shall supervise . . . .

Who is supervising, the Administrator or the Assistant? Wherever a pronoun could have more than one reference, clarify the meaning by repeating the identifying noun.

After the Administrator appoints an Assistant, the Assistant shall supervise . . . .

The better versions in these examples use language to state the meaning more clearly. This choice is preferable to simply adding more explanatory words. Although many drafters try to clarify by including extensive lists, doing this creates long sentences and often puts more words between the subject and verb; the solution thus becomes more of a problem than the original. The following rules provide guidance for resolving these problems.[64] But the first step is to state your points clearly.

Organize Content of the Chapter Logically

Disorganization of a chapter's sections reduces its accuracy by making it difficult for readers to know whether they have found every applicable section of the statute. If the readers do not have all the relevant sections, they may make decisions based on incomplete understandings or inaccurate readings. For example, Wisconsin Statutes'

Court, *see* Singer, *supra* note 33, at § 32A:4.

64. Mary Barnard Ray and Jill J. Ramsfield, *Getting It Right and Getting It Written* 2–3 (3d ed. 2000).

Chapter 80, titled Laying Highways, seems clear. The organization of this chapter, however, defies understanding, and its accuracy is questionable because of the number of sections that are related but spread throughout the chapter. For example, sections .01, .02, .03, .33, .38, .39, and .40 all concern creating highways. Sections .08 and .64 address highway width. Sections .09, .10, .30, and .65 address highway damage. Readers concerned with any of these issues must read the entire chapter, or at least the entire table of contents, to find every section relating to the relevant issue. Many readers will not spend the time to read so carefully, and they will miss sections related to the topics with which they are concerned.

Statutory disorganization sometimes results from the repeated amendments to statutes. To minimize this problem when drafting amendments, pay particular attention to selecting the appropriate location in the chapter for the amendment. If you are creating a new section or new chapter, try to keep all related sections in one place. This increases the likelihood that the statute will accurately indicate to the reader what actions can or must be taken.

Use Sentence Structure that Reflects the Content's Logical Structure

Consider the content of your statute or regulation and then use sentence structure to increase accuracy. When the sentence structure corresponds to the logical structure of the content, the reader will be able to understand the statute more easily and its accuracy will be increased.

To do this, first decide what is the main point and what is supporting or explanatory information. Put the main idea in the main clause, moving dependent ideas to dependent clauses. For example, the following provision places the point of the section in the main clause and adds supporting information in a dependent clause.

> Benefits shall be paid to each unemployed and eligible employe from his [or her] employer's account, under the conditions and in the amounts stated in . . . this chapter.[65]

This structure indicates to the reader quickly and directly the main point and the elaboration.

When you need to explain the context of your main point, use an introductory phrase. This structure serves as a transition by showing the reader how the previous sentence leads to the following one.

> If the Supreme Court directs that the order of the Commission be modified or set aside, the order of the Commission . . . shall become final. . . .[66]

The structure can also indicate preliminary information necessary for understanding the main point contained in the main clause.

65. Wis.Stat. § 108.025.   **66.** 15 U.S.C. § 45(h).

> Except as provided in sub.(6), this section does not prohibit an employer from requesting an employee to submit to a polygraph test if all of the following conditions apply: . . . . [67]

The reader immediately understands the limitation on this section by reading the introductory phrase.

The introductory phrase needs to be structured clearly, ending with a comma placed just before the subject. For example, consider how the following introductory phrase is unclear because its ending is unclear.

> If an inmate is placed in temporary lockup by a security supervisor, the security director, the superintendent, or the person in charge of the institution on that day shall review this action on the next working day.

The problem with this sentence structure is that the comma following the introductory phrase is lost in the list of individuals separated by commas. As a result, there is some ambiguity about who is placing the inmate in temporary lockup. An easy way to clarify this is to use the "if . . . then" format for this sentence, placing "if" at the beginning of the introductory phrase and placing "then" before the main clause. This sentence structure introduces the situation in which the rule comes into play and then states the rule.

> **If an inmate is placed in temporary lockup by a security supervisor,** *then* **the security director, superintendent** . . . .

The sentence structure in the following example obscures the meaning of the statute and makes it difficult to understand.

> No person, firm or corporation shall engage in the business of manufacturing or bottling or distributing at wholesale or selling at wholesale to retail establishments for the purpose of resale any soda water beverages without a license from the department. [68]

In this sentence structure, the main idea is split by a long list. Rewriting the statute to put the entire main clause together would clarify the sentence.

> **A person, firm, or corporation must have a license from the department to manufacture or bottle soda water beverages, to distribute soda water beverages at wholesale, or to sell soda water beverages at wholesale to retail establishments for the purpose of resale.**

This redrafting puts the main point in the subject and verb, puts that subject and verb together, and puts the dependent list in a dependent clause that clarifies the restriction stated in the statute. [69]

---

67. Wis.Stat. § 111.37(5)(a).

68. Previous version of Wis.Stat. § 97.34.

69. Additionally, the original is stated negatively, which makes it even more diffi- cult to read. Whenever possible, state your points in the affirmative, as will be discussed in detail in the jury instructions chapter.

In the past, many statute drafters have followed the pattern of (1) naming the group of people, things, or events the statute addresses and (2) stating something about that group. We do not encourage that approach. Although this two-part organization seems logical when stated, in practice it frequently creates sentences that are actually quite unclear. This happens because of a conflict between the structure of English and the nature of the law. English puts the subject of the sentence first when using natural order, so putting the group at the beginning leads to making the group the subject. But the group the statute addresses usually takes many words to define: "Any public restaurant that is open on Sundays and has as part of its frequent clientele groups of diners that include persons under the age of eighteen or who employs people who are under the age of eighteen must provide . . . ." This means that the subject consists of many words, which pushes the verb farther and farther away. By the time the readers reach the verb ("must provide"), they are too overwhelmed with detail to absorb the main point of the sentence. Thus any logic which might have been present is lost in the grammatically cumbersome sentence which this order created. To avoid this problem, we have chosen an approach that creates a clearer subject and verb, moving the detail to the end of the sentence where the reader can more readily understand it.

Use Correct Punctuation

Punctuation plays a major role in clarifying the meaning of sentences. Ambiguous punctuation in sentences can make the meaning of a statute unclear. For example, section 1951(b)(2) of the Hobbs Act states:

(b) As used in this section—

. . .

The term "extortion" means the obtaining of property from another, with his consent, induced by the wrongful use of actual or threatened force, violence or fear, or under color of official right.[70]

Because the punctuation is unclear, in a prosecution for extortion, the question remains open whether the government has to prove that the property was induced by the public official or simply that it was obtained under color of official right.[71] The defendant would argue that the punctuation of the clause gives it the following meaning: "with his consent, *induced (1) by* wrongful use of actual or threatened force, violence, or fear, or (2) under color of official right." In contrast, the government would argue that the punctuation of the statute gives it a different meaning: "with his consent, *(1) induced by* wrongful use . . . or (2) under color of official right." Whether a conviction is obtained will depend on which meaning the court uses. By punctuating to divide separate points into separate clauses, the meaning of the statute would be clear.

70. 18 U.S.C. § 1951 (2002).   **71.** Eskridge, *supra* note 29, at 917–18.

Additionally, incorrectly punctuated sentences are unclear because they are hard to read. As this example shows, the punctuation of the statute obscures its meaning and needs to be revised.

> Owners of lands who do not maintain and keep in repair lawful partition fences may not recover any damages for trespasses by the animals of owners of any adjoining lands with whom partition fences might have been maintained if such lands had been enclosed; but the construction of such a fence does not relieve the owner of swine, horses, sheep or goats from liability for any damage they commit upon the enclosed premises of an adjoining owner.[72]

One problem is that, in one long sentence, the statute regulates two entirely different actions. Remember to limit each sentence to one thought. Simply dividing this sentence into its two separate parts would help to clarify its meaning significantly.

> **Owners of lands who do not maintain and keep in repair lawful partition fences may not recover any damages whatever for trespasses by the animals of owners of any adjoining lands with whom partition fences might have been maintained if such lands had been enclosed. The construction of a partition fence, however, shall not relieve the owner of swine, horses, sheep or goats from liability for any damage they commit upon the enclosed premises of an adjoining owner.**

Because each separate point now is contained in a separate sentence, the reader can more accurately understand the statute and conform his or her behavior to its demands.

Clarity

While accuracy ensures that a statute will mean what you intended, clarity increases the odds that the statute will be read accurately. Three ways to increase clarity are

- use words the reader understands,
- prefer straight-forward organization, and
- omit information that does not add needed content.

Use Words the Reader Understands

When drafting statutes, you are trying to communicate with a reader who is turning to the statutes to determine what actions are allowed, required, or prohibited. The reader can glean this information more readily when you use words your reader understands.

Use words that will be understood readily by lay readers, because they are among the people who will be reading your statutes. Additional-

---

72. Wis.Stat. § 90.04. The version of this statute in effect when the first edition of this book was published imposed liability only on owners of swine; apparently, hors- es, sheep and goats caused enough damage in the interim to become covered by the statute. Unfortunately, in that revision, the sentence was not divided.

ly, these words are more likely to be clear under the plain meaning doctrine, so courts will interpret your language correctly. This is not the place to consult your thesaurus. For example, the following federal regulation on voting by members of the armed forces would be much clearer if more familiar words were used.

> It is recommended, in order to minimize the possibility of physical adhesion of State balloting material, that the gummed flap of the State envelope supplied for the return of the ballot be separated by a wax paper or other appropriate protective insert from the remaining balloting material, and, because such inserts may not prove completely effective, that there also be included in State voting instructions a procedure to be followed by absentee voters in instances of such adhesion of the balloting material, such as a notation of the facts on the back of any such envelope, duly signed by the voter and witnessing officer.

The unfamiliar wording raises unnecessary questions in the reader's mind. In lines one and two, does "physical adhesion" mean the same thing as "sticking"? Does "such adhesion" in line eight mean the same thing? Using "sticking" throughout would make the statute clear because it would be more readable. In line four is "appropriate" protective insert needed to differentiate an "appropriate" protective insert from an "inappropriate" protective insert? If not, why introduce that possibility by using the modifier "appropriate"? Changing the language to make it less stilted would help clarify this almost incomprehensible statute.

Additionally, do not vary your word choice by using several different words to refer to the same thing. This variation confuses the reader, who is not sure whether the words are intended to refer to the same things or to different things. For example, consider an earlier version of Wis.Stat. § 90.10.

> In case any person shall neglect to repair or rebuild any partition fence which by law he ought to maintain, the aggrieved party may complain to two or more fence viewers of the town, who, after giving notice as provided in s. 90.07, shall examine the same. If they determine that the fence is insufficient, they shall signify the same to the delinquent party and direct him to repair or rebuild the same within such time as they shall deem reasonable. If such fence shall not be repaired or rebuilt within the time so fixed, the complainant may repair or rebuild the fence and recover the expense as hereinafter provided.[73]

The drafter uses "any person" in the first line and "delinquent party" in the sixth line when referring to the person who does not repair or rebuild the partition fence. The drafter also uses "aggrieved party" in the second line and "complainant" in the eighth line to refer to the

---

73. Wis. Stat. § 90.10. This statute was amended in 1997 and much of the confusing legalese (including "shall examine the same," "such fence," "signify the same," "such time," "as hereinafter provided") was eliminated. Internally consistent language, however, still was not used.

party who is affected by the person not maintaining the partition fence. This variation confuses for the reader, who must sort out who is whom.

Even more confusing than using different words for the same meaning is using the same word for different meanings. Having once deciphered the meaning of the word, the reader must then redefine the word when it is used later to convey a different meaning. In the example above, the drafter used "same" several times and its meaning changes from use to use: the first and third times "same" is used, it means fence; the second time "same" is used it refers to the insufficiency of the fence. By substituting different words for each meaning of "same," we can clarify the statute. If we make the changes noted here and eliminate the legalese, the statute is easier to read.

> **In case any person shall neglect to repair or rebuild any partition fence which by law he ought to maintain, the aggrieved party may complain to two or more fence viewers of the town, who after giving notice as provided in § 90.07, shall examine the fence. If they determine that the fence is insufficient, they shall signify its insufficiency to the person and direct him to repair or rebuild the fence within a reasonable time. If the fence is not repaired or rebuilt within the time the fence viewers fix, the aggrieved party may repair or rebuild the fence and recover the expense of doing so as provided below.[74]**

Making small changes in wording adds up to a substantially clearer statute.

Prefer Straight–Forward Organization of Content

Good organization can significantly affect whether the statute is understandable. This organization should be not only logical, as discussed earlier, but also as simple and straight-forward as possible. For example, the statute above on voting for armed forces personnel was confusing because its organization was not clear to the reader; logically distinct ideas were combined. Reorganizing could clarify the content.

> **It is further recommended**
>
> > **(1) that the gummed flap of the return envelope for the ballot be separated from the balloting material by waxed paper or other protective insert to minimize the possibility that the balloting material will stick together; and**
> >
> > **(2) that the voting instructions include a procedure to be followed by the voter if the balloting material does stick together, such as noting the facts on the**

---

74. Another revision that needs to be made is to make this statute gender-neutral. Thus, you would change the statute either to use nouns instead of pronouns, make the subject plural (with pronouns also plural) or include "he or she." The 1997 revision used nouns, such as "that person" and "the delinquent party," to solve this problem.

back of the envelope, and having it signed by the voter and the witness.

The following statute is poorly organized because it tries to do too much in one sentence. This problem is typical in statutes where drafters try to include all the information necessary for one statutory section in one sentence.

Whenever any highway has been divided into two roadways by an intervening unpaved or otherwise clearly indicated dividing space or by a physical barrier so constructed as to substantially impede crossing by vehicular traffic, the operator of a vehicle shall drive only to the right of such space or barrier and no operator of a vehicle shall drive over, across, or within any such space or barrier except through an opening or at a crossover or intersection established by the authority in charge of the maintenance of the highway, except that the operator of a vehicle when making a left turn to or from a private driveway, alley or highway may drive across a paved dividing space or physical barrier not so constructed as to impede crossing by vehicular traffic, unless such crossing is prohibited by signs erected by the authority in charge of the maintenance of the highway.[75]

This statute section covers three points; each needs to be handled separately. The first point is that the driver is to drive only on the right side of a divided highway. The next point is that drivers must not cross the median except through an authorized opening. The final point is that there is an exception for left turns. The statute would be clearer and its meaning more understandable if it were divided into at least three sentences, each explaining a separate point, and the language were revised.

If any highway is divided into two roadways by an intervening, unpaved, or otherwise clearly indicated dividing space or by a physical barrier constructed to substantially impede crossing by vehicular traffic, then the operator of a vehicle shall drive only to the right of that space or barrier. No operator of a vehicle shall drive over, across, or within the divided space, except at a crossover, intersection, or other opening established by the authority in charge of highway maintenance. However, the vehicle operator may make a left turn to or from a private driveway, alley or highway; or may drive across a paved dividing space, unless the crossing is prohibited by signs erected by the authority in charge of highway maintenance.

Preferring straight-forward organization by dividing points into separate sentences will increase clarity and thereby help the reader understand the statute's meaning.

---

75. Wis.Stat. § 346.15.

Omit Unneeded Words

Statutory sections should be as lean as possible; unnecessary words can confuse the reader and unnecessary passive voice can hide the actor. Do this by

- using affirmatives rather than negatives;
- using possessives when possible to delete prepositional phrases; and
- using active voice instead of passive.

Using affirmatives rather than negatives eliminates the unneeded words and increases understandability. For example, the following statute is hard to understand.

> Owners of lands who do not maintain and keep in repair lawful partition fences may not recover any damages whatever for trespasses by the animals of owners of any adjoining lands with whom partition fences might have been maintained if such lands had been enclosed; but the construction of such a fence, however, shall not relieve the owner of swine, horses, sheep or goats from liability for any damage they commit upon the enclosed premises of an adjoining owner.[76]

The use of excess negatives forces the reader to take more time to discern the meaning of the statute. Negatives not only result in unnecessary words, but also include unneeded logical steps that the reader must sort out. In contrast, the following example eliminates negatives whenever possible, reducing the confusion.

> **Owners of lands who maintain and keep in repair lawful partition fences shall be entitled to recover damages for trespasses by animals of owners of any adjoining lands. The construction of a partition fence, however, shall not relieve the owner of swine, horses, sheep, or goats from liability for any damage those animals commit upon the enclosed premises of an adjoining owner.**

Redrafting this section requires care. There is a tendency to change the second sentence to make it parallel to the first: "Owners of swine ... who construct ... are not relieved...." But this causes ambiguity and a chuckle as well, because it becomes unclear whether the owners or the swine are constructing the fence. Whenever you revise your language, be sure the revision does not cause confusion in some other way.

Another way to remove unneeded content is to remove unneeded prepositional phrases. Using possessives to clarify the link between words allows you to delete prepositional phrases. For example, consider the phrase "the animals of owners of any adjoining lands." It is possible to revise that phrase to "the animals of adjoining landowners" or "adjoining landowner's animals." Similarly, you can use single words to indicate possession, instead of using prepositional phrases. This same

---

76. Wis.Stat. § 90.04.

section begins with "Owners of lands." It is more direct and clear if you revise this to say "Landowners."

In the push to eliminate unneeded language, however, do not give conciseness unfettered freedom. Some prepositional phrases are necessary to prevent a string of nouns that becomes dense and difficult to read. For example, if you eliminated all prepositional phrases in the statute, you could create "landowners' lawful partition fence construction," which would not be more readable. You could solve this problem by instead writing "landowners' construction of lawful partition fences."

Seek a readable balance. The following section of the armed forces balloting statute contains too many prepositional phrases.

> It is recommended, *in* order to minimize the possibility *of* physical adhesion *of* State balloting material, that the gummed flap *of* the State envelope supplied *for* the return *of* the ballot be separated *by* a wax paper or other appropriate protective insert *from* the remaining balloting material . . . .

This statute could be revised to eliminate many of these phrases.

> **To minimize the possibility of State balloting material sticking, the State envelope's gummed flap should be separated by a waxed paper insert** . . . .

This revision directly states the point, omits unneeded words, and thus clarifies the needed content.

Another way to clarify this statute, and others, is to minimize the use of the passive voice, especially because it often leaves the actor unidentified.[77] A statute's purpose is to indicate behavior that is permitted, regulated, or prohibited. This purpose will be clearer if you include the actor in the statute. For example, in the armed forces statute, the passive voice is used repeatedly. This usage makes it unclear who is supposed to do what. The statute starts with "It is recommended." By whom? It goes on to say that a procedure "be included." By whom? Using the active voice would clarify the actors and would help the reader understand what he or she was told to do.

> **The U.S. government recommends that, in order to minimize . . . . Additionally, the state voting instructions should include a procedure to be followed** . . . .[78]

CONCLUSION

The steps explained indicated in this chapter will help you draft statutes that provide meaningful assistance to those reading them. By

---

77. The passive voice occurs when the actor is eliminated from the sentence, such as saying "The ball was kicked" or "The ball was kicked by John" rather than "John kicked the ball."

78. Other passive constructions, such as "be separated by a wax paper . . .", occur in the statute. Some of these are difficult to remove because the actor is unidentified or unnecessary. This example makes clear that it is not always necessary or even helpful to remove all passive voice. *See e.g.,* Ray and Ramsfield, *supra* note 64, at 248–50.

interviewing your client, researching the law, learning about legislative history and canons of construction, and selecting needed clauses, you ensure that the statute thoroughly covers its intended situations and will be understandable when applied to new ones. By focusing on accuracy and clarity when drafting and by using the suggestions for revision listed above, you increase the likelihood that the statute will convey its intended meaning and will be understood by those using it.

Exercise 1

You are a private practitioner who also works on a contract basis as a city attorney for a small city in South Dakota. The city has just installed its first traffic light and wants to enact the appropriate traffic ordinance. They will pay you for one hour's work. Draft the ordinance.

Exercise 2

You work for the legislature drafting service of the Arkansas legislature. A state legislator is concerned about how difficult the following statutes are to understand and has asked you to revise them to improve comprehension.

999.075   Overtaking and passing bicycles and motor buses.

(1) The operator of a motor vehicle overtaking a bicycle proceeding in the same direction shall exercise due care, leaving a safe distance, but in no case less than 3 feet clearance when passing the bicycle and shall maintain clearance until safely past the overtaken bicycle.

(2) Except as provided in s. 999.48, if the operator of a motor vehicle overtakes a motor bus which is stopped at an intersection on the right side of the roadway and is receiving or discharging passengers, the operator shall pass at a safe distance to the left of the motor bus and shall not turn to the right in front of the motor bus at that intersection.

999.08   When overtaking and passing on the right permitted.

The operator of a vehicle may overtake and pass another vehicle upon the right only under conditions permitting such movement in safety and only if the operator can do so without driving off the pavement or main-traveled portion of the roadway, and then only under the following conditions:

(1) When the vehicle overtaken is making or about to make a left turn: or

(2) Upon a street or highway with unobstructed pavement of sufficient width to enable 2 or more lines of vehicles lawfully to proceed, at the same time, in the direction in which the passing vehicle is proceeding; or

(3) Upon a one-way street or divided highway with unobstructed pavement of sufficient width to enable 2 or more lines of vehicles lawfully to proceed in the same direction at the same time.

Assignment 1

Your firm has been hired by Smallville, which is a small town on the edge of Metropolis, to draft some ordinances for their city council's consideration. The Smallville council wants the town to retain its small town values, even though it is becoming a suburb of the larger nearby city, and they want you to draft an ordinance similar to the one below, which they got from another town. Smallville, however, wants to have an ordinance for funeral processions only, omitting the military convoy information. Your firm also has a reputation for drafting outstandingly clear regulations; that's why Smallville hired them. So you want to revise the language to make the statute understandable to the average reader, as well as being legally precise.

999.20   Right-of-way of funeral processions and military convoys.

(1) Except as provided in sub. (4), the operator of a vehicle not in a funeral procession or military convoy shall yield the right-of-way at an intersection to vehicles in a funeral procession or military convoy when vehicles comprising such procession have their headlights lighted.

(2) The operator of a vehicle not in a funeral procession shall not drive the vehicle between the vehicles of the funeral procession, except when authorized to do so by a traffic officer or when such vehicle is an authorized emergency vehicle giving audible signal by siren.

(3) Operators of vehicles not a part of a funeral procession or military convoy shall not form a procession or convoy and have their headlights lighted for the purpose of securing the right-of-way granted by this section to funeral processions or military convoys.

(4)(a) Operators of vehicles in a funeral procession or military convoy shall yield the right-of-way in accordance with s. 999.19 upon the approach of an authorized emergency vehicle giving audible signal by siren.

(b) Operators of vehicles in a funeral procession or military convoy shall yield the right-of-way when directed to do so by a traffic officer.

(c) The operator of the leading vehicle in a funeral procession or military convoy shall comply with stop signs and traffic control signals, but when the leading vehicle has proceeded across an intersection in accordance with such signal or after stopping as required by the stop sign, all vehicles in such procession may proceed without stopping, regardless of the sign or signal.

999.205 Owner's liability for vehicle failing to yield the right-of-way to a funeral procession.

(1) The owner of a vehicle involved in a violation of s. 999.20 (1) for failing to yield the right-of-way to a funeral procession shall be liable for the violation as provided in this section.

(2) The operator of a lead vehicle or a motorcycle escort in a funeral procession who observes a violation of s. 999.20 (1) for failing to yield the right-of-way to a funeral procession may prepare a written report indicating that a violation has occurred. If possible, the report shall contain the following information:

  (a) the time and the approximate location at which the violation occurred.

  (b) the license number and color of the vehicle involved in the violation.

  (c) identification of the vehicle as an automobile, station wagon, motor truck, motor bus, motorcycle or other type of vehicle.

(3) Within 24 hours after observing the violation, the operator of the lead vehicle or motorcycle escort may deliver the report to a traffic officer of the county or municipality in which the violation occurred. A report that does not contain all the information in sub.(2) shall nevertheless be delivered and shall be maintained by the county or municipality for statistical purposes.

(4)(a) Within 48 hours after receiving a report containing all the information in sub.(2), the traffic officer may prepare a uniform traffic citation under s. 999.11 and may personally serve it upon the owner of the vehicle.

  (b) If with responsible diligence the owner cannot be served under par.(a), service may be made by leaving a copy of the citation at the owner's usual place of abode within this state in the presence of a competent member of the family at least 14 years of age, who shall be informed of the contents thereof.

  (c) If with reasonable diligence the owner cannot be served under par.(a) or (b) or if the owner lives outside of the jurisdiction of the issuing authority, service may be made by certified mail addressed to the owner's last-know address.

(5)(a) Except as provided in par.(b), it shall be no defense to a violation of this section that the owner was not operating the vehicle at the time of the violation.

  (b) The following are defenses to a violation of this section:

(1) that a report that the vehicle was stolen was given to a traffic officer before the violation occurred or within a reasonable time after the violation occurred.

(2) if the owner of the vehicle provides a traffic officer with the name and address of the person operating the vehicle at the time of the violation and the person so named admits operating the vehicle at the time of the violation, then the person operating the vehicle and not the owner shall be charged under this section.

Assignment 2

You are the attorney for the Florida legislature. After several very public lawsuits against hospitals related to their compliance with the following Florida law, legislators realized that the hospitals were having trouble interpreting the law and thus understanding how to comply with the law. As a result, the legislators have decided that the following statute needs to be revised to be clearer about who does what when, and about when different actions are required. They have asked you to revise this statute to make it more understandable, but not to change the meaning of the statute.

Florida Statutes § 395.0197

PART I. HOSPITALS AND OTHER LICENSED FACILITIES

Internal risk management program

(1) Every licensed facility shall, as a part of its administrative functions, establish an internal risk management program that includes all of the following components:

(a) The investigation and analysis of the frequency and causes of general categories and specific types of adverse incidents to patients.

(b) The development of appropriate measures to minimize the risk of adverse incidents to patients, including, but not limited to:

1. Risk management and risk prevention education and training of all nonphysician personnel as follows:

   a. such education and training of all nonphysician personnel as part of their initial orientation; and

   b. at least 1 hour of such education and training annually for all nonphysician personnel of the licensed facility working in clinical areas and providing patient care.

2. A prohibition, except when emergency circumstances require otherwise, against a staff member of the licensed facility attending a patient in the recovery room, unless the staff member is authorized to attend the patient in the recovery room and is in the company of at least one other

person. However, a licensed facility is exempt from the two-person requirement if it has:

a. live visual observation;

b. electronic observation; or

c. any other reasonable measure taken to ensure patient protection and privacy.

(c) The analysis of patient grievances that relate to patient care and the quality of medical services.

(d) The development and implementation of an incident reporting system based upon the affirmative duty of all health care providers and all agents and employees of the licensed health care facility to report adverse incidents to the risk manager, or to his or her designee, within 3 business days after their occurrence.

BIBLIOGRAPHY

Cooper, Frank E., *Writing in Law Practice*. Indianapolis: Bobbs–Merrill Co., 2d ed. 1963.

Crepsi, Gregory Scott, *The Influence of a Decade of Statutory Interpretation Scholarship on Judicial Rulings: An Empirical Analysis*, 53 S.M.U.L.Rev. 9 (2000).

Dickerson, Reed, *The Fundamentals of Legal Drafting*. Boston: Little, Brown and Company, 1986.

Dickerson, Reed, *Materials on Legal Drafting*. St. Paul: West Group, 1981.

Dickerson, Reed, *Legislative Drafting*. Boston: Little, Brown and Company, 2d ed. 1977.

Eskridge, Jr., William N., Philip P. Frickey, and Elizabeth Garrett, *Cases and Materials on Legislation: Statutes and the Creation of Public Policy*. St. Paul: West Group, 3d ed. 2001.

Eskridge Jr., William N., Philip P. Frickey, and Elizabeth Garrett, *Legislation and Statutory Interpretation*. New York: Foundation Press, 2000.

Filson, Lawrence E., *The Legislative Drafter's Desk Reference*. Washington D.C.: Congressional Quarterly, 1992.

Frickey, Philip P., *Revisiting the Revival of Theory in Statutory Interpretation: A Lecture in Honor of Irving Younger*, 84 Minn.L.Rev. 199 (1999).

Holder, Russell, *Comment: Say What You Mean and Mean What You Say: The Resurrection of Plain Meaning in California Courts*, 30 U.C. Davis L.Rev. 569 (1997).

Kuzara, Christine M., *Plain English in Legislative Drafting*, 62 Mich.Bar J. 980 (Nov. 1983).

Llewellyn, Karl N., *Remarks on the Theory of Appellate Decision and the Rule or Canons About How Statutes Are To Be Construed*, 3 Vand. L.Rev. 395 (1950).

Looking It Up: Dictionaries and Statutory Construction, 107 Harv.L.Rev. 1437 (1994).

Manning, John F., *Legal Realism and the Canons' Revival*, 5 Green Bag 2d 283 (2002).

Marcello, David A., *The Ethics and Politics of Legislative Drafting*, 70 Tul.L.Rev. 2437 (1996).

Mikva, Abner J. and Eric Lane, *An Introduction to Statutory Interpretation and the Legislative Process*. New York: Aspen Law & Business, 1997.

Nutting, Charles Bernard, *Legislation: Cases and Materials*. St. Paul: West Group, 1978.

Peacock, James Craig, *Notes on Legislative Drafting*. Washington D.C.: REC Foundation, Inc., 1961.

Pratt, Diana V., *Legal Writing: A Systematic Approach*. St. Paul: West Group, 3d ed. 1999.

Ray, Mary Barnard, and Jill J. Ramsfield, *Getting It Right and Getting It Written*. St. Paul: West Group, 3d ed. 2000.

Read, Horace Emerson, *Materials on Legislation*. Mineola, N.Y.: The Foundation Press, Inc., 1982.

Schacter, Jane S., *The Confounding Common Law Originalism in Recent Supreme Court Statutory Interpretation: Implications for the Legislative History Debate and Beyond*, 51 Stan.L.Rev. 1 (1998).

Singer, Norman J., 1A *Statutes and Statutory Construction*. St. Paul: West Group, 6th ed. 2002.

Statsky, William P., *Legislative Analysis and Drafting*. St. Paul: West Group, 2d ed. 1984.

Talmadge, Philip A., *A New Approach to Statutory Interpretation in Washington*, 25 Seattle Univ.L.Rev. 179 (2001).

Tiefer, Charles, *The Reconceptualization of Legislative History in the Supreme Court*, 2000 Wis.L.Rev. 205.

Chapter 4

JURY INSTRUCTIONS

While drafting statutes involves creating law, drafting jury instructions involves explaining existing law to nonlawyers. It may require less research time than statutes, but substantially more drafting time. Drafting effective instructions also requires accuracy and clarity, but it also requires more because the purpose of jury instructions differs substantially from that of statutes.

Jury instructions are generally viewed as important, sometimes even the most critical part of the trial.[1] Except for those given at the beginning of the trial to help explain the jury's tasks during the trial, most jury instructions are given at the crossroads in a trial, when the focus is shifting from the witness box to the jury box and when the jury is turning from listening to deciding. Furthermore, the instructions stand between many tasks and participants: between advocating and informing, between two communicators (the judge and the attorneys), between readers who see the instructions (the judges) and those who only hear them (the jury, in some states[2]), and between lay readers (the jury) and technical readers (the appellate courts).

The intersection of all these aspects makes drafting instructions complex.[3] Perhaps this is why a successful set of instructions, one approved by reviewing courts and understandable for the jury, is rare. "When I read instructions to the jury, I hope that I will see a light go on in the juror's eyes, but I never do."[4]

1. John Kennelly, *Closing Arguments: Instructions are the Key,* 6 Trial Law. Guide 53 (1962); Ronald W. Eades, *The Problem of Jury Instructions in Civil Cases,* 27 Cumb. L.Rev. 1017, 1017 (1996/1997).

2. Some states give a copy of the jury instructions to the jury, but some expect the jurors to follow the instructions based only on the judge's oral presentation of those instructions.

3. Dean E. Hewes and Sally Planalp, *The Individual's Place in Communication Science* in *Handbook of Communication Science* 147 (C. Berger and S. Chaffee, eds. 1987).

4. Personal communication from an Oregon trial judge, quoted in Laurence J. Severance and Elizabeth F. Loftus, *Improving the Ability of Jurors to Comprehend and Apply Criminal Jury Instructions* 17 L. & Soc'y 153, 154–55 (1982).

In essence, the trial judge may have a choice between two evils: (a) instructions that properly state the law but which some jurors may not understand; and (b) instructions that nearly all jurors understand but which do not properly state the law. Error (a) is probably preferable to error (b).[5]

Rather than despairing about the complexity of the situation, however, work your way through the various considerations involved, making informed choices, improving the status quo, and you will reach your goal.

The first section of this chapter delineates the general considerations involved in choosing and revising instructions. The second section covers specific techniques you can use to implement the decisions you made in light of those considerations. The final section summarizes these techniques in a checklist to give you an overview of the process as a whole.

GENERAL CONSIDERATIONS WHEN CHOOSING AND REVISING INSTRUCTIONS

Jury instructions have changed substantially since the 1930s,[6] and significant improvements have occurred.[7] Throughout your legal career, you may see additional improvements as the legal system continues to learn more about how jurors process information. Although improvements continue, much of the literature in this area has focused on problems with the jury instructions currently in use.[8] Linguists have tested instructions, have found disturbingly low levels of understanding within juries, and have attributed these problems to writing structures.[9] Others have complained that the length of instructions makes it impossi-

5. J. Clark Kelso, *Final Report of the Blue Ribbon Commission on Jury System Improvement*, 47 Hastings L.J. 1433, 1516 (1996). *But see*, Kimball R. Anderson and Bruce R. Braun, *The Legal Legacy of John Wayne Gacy: The Irrebuttable Presumption That Juries Understand and Follow Jury Instructions*, 78 Marq.L.Rev. 791 (1995)(arguing that error (a) is worse and unacceptable, especially when imposing the death penalty based on a court-approved presumption of juror understanding, despite direct empirical evidence to the contrary).

6. In the 1930s, Judge William J. Palmer began working on jury instructions in California. In 1955, the state of Illinois began its study of jury instructions and eventually developed the first patterned (or model) jury instructions.

7. Over the past years, Montana added a communications specialist to their jury instructions drafting committee, and the Oregon, Connecticut, Florida, and California judiciaries held conferences, ran pilot projects, and have done other work to improve jury instructions.

8. For a particularly helpful review of the history and development of jury instructions, *see,* Harvey Perlman, *Pattern Jury Instructions: The Application of Social Science Research*, 65 Neb.L.Rev. 520 (1986). *See also*, Walter W. Steele, Jr. and Elizabeth G. Thornburg, *Jury Instructions: A Persistent Failure to Communicate*, 67 N.C.L.Rev. 77 (1988); Eades, *supra* note 1, at 1017.

9. One of the first systematic studies in this area is described in Robert and Veda Charrow, *Making Legal Language Understandable: A Psycholinguistic Study of Jury Instructions*, 79 Col.L.Rev. 1306 (1979). For an updated summary of research on jury instructions, *see* Bethany K. Dumas, *Jury Trials: Lay Jurors, Pattern Jury Instructions, and Comprehension Issues*, 67 Tenn. L.Rev. 701 (2000). For an interesting discussion between lawyers and linguists on jury instructions, *see Law and Linguistics Conference Proceedings*, 73 Wash.U.L.Q. 800, 953–970 (1995).

ble for the jury to comprehend its task.[10] Still others have complained about the judges' presentation of the instructions[11] and the time at which instructions are presented in the trial.[12] As the following judge's description illustrates, it is not a pretty scene.

> Probably the most discouraging part of the trial is the time when the judge tries to cram into twelve non-legal minds all the law applicable to the case at hand. The blank expressions on the faces of citizen jurors [are] pitiful. They [are matched] only by the bleak look of the judge [while plodding] through the legal terminology that [the judge] knows is making little if any impression on [the] listeners. Yet, the law continues to go under the assumption that this type of material is clearly understood and applied to trials that are of the utmost importance to the participants.[13]

Understanding the problems involved, however, can help you take the steps necessary to improve the jury instructions used in your trials. Issues you need to consider fall into two broad areas:

- those judges address when reviewing submitted instructions or preparing their own instructions, and

- those litigators address as they prepare instructions for the judge's review.

Considerations of the Judiciary

Although attorneys propose instructions to the judge, he or she is ultimately responsible for jury instructions. The judge decides what instructions to give the jury, reads the instructions as coming from the judge rather than the attorneys, and is finally responsible for making sure the jury receives all the instructions they need to reach a verdict and to avoid appealable error. The last two tasks can be at odds. "A trial judge must long for the ability to use two completely different vocabularies in addressing juries and in addressing the appellate courts. However, that is not the system in which trial judges operate."[14] This contradiction can either lessen or increase your chances for revising pattern instructions. For example, to avoid appealable error, a judge may think the unchanged model jury instruction is safer, simply because the judge then

10. Perlman, *supra* note 8, at 537; *see also*, Douglas G. Smith, *Structural and Functional Aspects of the Jury: Comparative Analysis and Proposals for Reform*, 48 Ala. L.Rev. 441, 529 (1997).

11. William Schwarzer, *Communicating with Juries: Problems and Remedies*, 69 Cal.L.Rev. 731, 756 (1981); Christopher N. May, *"What Do We Do Now?": Helping Juries Apply the Instructions*, 28 Loy. L.A.L.Rev. 869, 870 (1995).

12. Schwarzer, *supra* note 11, at 755; *see also* Neil P. Cohen, *The Timing of Jury Instructions*, 67 Tenn.L.Rev. 681 (2000).

13. Raymond Buchanan, *The Florida Judge–Jury Communications Project,* 8 Bridge.L.Rev. 297, 298 (1987).

14. J. Clark Kelso, *supra* note 5, at 1515. "Ultimately, the trial judge must be cognizant of what the sophisticated appellate audience demands, and if that audience demands language that is too complex for the ordinary juror, the trial judge has no choice but to comply (even when the trial judge knows that the result of complying is to confuse the jury.)" *Id.*

can rely on the understanding of specialists in instructions.[15] In contrast, that judge may suspect that a previously established instruction in a particular case will not be clear to the jury without modification.[16] Judges work to balance these two forces. "The courts' primary concern should be an effort to empower the jury to understand and apply the law in a holistic and contextual way."[17]

In general, concerns for clarity and the ability to stand up under appeal are better served by revising instructions. Even the drafters of model jury instructions agree: "Model instructions can be most useful as servants. There is danger in letting them become masters."[18] In light of all this, receiving revised instructions from the attorney is an improvement appreciated by many courts.

> [E]ven technically correct instructions should be reviewed with an eye to their comprehensibility. The test should not be simply whether the instruction was substantially correct, but whether it enabled the jury to reach a fair and informed verdict. An egregious departure from this standard should concern appellate courts as much as a traditional legal error in the instructions.[19]

Although some jurisdictions require that pattern jury instructions be used verbatim,[20] appellate courts generally do not strike down revised instructions if the content remains correct.[21] Indeed judges have praised instructions that have been adapted to specific situations.

> At its best [the jury instruction] is a simple, rugged communication from a trial judge to a jury of ordinary people, entitled to be appraised in terms of its net effect. Instructions are to be viewed in

---

15. *See* Graham Douthwaite, *Jury Instructions, Pattern and Otherwise,* 29 Def. L.J. 335 (1980).

16. For example, the 1991 and 1992 Pattern Jury Instructions Committees used language from 1954 and 1984 North Dakota Supreme court cases for an instruction on being "under the influence of intoxicating liquor," despite the fact that the court's language was intended to communicate with judges and lawyers, not with laypersons. Gail Hagerty, *Instructing the Jury? Watch Your Language!,* 70 N.Dak.L.Rev. 1007, 1017–18 (1994).

17. Elizabeth G. Thornburg, *The Power and The Process: Instructions and the Civil Jury,* 66 Fordham L.Rev. 1837, 1839 (1998). For a survey of South Carolina judges on this conflict, *see* Roger M. Young, *Using Social Science to Assess the Need for Jury Reform in South Carolina,* 52 S.C. L.Rev. 135, 181–82 (2000).

18. Douthwaite, *supra* note 15, at 347.

19. Schwarzer, *supra* note 11, at 758. This article might be a useful supporting source if you are arguing to the court for a revision of a model instruction. *But see* the introduction to the 6th Edition of California Jury Instructions: Criminal xviii (1996): "We who make up this committee are acutely aware of the criticism often made that instructions are difficult for jurors to comprehend and apply. We do try to use language that will be understandable. However, in the last analysis, we must use the language that the Legislature gives us, and the language that will meet the legal requirements of the appellate courts."

20. J. Clark Kelso, *supra* note 5, 1512 n.112 (citing Illinois Supreme Court Rule 25–1 (which is now 239(a) (2001)) which states: "Whenever Illinois Pattern Instructions (IPI) contain an instruction applicable in a civil case, . . . the IPI instruction shall be used, unless the court determines that it does not accurately state the law." *See also* Mich. Court Rule 2.516(D)(2); New Mex. Sup. Court Rule 1–051(D); Mo. Sup. Court Rule 70.02(b); Colo. Rules of Civ. Proc. 51.1(1)).

21. Kevin F. O'Malley, Jay E. Grenig, and William C. Lee, *Federal Jury Practice and Instructions* § 7.02 (5th ed. 2000).

this common-sense perspective, and not through the remote and distorting knothole of a distant appellate fence.[22]

Judges are also considering greater use of other components of jury instruction, such as special verdicts or instructive interrogatories (where the jury answers specific questions but also renders a general verdict).[23] By guiding the jury to answer a series of specific questions, the special verdict shows the jury precisely what they need to determine to deliver a verdict. These specific findings in turn establish a clearer record for any appellate questions that may arise. So, for example, rather than asking the jury to find for the consumer (plaintiff) or the manufacturer (defendant) on the issue of breach of a duty in a products liability case, the judge might ask a jury to decide the following questions.

1. Did the manufacturer exercise ordinary care in the design, construction, and manufacture of its product so that the product was safe for its intended use?

2. In exercising ordinary care, did the manufacturer make all reasonable and adequate tests and inspections of its product to guard against any defective condition that would render it unsafe?

3. Did the manufacturer exercise ordinary care in warning consumers of dangers which it knew or should have known are associated with use of its product?[24]

This series of questions avoids allowing the jury to find for the plaintiff out of sympathy for his or her plight without first determining whether the defendant was at fault. Some commentators believe this is one of the special interrogatory's drawbacks: it may prevent the jury from "doing justice."[25] Whether to use the special interrogatory or general verdict is usually a decision made by the court in conjunction with trial counsel.[26]

If you become a judge yourself, you will have an opportunity to address some of these considerations directly. If you are a practicing attorney, you will work within the limits set by the preferences of your judge and by the regulations of your jurisdiction.

Considerations of the Litigator

As a litigator, you will routinely submit jury instructions to the judge, who then chooses which instructions to submit to the jury.

22. *Time, Inc. v. Hill,* 385 U.S. 374, 481 (1967) (Fortas, J. dissenting).

23. Robert Berdon, *Instructive Interrogatories: Helping the Civil Jury to Understand,* 55 Conn.B.J. 179 (1981); and Robert Berdon, *Instructive Interrogatories: One Method to Aid the Jury,* 8 Bridge.L.Rev. 385 (1987).

24. Based on Wis.Civ.J.I. 3240–3242.

25. Eades, *supra* note 1, at 1025 (arguing that "[l]imiting the jury's authority to do justice casts doubt on the jury system and individual jurors." *Id.*) For a discussion on why keeping the general verdict is desirable, *see* Thornburg, *supra* note 17, at 1858–93.

26. David D. Noce, *Jury Instructions Drafting Workbook* 12 (1999)(citing the ABA Civil Trial Practice Standards for the suggestion that judges permit counsel to collaborate and agree on the type of verdict used where possible, and when stipulation is impossible, permit counsel to argue their views to the judge).

Although attorneys sometimes leave the choice of instructions to the judge when they think the standard ones are sufficient, instructions are too important to omit from your advocacy. When you submit instructions, you are both advocating for your client and acting as a servant of the court. You advocate when you choose instructions that show the jury (1) how they can find in favor of your client, (2) why damaging information is not critical to the outcome of the case, and (3) why favorable facts are critical. You want to revise the instructions you have chosen to communicate the applicable law clearly so the jury will see how it supports your position.

The first consideration in your jury instructions is that they are written to be given to the jury by a neutral party, the judge. This means you need to exercise some caution in preparing instructions. For example, when dealing with an unsettled area of law, prepare instructions early in the process; do not wait until the trial is in progress to address the critical issues that need to be resolved before the judge can use these instructions. Also prepare alternative requests, so you have some recourse if the court does not choose your primary instruction.[27] Similarly, in your instructions use clear-but-neutral descriptions that the judge would use, avoiding any biased words and any statements implying that your client should win. Finally, do not omit an instruction just because you would prefer that it were not needed. Instead, prepare your own version so the judge has an alternative to consider when reading the instruction your opponent prepares on that point.

Another consideration is what format to use when providing instructions; usually this means choosing between a special verdict (or instructive interrogatories) or a general verdict. Instructive interrogatories are generally useful when the jury's sympathy is likely to run against your client, but the law runs in your favor. The instructive interrogatory limits the jury's focus to more specific questions so the jury may find that their sympathies are not relevant to answering some or all of the interrogatories. In contrast, a general verdict allows the jury broader discretion in the factors it considers relevant when deliberating. For example, an attorney representing a corporation in a strict liability case might request an instructive interrogatory that asks for findings on the specific elements of the claim rather than asking for an overall verdict about whether the plaintiff should receive compensation. The plaintiff's attorney might request a general verdict that allows the jury more scope to act on its sympathy for the person injured.

How you approach developing your jury instructions depends in part on your jurisdiction. When your state has model jury instructions, as do most states, you begin by choosing those. Then, as allowable, you adapt them to fit your situation and to increase understandability. If your jurisdiction allows the jury to have a copy of the instructions, revise the instructions to make their organization visually clear. If the jury does not receive a copy, revise them so they are easy for the judge to read

---

27. O'Malley, *supra* note 21, at § 7.03.

clearly to the jury. This increases the chance that the judge will communicate, through inflection and pause, the organization you have given to the instructions. In turn, the jury will hear the organization more clearly and find the content easier to absorb. To communicate this organization to the judge, introduce listed items with visual clues, such as tabulation and parenthetical numbers. To communicate the organization to the jury, use verbal clues, such as introductory phrases before lists.

Your approach also depends on how your state uses model instructions. Although some states require you to use these model instructions with few modifications,[28] most encourage modifying the model instructions to fit the case at bar. "[T]he fact that pattern jury instructions are available should not preclude a judge from modifying or supplementing pattern instructions to suit the particular needs of an individual cases.... [P]attern instructions should be modified or supplemented by the court when necessary to fit the particular facts of a case."[29]

There is good reason for this modification. Model instructions are necessarily written to fit any possible situation. By applying to every general situation, they apply to no particular one. The introduction to the Wisconsin Model Civil Jury Instructions makes the limitations of model instructions explicit.

We forcefully disclaim that:

- It is free from error, completely accurate, or a model of perfection in form, statement, or expression.

- It is presented as a standard of instructions pattern to be blindly and unquestionably followed.

    . . .

- It will remove all need for the trial judge's industry and ingenuity in the preparation of instructions.

    . . .

- It will lessen the duties of the trial attorneys with respect to the preparation and submission of timely written instructions.

    . . .

- It forestalls any constructive suggestions for its improvement.

- It is as clear, concise, and correct as it can or ought to be.[30]

Furthermore, using an unmodified jury instruction, which covers many situations rather than your client's particular one, contradicts the

---

28. Douthwaite, *supra* note 15, at 348–49 (footnotes omitted).

29. *Forecite: Latest Developments in California Criminal Jury Instructions* 1 (Thomas Lundy, ed., Cumulative Supp. 1997)(citing *ABA Standards for Criminal Justice, Discovery and Trial by Jury* 236–37 (3d ed. 1996)). However, some pattern instructions are so well respected that, for example, the Standards of Judicial Adminis-

tration in California recommend use of BAJI or CALJIC instructions unless the judge finds that a different instruction would "more adequately, accurately or clearly state the law." J. Clark Kelso, *supra* note 5, at 1512.

30. A.W. Parnell, Chairman, Jury Instructions Committee, Introduction to the 1960 Edition of the Wisconsin Model Jury Instructions.

basic rules of effective public speaking, going back to Aristotle. Effective speakers know that listeners remember concrete images, so they use anecdotes and images to clarify their points. The model instructions do not allow for this because specifics arise from the facts of individual cases. Therefore, if the jury is to be expected to understand and apply the law to a particular situation, the instructions must be modified to explain the law clearly, concretely, and specifically.[31]

Precisely because accurately modified instructions are clearer, some attorneys request vaguer, pattern instructions when the sympathy runs in favor of their client but the law does not. The reasoning behind this was bluntly stated by Jamison Wilcox, although he did not particularly favor it.

> Simply put, when instructions are ineffective, the rules of law are ineffective in exercising their appropriate influence over the jury. Jurors then act more on their feelings and prejudices, and less on the law, than they do when effectively instructed.[32]

Nevertheless, choosing to retain vague instructions is risky for two reasons. First, people's "feelings and prejudices" often are not predictable; you might be lighting the fuse of a loose cannon. Second, "[a]n instruction which will win a lawsuit but will not stand up on appeal is worse than no instruction at all."[33] The better choice is to adapt the model instructions to your case, taking pains to maintain accuracy and still clarify how the law supports the result your client wants.

The task of drafting jury instructions raises many questions for judges and litigators alike, questions that sometimes conflict, sometimes coordinate, but always interact. When writing jury instructions, you will make many complex decisions. To help you make these decisions comfortably and competently, you need a clear sense of what makes jury instructions readable and how to achieve it.

We spend little time in this chapter discussing methods for drafting original jury instructions for two reasons. First, most states have comprehensive model jury instructions and it is unusual not to find a model instruction that addresses the issues raised in your case.[34] Second, the techniques you use to draft original instructions are similar to the ones you take in revising model instructions, with one significant difference: if you are drafting an original instruction, you must supply the necessary legal content. When drafting an instruction rather than revising a model,

---

31. For a proposal encouraging judges to use their right to summarize evidence (permitted in the federal system and at least forty states) to "weave in the facts, the evidence, or the parties' contentions, so that the law is presented to the jury in the context of the specific case," *see* May, *supra* note 11, at 892–901.

32. Jamison Wilcox, *The Craft of Drafting Plain–Language Jury Instructions: A Study of a Sample Pattern Instruction on Obscenity,* 59 Temp.L.Q. 1159, 1183 (1986).

33. Edward J. Devitt and Charles Blackmar, *Federal Jury Practice and Instructions* 241 (3d ed. 1977).

34. Even if your state requires you to use its pattern instructions, you may be faced with situations where your case is making new law or raising issues that have not been addressed by the pattern instructions. Because model instructions are routinely updated, however, this does not happen all that frequently.

begin by writing a rough draft including all needed content. For example, if you are writing an instruction on a novel theory of law or based on a newly passed statute, include all the elements necessary to establish whether the theory is met or the statute's requirements are established by the facts. Then revise, just as you would revise model instructions.

TECHNIQUES FOR CHOOSING AND REVISING INSTRUCTIONS

Because people untrained in the law must understand jury instructions, you need to focus on understandability when writing them. The jury's task is complex,[35] so unclear passages and missignals in the instructions are very likely to cause confusion. For this reason, all your revisions should make those instructions more understandable.

To attain understandability, instructions need to be readable, clear, and unambiguous. Jury instructions can meet this goal, although they often do not. For an example of their common failings, read the following instruction aloud at a normal rate of speech.

> If you find that, by reason of public improvements already made or planned to be made in the immediate future, special benefits have accrued to the remaining property of the plaintiff, so as to affect its market value, you should offset the fair market value of such special benefits against the severance damages, if any, found by you, or against the value of the land taken, but in no event should you allow special benefits in excess of the damages.
>
> A special benefit, as used in the foregoing instruction, is a benefit that in fact enhances the value of the land not taken either because the public project improves the physical condition of the remaining land, or because the public project, by its proximity to the remaining land, immediately increases the market value of the land for an existing use or for a different and more profitable use.[36]

It is hard to imagine a juror understanding and correctly applying the law after listening to that instruction read aloud once. While it is easy to see the problem with this example, it is harder to know exactly what, in terms of rewriting, will solve the problem. The rest of this section focuses on showing you how to improve both the instructions you draft yourself and those you find in pattern instruction books.

The following revision avoids many of the problems plaguing the instruction above. Read this version aloud to appreciate the difference.

> **Sometimes the expansion of a park will increase a lot's market value, even though that expansion took some of the lot's land. This can happen if any of following three things occur:**
>
> **(1) if the expansion improved the physical condition of the lot,**

---

35. Hewes and Planalp, *supra* note 3, at 161.

36. Wis.Civ.J.I. 8115.

(2) if the lot is more valuable because it is close to the park's expansion, or

(3) if an owner can now put the lot to a different and more profitable use.

If you find that the market value of Mr. Oliveras's lot has or will increase because of the park's expansion, then you should subtract that increase from the damages you determined. If you find that this increase in market value is greater than the damages you determined, then you should decide that the damages are zero.

But even if the increase in market value is greater than the damages you determined, you should not subtract anything from the value of the land actually taken from Mr. Oliveras's lot for the park's expansion.

To avoid some of the problems in the original, this revision uses several writing techniques to make the content clearer.

- It personalizes the instructions, so the jury can understand more readily how the law applies to this situation.

- It substitutes plain English for unfamiliar words whenever possible.

- It uses more understandable sentence structure.

- It keeps the subject and verb close together, uses clearer structural signals, and avoids long introductory phrases that would put confusing details before the main point.

Taken together, these individual techniques work substantial changes in the instruction's overall readability. The following subsections explain each technique, taking you through a plan of attack for clarifying jury instructions.

Before turning to those techniques, also consider when to prepare jury instructions. On this, the authorities are in agreement: frame jury instructions as soon as possible, once you know the case will be going to trial.[37] Doing so helps you focus on the points you need to make to win your case. It also helps you work out the wording of those points, so throughout the trial you can point toward the conclusion you want the jury to reach. You have much to gain and nothing to lose by starting early. Before the trial, you need to prepare any pretrial instructions you want the judge to read to the jury to help explain how the upcoming trial will be presented and explain the general rules the jury should keep in

37. A.H. Reid, *The Law of Instructions to Juries in Civil and Criminal Cases* 483 (3d ed. 1960). "Some courts request that the parties submit their instructions at the outset of the trial; others after all the evidence is in. Generally, approval of jury instructions occurs before closing arguments, so that the parties know better how to structure their last appeal to the jurors." Mark A. Dombroff, *Burdens, Inferences and Presumptions: A Tactical Perspective*, 8 Trial Dipl.J. 36 (1985).

mind while considering the opening statements and presentation of the evidence.[38]

Choosing Instructions

When choosing instructions, you need to request all the necessary instructions to avoid waiving them, but nevertheless you must be selective. You may find it helpful to consult or create a checklist for the type of case you have to make sure you have considered all the issues you should raise during the trial.[39] A general guide is do not tell the jury things they may not need to know.[40] In your initial proposal for instructions, for example, do not include instructions for the jury to disregard the opposition's objections. Request those only after significant objections are made. When selecting instructions, keep the list as short as possible.[41] This is important because the jury, if overwhelmed by the amount of instruction, may give up and decide the case on its own.

The important points must not be lost in a mass of jury instructions. In general, keep the instructions to thirty minutes reading time (the length of the average sermon), shorter if possible.[42] You do need to prepare legally sufficient instructions, but this may not require a quantity of instructions.[43] Occasionally, you may need to choose from several applicable model instructions, perhaps even between those for civil and criminal cases. For example, in a criminal case, you may need an instruction to address the idea of "falsis in uno," the idea a jury may find a witness's testimony to be false generally if it has been shown to be false on a particular point. Perhaps your state has a model instruction on this point in its civil instructions, but not its criminal instructions. Rather than creating a new criminal instruction, consider adapting the civil model instruction to fit the circumstance. You may also need to

---

38. Preinstruction may enhance what the jury remembers because "attention and memory processes are more acute" when jurors better understand the trial process and their role. Both judges and commentators encourage preinstruction. *See* Smith, *supra* note 10, at 531–37. Although presenting jury instructions just before deliberations makes sense, due to the principle of recency, it would also help juries have some idea of their job before they begin–"when was the last time anyone learned the rules of a game *after* it was played?" Dumas, *supra* note 9, at 737. Most pattern instruction books include preliminary instructions (usually on the nature and organization of the trial process, burdens of proof, duty of the jury, credibility of witnesses, bench conferences, taking notes, etc). For a list of instruction topics and sources for preliminary instructions, *see* Noce, *supra* note 26, at 40–45.

39. For an example checklist for a criminal trial, *see Forecite: Latest Developments in California Criminal Jury Instructions–*

Practice Guide 6–18 (2d ed. 1994). Additionally, model jury instructions for specific types of cases have been published. *See Model Jury Instructions: Business Torts Litigation* (American Bar Association 3d ed. 1996); *Model Jury Instructions: Employment Litigation* (American Bar Association 1994).

40. Anthony Partridge, *When Judges Throw Gibberish at Jurors,* 8 Update of L.Rel.Ed. 7 (1974).

41. Reid, *supra* note 37, at 484.

42. Berdon, *Instructive Interrogatories, supra* note 23, 8 Bridge.L.Rev. at 390. "Few cases, if properly prepared, should require instruction taking more than twenty to thirty minutes to read." Schwarzer, *supra* note 11, at 747. Also see Judge Learned Hand's comments supporting a trial judge's rejection of 366 requests for instructions in *United States v. Cohen,* 145 F.2d 82, 93 (2d Cir. 1944).

43. Reid, *supra* note 37, at 484–85 n. 1.

draw from both civil and criminal model instructions in quasi-criminal actions, such as some violations of municipal ordinances.

When choosing specific jury instructions, include instructions that:

- explain law critical to your theory or theories;

- explain your theories for damages, if applicable;

- include a special verdict if advantageous to your client;

- make your case hold up on appeal;

- forestall misunderstanding if you are quite sure something at trial will be likely to be misunderstood or misinterpreted by the jury;

- you believe the judge will want to submit and you want to revise to fit clearly with your client's position; and

- are needed to present a clear charge to the jury.

You will take the first four steps by determining what arguments you will make and what evidence you will present. Those steps are an adaptation of the research and thought you invest as you write the research memo, the brief, or both. When choosing instructions, look to your jurisdiction's model instructions on your critical theories. The commentary accompanying these instructions may provide helpful guidelines and may also tell you what instructions are legally essential.[44]

As you move to step five, consider what aspects of the law or the case are likely to be confusing to a jury, and select instructions that forestall confusion. For example, assume you are representing the plaintiff in a negligence case in which the plaintiff slipped on a patch of ice in the defendant's driveway. Assume the defendant had scraped the ice off as best he could; there were patches of ice but also enough clear spots so the plaintiff could have avoided the ice. Finally, assume there were only two witnesses at the trial, the defendant and the plaintiff. In this case, along with the legally necessary instructions for negligence, you might include an instruction on comparative negligence. Because your opponent will raise this issue, you should include your version of this instruction so the judge can consider an instruction that is more favorably worded for your client.

44. For example, Schwarzer, *supra* note 11, at 748–49, states the following about a criminal case:

Case law suggests that, depending on the context, instructions on the following subjects may be mandatory regardless of whether they are requested:

1. Each essential element of the offense charged that is in issue and particularly the requisite intent;

2. The burden of proof and probably the presumption of innocence;

3. The need for caution in accepting uncorroborated testimony of an accomplice or an informer, at least where it may be suspect;

4. In a multiple conspiracy case, the restriction against using evidence from one conspiracy to prove another; and

5. The limitation on the use of a confession as evidence when voluntariness is in question.

Under the last two steps, include instructions you know the judge will want to include, either because this judge always includes them or because they are common in your jurisdiction. These may be the instructions you revise least, because it is hard to overcome the traditional wording. But try to revise them when the instruction's language does not communicate accurately to the jury.

When submitting the instructions, follow the format requested by the judge or required by local court rules.[45] If you are unsure of the judge's preferred order of instructions, begin each instruction on a separate sheet of paper with the instruction number or title on the top of the page.[46] This allows the judge to re-order the instructions, insert others, or delete instructions easily. When you have each instruction typed, make its layout easy to read, using tabulation and double spacing as needed. This will help the judge, but it will also help your case by getting a clearer reading of your instructions to the jury. If your jurisdiction permits jurors to have a copy of the instructions, provide two sets of instructions: one for the judge and one for the jury.[47] With the instructions for the judge, also include relevant citations supporting the proposed instruction, which may come from statutes, appellate cases, dictionaries, law review articles, or other sources. This chapter's bibliography is a good starting point for finding this support.

Many communications experts suggest that judges and lawyers consider providing instructions to the jury using visual aids, such as diagrams, charts, or decision trees.[48] One commentator states: "Nothing could be worse, from a communications science perspective, than having these instructions read verbatim, in an official monotone, by a berobed judge to captive jurors."[49] Given the increasing use of multimedia aids in presenting evidence,[50] consider whether the judge and opposing counsel would permit you to provide the judge with a computer-generated visual presentation of the instructions, using the roadmaps suggested above, for the jury to follow while the judge is reading the instructions.

Revising Instructions

When you have selected the instructions, your next task is to revise those instructions for understandability. "Jury instructions . . . are on average more successful as each additional drop of abstruseness or complexity is wrung out of them."[51] One way to approach this task

---

45. Some local court rules set out specifications for jury instructions, including a requirement that they be submitted on computer disk so the judge can easily put together proposed instructions with standard instructions. O'Malley, *supra* note 21, at § 7.03 n.30.

46. Noce, *supra* note 26, at 9. Or you can include a line at the top that permits numbering to be inserted by the judge or the clerk. *Id.*

47. *Id.*

48. Dumas, *supra* note 9, at 738.

49. *Id.*

50. *See* Julie K. Plowman, *Note: Multimedia in the Courtroom: A Valuable Tool or Smoke and Mirrors?*, 15 Rev.Litig. 415 (1996).

51. Wilcox, *supra* note 32, at 1177.

without feeling overwhelmed is to divide the revision into the following ten steps.[52]

Ten Steps for Revising Jury Instructions

- Delete any irrelevant information.

- Personalize the instructions.

- Substitute common spoken English wherever possible.

- Define any critical, uncommon words.

- Find all the lists in your instructions, structure each of them clearly, and move each list to the end of the sentence.

- Make sure all signal words are clear.

- Use verbs instead of nouns stating action.

- Put modifying phrases next to the words they modify.

- Delete unneeded negatives.

- Divide or simplify any remaining complicated sentences.

Learning to use each of these techniques will give you the ability to improve the understandability of your instructions.

Delete Any Irrelevant Information

When using model instructions from your jurisdiction, delete any information irrelevant to your case.[53] For example, if your case involved a limousine, you would instruct as follows.

Any driver hired by a limousine service ....

rather than keeping all of the language in the original model instruction.

Any driver hired by a company that provides taxicabs, commercial vans, limousines, private trolleys, chartered buses, or other motorized vehicles for public transportation ....

This technique alone will make the instruction more focused on the case in question, and thus clearer. It also should reduce the length of the instruction and thus jurors' misunderstanding.[54]

---

52. Consider writing instructions using the framework that journalists use. They write the way experts advise for making jury instructions understandable because they write for people with varied backgrounds and levels of education. *See* Hagerty, *supra* note 16, at 1019.

53. "Make things as simple as possible—but no simpler." Richard Hatch, *Busi-ness Communication: Theory and Technique* 77 (1977), quoting Albert Einstein.

54. As the number of relevant dimensions or variables in a problem increases, the complexity of the problem increases and also the chance for error. Lyle E. Bourne, Jr., *Human Conceptual Behavior* 52 (1966).

Personalize the Instructions

If allowed in your jurisdiction, personalize the instruction by adding the names of the persons, places, and things involved. This helps the jury by presenting a more concrete picture of the facts they must determine. For example, use the following instruction,

> **You must decide whether Mr. Oliveras should receive severance damages. If you decide that he should receive these damages, you must also decide how much money he should receive. When deciding these two questions, you should consider all the credible evidence relating to two things: (1) Mr. Oliveras's claim that his lot's market value was reduced when the state changed the highway's grade, and (2) any other facts shown during the trial that affect the market value of his lot.**

rather than the original, more abstract model.

> In making your determination of severance damages, if any, you will consider all the credible evidence bearing upon the claimed diminution in market value of the land remaining (as a result of the change of grade of the highway), as well as all other facts and circumstances shown, by the credible evidence in the case, to affect the market value of the remaining land.[55]

Personalizing jury instructions helps the jury comprehend and use new information. Messages directed to persons inexperienced in the topic at hand are more effective when "links between actions and goals are stated explicitly."[56] Similarly, explanations of the law are more effective when linked explicitly to the specific facts of the case.

As you personalize, avoid phrasing that assumes guilt or innocence. For example, write

> **To determine whether the defendant failed to yield the right of way, you must answer the following questions. . . . If your answer to all of the questions is "yes," then you should find that the defendant did fail to yield the right of way. If, however, your answer to any one of the questions is "no," then you should find that the defendant did not fail to yield the right of way.**

rather than

> You should find that the defendant failed to yield the right of way if
> . . . .

To keep jury instructions neutral, avoid using "you should find" at the beginning of a sentence; some judges are concerned that the phrase steers the jury toward a certain outcome.[57] The judge must be able to accept your instruction as a neutral statement of law.

---

55. Wis.Civ.J.I. 8110.

56. Hewes and Planalp, *supra* note 3, at 160.

57. O'Malley, *supra* note 21, at § 7.02.

Substitute Common Spoken English Wherever Possible

Substitute common language, or plain English, for legalese whenever you can. For example, write

> **You should also be aware that, during the course of a trial, the lawyers will often refer to and read from depositions. Depositions are *written copies* of testimony taken *after the lawsuit began but before this trial began.***

rather than

> You should also be aware that, during the course of a trial, the lawyers will often refer to and read from depositions. Depositions are *transcripts* of testimony taken *during the pendency* of a lawsuit.[58]

Generally choose words used in everyday speech.[59] After you choose the clearest word, use that same word for the same idea throughout the instructions. This should help the reader understand how points are related. For example, write

> **The statutes further provide that when two *cars* approach an intersection, ... If you find that the Smith *car* and the Jones *car* both ....**

rather than

> The statutes further provide that when two *vehicles* approach or enter an intersection.... If you find that the *automobiles* in question ....[60]

You may need to keep a legal term when it states the standard. For example, keep such words as "reasonable doubt" or "evidence that is clear, satisfactory, and convincing." But avoid defining these terms in words that are equally confusing. For example, consider the following substitutions.

For this unfamiliar word	substitute this word.
engendered	born of
captious	trivial
requisite	required[61]

If you are working with a judge who is skittish about varying the wording of model instructions, try retaining key words from the original instruction and focusing instead on inserting clearer signal words and using clearer structure. Often readers will not see the structural changes as critical, yet those structural changes can greatly increase the clarity of the content.

---

58. Previous version of Wis.Civ.J.I. 50. The latest revision eliminated "during the pendency."

59. "The use of legal terminology in instructions should likewise be avoided." O'Malley, *supra* note 21, at § 7.02.

60. Wis Civ.J.I. 1157.

61. Dumas, *supra* note 9, at 733. She is referring to language contained in an earlier version of Tennessee's pattern instruction on reasonable doubt. *Id.* at 726. See her suggested revision at 732–33.

Define Any Critical, Uncommon Words

After you have identified terms that are necessary but perhaps unfamiliar, you can add definitions. Because the instructions will be read, you will probably not choose parentheses to mark your definition. You may, however, use a separate sentence, as in this example:

"Beyond a reasonable doubt" means . . . .

Or you might be able to use an added clause, if this does not make the sentence too complex, as in:

"beyond a reasonable doubt," or . . . .

These approaches allow you to maintain your focus on the main point while explaining your term.

Find All Lists in Your Instructions, Structure Each of Them Clearly, and Move Each List to the End of the Sentence

To structure lists clearly, begin by explaining the structure and purpose of the list in an introductory phrase. For example, you may begin with the following.

In order to find the defendant guilty, you must find that all three of the following are true:

This introduction tells the jury when it must use the information (to find the defendant guilty), how many items are in the list (three), and how the list is structured (they must find all items, not just any one). With this overview in mind, each juror has a better chance of remembering the information so he or she can apply it.

End the sentence after the list. A list presents the reader with enough information for one sentence. For example, write the following version (which uses some of the other techniques as well),

> **In some situations, the law allows a jury to infer that a defendant was negligent in making an item based solely on the evidence of the accident caused by that item. In this case, if you find both of the following to be true, you may infer that Ms. Henderson was negligent when she wove the plant hanger that broke:**
>
> **(1) Ms. Henderson had exclusive control of the production of the macrame plant hanger that broke when the plant was placed in it, and**
>
> **(2) the hanger would not have broken when a plant was placed in it if Ms. Henderson had exercised the ordinary care a macrame weaver should exercise.**

rather than the original

> If you find that defendant had exclusive control of the production of the items involved in the accident and if you further find that the accident claimed is of a type or kind that ordinarily would not have occurred had the defendant exercised ordinary care, then you

may infer from the accident itself and the surrounding circumstances that there was negligence on the part of the defendant.

Finally, look at the items in the list and make sure they are all needed, logically parallel, and written in parallel form.

If you find that Ms. Jamison exercised due care, then you must find in her favor. To find that Ms. Jamison did exercise due care, you must find all of the following:

(1) she noticed the warning sign on the sidewalk,

(2) she stepped carefully around the blockade,

(3) she at no time walked within the area marked as dangerous,

(4) she . . . .

Because lists are essential to many instructions, taking time to structure and word each list carefully helps you ensure the instruction's clarity.

Use Signal Words as Needed to Clarify Structure

Clear signals of sentence organization operate like the glowing flashlight covers used by parking lot attendants at a stadium to direct you to your parking spot. One waves you left, another right, through the lot to the next available space. Similarly, signals guide the reader or listener through an instruction, past explanations, through conditions, and ultimately to the main point.[62] Examples of such signals are "if" and "then," "only if," "all of the following," and "after." Although punctuation and visual aids serve as signals in other writing, they offer little help with the oral challenge of jury instructions (unless the jury is given a copy of the instructions in your jurisdiction).

You will probably find you use more verbal signals in jury instructions than in other writing. For example, the following instruction makes effective use of a series of signals.

> **If you choose to, you *may* take notes about the evidence during this trial. *But* it is your choice. *If* you do take notes, *then* you *must* be careful that taking those notes does not distract you from carefully listening to and observing the witnesses.**

Compare it with the following.

> You are not required to but you may take notes of the evidence during this trial. . . . In taking notes, you must be careful that it

62. Indeed, their power is so strong that they sometimes override content. In an experiment in 1984, students were instructed to cut in front in a line at the copying machine; the variable was whether they offered no reason, said "because I am in a rush," or added the redundant "because I have to make some copies." The number of persons allowing the student to cut in front was higher when the student added a "because" phrase, but was equally high with either of the two "because" phrases. Herbert W. Simons, *Persuasion: Understanding, Practice, and Analysis* 55 (2d ed. 1986).

does not distract you from carefully listening to and observing the witnesses.[63]

You also might write the following

A hospital employee has the duty to provide a patient with *whatever* services, care, and attention that patient reasonably requires under the circumstances.

or this

***If* a patient in a hospital has a reasonable need for any required services, care, or attention, *then in that case* a hospital employee has the duty to provide them.**

rather than this

A hospital employee has the duty to provide *such* services, care, and attention *as* a patient reasonably required under the circumstances.

These clear signals are particularly helpful when the law differs from what the jury might expect; the signals help increase the chance that the jury will see the distinction being made.[64] In some jurisdictions, the jury does not receive written copies of instructions. If this is so in your jurisdiction, then you need to be especially sure that you use clear verbal signals. Your listeners must be able to hear the organization of the instructions because they will not have the text as a reference while deliberating.

Use Verbs Instead of Nouns Stating Action

Using verbs rather than nouns makes it easier for the jury to hear what you mean.[65] Verbs communicate an action, something that the listener can imagine. This vision creates a more concrete image, so the point is more easily remembered. Use verbs to state actions important to the meaning of the sentence. If you cannot use a verb, state the meaning as the object of some form of "to be," a linking verb. Avoid nominalization, or making the verb into a noun. For example, write

If the employee *failed* to perform this duty, the hospital *is negligent.*

rather than

A failure to perform this duty is negligence.

Nouns that state actions are less effective because they are harder to understand. It takes a reader or listener longer to process these nominalizations than verbs, suggesting that the reader has to work harder mentally to understand the word's meaning.[66] Out of consideration, you can do this work for your jury.

---

63. Based on Wis.Civ.J.I. 61.

64. "Messages targeted to naive readers might be designed to emphasize how the new information is different from what they might expect." Hewes and Planalp, *supra* note 3, at 160.

65. Rulon Wells, *Nominal and Verbal Style* in *Style in Language* 213–20 (T. Sebeok ed. 1960).

66. Charrow and Charrow, *supra* note 9, at 1321–22. One example is to revise "failure of recollection is a common experience" to read "people often forget things"

Put Modifying Phrases Next to the Words They Modify

The human mind can keep only a limited number of things in active thought at one time.[67] Group your information. Because modifying phrases are commonly used to group information, your handling of these phrases is important.

Modifying phrases are groups of words that work together to add information about another word. For example, "of the participants" is a modifying phrase in "one of the participants," and "with evidence that is clear and convincing" is a modifier in "must convince you beyond a reasonable doubt with evidence that is clear and convincing." The latter example illustrates the problem; "with evidence ..." modifies "convince," but that is not easy for the reader or listener to understand because other words intervene. Although you cannot always place a modifying phrase next to the word it modifies, do so whenever possible. For example, the first instruction that follows is easier to understand than the second.

in other previous use of the premises

rather than

in the previous use of the premises by others

Similarly, the following sentence is easier to understand if the modifiers are untangled.

An owner of an automobile when granting permission to another for use of the automobile may restrict or limit the length of time or the kind of use to which the automobile is to be put by the one borrowing it.

When granting permission for another to use an automobile, the owner of that automobile may place restrictions on the automobile's use. The owner may limit the length of time the one borrowing it may use it. The owner may also restrict the purposes for which the automobile may be used.

If you have trouble placing modifiers next to the word modified, consider whether you are trying to put too much information in one sentence. If so, divide the sentence, as discussed in a later section.

Delete Unneeded Negatives

Just as in statutes, use negatives only when needed. Because negative statements take longer for the reader or listener to process,[68] they decrease the understandability of the content. You will need to use some negatives in your instructions, but you can minimize their use. For

---

with no loss in meaning. *See* Peter M. Tiersma, *Jury Instructions in the New Millennium*, 36 Ct.Rev. 28, 29 (1999) (citing *California Jury Instructions, Criminal* 2.21.1 (6th ed. 1996)). Unfortunately, the 2001 revision did not change this wording. *See id.* at 2.21.1 (6th ed. Supp. 2002).

67. Research suggests that adults may remember as few as five or as many as seven groups of information. Carl Bereiter and Marlene Scardamalia, *The Psychology of Written Composition* 93–176 (1987).

68. Charrow and Charrow, *supra* note 9, at 1324–25, 1337.

example, instead of writing "if you determine that the defendant could not have failed to be able to see," write "if you determine that the defendant must have been able to see." Subtler forms of the negative are particularly difficult to understand,[69] so especially minimize the use of words listeners will not recognize as negative. Examples of these negatives include "unless" or "failure," and negative prefixes, such as "un-." By doing what you can to reduce negatives, you reduce the burden on the jury.

Use only one negative at a time. For example, write

> **An "implied warranty" is a warranty that arises legally from either the parties' acts or circumstances of the transaction. It requires no intent or particular language or action by the seller to create it.**

> **The warranty, however, does not apply to any use. If the user of the product put it to some use other than that for which it was sold, the warranty will not apply. If the user did not use it according to the directions, the warranty will not apply.**

rather than

> An "implied warranty" is a warranty that arises by operation of law from the acts of the parties or circumstances of the transaction. It requires no intent or particular language or action by the seller to create it.

> There is no breach of warranty if the product sold is put to a use for which the product was not intended or used not in accordance with the directions given as to its use.

Divide or Simplify Any Complicated Sentences Still Remaining

Finally, make sure you do not have too much action in one sentence. Divide important points to explain the law one step at a time. For example, in the earlier revision of an instruction with many negatives, the instruction was divided into several shorter sentences.

> **The warranty, however, does not apply to any use. If the user of the product put it to some use other than for which it was sold, the warranty will not apply. If the user did not use it according to the directions, the warranty will not apply.**

rather than

> There is no breach of warranty if the product sold is put to a use for which the product was not intended or used not in accordance with the directions given as to its use.

Your goal here is not simply to make sentences shorter, but to make sure they do not include more concepts than the jury can manage at once. Because a person can process only a limited amount of information

---

69. *Id.* at 1325.

in one reading of a sentence, you must limit the number of ideas in each sentence. If you include too many, you force the reader or listener to forget some of the information,[70] no matter how carefully you have placed your modifying phrases.

Shorter sentences also help the judge, who has to read these sentences aloud; he or she needs to reach the period before reaching the end of a breath. This step is last because it allows you to check for long sentences after your other revisions are made, so long sentences have no opportunity to insinuate their way back into your instructions. Reading the text for long sentences also allows you to move away from looking at individual words and move back to looking at the overall effect of the instructions. This review is your opportunity to see if you have synthesized the ten techniques into a workable whole. It also allows you to appreciate the cumulative benefits of many small improvements, an awareness that will be useful when you work with longer units of text, such as arguments and research reports.[71]

CONCLUSION

The following checklists summarize the techniques discussed in the chapter.

Jury Instruction Checklist

When choosing jury instructions, do the following.

- Include instructions that explain the law critical to your theory or theories.

- Include instructions that explain your theories for damages, if applicable.

- Determine whether a special verdict would be advantageous to your client and, if so, draft this.

- Include instructions needed to make your case hold up on appeal.

- If you are quite sure that something at trial will be likely to be misunderstood or misinterpreted by the jury, choose instructions to forestall their misunderstanding. Examples of this would be when the defendant does not testify or when the opposition will emphasize some fact that you argue is irrelevant. If the problem only might arise, wait and submit the instruction later if needed.

---

70. George Gopen, *Let the Buyer In Ordinary Business Beware: Suggestions for Revising the Prose of the Uniform Commercial Code,* 54 U.Chi.L.Rev. 1178 (1987).

71. For other techniques to consider, *see also* Peter Tiersma, *Reforming the Language of Jury Instructions,* 22 Hofstra L.Rev. 37, 48–52 (1993); Dylan Lager Murray, *Plain English or Plain Confusing?,* 62 Mo.L.Rev. 345, 350–63 (1997); Hagerty, *supra* note 16, at 1018–20; Dumas, *supra* note 9, at 729–37.

- Include any general instructions that you believe the judge will want to submit and that you want to revise to fit clearly with your client's position.

- Include any other instructions needed to present a clear charge to the jury.

When revising the instructions you have chosen, follow these steps.

- Delete any irrelevant information.

- Personalize the instructions.

- Substitute common spoken English wherever possible.

- Define any critical, uncommon words.

- Find all lists, structure them clearly, and move each list to the end of a sentence.

- Make sure all signal words are clear.

- Use verbs instead of nouns when stating actions.

- Put modifying phrases next to the words they modify.

- Delete unneeded negatives.

- Divide or simplify any remaining complicated sentences.

Exercise 1

Revise the following jury instruction on bad faith by an insurance company so that it is more understandable for the jury. This jury will not receive a written copy of the instruction, so you must make your organization clear for the listener.

Wisconsin Jury Instruction—Civil

Bad faith by insurance company: Assured's Claim

To prove bad faith against (insurance company), the (Plaintiff) must establish that there was no reasonable basis for the insurance company's denying (Plaintiff's) claim for benefits and that (insurance company), in denying the claim, either knew or recklessly failed to ascertain that the claim should have been paid.

Bad faith on the part of an insurance company towards its insured is the absence of honest, intelligent action or consideration of its insured's claim.

Bad faith exists if, upon an examination of the facts found by you, you are able to conclude that (insurance company) had no reasonable basis for denying (Plaintiff's) claim.

In answering this question, you may consider whether (Plaintiff's) claim was properly investigated and whether the results of the investigation were given a reasonable evaluation and review. If you find that (insurance company) either refused to consider the (Plaintiff's) claim for damages, made no investigation, or conducted its investigation in such a way as to prevent it from learning the true facts upon which the (Plaintiff's) claim is based, the insurance company can be found to have exercised bad faith. This is because you may infer from these facts a reckless disregard on the insurance company's part to learn that there was no reasonable basis for it to deny (Plaintiff's) claim.

If, on the other hand, you find that the insurance company, after conducting a thorough investigation of the facts and circumstances giving rise to the (Plaintiff's) claim, reasonably concluded that the claim is debatable or questionable, then there is no bad faith even though it refused to pay the claim.

Exercise 2

Revise the following jury instruction so that it is more understandable by the jury. This jury will receive a copy of the jury instruction so make sure that you provide visual keys to organization as well as written ones.

When A Person is Faced with an Emergency

A person faced with an emergency and who acts without opportunity to consider the alternatives is not negligent if [he, she] did not make the safest choice or exercise the best judgment. A mistake in judgment or wrong choice of action is not negligence if the person is required to act quickly because of danger. This rule applies where a person is faced with a sudden condition, which could not have been reasonably anticipated, provided that the person did not cause or contribute to the emergency by [his, her] own negligence.

If you find that the [defendant, plaintiff] was faced with an emergency and that [his, her] response to the emergency was that of a reasonably prudent person, then you will conclude that the [defendant, plaintiff] was not negligent. If, however, you find that the situation facing the [defendant, plaintiff] was not sudden, or should reasonably have been foreseen, or was created or contributed to by the [defendant's, plaintiff's] own negligence, or that the [defendant's, plaintiff's] conduct in response to the emergency was not that of a reasonably prudent person, then you may find that the [defendant, plaintiff] was negligent.

Assignment 1

Facts

On August 11, 20__, Michael Trenton and his friend Jackson Harper, both 11, were riding Jackson's new bicycle near their homes in Minnehaha, Montrose (our jurisdiction). Michael was steering and pedaling, and Jackson, who was carrying two baseball gloves and a ball, was balanced on the seat of the bicycle. They were traveling west along Cedar Street, which runs parallel to railroad tracks owned and maintained by Colgate Railroads, Inc.

As they were crossing Monroe Street, which intersects the railroad right of way, Jackson spotted a dead animal in the middle of the tracks. He yelled to Michael to turn onto the tracks to investigate. They both climbed off the bike in the middle of the crossing and, as they were bending down to look more closely at the opossum, they heard the first blast of the train horn. Jackson looked up, saw the train's headlight in the distance, and told Michael that they had "plenty of time" before it got to them. They poked at the opossum with a stick for "a few more seconds" and then climbed back on the bike. They began to head back to Cedar Street, but the front wheel of the bike became caught in the tracks and stopped them short. They both jumped off the bike and attempted to free it from the tracks but were unable to do so. Michael yelled to Jackson to "come on" as the train was bearing down on them, blowing its horn, but Jackson refused to leave his new bike. Michael, in exasperation, took a final yank on the bike and it came loose; both boys jumped back on the bike and Michael began to pedal but not quickly enough. The train, though slowing, swept through and caught the rear fender of the bike, dragging the bike and both boys along with it, somehow keeping the bike nearly upright. The boys, scared stiff, held onto the bike. Michael fell off after 20 yards and rolled down an embankment, breaking his leg in two places. Jackson held on for another 15 yards and then fell down a steeper slope, dislocating his shoulder and suffering compound fractures of his right arm and a concussion.

The railroad crossing where the train caught the bike was equipped with warning bells and gates that dropped to prevent traffic from crossing during the approach of a train. Witnesses close to the scene reported that they first heard the warning bells or saw the gates drop about 5–7 seconds before the boys were struck.

Assignment

You are defending Colgate Railroads in a lawsuit brought by the boys and their parents; the case has gone to trial. Your client's defense is that the boys' negligence exceeded that of the railroad. Evidence at trial included expert testimony by both sides on the requirements for train warning bells and gates, and the compliance with those requirements by Colgate.

You have found the following pattern jury instructions in Montrose. Your assignment is to (1) revise them for clarity and to fit your case, and (2) put them in the order that you would like them to be read to the jury. (There would be many more instructions used for your trial, but your assignment is to redraft only these four.)

Remember, Judge Elvia Perez will allow us to revise to improve readability and juror understanding. But she is always concerned that the statement of the law remain accurate because she hates to be reversed on appeal. Thus, makes sure that the legal requirements stated in the original get included accurately in your revision.

Format

Start each instruction on a new sheet of paper. Put the instructions in the order in which you want them read.

DAMAGES—INJURY TO MINOR—SUIT BY PARENTS AND MINOR—MEASURE OF DAMAGES

This lawsuit involves two separate claims, one, a claim by _____, a minor, for damages for injuries allegedly caused by the defendant, and a claim by the minor's parent[s] for medical expenses incurred [and for loss of earnings and services of the minor during minority].

If you find that the minor and the parent[s], or either of them, are entitled to recover from the defendant[s], you must award to the party or parties entitled to recover, damages in an amount that will reasonably compensate such party or parties for each of the following elements of claimed loss or harm, [subject to being reduced, as you will be instructed, if you should find that the minor or the parents were contributorily negligent,] provided that you find it was [or will be] suffered by the minor or the minor's parent[s] and caused by the act or omission upon which you base your finding of liability.

The amount of the award to said parent[s] shall include the reasonable value of medical [hospital and nursing] care, services, treatment and supplies reasonably required and actually given in the treatment of said minor, such monetary loss, if any, as the parent[s] [has] [have] suffered and [is] [are] reasonably certain to suffer in the future by being deprived of the services, if any, [which the minor would have performed during the period of minority] and such loss of the child's earnings, if any, as said parent[s] may have suffered by reason of the fact, if it be a fact, that the injury in question has caused [their] [his] [her] child, _____, to be unable to pursue [his] [her] occupation or a gainful employment. In determining that amount, you must find what portion of such earnings as earned by the minor would have accrued to the financial advantage of the parent[s].

[Also such sum as will compensate said parent[s] reasonably for whatever loss, if any, [they] [he] [she] [are] [is] reasonably certain to suffer in the future, until the child reaches the age of 18, caused by any loss of earning capacity caused said child by the injury in question.]

POSSESSOR'S LIABILITY FOR CONDITION OR USE OF PREMISES—STANDARD OF CARE—RAILROAD CROSSING

The (owner, possessor) of (land, a building) has a duty to use reasonable care to keep the premises in a reasonably safe condition for the protection of all persons whose presence on the premises is reasonably foreseeable by the (owner, possessor) of (land, a building). Specifically, it is the duty of a railroad company to exercise reasonable care at public highway crossings to warn and to avoid injury to persons traveling upon the highway and crossing the railroad tracks.

In order to recover, plaintiff must prove that the premises were not reasonably safe, that defendant was negligent in not keeping the premises in a reasonably safe condition, and that defendant's negligence in allowing the unsafe condition to exist was a substantial factor in causing plaintiff's injury.

You must first consider whether the premises were reasonably safe. If you decide that the premises were reasonably safe, you will find for defendant and proceed no further ([add where appropriate:] (on this claim)). If you decide that the premises were not reasonably safe, you will proceed to consider whether defendant was negligent in permitting the unsafe condition to exist.

Negligence is the failure to use reasonable care. Reasonable care means that degree of care which a reasonably prudent (owner, possessor) of (land, a building) would use under the same circumstances. Negligence includes both a foreseeable danger of injury to another and conduct which is unreasonable in proportion to the danger. In deciding whether defendant was negligent, you must weigh the likelihood and seriousness of the risk of injury against the defendant's having to carry the burdens involved in maintaining the premises. The amount of caution required of the railroad company in the exercise of reasonable care must be commensurate with the hazards and dangers which are apparent to it or should be apparent to a reasonably prudent person under circumstances similar to those shown by the evidence.

The reasonableness of defendant's conduct also depends upon whether defendant should reasonably have foreseen the presence of plaintiff or someone like plaintiff on the property. In deciding whether plaintiff's presence should have been reasonably foreseen by defendant, you must consider the time, place, and circumstances of plaintiff's presence (on defendant's property, in defendant's building). In deciding that question, you should consider the nature and location of the property, and whether [add or delete any items as appropriate to the evidence] plaintiff entered the property for a purpose for which the property was open to the public; plaintiff entered the property for a purpose which was related to defendant's business; plaintiff had defendant's consent to (enter, remain on) the property; plaintiff was invited in as defendant's guest; (plaintiff regularly used the property or was there for a significant period of time.)

In order to find that defendant's conduct was negligent, you must find that plaintiff's presence was foreseeable and either that defendant knew of the unsafe condition long enough before plaintiff's injury to have permitted defendant in the use of reasonable care to have it corrected, or to take other suitable precautions, or to give adequate warning, and did not do so or defendant did not know of the condition but in the use of reasonable care should have known of it and corrected it (or taken other suitable precautions, or given adequate warning). If you find that plaintiff's presence was not foreseeable or that defendant did not know of the condition and that by the use of reasonable care defendant would not have been able to discover and correct it, or if you find that defendant knew of the unsafe condition but took suitable precautions or gave plaintiff an adequate warning, you will find that defendant was not negligent.

OPENING INSTRUCTIONS

Members of the jury, the court will now instruct you on the principles of law, which you should follow when considering the evidence and reaching your verdict. As you apply these instructions, keep the following principles in mind. First you should consider the instructions as a whole when applying them to the evidence. You should also consider all the instructions. The fact that the instructions are given in one particular order does not mean one is more important than the other.

Take the law given in these instructions and apply that law to the facts in the case before you that are properly proven by the evidence. Consider only the evidence allowed by the court during this trial and the law as given to you in these instructions and use these alone to guide you to reach your verdict, using your soundest reason and best judgment.

You, the jury, are the sole judges of the facts, and the court is the judge of the law only. If any one of you has an impression of my opinion as to whether the defendant is guilty or not guilty, disregard such impression entirely. Decide the issues of fact only on your view of the evidence.

DUTY OF PASSENGER FOR OWN SAFETY—CROSSING TRACKS

One who is simply a passenger in a vehicle that is approaching a railroad crossing and has no right to the control or management of such vehicle nevertheless has the duty to exercise the same ordinary care for [his] [or] [her] own safety and protection as a person of ordinary prudence would take under the same circumstances. You must determine from all of the evidence what conduct might reasonably have been expected of a person of ordinary prudence if that person of ordinary prudence were in the same circumstances.

In the absence of some fact brought to the passenger's attention which would cause a person of ordinary prudence to act otherwise, such passenger is not charged with the responsibility [of observing the condition of the traffic on the highway] [of ascertaining whether or not a train is approaching] [of warning the driver of the presence of railroad tracks or of an approaching train]. However, if a passenger is aware that the driver is not looking for [trains] [other vehicular traffic] or is driving the vehicle in a negligent manner or is violating the law, or that [an engine, train or car] [another motor vehicle] is approaching [on the tracks] [the intersection] and is so close as to constitute an immediate hazard to those in the passenger's vehicle, the passenger has the duty of doing whatever a person of ordinary prudence in the same situation would do to inform or warn the driver in an effort to prevent an accident.

Contributory negligence, if any, by the passenger does not bar recovery against the defendant but the total amount of damages to which the passenger would otherwise be entitled shall be reduced in proportion to the amount of negligence attributable to the passenger. The tracks of a railroad are in themselves a warning of danger. Before a person drives a vehicle [into] [enters upon] the space which would be occupied by a train if it were to pass over such tracks, it is [his] [or] [her] duty to use every reasonable opportunity to look and listen for the approach of train, engine or car on the tracks, and to yield the right of way to any approaching train, engine or car so near as to constitute an immediate hazard. What is included in the term "every reasonable opportunity" depends on all the surrounding circumstances, as they would be met and viewed by a person of ordinary prudence, if the person occupied the same position as the one whose conduct is in question. [No failure of duty or of the customary practice on the part of those in charge of a train or of anyone handling or supervising any phase of its operation, such as a failure to sound the bell, siren or whistle as required by law [or] [_____] excuses a person going upon a track area from the duty to use ordinary care for his or her own protection.]

Assignment 2

Your firm represents Jim and Kate Putnam, parents of the deceased, as part of their action for the wrongful death of their daughter. Specifically, you are helping the firm prepare jury instructions for the Putnams' suit against City General under the tort of spoliation of evidence.

Heather Putnam was a nineteen-month-old, otherwise healthy girl who was having surgery to correct a drooping eyelid, a relatively routine out-patient surgery. She was admitted to City General on August 4, (20__), and underwent surgery on that same day. Dr. Bradley Ferella administered general anesthesia to Heather using a ten-year-old halothane vaporizing equipment that was owned by City General.

Dr. Ferella set the rate at which the anesthesia should be vaporized by turning a dial to the appropriate setting. Unbeknownst to Dr. Ferella, the vaporizer emitted the anesthesia at a higher rate than was indicated by the dial. Although newer vaporizers include a gauge that shows the actual rate at which the anesthesia is being vaporized, this vaporizer was an older model that did not have the gauge. In a few minutes, Heather's vital signs began to deteriorate, and the surgeon reported that there was abnormally little bleeding at the incision site, which indicates that the heart is not functioning properly. Dr. Ferella then administered an IV to increase Heather's heart rate and blood pressure. He had difficulty getting the IV needle inserted, and thus was distracted from Heather's vital readings for a time. Meanwhile, Heather's heart rate fell to 60 and her blood pressure to 0. She then suffered cardiac arrest. She was placed on a respirator, but no brain activity was subsequently detected. Ten days later, Heather was pronounced dead and life support was disconnected.

The Putnams filed a negligence claim against City General and Dr. Ferella. They settled with Dr. Ferella, but proceeded with the suit against City General. During discovery, they learned that Dr. Ferella had directed City General anesthesia technician, Geri Kodesh, to have the vaporizer checked by the manufacturer, Alpha. When Kodesh contacted Alpha, she did not tell them that the vaporizer had been involved in an incident that might lead to a lawsuit. The vaporizer was sent to Alpha, and Alpha's technician, Dan Seidel, checked it. He determined that the vaporizer was indeed emitting anesthesia at a rate 30% higher than indicated by the dial. Seidel wrote his findings in a Field Service Report, which Kodesh signed. City General risk management received a copy of this report. City General at no time notified Alpha of the risk of a lawsuit as a result of the vaporizer's malfunction. Two months after the incident, Alpha dismantled the vaporizer, thus destroying evidence of the cause of the vaporizer's loss of calibration.

Through discovery and a deposition of Setyadi Bo–Noz, Alpha's product safety manager, we learned the following. Alpha's tests showed that the vaporizer had no internal cause for its loss of calibration. Vaporizers only go out of calibration for external reasons, such as an incorrect or contaminated anesthesia. Further tests could have been done on the vaporizer to determine the reason it had gone out of calibration and emitted excess anesthesia. Alpha did not learn of the accident involving Heather until several months after the vaporizer had been dismantled. Alpha would not have dismantled the vaporizer if it had known of the accident.

The Putnams are now bringing a second action against City General for intentional destruction of the vaporizer (spoliation of evidence), alleging that City General knew of the potential civil claim against the manufacturer of the vaporizer, and thus City General had a duty to preserve the evidence. They failed to do this and thus impaired the Putnam's ability to bring an action against Alpha.

Revise the following three instructions for the Putnam case. Also create an instruction for spoliation of evidence for the case using the elements contained in the cases listed below. Begin each instruction on a separate page (although some may take more than one page). Also put the instructions in the most logical order.

Use only the following law in your research unless your teacher advises otherwise.

- *Continental Ins. Co. v. Herman*, 576 So.2d 313 (Fla. Dist. Ct. App. 1990).

- *Bondu v. Gurvich*, 473 So.2d 1307 (Fla. Ct. App. 1984), *rev. denied*, 484 So.2d 7 (Fla. 1986).

- *Miller v. Allstate Ins. Co.*, 573 So.2d 24 (Fla. Dist. Ct. App. 1990).

- *Grove's Fresh Distrib. v. Flavor Fresh Foods, Inc.*, 720 F. Supp. 714 (N.D. Ill. 1989).

- *Stanton v. Astra Pharm. Prods.*, 718 F.2d 553 (3d Cir. 1983).

- 21 U.S.C. 360i(b)(1)(A) and (D).
- Fla. Stat. 395.0197.
- Fla. Admin. Code Ann. 59A-10.0065.

BROAD FUNDAMENTAL PRINCIPLES OF LAW

I shall at this time touch upon certain broad fundamental principles of law applicable to all civil cases in order to assist you further in understanding and following the evidence and law in this case and in your deliberations as jurors. Now that you have heard all of the evidence in this case and the arguments of counsel, I will instruct you as to the law applicable to this case.

The court is the judge of the law, and I will instruct you in full as to the law applicable to the case and will then submit verdict forms to you for your consideration. Please keep in mind that it is your absolute duty to accept the law as defined in these instructions and to follow it regardless of your own feelings about the case or anything else that might interfere.

Some jurors find themselves surprised or upset at the law which the Court gives them, because it is not as the jurors might expect the law to be. If that happens to you, please understand that your oath requires you to follow my instructions on the law just as I give them to you and that you cannot change it because it is not as you expected or think it ought to be under the circumstances. You must follow my instructions as to the law.

You are the judges of the facts in this case, and in that connection you are the judges of the credibility of the witnesses and the weight to be given to their testimony. It is my duty to inform you of the applicable law. It is also my duty to determine what evidence you may consider. Since you have now heard all the evidence in this case, and the arguments of counsel, and when you have received the written instructions from me as to the law, it will be the duty of the jury to determine the facts in the case from the evidence presented and the Court's instructions.

FAILURE TO PRODUCE EVIDENCE OR A WITNESS

If a party to this case has failed [to offer evidence] [to produce a witness] within his power to produce, you may infer that the [evidence] [testimony of the witness] would be adverse to that party if you believe each of the following elements:

1. The [evidence] [witness] was under the control of the party and could have been produced by the exercise of reasonable diligence or effort on the part of that party.

2. The [evidence] [witness] was not equally available or accessible to an adverse party.

3. A reasonably prudent person under the same or similar circumstances would have [offered the evidence] [produced the witness]

if he believed [it to be] [the testimony would be] favorable to him.

4. No reasonable excuse for the failure has been shown.

CAUTIONARY INSTRUCTIONS

Faithful performance by you of your duties is vital to the administration of justice.

Arguments, statements, and remarks of counsel are intended to help you in understanding the evidence and applying the law, but are not evidence. If any argument, statement or remark has no basis in the evidence, then you should disregard that argument, statement or remark. [However, there is one exception to this rule: an admission of a fact by counsel is binding on his client.]

It is your duty to determine the facts, and to determine them from the evidence produced in open court. You are to apply the law to the facts and in this way decide the case. Neither sympathy nor prejudice should influence you. Your verdict must be based on evidence and not upon speculation, guess or conjecture.

In deciding whether any fact has been proved, it is proper to consider the number of witnesses testifying on one side or the other as to that fact, but the number of witnesses alone is not conclusive if the testimony of the lesser number is more convincing.

You are the sole judges of the credibility of the witnesses and of the weight to be given to the testimony of each of them. In determining the credit to be given any witness you may take into account his ability and opportunity to observe, his memory, his manner while testifying, any interest, bias or prejudice he may have, and the reasonableness of his testimony considered in the light of all the evidence in the case

The law applicable to this case is contained in these instructions and it is your duty to follow them. You must consider these instructions as a whole, not picking out one instruction and disregarding others.

The (corporate)(_____ (other legal entity, e.g., bank)) (plaintiff) (defendant) _____ (party's name) in this case is entitled to the same fair and unprejudiced treatment as an individual would be under like circumstances, and you should decide the case with the same impartiality you would use in deciding a case between individuals who were involved in the lawsuit.

Neither by these instructions nor by any ruling or remark which I have made do I or have I meant to indicate any opinion as to the facts.

BIBLIOGRAPHY

Anderson, Kimball R. and Bruce R. Braun, *The Legal Legacy of John Wayne Gacy: The Irrebuttable Presumption That Juries Understand and Follow Jury Instructions*, 78 Marq.L.Rev. 791 (1995).

Berdon, Robert I., *Instructive Interrogatories: Helping the Civil Jury to Understand*, 55 Conn.B.J. 179 (1981).

Berdon, Robert I., *Instructive Interrogatories: One Method To Aid the Jury*, 8 Bridge.L.Rev. 385 (1984).

Bereiter, Carl and Marlene Scardamalia, *The Psychology of Written Composition*. Hillsdale, NJ: Lawrence Erlbaum Associates, 1987.

Berger, Charles R. and Steven H. Chaffee, *Handbook of Communication Science*. Newbury Park, CA: Sage Publications, 1987.

Bourne, Lyle E., Jr., *Human Conceptual Behavior*. Boston: Allyn and Bacon, 1966.

Buchanan, Raymond W., *The Florida Judge–Jury Communications Project*, 8 Bridge.L.Rev. 297 (1984).

Charrow, Robert P. and Veda R., *Making Legal Language Understandable: A Psycholinguistic Study of Jury Instructions*, 79 Colum.L.Rev. 1306 (1979).

Cohen, Neil P., *The Timing of Jury Instructions*, 67 Tenn.L.Rev. 681 (2000).

Devitt, Edward J. and Charles Blackmar, *Federal Jury Practice and Instructions*. St. Paul: West Group, 1977.

Dombroff, Mark A., *Burdens, Inferences and Presumptions: A Tactical Perspective*, 6 Trial Dip.J. 36 (1985).

Douthwaite, Graham, *Jury Instructions, Pattern and Otherwise*, 29 Def. L.J. 335 (1980).

Dumas, Bethany K., *Jury Trials: Lay Jurors, Pattern Jury Instructions, and Comprehension Issues*, 67 Tenn.L.Rev. 701 (2000).

Eades, Ronald W., *The Problem of Jury Instructions in Civil Cases*, 27 Cumb.L.Rev. 1017 (1997).

Forecite: Latest Developments in California Criminal Jury Instructions. Santa Rosa, CA: Forecite Legal Publications, Thomas Lundy, ed., Cumulative Supp. 1997. and 2002 Supp.

Forecite: Latest Developments in California Jury Instructions—Practice Guide. Santa Rosa, CA: Forecite Legal Publications, Thomas Lundy, ed., 1994.

Gopen, George, *Let the Buyer in Ordinary Course of Business Beware: Suggestions for Revising the Prose of the Uniform Commercial Code*, 54 Univ.Chi.L.Rev. 1178 (1987).

Hatch, Richard, *Business Communication: Theory and Technique*. Chicago: Science Research Associates, Inc., 1977.

Hagerty, Gail, *Instructing the Jury? Watch Your Language!*, 70 N.Dak.L.Rev. 1007 (1994).

Hewes, Dean E. and Sally Planalp, *The Individual's Place in Communication Science* in *Handbook of Communication Science* 147 (C. Berger and S. Chaffee, eds. 1987).

Kennelly, John, *Closing Arguments: Instructions are the Key*, 6 Trial Law. Guide 53 (1962).

Kelso, J. Clark, *Final Report of the Blue Ribbon Commission on Jury System Improvement*, 47 Hastings L.J. 1433 (1996).

May, Christopher N., *"What Do We Do Now?": Helping Juries Apply the Instructions*, 28 Loy.L.A.L.Rev. 869 (1995).

Mellinkoff, David. *Legal Writing: Sense and Nonsense.* St. Paul: West Group, 1982.

Mellinkoff, David. *The Language of the Law.* Boston: Little Brown and Company, 1990.

Model Jury Instructions: Business Torts Litigation. Chicago: American Bar Association, 3d ed. 1996.

Model Jury Instructions: Employment Litigation. Chicago: American Bar Association, 1994.

Murray, Dylan Lager, *Plain English or Plain Confusing?*, 62 Mo.L.Rev. 345 (1997).

Noce, David D., *Jury Instructions Drafting Workbook.* St. Paul: West Group, 1999.

O'Malley, Kevin F., Jay E. Grenig, and William C. Lee, *Federal Jury Practice and Instructions.* St. Paul: West Group, 5th ed. 2000.

Parnell, A.W., Chairman, Jury Instructions Committee, Introduction to the 1960 Edition of the Wisconsin Model Jury Instructions.

Partridge, Anthony, *When Judges Throw Gibberish at Jurors*, 8 Update on L.Rel.Ed. (1984).

Perlman, Harvey S., *Pattern Jury Instructions: The Application of Social Science Research*, 65 Neb.L.R. 520 (1986).

Plowman, Julie K., *Note: Multimedia in the Courtroom: A Valuable Tool or Smoke and Mirrors?*, 15 Rev.Litig. 415 (1996).

Reid, Judge A.H., *The Law of Instructions to Juries in Civil and Criminal Cases.* Indianapolis: Bobbs–Merrill, 1960.

Schwarzer, William W., *Communicating with Juries: Problems and Remedies*, 69 Cal.L.Rev. 731 (1981).

Sebeok, Thomas, A. ed., *Style in Language.* Cambridge, MA: M.I.T. Press, 1960.

Severence, Lawrence J. and Elizabeth F. Loftus, *Improving the Ability of Jurors to Comprehend and Apply Criminal Jury Instructions*, 17 L.Soc'y 153 (1982).

Simons, Herbert W., *Persuasion: Understanding, Practice, and Analysis.* New York: Random House, 2d. ed. 1986.

Smith, Douglas G., *Structural and Functional Aspects of the Jury: Comparative Analysis and Proposals for Reform*, 48 Ala.L.Rev. 441 (1997).

Steele, Walter W. and Elizabeth G. Thornburg, *Jury Instructions: A Persistent Failure to Communicate*, 67 N.C.L.Rev. 77 (1988).

Thornburg, Elizabeth G., *The Power and the Process: Instructions and the Civil Jury*, 66 Fordham L.Rev. 1837 (1998).

Tiersma, Peter M., *Jury Instructions in the New Millennium*, 36 Ct.Rev. 28 (1999).

Tiersma, Peter M., *Reforming the Language of Jury Instructions*, 22 Hofstra L.Rev. 37 (1993).

Wells, Rulon, *Nominal and Verbal Style* in *Style in Language* 213 (T.Sebeok ed. 1960).

Wilcox, Jamison, *The Craft of Drafting Plain–Language Jury Instructions: A Study of a Sample Pattern Instruction on Obscenity*, 59 Temp.L.Q. 1159 (1986).

Young, Roger M., *Using Social Science to Assess the Need for Jury Reform in South Carolina*, 52 S.C.L.Rev. 135 (2000).

Chapter 5

CONTRACTS

If writing legal documents were sporting events, then writing contracts would be a long distance, high hurdles, relay race. It would be long distance because the drafter must often express the parties' expectations and duties toward one another over the long term, given numerous unexpected contingencies.[1] It would be the high hurdles because lurking everywhere are problems that can cause the drafter to land on the wrong foot, lose his or her stride, and crash into a barrier. Finally, it would be a relay race because the parties and the drafter must work in synchronized motions to ensure that the result is one everyone desires, and the drafter creates a contract that all the parties will sign. To succeed, the drafter must produce a contract signifying the mutual understanding of the parties, and thus the drafter must work with the parties to complete this team event. But you can complete the event successfully if you carefully complete all the needed steps.

A contract is private legislation between the parties. It delineates the obligations of all parties to the contract, defines when the parties' interactions begin and end, and provides for the contingencies that may arise during the contractual term, especially if it is a long-term contract. The parties want this private legislation to shape their agreement.

Making this private legislation work requires an unrelenting willingness to take care while drafting. If the parties disagree about even so much as one word, they can find themselves facing expensive and lengthy litigation, as happened in a case resulting from a misunderstanding between the parties about what was meant by "chicken" in a purchase contract.[2] The contract was dated May 2, 1957; the court's decision was delivered in 1960. Three years were spent and a full trial was held, only to have the plaintiff's case dismissed. If the parties had

---

1. These are known as "relational" contracts, as distinguished from one-time, discrete exchanges. *See* Ian R. Macneil and Paul J. Gudel, *Contracts: Exchange Transactions and Relations, Cases and Materials* (3d ed. 2001).

2. *Frigaliment Importing Co. v. B.N.S. International Sales Corp.*, 190 F.Supp. 116 (S.D.N.Y.1960).

included a definition section in their contract and had taken the time to come to an agreement on the meaning of "chicken," they could have avoided the expense and aggravation of being embroiled in a lawsuit for three years.

Careful drafting of the contract can help the parties ascertain what they actually want from the agreement and whether they will be able to achieve their objectives. For example, if the parties above had tried to clarify what each meant by "chicken," they might have discovered they were unable to come to an agreement. Having determined that, they could have gone their separate ways and contracted with others to provide the goods desired, rather than discovering their disagreement during the course of the contract and then having to litigate.

Careful choice of other terms, such as articles, prepositions, and conjunctions, also could have avoided litigation that has occurred hundreds of times.[3] For example, the meaning of "about" had been litigated in more than 150 cases by 1930.[4] Courts have used at least thirteen methods to interpret the meaning of words in various contexts, including literal interpretation, etymology, technical meaning, dictionary meaning, context, and interpretation based on intent or fact.[5] The varying interpretations that can be accorded to even one word illustrate how important each word is to the meaning of a contract.

This chapter focuses on teaching you writing techniques needed to write a contract that conveys your client's meaning. First, it discusses the general writing concerns you must address when drafting a contract. Then it explains the steps you need to complete before starting to draft and the steps needed during the drafting process. This chapter also includes a checklist of some of the clauses you should consider including in your contract. By using a checklist, you will be able to draft contracts across a wide range of specific situations and be assured that you have included the clauses needed in each situation.

This chapter, however, cannot cover all the points presented in the myriad books and articles addressing contract drafting. Some of these sources provide examples of selected contract provisions; some address the special concerns for drafting specific types of contracts, such as works-in-progress or entertainment contracts.[6]

WRITING TECHNIQUES FOR CONTRACTS

Like statutes and jury instructions, contacts need careful word choice and sentence structure. But contracts also focus on large-scale concerns. Two primary concerns vital to effective contract drafting are

---

3. Note, *Avoiding Inadvertent Syntactic Ambiguity in Legal Draftsmanship,* 20 Drake L.Rev. 137, 138 (1970).

4. *Id.* at 138, n.11.

5. *Id.*

6. We have listed sources in the bibliography at the end of the chapter to provide you with further information about particu-lar drafting problems. This chapter does not include examples of particular contract provisions; look to a form book for that assistance. But always remember to revise the clauses you find in the form books so that they apply to your client's particular situation.

thoroughness and consistency. Thus, the contract will thoroughly cover all the details that comprise the parties' expectations of their agreement and will state that agreement consistently throughout. Both concerns foster the same result: the contract, as a written document, accurately presents the relationship the parties will have over the life of the contract.[7]

Thoroughness

Thoroughness results from spending time thinking through the purposes of the contract. To achieve thoroughness, ask yourself questions such as these.

- How much protection can your client afford?

- What needs to be included to state the parties' working relationship if all goes well?

- What are the concerns of each party and what is needed in the contract to meet those concerns?

- What are the possible problems that could arise? Of these, which ones need to be handled in the contract, and which ones could be left for the parties to resolve?

- What needs to be included to resolve any of these problems?

- What changes or events in the future may affect the performance of the contract?

- What remedies are needed in the event of breach or default?

- What miscellaneous clauses need to be included to make the agreement function?

Asking yourself these questions will help you envision everything you need to include, allowing you to enhance the thoroughness of the contract.

Consistency

Consistency results from ensuring that each provision corresponds to the total agreement between the parties and meshes with the other provisions in the contract. Address consistency concerns when rewriting and revising. At these stages, ask yourself questions such as the following.

- Is each term, heading, and provision used consistently throughout the contract?

- Are all sections organized consistently throughout the contract?

- Are both parties' duties handled consistently?

---

7. But this agreement must remain flexible over time. "A deal is a living thing, a contract is static. And the purpose of a contract is to support the living, evolving deal, not to supplant it." Mark H. McCormack, *The Terrible Truth About Lawyers: How Lawyers Really Work and How to Deal With Them Successfully* 17 (1987).

- Are the results of breach or default consistent throughout the contract and for each party?

- Are remedies for breach or default consistent throughout the contract?

- Are all numbers and dates consistent throughout the contract?

Asking yourself these questions will allow you to revise the contract so it will be internally consistent. You must review each clause of the contract to ensure that it is congruent with the other clauses.

This consistency can be difficult to achieve, especially when you start with provisions from other contracts or from form books. It is not necessarily a problem to adapt provisions from other contracts you have drafted. Often these provisions have been effective in the past, and you will have revised them often enough so they accurately state what the parties want to accomplish. But check the inserted provisions to be sure you do not add new, and thus, inconsistent terms. Be particularly careful about using provisions you did not draft. Other contracts may include clauses that may not have been drafted with sufficient care. Remember, the agreement you are drafting is unlike the agreement between any other parties.

This agreement is even unlike other contracts previously drafted for the same parties. The factual situations and legal parameters are always changing and, because of this, a provision that effectively stated one aspect of the parties' agreement five years ago, or even five months ago, may no longer effectively do so. Most likely things have changed, which is why the parties want a new contract. If you start with a previous contract between the parties, consider starting from the draft that your client initially submitted to the other side because "it presumably represents the drafting side's most coherent statement of its position, before the waters were muddied by negotiations."[8]

Form provisions are also of limited usefulness because they were not written with your parties in mind. Form books are drawn from a number of sources. As a result, they can contain provisions that are incomplete, unedited, or drawn from litigated cases.[9] When drawn from opinions, they did not do what they were intended to do, which was to keep the parties out of court. Never include a provision you do not understand just because you found it in a form book or other sample contract. If, as is likely, your client asks you about that particular provision, you will have the embarrassing job of telling him or her that you do not know its meaning or purpose.

8. Kenneth A. Adams, *Legal Usage in Drafting Corporate Agreements* 132 (2001). Comparing that draft with the resulting final contract may, however, indicate improvements that resulted from those negotiations. *Id.*

9. Harry J. Haynsworth IV, *How to Draft Clear and Concise Legal Documents,* 31 Prac.Law. 41, 44 (1985). *See* Robert A. Feldman and Raymond T. Nimmer, *Drafting Effective Contracts: A Practitioner's Guide* App. A (2002), which provides litigated language from various contract provisions that you can consider when drafting to avoid the problems encountered.

In summary, while previously drafted provisions may provide a solid starting point for drafting,[10] you must alter each provision so it explicitly addresses the needs of the parties in this given situation at this particular time with an eye toward the future. Although computer programs can help with document assembly, effective contract drafting requires careful thought.[11]

STEPS FOR DRAFTING THE CONTRACT

The process for drafting a contract resembles the process for all writing projects. For example, there are five stages of the writing process: prewriting, writing, rewriting, revising, and polishing.[12] Similarly, after developing a plan of organization, there are five steps in drafting a contract or other legal instrument: preparing a first draft, revising, making across-the-board checks, checking with others, and applying the polish.[13] While these two processes include different terms and steps, both processes essentially proceed step by step.

As both processes show, drafting a thorough and consistent contract will take many steps. No one can reliably remember every thing needed in the contract at one time. Keeping your client out of court and accurately conveying the parties' agreement requires serious thought throughout the writing process.

Steps for Drafting a Contract

- Research the parties' relationship and the law.

- Think through what is needed in the contract.

- Write either a draft or outline, concentrating on setting out the entire agreement between the parties.

- Rewrite, concentrating on logical and clear organization of major elements.

- Revise, concentrating on thoroughness and consistency.

- Obtain editing assistance from someone else.

- Polish for clarity.

---

10. Many forms are available via web sites, in books, or found on CD–ROM. For a good listing of these sources, *see* James W. Martin, *Fifty Tips for Writing the 21st Contract that Stays Out of Court*, 16 Prac. Real Est.Law. 41, 42 (Nov. 2000).

11. Computer-based "document-assembly systems" are, however, providing increasing assistance to lawyers working in large firms or companies that can afford them. This software integrates template documents with a text editor or word processing system to create a document from a template. See Adams, *supra* note 8, at 135–36, and information available at http://www.newchange.com.

12. Mary Barnard Ray and Jill J. Ramsfield, *Legal Writing: Getting It Right and Getting It Written* 416 (3d ed. 2000).

13. Reed Dickerson, *The Fundamentals of Legal Drafting* 51–69 (1986).

We have arranged these steps in the order we find most useful. You should feel free, however, to adapt any drafting process to your own particular situation. For example, if you have drafted numerous contracts, you may find it easier to think through what to include in the contract before doing the research; this may make your research more focused. Or, if you find it difficult to think through the contract, you may find drafting or outlining the contract will better prepare you to think through what else to include.

Drafting contracts, like all writing at an advanced level, requires working through many steps before completing the project. But do not worry that completing these steps will take more time than is available given the demands of a busy practice. As you become more proficient at drafting contracts, you will still do each step of the process, but you will discover that each step takes less time to complete and sometimes will combine with other steps.

Research the Parties' Relationship and the Law

This step consists of two parts: learning what your client wants and learning the law. You will begin to determine what the client wants at your initial meeting. Ask your client to tell you the main points of the agreement between the parties. Whether in list, outline, or narrative form, this will help your client focus on the agreement's terms.[14] Also, "engage your client in 'what if' scenarios" that will help you anticipate potential factual situations that may face the parties and consider issues that you may not have otherwise considered.[15] One of the best tools for finding out the information you need is a healthy curiosity; ask about the details of the deal and its financial components, and most of the information you need will likely flow from that conversation.[16] It may take several meetings with your client, and perhaps with the other parties, to discover the heart of the contract: a mutual understanding between the parties.

Part of identifying this understanding will be learning whether there were any previous negotiations or contracts between the parties and, if so, what the terms were.[17] Another part is finding out whether the parties completed a previous contract successfully or had problems implementing it. Learning this information will help you determine the parties' current understanding. Even if your client has not had previous agreements with this party, find out whether similar contracts between your client and other parties exist and review them.[18]

You may also want to do background research about the parties and their business or industry. Becoming familiar with the nature of the

---

14. Martin, *supra* note 10, at 42. Make sure your client does not sign a "letter of intent" unless it clearly states it is not a contract, but simply an outline of points that may be included in the contract. *Id.* For a discussion of the enforceability of preliminary documents, *see* Feldman and Nimmer, *supra* note 9, at § 1.05[A].

15. *Id.*

16. *Id.* at § 1.02[B][4].

17. Frank E. Cooper, *Writing in Law Practice* 272 (2d ed. 1963).

18. Martin, *supra* note 10, at 42.

business involved is important because a court construing the contract will consider common trade practices for that business.[19] Your client will be able to give you this information during your initial meetings, or you can use such resources such as Standard & Poor's or Dunn & Bradstreet reports.[20] Also become familiar with your client's day-to-day business; otherwise, you may include requirements in the contract that your client simply cannot meet.[21]

Your client may ask you to draft a contract focusing on what he or she wants from the agreement without considering the other party's desires or goals, because your client wants to obtain the most favorable terms possible. Although you can attempt to do this, realistically your client's needs must mesh with the other party's concerns. Part of your job may be to remind your client that trying for absolute control or diminishing the other side's needs will not result in a satisfactory working relationship.[22] Help your client understand that part of achieving a favorable contract includes drafting a contract all the parties can accept. Otherwise, the more lopsided the contract, the greater the incentive for the disadvantaged side to try to disrupt or terminate the contract.[23] "The ultimate purpose of any contract is not to get a stranglehold on the other party but to formalize the understanding that is of real and proportionate benefit to both sides over time."[24] Determine what your client must have in the contract; what is his or her bottom line. Then determine what your client can give up and try to draft the agreement accordingly.[25]

You can, however, try to make the contract more favorable for your client. In corporate transactions, the party with the most to protect will usually do the initial draft.[26] When you draft the contract yourself, a "mildly coercive" effect favoring your client will result because the other side must then show why this contract does not state the parties' agreement.[27] As one commentator explains: "No matter which party the lawyer represents, he [or she] should seize every opportunity to produce

19. Cooper, *supra* note 17, at 272.

20. Michael L. Goldblatt, *Well-drafted Contracts Keep Client and You Out of Court. Here's How!*, 7 Prev.L.Rep. 14, 14 (June 1988).

21. The amount of time you will spend depends on several factors, including "the magnitude and complexity of the transaction, the lawyer's relationship with the client, time pressures, and economic constraints." Feldman and Nimmer, *supra* note 9, at § 1.02[B][4].

22. David Crump, *The Five Elements of a Contract: Avoiding Ambiguity in Them*, 43 Tex.Bar J. 370, 372 (April 1980).

23. McCormack, *supra* note 7, at 144.

24. *Id.* at 176.

25. Be careful not to try and improve the "deal" that your client has already accepted; do not use the drafting practice to obtain what the client did not bargain for or gave up, unless everyone clearly understands that you are acting in both the role of a drafter and a negotiator. Otherwise, you risk harm to your professional reputation with both your client and the other side. Kenneth P. Kopelman, *Some Thoughts re: Drafting Corporate Agreements–A Step by Step Approach* in *Drafting Corporate Agreements* 2, 23 (P.L.I. 1997–98).

26. Maryann A. Waryjas, *Universal Issues in Drafting Corporate Agreements* in *Drafting Corporate Agreements* 111, 114 (P.L.I. 2001–02).

27. David W. Maxey, *Fundamentals of Draftsmanship—A Guide in Preparing Agreements*, 19 L.Notes 87, 89 (Summer 1983).

the first draft. He [or she] who produces the first draft generally has the upper hand in the ensuing negotiations."[28] By drafting the agreement, you can set the tone between the parties from the start and can have some initial control over the parties' agreement. But be careful in setting the tone. It must not sound punitive, distrustful, or biased toward your client. You can destroy a deal even though the initial negotiations were successful, simply because of the way the contract sounds.

After researching the particular situation between the parties, identify the applicable law controlling the contract. The law may require particular provisions to protect your client's legal expectations or to prevent your client from being forced to litigate to solve a problem. To determine what law controls the contract, become familiar with the statutes of the state or states where the contract will be performed. For example, South Carolina requires the words "This agreement is subject to arbitration" to appear on the contract's first page for an arbitration clause to be enforced.[29] If you did not meet the requirements of this particular statute, an arbitration clause contained in a South Carolina contract would be rendered useless.

When drafting, also consider relevant common law or statutory canons of construction because the courts may use them to interpret the meaning of the contract.[30] As when writing statutes, you should be aware, however, that you can find a canon of construction that contradicts any other canon; therefore, a court can find canons to support any decision it chooses.[31] Besides the canons included below, you can find others in the applicable state statutes, in cases, or in reference books.[32]

Check both the common law and the statutory canons that the courts in your jurisdiction use most frequently so you can draft your contracts to meet the demands of those canons. Examples of common law canons are "the expression of one thing implies the exclusion of all others" and "an interpretation should always be made such that the instrument may stand rather than fall."[33] Examples of statutory canons

---

28. Feldman and Nimmer, *supra* note 9, at § 1.03[A][1](emphasis omitted). If you do not write the first draft, then take extra care reviewing the draft to make sure it states the agreement in a way that is acceptable to your client. For an excellent checklist of what to consider when reviewing another lawyer's draft, *see*, Louis M. Brown, *Reviewing and Revising Draft Transactional Documents* in Robert M. Hardaway, *Preventive Law: Material on a Non Adversarial Legal Process* 214–19 (1997).

29. Haynsworth, *supra* note 9, at 50–51.

30. Alan R. Perry, et al., *Introduction to Drafting California Legal Instruments* 45 (1983).

31. Most of these canons of construction are also used for interpreting statutes. *Cf.* Karl N. Llewellyn, *Remarks on the Theory*

of Appellate Decision and the Rules or Canons about How Statutes Are to be Construed, 3 Vand.L.Rev. 395, 401–06 (1950). Examples of canons that support both sides are provided in Chapter 3, Statutes or Rules.

32. Hollis Hurd, *Writing for Lawyers* 103–05 (1982).

33. Perry, *supra* note 30, at 46. These common law canons are usually expressed in Latin, although they are not actually Latin phrases, but rather are English dressed up in Latin words. For example, the first canon above is commonly referred to as "expressio unius est exclusio alterius." Hurd, *supra* note 32, at 105. Although they may be incomprehensible to classical scholars, courts know them and use them frequently when a contract needs to be interpreted.

include "the language of a contract is to govern its interpretation if the language is clear and explicit, and does not involve an absurdity" and "the whole of a contract is to be taken together, so as to give effect to every part, if reasonably practicable, each clause helping to interpret the other."[34]

Also become familiar with the following canon, because most courts will use it to interpret a contract: "in cases of uncertainty not removed by the preceding rules, the language of a contract should be interpreted most strongly against the party who caused the uncertainty to exist."[35] This canon usually means the court will construe the contract against the party who drafted it. Therefore, as drafter, you are responsible for any uncertainty caused by your contract, and that uncertainty will be imputed to your client.

When drafting, keep in mind the parol evidence rule you learned in contracts.[36] Your client may need your help to understand that discussions or promises between the parties not included in the contract probably will be unenforceable in court. Usually, the court will consider the contract to be the final, binding agreement of the parties.[37] Thus you must include all the provisions that will control the parties' agreement, including, if agreed to by the parties, an integration or merger clause which expressly states that the contract expresses their entire agreement. But also consider how the specific case law in your jurisdiction may affect interpretation of that and the other provisions of the contract.[38]

Think Through What Is Needed in the Contract

At this point, you have determined what the parties want and what the law requires. Nevertheless, do not rush into writing specific provisions. Make sure that you have a clear picture of what you hope to accomplish through the contract. Just as good teachers determine their objectives before teaching a class and good litigators consider the remedy

---

34. Cal.Civ.Code secs. 1638 and 1641.

35. Cal.Civ.Code sec. 1654.

36. When the parties have stated their agreement in writing, evidence of any oral agreement that might alter the written document in any way (vary, add, subtract) will usually not be accepted in court. There are some exceptions, such as for fraud. Paul H. Till and Albert F. Gargiulo, *Contracts: The Move to Plain Language* 11 (1979).

37. The strength of the parol evidence rule varies between jurisdictions, however, with some almost always excluding extrinsic evidence and others frequently permitting it to resolve ambiguities or to prove oral promises not included in the contract. *See* Eric A. Posner, *The Parol Evidence Rule, the Plain Meaning Rule, and the Principles of Contractual Interpretation*, 146 U.Pa.L.Rev. 533 (1998).

38. For example, the California Court of Appeal held that, when a contract included both an integration clause specifying that "no extrinsic evidence whatsoever may be introduced in any judicial or arbitration proceeding, . . ." and an arbitration clause requiring arbitration of all disputes arising under the contract, an arbitrator may not consider extrinsic evidence outside the contract. (This limitation on arbitrators is greater than that on judges in California where the parol evidence is not strongly enforced.) *See* David M. Rosman and Ronald P. Kaplan, *Without the Possibility of Parol*, 21 L.A.Law. 48, 96–98 (1998) *citing* Bonshire v. Thompson, 52 Cal.App.4th 803 (Cal.Ct.App. 1997) *modified* 53 Cal.App.4th 337a.

they want before drafting a complaint, good contract drafters must consider the contract's objectives before starting to draft.

To determine whether you understand the intent of the parties, think through the contract and decide its intended objective. This usually should happen before you set pen to paper or fingers to keyboard.[39] Focus on fully understanding the needs of the parties, the scope of the contract, and the length of the agreement. Stating the parties' entire agreement will be quite complex, and you must analyze that complexity to state the agreement clearly. You will recover this thinking time later.

Write a Draft or an Outline, Concentrating on Setting Out the Entire Agreement Between the Parties

At this stage, what you write or how you write is less important than that you write. "Good writing does not depend on whether you start in the right place; it depends on whether you do all you need to before you stop."[40] Work with a broad brush to outline what the parties are to do for themselves and for each other, what the focus of their agreement is, what the subject matter of the contract is, and how long the contract will continue.

Many authorities assert that using an outline is the best way to start writing; they especially encourage this for drafting contracts, which often have the same type of organization and headings as an outline. Others believe that writing a draft is the best first step. They either draft the actual language of particular provisions or draft language covering what upon revision will turn into several provisions and then organize the provisions later. As drafter, you will learn which method works best for you.

Try to include all the major sections you will need and portray accurately what you believe are the parties' intentions for each major section. Do not worry yet about the sentence structure, word choice, or even the large-scale organization. What is important is getting the gist of the agreement down on paper. The remaining steps will provide the revisions and polishing needed. While keeping your client's objectives in mind, try to consider all foreseeable contingencies and address those that do not seem too remote.[41] By considering all the problems that can arise and doing your best to resolve them, you will help your client stay out of court.

Write for the knowledgeable layperson; if a layperson can understand your contract, it is less likely to result in litigation.[42] Remember

---

39. Some people find it easier to think through an agreement by writing a rough draft. We are not intending to discourage that "write-to-think" style. Instead, we are simply warning that the process of thinking through the needs of the parties must occur at some point during the drafting process before revision.

40. Ray and Ramsfield, *supra* note 12, at 145.

41. Ludwig Mandel, *The Preparation of Commercial Agreements* 14 (1979).

42. Martin, *supra* note 10, at 45.

that laypeople will be carrying out the contract so they need to understand it.

Using a checklist, such as the one following, is the easiest way to ensure you have included all the required provisions. You may obtain other checklists by asking senior members of your firm for their contract checklists or by using formbooks or other books about drafting contracts.[43] Over time, you will want to develop your own checklist, drawing from the ones you have used and complete with your own sample provisions.[44]

The following checklist includes provisions you must consider including in all but the simplest of contracts. While this list is not exhaustive, it does present those provisions regularly found in most contracts.

Checklist of Common Contract Provisions

Initial Clauses

- Purpose or goals (sometimes known as recitals)
- Definitions
- Duration of the contract
- Statement of consideration

Duties of the Parties

- Statement of responsibility between parties to fulfill the agreement
- Payment to whom, by when, and any conditions for payment
- Time for performance
- Right to terminate, notice and timing of termination

Remedies

- Default or breach
- Time and manner for giving notice of breach
- Damages and liquidated damages
- Extensions, option to renegotiate or flexibility
- Specific remedies
- Mediation or arbitration before or instead of litigation
- Limitation of liability because of acts of God or other reasons

---

43. *See,* Cooper, *supra* note 17, at 274.

44. Consider creating checklists for different subject matters. For example, *see* Feldman and Nimmer, *supra* note 8, at § 1.02[B][5] for a sample checklist for the sale of commercial goods.

Assignability

- Delegation
- Assignability
- Permitting or prohibiting a change of parties

Timing

- Automatic renewal
- Time of the essence

Miscellaneous Clauses to Help the Contract Work

- Assumption of good faith
- Representations, warranties, or conditions; no other representations
- Headings not part of contract
- Incorporation of other documents
- Severability of terms
- Merger or integration clauses incorporating oral representations
- Choice of governing law and venue selection

Ending Clauses

- Acknowledgement clause
- Signatures
- Dates
- Testimonium clause

When drafting provisions, limit each provision to one subject. Focusing each provision on one point will help you increase the readability and clarity of the contract. Keeping each subject separate helps avoid ambiguity about what modifies what, helps keep the content easier to understand, and also contains damage if something goes wrong. Just as a bulkhead in a ship keeps a leak from sinking the whole ship, separate provisions and a severability clause can keep a contract from failing if any one clause becomes problematic. For example, the following provision from an insurance contract includes all information on personal property, regardless of who owns the personal property.

We cover personal property under the following situations.

1. We cover personal property owned or used by any insured while it is anywhere in the world.

2. At your request, we will cover personal property owned by others while the property is on the part of the residence premises occupied by any insured.

3. In addition, we will cover, at your request, personal property owned by a guest or a residence employee while the property is in any residence occupied by any insured.

Including unrelated matters in a provision is confusing. For example, the provision above is already complex and would have become confusing if the drafter had included the insurance company's liability for injuries to guests or residence employees. If you believe the contract needs to address related matters, state those matters in separate provisions and then include cross-references to those related provisions.[45] For example, at the end of the above provision, the drafter could add: "(Liability for injuries to guests and residence employees is covered in section D below.)"

Use active voice and clear verbs when drafting clauses relating to the actions each of the parties is going to take, such as "Acme grants the license to Smith" or "Doe purchases the shares."[46] Uses clear language, such as "will," "agrees to," or "promises" to express the duties of the parties to each other.[47] Use language such as "may" or "at Acme's discretion" to indicate when a party has discretion to take or not take action.[48] You may also include clauses that indicate prohibited actions, policies to be observed between the parties, conditional events, and representations or warranties.[49]

Large-scale organization is hard to get right if you look at only one computer screen at a time. So, at this stage of drafting, keep each provision on a separate page so you can rearrange the sections without difficulty.[50] With each provision on a separate page, you can reorder the pages quickly and repeatedly, moving them on the computer file only after you have settled on an organization you like. Also print out your provisions periodically and review their order. When all the sections are present and in place, remove the page breaks. This method also gives you a clearer sense of whether the major provisions have been included and allows for easy comparisons to your checklist.

In summary, at this stage concentrate on drafting the provisions for the contract and clarifying their content. Focus on being thorough, including everything needed to state the parties' agreement. When you

---

45. As you revise drafts, make sure that cross-references are updated as well. Your software likely has automatic cross-referencing functions that can track changes to your cross-references. Adams, *supra* note 8, at 92.

46. *Id.* at 18–20.

47. *Id.* at 22–33. Adams argues strenuously for using "shall" instead of "must" in these provisions, as does Scott J. Burnham, *Drafting Contracts* § 17.6.1 (2d ed. 1993); *but see* Joseph Kimble, *Plain Language–A Modest Wish List for Legal Writing*, 79 Mich. Bar J. 1574, 1576–77 (2000)(arguing

that "shall" has become so "corrupted by misuse" that "must" should be used instead). We prefer the terms in the text instead, to keep it clear that the contract was willingly undertaken, rather than imposed as a statute is.

48. Adams, *supra* note 8, at 33–35. These situations arise when you say "The indemnified party may . . . ," "If . . . occurs, then . . . Jones will be entitled . . . ," or "Acme is not required . . . ." *Id.*

49. *Id.* at 36–49.

50. Dickerson, *supra* note 13, at 62.

have most of the provisions drafted, your next step will involve the overall organization of the contract.

Rewrite, Concentrating on Logical and Clear Organization of Major Elements

When you begin to fix the organization of the contract, reorganize with the reader in mind, focusing on the sequence that is most functional for the contract's purpose. The best organization is often apparent from the internal logic of the contract itself. For example, in a real estate broker's agreement, the agreement could follow the transaction through its major components. The major sections would be organized as follows.

Sample Contract Organization

Introduction
- the parties
- the period of agreement

Duties
- the owner's obligations
- the broker's obligations
- the price at which the property will be offered
- the broker's commission
- the submission of the listing to a multiple listing service

Contingencies
- how to solve problems that arise

Miscellaneous
- the authorization for the "for sale" sign

Concluding
- the parties' signatures
- the date of the agreement

Organize to increase thoroughness and consistency. The broker's agreement above is both thorough and consistent because (1) it opens with the parties, (2) it moves to both parties' duties, (3) it then states the offering price and the broker's commission so both parties know what money is involved, (4) it states the niceties of the deal by including the multiple listing service; and (5) it concludes with the contingency, miscellaneous, and concluding provisions that are needed to fully state the contract. All the needed provisions are included and the contract consistently addresses both parties' needs.

You will facilitate thoroughness and consistency by grouping related provisions under general headings, which helps the reader understand the relationships of the various aspects of the contract. Use consistent language in the headings, but be careful when drafting headings not to depend on the headings to convey meaning. That meaning could be interpreted to contradict, limit, or expand the language stated in the particular provision. For example, in the broker's agreement, if a heading stated "Owner's obligations after the expiration of this agreement" but the provisions following the heading included references to the owner's obligations during the agreement, then the owner could argue that any obligations to be performed during the agreement were not binding because the heading only referred to obligations after the agreement expired. To avoid this problem, carefully draft your headings to portray accurately what is in each section or provision. Also consider inserting a provision saying headings are not part of the contract, such as the following.

> The table of contents and section headings in this Agreement are inserted only for reference. They are not intended to modify or define this Agreement.

To clarify your organization and to help readers locate particular provisions, include a table of contents at the beginning of the contract if the contract is over five pages long.[51] Many readers also find it useful to have numbered paragraphs, so it is easy to locate a particular provision.[52] Numbers also make cross-referencing easier, with phrases such as "see paragraph 14," to pinpoint the correct provision. In contrast, a cross-reference such as "see company's liability," could refer to several different provisions. Remember to double-check when polishing, however, to ensure that these cross-references correlate to the correct provisions.

This step of drafting ensures that your organization enhances the contract, rather than detracts from it. Your organization should show that the contract is more than a collection of individual provisions, but rather that those provisions are logically interrelated. You can unify the organization by having the provisions present the parties' agreement in logical sequence, grouping provisions under general headings, and using cross-references.

Revise, Checking Thoroughness and Consistency

The next step, revising, ensures that the wording also enhances the contract. As part of revising, complete two checks during this step. The first check, for thoroughness, is to review each provision to make sure that it completely covers everything needed to make its point and that the provisions together cover everything needed to state the contract between the parties.

The second check, for consistency, is to see that you have used each word or idea consistently throughout the contract. To make this check,

---

51. Others do not provide a table of contents until the contract reaches 20 pages or longer. *See* Adams, *supra* note 8, at 15.

52. Lawyers have strong opinions on numbering systems. *See, e.g., id.,* at 52–53, and Kimble, *supra* note 7, at 1574–75.

select an aspect of the contract and revise with only that aspect in mind. Read through the contract multiple times. Verify that you have used all terms consistently throughout the contract, checking individual terms to make sure they are used consistently and that no other term is substituted in any clause. Contracts are not the place for elegant variation. Using the same words throughout the contract may diminish it as great prose, but it will increase the chances of avoiding litigation.[53] Then identify any terms that could have more than one meaning in the context of the contract and revise their usage, giving each term only one meaning.

When needed, define any term that has a specific meaning for the contract that is different from its general use or is a technical word you cannot eliminate from the contract's language. Put these defined terms in the first section of the contract and consider putting all defined words in bold or in italics throughout the contract so the reader knows when to refer to the definition section. If you object to a separate definition section because it forces the reader to move back and forth between the body of the contract and the definition section, define the terms in context.[54] To include a definition in context, you could use any of the following methods:

Adjusted gross income, which is your total gross income minus deductions . . . .

Adjusted gross income (total gross income minus deductions) . . . .

. . . adjusted gross income. Adjusted gross income is your total gross income minus deductions.

But use definitions only when needed.

Use plain English in your contracts. Using plain English throughout the contract means choosing everyday terms and eliminating unnecessary technical words, terms of art, or legal jargon. While the plain English movement originally centered around consumer contracts, the movement has now expanded into contracts in general. Revise your language so it presents the parties' understanding as directly and clearly as possible.

Software may also help you when revising your drafts. For example, some programs can scan documents and highlight errors and inconsistencies, such as cross-references to sections that do not exist, defined terms that are not defined or are defined more than once, blanks that indicate language is missing, and variations in recurring phrases.[55] But be cautious. Just as you must not become too dependent on your word processing software's spell checkers or grammar checkers because they frequently do not catch words that are spelled correctly but not the

---

53. Pay special care to make sure that sections or provisions drafted by other specialists and inserted into the contract, such as tax, ERISA, or environmental provisions, are consistent both in substance and language with the rest of the contract. Waryjas, *supra* note 26, at 117.

54. Carl Felsenfeld and Alan Siegel, *Writing Contracts in Plain English* 98 (1981).

55. Adams, *supra* note 8, at 134, referring to software used by some firms. *See also,* Martin, *supra* note 10, at 45.

correct word, so too you should not become too dependent on editing software. You ultimately are responsible for ensuring that the contract is accurate and complete.

Obtain Editing Assistance From Someone Else

After you have completed these checks, the next step is to ask someone else to review the contract. Preferably the person who reviews your draft will be someone who also drafts contracts and perhaps has had some previous contact with your client, so he or she will be better able to focus on what the contract should say. Because readers give their best editorial critique on the initial review of a document,[56] you will make the best use of your colleagues' time if you seek the first review after having completed the content, organization, and revision steps. This will allow them to critique the contract with most of its substance in place.

When requesting the review, ask the reviewer to focus on determining whether the contract accurately, thoroughly, and consistently states the parties' needs and responsibilities. While this person may provide some general editing assistance to make the language more readable or legally accurate, his or her primary purpose is to determine whether you have stated the parties' objectives. You need to remind the reviewer of this purpose or the reviewer may spend his or her time editing minor points.[57]

To help the reviewer focus, consider providing a list of questions to clarify what you want the reviewer to do. By using these questions, the reviewer will be able to respond to your concerns more quickly and will not get off track. For example, you might ask the reviewer the following questions.

Sample Reviewer's Checklist

Thoroughness

- Are all routine duties covered?

- Are all contingencies adequately covered?

- Are any provisions so specific that they do not allow adequate flexibility?

Clarity

- Will the organization be clear to the users of the contract?

- Will the parties be able to read, understand, and accurately interpret the contract?

- Is the contract clear within the context of the parties' standard practices (construction industry, shipping, retail, insurance, etc.)?

---

56. Dickerson, *supra* note 13, at 67.

57. For more help in how to work with reviewers, see the section on this in Chapter 2, Process.

- Will the contract be clear to a court that does not understand the standard practices?

Consistency

- Are any terms used in ways that contradict standard usage and thus invite misunderstanding?
- Are all necessary cross-references included?
- Are the provisions internally consistent with one another?

Also consider reviewing this draft of the contract with the client.[58] Have your client read the contract and then explain to you his or her understanding of the agreement. As you listen, you can determine whether you have actually stated what your client wants from the agreement or need to make changes and corrections. Whether you review the contract with your client before or after polishing is a decision you must make, given your situation and your particular client. It may be wise, however, to obtain this review before polishing because, if major changes or corrections need to be made, it will save time to make those changes earlier in the process.

Polish for Clarity

Polishing, the final step, means focusing on the details. Doing this ensures the material presented is of high quality, which increases the likelihood the contract will achieve its purpose. Try to spend at least one revision polishing the language. As illustrated at the beginning of the chapter, words as seemingly innocent as prepositions or even articles have been the focus of numerous cases. Carefully read each provision to make sure each word accurately indicates what you believe are the parties' objectives.

The time you spend polishing will depend on the complexity of the contract and the needs and resources of your client. This step requires concentrating on writing rather than substance. For example, read the contract for subjects and verbs too far apart, misspellings, awkward sentence structure, and problems peculiar to your own writing, such as dangling modifiers, overuse of passive voice, or improper use of semicolons.[59] Correct any errors in your grammar, punctuation, usage, and word choice. Your reader will be focused on detail.[60] You must be too.

After polishing the language, put the contract aside for one day and then review it one more time for overall impression. In this final review, read through the entire contract quickly in one sitting. Look for contradictions between sections of the contract because, when polishing, you can often become too focused on the details and forget to look at the contract as an integrated document.

---

58. Larry A. Christiansen, *Drafting Contracts* 32 (1986); *see also* Martin, *supra* note 10, at 46.

59. Ray and Ramsfield, *supra* note 12, at 267–68.

60. *Id.*

CONCLUSION

By working step by step, you will be able to reach your goal. The contract will be thorough and consistent and will accurately state the parties' agreement.

Exercise 1

Your client, Amanda Benson, own a small shop which rents all different kind of tools and equipment to residential customers and a few other small businesses. She has been receiving complaints from her customers that the Damage Waiver provision in her form contract is difficult to read and understand. She is happy with the rest of the contract but agrees with her customers that the Damage Waiver provision is not as clear as it could be. She wants you to revise the provision below to make it easier to read and understand, without changing any of the rights and protections that she has under the current provision.

DAMAGE WAIVER

This section modifies Customer's responsibility for damage to the equipment, provided the Customer has not declined benefits of this section by initialing on the front of the contract and provided the Customer takes reasonable precaution to protect equipment. Dealer agrees, in consideration of Customer paying an additional fee based upon gross rental charges, to assume risk of damage to equipment as hereinafter limited. Customer agrees to immediately return damaged equipment to Dealer. The following risks are assumed by the Customer: (a) Loss by damage at 25% of current replacement value or repair cost of equipment. (B) Loss or damage resulting from overloading, exceeding rental capacity, misuse, abuse, or improper servicing of equipment at full current replacement value. (C) Loss due to theft, mysterious disappearance, or wrongful conversion by a person entrusted with equipment, at full current replacement value. (D) If 25% of replacement value is not paid by customer within 30 days of damage, the Damage Waiver becomes null and void and Customer is responsible for 100% of cost less Damage Waiver fee paid. (E) Damage Waiver does not release any person or entity except the customer. In this instance, Dealer reserve the right to collect from person or company causing damage. Customer may decline Damage Waiver provision by initialing in the appropriate place on the face of this contract. In such event, Customer shall be responsible for all loss of and damage to equipment. If Customer has insurance covering such loss or damage, customer shall exercise all rights available to him under said insurance, take all action necessary to process said claim, and Customer further agrees to assign said claims and any and all proceeds from such insurance to Dealer. Upon request of Dealer, Customer shall furnish the name of the insurance agent, insurance company, and complete information concerning insurance carried. Dealer's waiver of claims against Customer as herein set forth is contingent upon Customer's prompt notification of damage and return of equipment to Dealer.

Exercise 2

The senior partner in your firm, Lenore Bostick, is developing a user-friendly contract for a client, Peter Bagley, who has recently opened a new car dealership. Peter has gathered together several competitors' contracts and wants you to review them and help him draft the contract. Today, he is meeting with Lenore and they want to talk over the possible contract provisions when customers want to purchase the car at the end of the lease. Lenore is concerned that some of the contracts seem very user-friendly but do not adequately protect the dealer, and others seem to protect the dealer well but are very difficult to read and understand. Please review the following competitors' provisions on purchase after lease, write a summary of each provision's strengths and weaknesses, and then write a new provision that is both user-friendly while protecting the car dealership.

(A) **Lessee's Option to Purchase**

If I am not in default in my obligations under this lease, I have the option to purchase the vehicle "AS IS, WHERE IS" at the end of the lease term by adding $150 to the Residual Value. I agree to notify you 30 days prior to the scheduled end of the lease if I want to purchase the vehicle. After I pay the Purchase Option Price, plus official fees, taxes and any amounts necessary to prepare the vehicle to conform with legal requirements for sale, you will deliver title to the vehicle to me. I also understand this is a true lease and unless and until I exercise this purchase option, I have no ownership interest in the vehicle, its equipment, accessories or replacement parts, except my right to possess and use the vehicle under the terms and conditions of this lease.

(B) **Option to Purchase** (check applicable provision):

____ There is no option to purchase the Vehicle under this Lease.

____ You may purchase the Vehicle, but only at the scheduled end of the Lease, for $150.00 plus fees and taxes related to the purchase. To do so, you must notify us at least 30 days before the scheduled end of the lease.

(C) **Lease End Purchase Option Price**

$_____ plus official fees, taxes, and other charges (including repair costs) required by law. You have the option to purchase the Vehicle from Lessor in cash for the Purchase Option Price at the end of this lease. You do not have the option to purchase upon default or early termination.

(D) **Purchase Option:** You acknowledge that this is a true lease and you will not own or have any equity in the vehicle or its replacement parts unless you exercise the purchase option. You have the option to purchase the vehicle from us on an AS–IS WHERE–IS basis at scheduled termination. The purchase price will be the sum of:

(1) All amounts you owe under this Lease; and

(2) Any official fees and taxes imposed in connection with the purchase of the vehicle.

(E) **Purchase Option**

You can buy the Vehicle from us or our designated intermediary, "AS IS WHERE IS." If you want to buy the Vehicle, you will tell us at least 30 days in advance and will complete any documents we require for the purchase. At the end of the Lease Term, the purchase price will the Residual Value. Before the end of the Lease Term, the purchase price will be the remaining Net Balance. In either case, you will also pay any other amounts due under the Lease at the time of purchase and any official fees and taxes related to the purchase.

Assignment 1

Your client, John Hollis, has come to you for your help with two related matters. The first is to draft an offer to purchase and follow through with the closing on a real estate purchase. The second, and the contract assignment for class, is to draft a co-ownership agreement.

John is buying a one-half interest in a home—at 614 Constitution Lane—from Patty O'Leary, a sister of one of his friends. John and Patty are not in a romantic relationship; he will be a tenant in common with and a housemate of Patty's once he has completed the purchase. (Do not worry about any of the details of the purchase for this assignment— assume everything will go smoothly and John will become a co-owner without mishap.) However, he wants the co-ownership agreement to be in place before he actually becomes an owner of the property.

The co-ownership agreement must set out the rights and responsibilities of each co-owner and the consequences for not "following the rules" with respect to the following oral agreement that John and Patty have made.

- Either or both parties may live in the house whenever they wish and may take one of the two bedrooms.

- Either party may rent to a third person (generally when that party does not occupy the house—see the exception for sharing a bedroom).

- Both parties are equally responsible for the expenses of maintaining the house—property taxes, special assessments, and homeowner's insurance—as well as maintenance of and repairs to the property.

- Each party will be responsible for one-half (or a proportionate share) of any utilities during periods of occupancy as will any tenant of either party.

- An occupying party has the right to approve or disapprove of the other party's prospective tenant—general rules for tenants are no smoking, no pets of more than 20 pounds—and can also object because of incompatibility of lifestyle, but cannot withhold consent without a good reason.

- At the time any shared expense comes due, each party will write a check for his or her portion of the expense.
- Either party may have another person live with them in the house (with or without paying rent to that party) as long as the person shares a bedroom with the party, but in that case the utilities for the house will be divided by the total number of occupants and paid accordingly (the right of the other party to object to a prospective tenant does not apply to this situation).
- No improvements will be made to the property unless both parties agree and then payment shall be made with equal contributions from the parties or financed together.
- Either party may authorize a repair to the property.

John is not sure what to do about these areas:

- how to define an improvement as opposed to a repair or general maintenance, and
- what to do if one party refuses or is unable to pay for his or her portion of an expense (e.g., if the other party pays the bill, how will they be reimbursed?).

John and Patty have agreed that they will both pitch in to cover regular maintenance of the property—snow shoveling, raking, etc. They have also agreed to make written amendments to the co-ownership agreement when necessary.

John would like to include a clause that says if any provision of the agreement is later held to be unenforceable, the other provisions will survive.

The property is in Cottage Grove, Wisconsin, so Wisconsin law will apply. Don't worry about the income tax consequences for this assignment. Similarly you may ignore ordinances or rules regarding occupancy and zoning. Also ignore any concerns about life of the agreement, what happens when a party sells or gifts his or her interest, dies, etc.

Assignment 2

Lewis "Lucky" Osterson has hired you to create a contract for his new garden tiller business. His company, Lucky Auto and Small Engine Repair, 100 Main Street, Middletown, Vermont, has tuned and repaired garden tillers as a sideline for several years. During this time, Lucky has collected several dozen used tillers in good condition. Lucky has also been outraged by the experiences his friends have had with another rental company, which has a convoluted contract that always leads to his friends getting caught with hidden charges for minor things.

So Lucky has decided to provide a little competition, at least in the area of renting garden tillers. He plans to rent tillers by the day for $30.00. He will clean them when returned, and he will fill the gas tanks as needed. But he does want the user to be responsible to pay for damage, such as bent tines or missing parts. He also wants people to return the tillers on time, so he can then rent them out to others.

Lucky has given you a copy of a contract used by the local rental company, but he wants something simpler, fair to all parties, and more user-friendly. He also needs a contract only for renting tillers. He also does not want to risk major liability.

You can only charge Lucky a modest amount for this contract, which is another reason why the contract should not be too long or too complicated. Think through what needs to be clarified, what protections each party needs, and proceed from there. You do not need to research Vermont contract law; the focus on this assignment is organization and clear, consistent text.

Copy of Contract Given to You by Lucky

GOTTAHAVIT RENTAL COMPANY

5432 Commercial Avenue
Middleton, Vermont
1–555–555–5555

"If we don't have it, you can live without it!"

Clerk⎯⎯⎯⎯⎯⎯⎯⎯ Time Out ⎯⎯⎯⎯ Time In ⎯⎯⎯⎯

Time Due ⎯⎯⎯⎯ List of Equipment Rented ⎯⎯⎯⎯⎯⎯⎯⎯⎯⎯

Name⎯⎯⎯⎯⎯⎯⎯⎯⎯⎯⎯⎯⎯⎯⎯⎯⎯⎯⎯⎯⎯⎯⎯⎯⎯⎯⎯

Address ⎯⎯⎯⎯⎯⎯⎯⎯⎯⎯⎯⎯⎯⎯ Apt. ⎯⎯⎯⎯⎯⎯⎯⎯⎯⎯

City ⎯⎯⎯⎯⎯⎯⎯⎯⎯⎯⎯⎯⎯⎯⎯ State⎯⎯⎯⎯ ZIP⎯⎯⎯⎯

Phone number⎯⎯⎯⎯⎯⎯⎯⎯⎯⎯⎯⎯⎯⎯⎯⎯⎯⎯⎯⎯⎯⎯⎯⎯

Driver's license #⎯⎯⎯⎯⎯⎯⎯⎯⎯State ⎯⎯⎯⎯⎯⎯⎯⎯⎯⎯

Deposit amount⎯⎯⎯⎯⎯⎯⎯ Cash or Credit Card #⎯⎯⎯⎯⎯⎯⎯

Amount Due if delivered on time ⎯⎯⎯⎯ Unless declined, Customer accepts the damage waiver.

Damage Waiver: In consideration of Customer paying additional charge of 09% of gross rental charges to Dealer, said Dealer agrees to modify Section 10 (Damaged or Lost Equipment) hereinbelow. Refer to Section 11 hereinbelow for Damage Waiver provisions. By initialing hereon, Customer DECLINES benefits of Section 11, Damage Waiver and assumes full responsibility for damage to equipment.

Initials ⎯⎯⎯⎯ Damage Waiver is not insurance.

I have read and agree to the CONTRACT TERMS ABOVE AND BELOW, which constitute the entire agreement. There are no oral or other representations not included herein. I also hereby acknowledge receipt of a copy of this contract.

Signature⎯⎯⎯⎯⎯⎯⎯⎯⎯⎯⎯ Date ⎯⎯⎯⎯⎯⎯⎯⎯⎯⎯⎯

CONDITIONS OF THE RENTAL

1. **INSPECTION.** Customer acknowledges that he has had or will have an opportunity to personally inspect the equipment, and finds it suitable for his needs and in good condition, and that he understands its proper use. Customer further acknowledges his duty to inspect the equipment prior to use and notify dealer of any defects.

2. **REPLACEMENT OF MALFUNCTIONING EQUIPMENT.** If the equipment becomes unsafe or in disrepair as a result of normal use, Customer must discontinue use and notify dealer who will replace the equipment with similar equipment in good working order, if available. Dealer is not responsible for any incidental or consequential damages caused by delays or otherwise.

3. **WARRANTIES.** THERE ARE NO WARRANTIES OF MER-CHANTABILITY OR FITNESS, EITHER EXPRESS OR IMPLIED. There is no warranty that the equipment is suited for Customer's intended use, or that it is free from defects.

4. **HOLD HARMLESS AGREEMENT.** Customer assumes the risks of, and hold Dealer harmless for, any and all property damage and personal injures caused by the equipment and/or arising out of Customer's negligence.

5. **PROHIBITED USES.** Use of the goods in the following circumstances is prohibited and constitutes a breach of this contract:

   (a) Use for illegal purposes or in an illegal manner.

   (b) Use when the equipment is in bad repair or is unsafe.

   (c) Improper, unintended use or misuse.

   (d) Use by anyone other than Customer or his employees, without Dealer's written permission.

   (e) Use at any location other than the address furnished Dealer, without Dealer's written permission.

6. **ASSIGNMENTS, SUBLEASES AND LOANS.** Dealer may assign his rights under this contract without Customer's consent, but will remain bound by all obligations herein. Customer may not sublease or load the equipment without Dealer's written permission. Any purported assignment by the customer is void.

7. **TIME OF RETURN.** Customer's right to possession terminates on the expiration of the rental period and retention of possession after this time constitutes a material breach of this contract. TIME IS OF THE ESSENCE OF THIS CONTRACT. Any extension must be mutually agreed upon in writing.

8. **LATE RETURN.** Customer agrees to return the rented goods during Dealer's regular store hours, upon termination of the rental period. In the event the goods are not returned during the Dealer's regular business hours, Customer will pay for any damage to or loss of

the goods or equipment damage occurring between the return and the commencement of Dealer's next business day.

9. **DIRTY EQUIPMENT**. Customer agrees to pay a reasonable cleaning charge for equipment returned dirty.

*10. **DAMAGED OR LOST EQUIPMENT**. Customer agrees to pay for any damage to or loss of the goods, as an insurer, regardless of cause, while the goods are out of the possession of Dealer. Accrued rental charges cannot be applied against the purchase or cost of repair of damaged or lost goods. Equipment damaged beyond repair will be paid for at its Replacement Cost when rented. The cost of repairs will be born by Customer, whether performed by Dealer or, at Dealer's option, by others.

*11. **DAMAGE WAIVER**. This section modifies customer's responsibility stated in section 10 for damage, provided that the Customer has not declined benefits of section 11 by initialing on the front, and provided the Customer takes reasonable precaution to protect the equipment. Dealer agrees, in consideration of Customer paying an additional fee based upon gross rental charges, to assume risk of damage to equipment as hereafter limited.

Customer agrees to immediately return damaged equipment to Dealer. The following risks are assumed by the Customer:

    (a) Loss by damage at 25% of current replacement value or repair cost of equipment.

    (b) Loss or damage resulting from overloading, exceeding rated capacity, misuse, abuse, or improper servicing of equipment at full current replacement value or repair cost.

    (c) Loss due to theft, mysterious disappearance or wrongful conversion by a person entrusted with equipment, at full current replacement value.

    (d) If 25% of replacement value is not paid by customer within 30 days of damage, the Damage Waiver becomes null and void and Customer is responsible for 100% of cost less Damage Waiver fee paid.

    (e) Damage Waiver does not release any person or entity except the customer. In this instance, Dealer reserves the right to collect from person or company causing damage. Customer may decline Damage Waiver provision by initialing in the appropriate place on the face of this contract. In such event, Customer shall be responsible for all loss of and damage to equipment. If Customer has insurance covering such loss or damage, Customer shall exercise all rights available to him under said insurance, take all action necessary to process said claim, and Customer further agrees to assign said claims and any and all proceeds from such insurance to Dealer. Upon request of Dealer, Customer shall furnish the name of the insurance agent, insurance company, and complete information concerning insurance carried.

12. **LOADING AND UNLOADING GOODS**. Customer is responsible for loading and unloading the goods. If Dealer's employees assist in loading or unloading the goods, Customer agrees to assume the risk of, and hold Dealer harmless for property damage or personal injuries.

13. **USE OF GOODS**. Customer agrees that the goods shall be used only by persons competent in their operation and further agrees that the customer is solely responsible for providing competent operations. Customer further agrees not to operate the equipment in a careless or negligent manner.

14. **COLLECTION COSTS**. Customer agrees to pay all reasonable collection, attorney's and court fees, and other expenses involved in the collection of the charges or enforcement of Dealer's rights under this contract.

15. **REPOSSESSION**. Upon a failure to pay rent or other breach of this contract, Dealer may terminate this contract and take possession of and remove the goods from wherever they are, and Dealer and his agents shall not be liable for any claims for damage or trespass arising out of the removal of the goods.

16. **DISCLAIMER OF AGENCY**. Customer acknowledges that he is not the agent of Dealer for any purpose.

17. **DISCLAIMER OF MANUFACTURE**. The Dealer is neither the manufacturer of the goods nor the agent of the manufacturer.

19. **INDEMNITY**. Customer agrees to indemnify and reimburse dealer for all liabilities of Dealer arising out of the use of the goods or a breach of this contract by Customer.

20. **SEVERABILITY**. The provisions of this agreement shall be severable so that the invalidity, unenforceability or waiver of any of the provisions shall not affect the remaining provisions.

21. **TITLE**. Title to the rented property is and at all times shall remain with the Dealer. Only the parties hereto and such other persons whose names are endorsed hereon are authorized to use said property, and Customer will not permit said property to be used by any other person at any address other than the place designated hereon without the express written consent to Dealer.

22. **THEFT**. Dealer, at Dealer's discretion, may report property as stolen if held 10 day beyond "Due in" date or if conditions and circumstances indicate theft or fraud before that time.

23. **INHERENT RISKS**. Customer acknowledges and accepts the risks inherent and attendant in the use of the equipment rented hereunder and voluntarily assumes risk of injury to customer's bumper or vehicle.

24. **INSPECTION OF TRAILER HITCH**. Customer agrees to inspect the trailer coupling mechanism and safety chain before leaving Dealer's premises. Dealer is not liable for damage to customer's bumper or vehicle.

25. **ACCIDENT NOTIFICATION**. Customer will immediately notify Dealer in the event of any accident or damage to rented property.

26. **DAMAGE TO VEHICLES**. Dealer is not liable for damage to customer's car top or body of the vehicle done by installation or use of car top carrier or the items carried on them.

27. **RENTAL CHARGES**. The customer agrees to pay Dealer all rental, delivery, mileage, installation, and other charges and costs set forth herein, at the rates, schedules, and charges on file with Dealer.

BIBLIOGRAPHY

Adams, Kenneth A., *Legal Usage in Drafting Corporate Agreements*. Westport, CT: Quorum Books, 2001.

Bloss, Julie L., *How to Review a Contract*, 91 Case & Comment 38 (May/June 1986).

Brown, Louis M., *Reviewing and Revising Draft Transactional Documents (A Checklist)* in Robert M. Hardaway, *Preventive Law: Materials on a Non Adversarial Legal Process*. Cincinnati: Anderson Publishing Co., 1997.

Burnham, Scott J., *Drafting Contracts*. Charlottesville: The Michie Company, 1987.

Child, Barbara, *Drafting Legal Documents: Principles and Practices*. St. Paul: West Group, 2d ed. 1992.

Christiansen, Larry A., *Drafting Contracts*. San Diego: Kensington House Publications, 1986.

Cooper, Frank E., *Writing in Law Practice*. Indianapolis: Bobbs–Merrill Co., 2d ed. 1963.

Crump, David, *The Five Elements of a Contract: Avoiding Ambiguity in Them*, 43 Tex.Bar J. 370 (April 1980).

Cuff, Terence F., *Drafting Agreements*, 15 Barrister 41 (Winter 1988).

Daly, David T., *Plain Language–Top 10 Phrases Not to Use in a Contract–A Lesson from Dr. Frankenstein*, 78 Mich. Bar J. 186 (1999).

Daly, David T., *Plain Language–Why Bother to Write Contracts in Plain English?*, 78 Mich. Bar J. 850 (1999).

Dickerson, Reed, *The Fundamentals of Legal Drafting*. Boston: Little, Brown and Company, 1986.

Feldman, Robert A. and Raymond T. Nimmer, *Drafting Effective Contracts: A Practitioner's Guide*. New York: Aspen Law & Business, 2d ed. 2002.

Felsenfeld, Carl and Alan Siegel, *Writing Contracts in Plain English*. St. Paul: West Group, 1981.

Goldblatt, Michael L., *Well-drafted Contracts Keep Client and You Out of Court. Here's How!*, 7 Prev.L.Rep. 14 (June 1988).

Goodwin, Rodney L., *Drafting Buy–Sell Agreements to Protect Both Buyer and Seller,* 17 Taxation for Lawyers 124 (Sept./Oct. 1988).

Haynsworth IV, Harry J., *How to Draft Clear and Concise Legal Documents,* 31 Prac.Law. 41 (1985).

Hurd, Hollis T., *Writing for Lawyers.* Pittsburgh: Journal Broadcasting & Communications, 1982.

Kimble, Joseph, *Plain Language–A Modest Wish List for Legal Writing,* 79 Mich. Bar J. 1574 (2000).

Kopelman, Kenneth P., *Some Thoughts re: Drafting Corporate Agreements–A Step by Step Approach* in *Drafting Corporate Agreements.* New York: Practising Law Institute, 1997–1998.

Llewellyn, Karl N., *Remarks on the Theory of Appellate Decision and the Rules or Canons About How Statutes Are To Be Construed,* 3 Vand. L.Rev. 395 (1950).

Macneil, Ian R. and Paul J. Gudel, *Contracts: Exchange Transactions and Relations, Cases and Materials.* New York: Foundation Press, 3d ed. 2001.

Mandel, Ludwig, *The Preparation of Commercial Agreements.* New York: Practising Law Institute, 1978.

Martin, James W., *Fifty Tips for Writing the 21st Contract that Stays Out of Court,* 16 Prac. Real Est.Law. 41 (Nov. 2000).

Maxey, David W., *Fundamentals of Draftsmanship—A Guide in Preparing Agreements,* 19 Law Notes 87 (Summer 1983).

McCormack, Mark H., *The Terrible Truth About Lawyers: How Lawyers Really Work and How to Deal With Them Successfully.* New York City: Beech Tree Books, 1987.

Note, *Avoiding Inadvertent Syntactic Ambiguity in Legal Draftsmanship,* 20 Drake L.Rev. 137 (1970).

Perry, Alan R., et al., *Introduction to Drafting California Legal Instruments.* San Diego: Jenkins & Perry, 1983.

Posner, Eric A., *The Parol Evidence Rule, the Plain Meaning Rule, and the Principles of Contractual Interpretation,* 146 U.Pa.L.Rev. 533 (1998).

Ray, Mary Barnard and Jill J. Ramsfield, *Legal Writing: Getting It Right and Getting It Written.* St. Paul: West Group, 3d ed. 2000.

Rosman, David M. and Ronald P. Kaplan, *Without the Possibility of Parol,* 21 L.A.Law. 48 (1998).

Till, Paul H. and Albert F. Gargiulo, *Contracts: The Move to Plain Language.* New York City: AMACOM (American Management Associations), 1979.

Waryjas, Maryann A., *Universal Issues in Drafting Corporate Agreements* in *Drafting Corporate Agreements.* New York: Practising Law Institute, 2001–02.

Wollner, Kenneth S., *How to Draft and Interpret Insurance Policies.* West Bloomfield, MI: Casualty Risk Publishing, Inc., 2000.

Chapter 6

ISSUES

Writing a good issue statement is like building a bridge.[1] One end of the issue rests on the bedrock of the law. The other end rests on the bedrock of the facts. The center, which is the core legal question, spans the space between, joining the beginning and end together and making the issue a freestanding element in the memo.

When writing issues, you focus intently on one sentence, more so than in most legal writing. In one sentence, an effective issue encapsules the relevant law, the legal question, and the significant facts upon which a case will turn, focusing a discussion that will take pages to explicate and resolve.

An effective issue not only communicates the essential elements; it also communicates the nature of the question, which could be a question of which law applies, whether the law applies, or how it applies in this situation. Because the issue must communicate so much in one sentence and must communicate it clearly, each word is critical. Similarly, each part of the issue's sentence structure must communicate how the words relate logically to each other. Each punctuation mark must do its job precisely. This focused writing task provides you with an especially effective opportunity for intensive practice with the small-scale writing skills of word choice and word order.

The most effective sentence structure for an issue will be a variation on a general structure. This chapter teaches you first how to put together that general sentence structure and then how to vary the wording and phrase structures within that structure to serve different purposes. The chapter discusses each component of the issue in turn: the law, the core question, and the facts.

Your task is to choose the most effective way to build each component so the whole issue is a unified, solid structure. This remains your task in writing both objective and persuasive issues. For that reason, this

---

1. Mary Ann Polewski contributed many of the ideas, examples, explanations, and assignments in this chapter.

chapter also discusses how to move from objective to persuasive issues, treating these two kinds of writing as variations on a common theme. The chapter provides specific techniques useful for emphasizing points in your persuasive issues.

Organizing an excellent issue can seem overwhelming at times because writers often feel pulled by contradictory objectives. The issue includes several pieces, each of which can be complex. Yet it is traditionally written in one sentence and it needs to be readable. These objectives seem to be necessarily at odds. To help you master this complexity, this chapter presents a format for the three components of issues (the law, core question, and facts) that allows for substantial complexity while maintaining a readable structure.

STRUCTURING THE SENTENCE

When structuring your three components into a one-sentence issue, try putting the law at the beginning and the facts at the end, with the core question as the central subject and verb in between. Although other orders are possible and are commonly used, this order is most useful because it works best logically and grammatically. The three-part nature of the issue means the sentence must include two major dependent phrases (one for the law and one for the facts) and one independent clause (the core question). In turn, this means that one phrase should be placed at the beginning of the sentence and one at the end. Other possibilities are unworkable. In a structure this complicated, making one of the phrases an intrusive phrase within the independent clause would decrease readability too much. The other possibility, putting two phrases in series at the beginning or end of the sentence, would also be too complicated because the two units would blur together visually and grammatically.

The choice then becomes whether the law or the facts should come first. Because the facts often require a list and because lists are most readable at the end of a sentence, placing the facts at the end will usually be more readable. It is also more logical to put the law at the beginning and the facts at the end; this order moves the issue from general to specific, leading the reader from the basic understanding of the law into the particularities of the issue at hand. Finally, beginning with the law provides appropriate emphasis, because the law is the foundation, or bedrock, of the issues's existence.

For all these reasons, this general structure is the best for beginning to form your issue.

Under [law], is [core question] when [facts]?

Under Wisconsin's wrongful death statute, which applies to a "death caused in the state,"is a death caused in the state when the victim was shot in the chest by a fellow bow hunter while in Wisconsin but died when the ambulance transporting him to the hospital was involved in a accident on a Minnesota highway?

Because this structure helps you unify and communicate the three key components of the issue, it allows you to rearrange those components quickly and easily.

The three-part question structure is easily adapted to various structural challenges. For example, usually the facts take longer to explain than the law, so the facts fit well at the end of the issue. But when the facts are short and the law is more complex, you can easily move the law component to the end of the sentences to maintain readability.

> Is a farm pig a domestic animal under Wis. Stat. § 174.01, which applies to "any horses, cattle, sheep, lambs or other domestic animals"?

Although this three-part question is not the only way to structure an issue, it provides a readable and organized starting point. The three parts enable you to state even the most complex issue as a grammatically complete question. In contrast, the "whether" structure, even at its best, can create only a grammatical fragment, never a complete sentence. Additionally, an issue beginning with "whether" forces the writer to use a complex phrase as a subject. The writer begins at a disadvantage, having to overcome a structure that is innately hard to read.

> Whether an uninsured motorist who is a legal resident of New Hampshire but currently living in Vermont while attending college and who injures a Vermont driver in an accident occurring in New Hampshire can be held liable under Vermont's statute concerning applicability of "financial responsibility laws to nonresidents ... and accidents in other states."

"Whether" clauses are complex, and they drive the verb away from its grammatical subject. In contrast, placing the facts at the end of the sentence allows you to keep the subject and verb together.

> **Under Vermont Statute 999.99 concerning applicability of "financial responsibility laws to nonresidents ... and accidents in other states," can an uninsured motorist be held liable when the motorist is a New Hampshire resident, when the motorist currently lives in Vermont while attending college, when the injured person is a Vermont resident, and when the accident occurred in New Hampshire?**

When describing a body of common law, you may be able to insert the law and facts after the core question because the law can be stated simply.

> **Does a city bus driver have a duty of care under Alaska tort law when** ....

But you could also retain the following structure.

> **Under Alaska tort law, does a city bus driver have a duty of care when** ....

By clearly identifying each component, you can vary your issues' structure without sacrificing precision or clarity. With or without the varied order of components, the three-part question is still the most useful starting point for your issue. It helps you create an issue that is both clear and complete, both precise and readable.

DEVELOPING THE ISSUE AS THREE COMPONENTS

For many writers, developing an issue is easier if they approach each component separately. After developing the components, they can revise each until all three are unified into one effective issue. Even if you prefer to start with the whole issue rather than separate parts, learning more about the construction of those parts will help you improve your issues.

Phrasing the Law

The law component provides the context for the whole issue. Memos are written for legal readers, and those legal readers are trained to interpret information based on the applicable laws. If you do not tell the reader what law applies, that reader must infer what law applies to the issue. If the reader makes the wrong inference, he or she will misunderstand the issue and is likely to reach the wrong substantive answer. You will avoid this risk of misunderstanding, and save your reader some work, if you clarify that law in the beginning.

The law component may set the issue in the context of a broad area of the law, such as contracts, or may set the issue in a specific area of the law, such as a subsection of a particular statute, constitutional provision, or administrative rule. It usually includes the jurisdiction.

The law is contained in an introductory phrase either alone or accompanied by a modifying phrase. This component can be as short as four words or much longer. The longer it is, the more carefully it must be written, for any long introductory phrase is hard for a reader to absorb. Include the law as an introductory phrase with a comma placed at the end. That comma signals the end of the introductory information and the imminent appearance of the sentence's subject.

Under the New York Pharmacist Examinations Statute,

When the law includes more than one part, you may need to include an appositive[2] within the introduction.

Under the statute concerning judicial administrative districts, Wis. Stat. § 757.60,

Under Wis.Stat. § 29.427, which regulates the possession and sale of live skunks,

Under Nebraska's Opening Letters statute, which prohibits opening a letter without the sender's or the addressee's consent,

Try to keep the two phrases as concise as possible. The combination of an introductory phrase and a dependent clause will bog down the issue if

---

2. An appositive is set off by commas and is a noun or phrase that comes right after a noun and describes that noun.

both are long. Your wording of the law component involves choosing between many specific options; when making those choices, be guided by your objectives of readability and precision.

Incorporating Case Law or a Group of Enacted Laws

A law component based on common law is relatively simple to structure. It can include four simple terms, as the examples below illustrate.

Basic Law Components Using Common Law			
introductory word	*jurisdiction*	*area*	*law*
Under	Washington	contract	law
According to	North Carolina	negligence	common law
Applying	federal	commodity trade	custom

The area of law described may be as broad as "contract law" or as specific as "the doctrine of res ipsa loquitur," but it should be as specific as possible. Rather than stating "tort law," you may be able to specify "negligence," "battery," or "false imprisonment." You may even be able to specify the sub-issue within the broader category.

Under the restraint element of Hawaii false imprisonment law,

Do not use overly broad labels such as "Under Texas case law" or "Under Ohio common law." Those descriptions are too general to give the reader an adequate legal framework. Be as specific as possible, introducing the legal terms applicable to the issue, even though you cannot narrow the area down to one particular element or statute.

The law component does not include names of cases or citations to them. Few cases are so well known that the citation alone will convey the area of law you want to identify. Even when the cases are well known, a case seldom stands for one proposition only, so reference to it would be ambiguous.

Incorporating a Single Enacted Law

You have more choices when writing an issue based on a specific statute or other type of enacted law. In this situation, the law component will usually include some combination of the following components.

Possible Components of Enacted Law	
Citation	Wis. Stat. § 895.03
Title	recovery for death by wrongful act
Paraphrased title	wrongful death statute
Description	which applies to deaths caused by a wrongful act
Reference to key language	which requires that a wrongful death be "caused in this state,"

The possible combinations of these components are many, as the following table illustrates.

Possible Combinations of These Components and Their Uses		
sample	components	when useful
Under Wis. Stat. § 895.03, Recovery for Death by Wrongful Act,	• citation • title	• when the statute's title is familiar to the reader and • when the issue cannot be more specifically focused.
Under Wis. Stat. § 895.03, the wrongful death statute,	• citation • paraphrased title	• when the title is cumbersome or unclear and • when the issue cannot be more specifically focused
Under Wis. Stat. § 895.03, which requires that a wrongful death be "caused in this state,"	• citation • reference to key language	• when your issue revolves • when your issue revolves around the interpretation of a specific part of the statute
Under Wis. Stat. § 895.03, which applies to deaths caused by a wrongful act	• citation • description	• when your issue revolves • around one aspect of the statute but not a quotable part
Under the Wisconsin wrongful death statute, Wis. Stat. § 895.03,	• paraphrased title • citation	• when the paraphrased title is more familiar than the citation and when the citation will not interrupt the flow of the issue statement
Under the Wisconsin wrongful death statute, which requires that the death be "caused in this state,"	• paraphrased title • reference to key language	• when your reader does not require the citation in the issue and • when the key aspect of the law can be quoted
Under Wisconsin's statute for recovery for death by wrongful act,	• title	• when the title is more familiar than the citation and • when your reader does not require the citation in the issue.
Under Wisconsin's statute for recovery for death by wrongful act, which applies to defendants whose negligence has caused a death,	• title • description	• when the title is more familiar than the citation, • when your issue revolves around one aspect of the statute but not a quotable part, and • when your reader does not require the citation in the issue

In general, do not use a citation alone for the law component. A citation alone does not give the reader enough information to be useful, even if the reader recognizes the statute number. Combining the citation with a title or description will provide the necessary information.

Some writers and readers believe the citation must be included because it provides essential information, while others find it distracting and unnecessary in the issue. Beyond this general position, you may find specific circumstances require different choices. Court rules may require you to include the citation. The complexity or length of the issue may make omitting the citation desirable. If the issues are used for indexing your firm's memo bank, the citation may be essential to the retrieval system. If you include a citation, be sure to use proper citation form and to comply with any rules imposed by the court or your firm.

Unlike citations, titles may be used alone if the title is clear and specific enough to inform the reader of the legal foundation for the issue.

Applying Michigan's *compulsory school attendance statute,*

Under the Georgia statute concerning *judgments docketed in other counties,*

Enacted laws generally include titles, although the title's wording does not carry any weight when interpreting or analyzing the enacted law.[3] Attorneys can use these titles as references that are more readily understood than citations.

Often, however, the title is too difficult to read without modification, as happens in the following examples.

Under the Wisconsin buttermaker and cheesemaker license statute,

According to Florida's false, misleading or deceptive insurance solicitation statute,

In this circumstance, the title's language may still be used if it is rephrased so the detail comes at the end of the phrase. Other titles may need to be partially paraphrases to work as a readable introductory phrase. In the following table, the title of a statute is given on the left, and an example of a restructured or paraphrased introductory phrase is on the right.

Actual title	Introductory phrase including the title restructured or rephrased
buttermaker and cheesemaker license statute,	Under the Wisconsin statute concerning buttermaker and cheesemaker licenses,
insurance solicitation that is false, misleading or deceptive,	According to the Florida statute addressing false, misleading or deceptive insurance solicitation,
operating vehicle without owner's consent	Under the Kentucky statute concerning operating a vehicle without the owner's consent,
jurors, how paid	Under the Colorado statute for paying jurors,

Many titles of enacted laws will not provide enough information for the reader. Other titles will give more information than is needed for the issue. Add or delete information as needed to make your law component clear, and then revise it as needed to make it grammatical and readable.

---

3. As discussed in Chapter 3 on statutes, the title of a provision is generally not part of the enacted law that it introduces.

Introductory phrase using actual title	Introductory phrase restructured to fit a specific issue
Under the New Mexico statute requiring obedience to traffic signs and signals, right of way of funeral processions and military convoys;	Under New Mexico's right of way statute for military convoys,
Under Vermont's statute concerning applicability to nonresidents, unlicensed drivers, unregistered motor vehicles and accidents in other states,	Applying the Vermont statute concerning the applicability of financial responsibility laws to unlicensed drivers,

At some point, the title is so changed from the original that it becomes more of a description than a title, a natural progression to the next option for stating the law.

The description may include some words from the title, but the writer's goal is not to be faithful to the title. Rather, the goal is to be faithful to the meaning of the law itself. Descriptions are most useful when

- you want to include extensive information about the law,
- you want to focus the reader's attention on particular language or on a particular element, or
- the title of the provision does not give needed information.

Place a description in a dependent clause following an introductory phrase containing either a citation or a title. For example, the description may begin with any of the following terms: *requires, describes, addresses, prohibits, allows, states.* Use the term that suggests the meaning you want to convey.

Examples of Useful Descriptions	
Purpose	Example
Including extensive information	Under Wis. Stat. § 942.05, which prohibits opening a letter without the sender's or the addressee's consent,
Focusing the reader's attention on particular language	Under the Wisconsin wrongful death statute, which requires that the death be "caused in this state,"
Providing information not given in the title	According to Oregon's poisons statute, which describes the procedure for delivering highly toxic substances without a prescription,

In summary, the law component of the issue is more than a formulaic introduction to the issue. By shaping the law carefully, you begin focusing the issue for the reader, even before he or she has read the core question.

Focusing the Core

The core of the issue contains the central legal question, making it the central structure of the sentence: the subject, verb, and object. This core connects the law and facts, both logically and grammatically. Though short, this core deserves substantial attention.

Avoid wasting the core on unimportant terms. Generic core questions such as "is the defendant liable" add no substantive information about the issue; that subject and verb could be used in any civil action. Instead, use the core question to focus the reader's attention on the critical aspect of the law that must be applied to the facts.

When choosing the subject, search for a legal term upon whose definition the issue turns, because that term is often your best subject. Often it will be a subcategory of the legal concept introduced in the law component. For example, if the law component was "Under North Dakota's first-degree murder statute, which defines 'intent to kill,'" your core question might zero in on the word "intent."

is *intent* established by

If your law component was "Under Kansas common law regarding intentional tort," your core question might focus on "injury" or "reasonable apprehension."

was the plaintiff's apprehension that the defendant would strike her *reasonable* when

Occasionally this critical legal term will work better as the object rather than the subject.

does the evidence establish *intent* when

By placing this term in your core question, you focus the reader on the precise legal question. You gain clarity and conciseness.

The verb can also reflect the issue's focus. If the issue focuses on whether a legal concept applies to the particular set of facts, often you will use a linking verb (usually a form of "to be"), which is the grammatical equivalent of an equals sign. For example, if the question is whether shouting epithets equals a threat of harm, the core question might be "is shouting sufficient," as the following example illustrates.

is shouting insults alone sufficient to establish a threat of harm when

Although using "to be" is often criticized for leading to inactive writing, this use of the verb is anything but passive. The linking verb joins a legal term and a word or phrase summarizing the key facts. This core question then bridges the gap between law and facts by pulling the key term from each of those elements and fusing them into a legally significant and grammatical unit. In some cases, the verb can be an action that carries the central legal concept. For example, in a property case, the following core question might best focus the issue.

does a landlord *breach* the implied warranty of habitability when

The central concern in the core of the issue is that this legal and grammatical center of the sentence expresses the core question of the issue, the exact point where the law and facts meet. It also provides an analytical tool that helps move the reader to apply the law to the legally significant facts.

Organizing the Significant Facts

The fact component of the issue usually involves more than one fact. Since issue statements are traditionally written as one sentence, that means you will organize facts in some sort of list. Thus issue statements will require the same techniques you used to structure lists in jury instructions.

1. Group listed items logically.

2. Use clear signals to show the reader how the list is structured.

3. Order the items logically.[4]

The most challenging step in organizing lists is determining the most logical grouping for those facts. But, after you have chosen the best grouping, remember to finish the job well. Be sure to use parallel structure for your listed items, and to punctuate your list correctly.[5]

Structuring a Simple List

If the facts tell a unified story, chronological order might be best. For example, if you were describing a series of events leading to injury, you might write the following facts.

> when she slipped on the ice, lost her balance and fell sideways, reached out with her left arm to break her fall, and wrenched her left shoulder as the arm twisted beneath her?

Within this chronology of events, individual events often need to be grouped to increase clarity. Background facts are grouped with more significant events, so the reader can distinguish which events are most important to the narration. For example, the previous set of facts groups "losing her balance" with "falling" and groups the legally significant result ("wrenching her arm") with the supporting detail about the event that caused that injury ("as the arm twisted beneath her"). Grouping facts within the list presents a series of small scenes that, together, tell the story. This can be quite effective as long as the groups do not become too complicated. When that happens, the reader loses the sense of sequence and overall clarity is lost, as the following example shows.

> when, slipping on the ice, she lost her balance and fell sideways, reached out with her left arm as she attempted to break her fall, and suffered the pain of a wrenched left shoulder as the arm twisted beneath her?

An effective chronology stays focused on the main sequence of events. It is not so complicated that the reader loses the main point, as in the

---

4. See Chapter 4 on jury instructions.

5. For details on punctuating lists correctly, see a grammar text or Mary Barnard

Ray and Jill J. Ramsfield, *Getting It Right and Getting It Written* 192–96 (3d ed. 2000).

previous example. Neither is it so fragmented that the story loses its focus, as in the following version.

> when she slipped on the ice, lost her balance, fell sideways, reached out with her left arm, tried to break her fall, twisted her arm beneath her, and wrenched her left shoulder?

In summary, even the chronological organization of the facts requires careful thought about the significance of the facts.

If, more than telling a story, the facts relate to two topical groups, then you may need to reflect those groups in the structure of your list. In the following set of facts, for example, the facts fell into two legally significant groups: (1) the landlord's failure to initiate repairs and (2) the landlord's failure to respond to the many warnings that repairs were needed.

> when the landlord failed not only to inspect the stairs regularly, but also to repair them at the tenants' request, to answer the building supervisor's inquiries about the stairs, and to complete the repairs required by city inspectors?

When using a topical structure, include grammatical signals to reflect the logical relationship of your groups. The previous list signaled its groupings with the coordinating phrases "not only" and "but also." Often the relevant facts divide into two logical groups because some facts support a favorable answer to the issue, while others support the opposite answer. In this situation, you may want to organize two groups and divide them with a term indicating the contrast, usually "but."

> when the driver did slow his vehicle in the construction zone and was aware of the officer's presence at the intersection, *but* failed to heed that officer's warning whistles, turned into the unpaved street, drove past warning barricades, and steered his vehicle into the open trench?

This simple act of grouping facts can add meaning to the issue, suggesting that the two groups represent different points to be made.

Occasionally, the facts in the list will not require any particular topical or chronological order. In that situation, consider putting the simpler facts first and the most complicated ones last to improve readability.

> **caused by the failure to turn off the water, repair the leaking faucet, post warning signs, or take any steps to prevent the ice from building up on the sidewalk?**

rather than

> caused by the failure to turn off the water, repair the leaking faucet, take any steps to prevent the ice from building up on the sidewalk, or post any warning signs?

Readability is increased when the longest element is last. The reader is able to understand the structure and general content of the sentence before reading the most complex component.[6]

In summary, any grouping you use should reflect the logical categories created by the relevant law, rather than using a grouping solely for your convenience. Illogical groupings are likely to mislead the reader about the facts' significance.

Structuring More Complex Lists

When the list becomes more complex, you may need to insert stronger signals of the lists' organization. One option is tabulation.

Under New Jersey contract law, is a liquidated damages clause enforceable when:

(1) the clause was in a standard real estate contract for the sale of a $200,000 home;

(2) the clause required the buyer to forfeit $16,000 when he breached the contract;

(3) the seller incurred over $4,200 in expenses because of the buyer's breach;

(4) the seller lost the opportunity to buy another home on which she had made an offer; and

(5) the seller has not been able to sell her home in the seven months since the breach?

Tabulation helps the reader find his or her way through the complicated facts by providing visual signals of the organization.

A second way to handle this situation is to give two or three key facts and then indicate that there are more.

Under the New Jersey rule that liquidated damages clauses are enforceable if reasonable under the totality of the circumstances, is a $16,000 liquidated damages clause reasonable in a standard real estate contract for the purchase of a $200,000 home when the seller suffered losses because of the buyer's breach, *including* $4,200 in out-of-pocket expenses?

A third approach is to state general categories of facts, rather than specifics.

Under the New Jersey rule that a liquidated damages clause is enforceable if it is reasonable under the totality of the circumstances, is a clause reasonable in a standard real estate contract when the seller incurred expenses because of the buyer's breach and when the seller lost the opportunity to buy a home she wanted?

The final option is to divide the issue into sub-issues.

6. Daniel J. O'Keefe, *Persuasion: Theory and Research* 217 (2d ed. 2002).

Under New Jersey contract law, which states that a liquidated damages clause meets the test of being reasonable under the totality of the circumstances if three factors are satisfied, does the liquidated damages clause in Ms. Johnson's standard real estate contract for the sale of her home satisfy the three factors?

1. Was the liquidated damages clause not a penalty for breach when it required an $16,000 forfeiture on the sale of a $200,000 home and the parties negotiated the amount of damages at arms length?

2. Was it impossible to estimate accurately the loss from a breach when the parties did not know at the time they negotiated the contract whether Ms. Johnson would try to buy another home, what expenses she would incur while preparing to move, or that she would be unable to sell the house for more than seven months?

3. Did the $16,000 liquidated damages clause accurately forecast the harm to Ms. Johnson when her damages included forfeiting $4,200 in earnest money on the new home she offered to purchase, losing the opportunity to buy a home that uniquely suited her needs, and incurring expenses while preparing to move?

This format is likely to be needed only for extremely complex issues, where both the law and the facts are multi-faceted. Before using this approach, consider whether your issues would be clearer if written separately, rather than as sub-issues.

In summary, when writing the facts, you are basically applying your skills at structuring a list. But because of the many twists facts can take, you may try several options before you find one that communicates your facts clearly and precisely. Nevertheless, a clear focus on the facts will make it much easier for the reader to understand the significance of all the details in your issue and discussion section.

DEVELOPING THE ISSUE AS A WHOLE

Although some writers work more efficiently by focusing on each component of the issue in turn, others cannot begin this way. Instead, they need to begin with a general outline of the overall issue; then they can work out the details later. If you like to begin with a general outline, we offer the following process.

The following table explains the process and shows you how it would apply in a real situation. For example, assume Oregon has a worker's compensation act that provides benefits for all workers who suffer "accidental injuries arising out of and in the course of their employment." Our client, a teacher, was injured when he attempted to put out a fire he discovered while working in the building where he was employed. He applied for benefits, but they were denied by the compensation board on the grounds that his injuries were a result of his own mistake, and that his duties as an employee did not include attempting to extinguish fires. See how the following process helps you draft the issues involved.

Step	Example		
1. Ask yourself the general question.	Is our client entitled to benefits?		
2. Divide it into separate ideas		Is our client	entitled to benefits?
3. Add more specifics to each idea.		• a teacher • injured when he attempted to put out a fire • it was an oil-based fire on the stove in the teachers' lounge he discovered the fire • he threw water on the fire and the oil spattered on him • there was a fire extinguisher nearby	• Workers Compensation benefits • because he was at work when it happened, • when he isn't a firefighter • he didn't call the fire department first • he didn't use the fire extinguisher provided by the stove
4. Identify the relevant law and add that to the issue.	Under the State Worker's Compensation Act,		
5. Look more closely at the relevant law and identify the particular phrases that apply.	"accidental injuries arising out of and in the course of their employment"		
6. If several phrases apply, divide the information into separate issues.	"accidental injuries"	• he attempted to put out an oil fire with water, • he didn't use a nearby extinguisher	
	injuries that occur "in the course of their employment"	• he discovered a fire in the teachers' lounge after regular school hours	
		• he attempted to put it out himself, even though he is not a firefighter	
7. Assemble the pieces and then revise each issue for accuracy and clarity.	Under the Oregon Worker's Compensation Act, which applies to employees suffering "accidental injuries" at work, was a teacher's injury accidental when the teacher discovered burning oil on a stove in the teachers' lounge, failed to use a fire extinguisher nearby and instead threw water on the fire, which caused the oil to spatter and burn the teacher on the arms and face?		
	Under the Oregon Workers' Compensation Act covering employees for injuries "arising out of and in the course of their employment", was a teacher "in the course of his employment" when he was working in the school after regular hours and attempted to put out		

Step	Example
	a fire he discovered himself rather than calling for help, even though he is not a firefighter?
8. Revise the pieces for readability.	Under the Oregon Worker's Compensation Act covering "accidental injuries" that occur at work, was a teacher's injury "accidental" when the teacher threw water on a pot of burning oil, rather than using a nearby fire extinguisher, and suffered burns when the oil spattered?
	Under the Oregon Workers' Compensation Act, which applies to injuries "arising out of and in the course of [a worker's] employment", was a teacher acting in the course of his employment when he was at the school after regular working hours, when he discovered a fire there and when he attempted to put out the fire rather than calling the fire department?

At this stage, you have a good preliminary issue to help you focus as you create first drafts of your facts and discussion sections.

It is unlikely, however, that you will have successfully drafted a final version of your issue in this one try. It is even unlikely that you can accomplish it in one series of tries. Instead, draft your issues early in the memo writing process. Then return to those issues periodically, revising them as your understanding of the law and facts is revised and sharpening the issue's focus as your research is focused. Drafting your issues is likely to be both the first and last step in your process of writing a memo.[7]

UNIFYING THE ISSUE

After you have combined and refined the components of your issue, check to make sure it is unified. All three components should be focused on the same legal question. Although that goal seems obvious, writers routinely overlook it, and as a result they create issues that sound clear and smooth but fail to clarify the crux of the legal problem. Thus they fail to move beyond adequacy to excellence. For example, the following issue is structured clearly, but is not unified.

> Under New Jersey contract law, which will enforce a clause requiring liquidated damages but not punitive damages, does a liquidated damages clause meet all three elements of the test when the clause required the breaching party to pay 8% of the contract cost, when the parties could not estimate the cost of a breach when the contract was negotiated, and when the actual damages included $4,200 in out-of-pocket cost and the lost opportunity to buy another house?

Rather than being focused, this issue shifts its focus in each component. The law sets up a contrast between liquidated and punitive damages, but the core question does not pursue that point. The core question focuses on a three-part test, but neither the law nor the facts deal with those three elements. Finally, the facts address the amount and kind of damages suffered, but does not explain the sources of those amounts or

7. William P. Statsky and R. John Wernet, Jr., *Case Analysis and Fundamentals*   *of Legal Writing* 188 (4th ed. 1995).

their relation to the legal standards suggested earlier. The effect of this issue is reminiscent of a Picasso portrait—interesting and evocative perhaps, but hardly a clear portrait of the problem from a single legal perspective.

Under New Jersey's rule that permits liquidated but not punitive damages, is a damages clause punitive when it requires the breaching buyer of a house to pay $16,000, and when the seller's actual damages included only $4,200 in out-of-pocket cost and the lost opportunity to buy another house?

As you develop each part of your issue, strive for accuracy, clarity, and readability. Then, as you combine those parts, strive for unity. Revise each of the three components of your issue until the all strike the same target, directing your reader to the core of the legal problem your memo or brief addresses. When you achieve this, you will have created a single sentence that reveals the exact question upon which the outcome will turn. You will have provided your reader with a useful, efficient insight into the legal problem, and yourself with a guide that helps you structure and evaluate all the other parts of your document.

STRUCTURING THE BRIEF ANSWER

The two main purposes of a brief answer are to answer the question and to foreshadow the main points that will be covered in the discussion. It is generally difficult to accomplish both of those purposes in one sentence, so your brief answer is likely to require more than one sentence. The first phrase or sentence of your brief answer gives the reader your answer to the issue and echoes some of the language of that issue. Any subsequent phrases or sentences outline the reasoning behind the answer and echo the organization of the discussion that is to come.

Issue

Under Wyoming law on superseding causes, which includes foreseeability as an element, was the gang's act of chasing Tommy into the street unforeseeable when gangs had never been present in the neighborhood before, although some parents knew of gang members verbally harassing students?

Brief Answer

Probably yes. The gang's act of chasing Tommy into the street was an unforeseeable superseding cause, which would relieve the District of liability. The gang's presence and behavior could not have been foreseen based on past events, and thus the incident was unforeseeable.

The most frequent error made when writing brief answers is not including any sense of the legal reasoning behind the answer.

Probably yes. The gang's act of chasing Tommy into the street satisfies the first element of a superseding cause, which would relieve the District of liability.

Without the reasoning behind the answer, the reader must read the discussion section on faith that you will provide the reasoning there. When you include the reasoning in the brief answer, you allow the reader to gain a fuller view of the answer; he or she can then read the discussion section with a solid understanding of the analysis you present.

MOVING FROM OBJECTIVE TO PERSUASIVE WRITING

The difference between objective and persuasive issues is one of purpose rather than of style. You change the wording in your issue in response to the changes in your purpose. When writing an objective issue, for example, your purpose is usually to reveal to the reader the single question that makes the outcome of a legal situation less than obvious. You are explaining what is debatable, given the particular facts you have. If there were no debatable point, you would probably not have been asked to write a formal memo. In contrast, when you write a persuasive issue, you are explaining the single question that, when answered, will explain why your client should prevail. You are explaining why the issue is not really that debatable, given the facts you have. Ironically, then, a good persuasive issue should appear to be simpler than an objective issue, even though in reality the issue may not be simple at all.

To achieve this purpose, you must think about the legal reasoning that favors your side of the argument, and in your issue you must communicate that this reasoning is the standard the court should use. When stating the law component, for example, word it to emphasize a particular legal concept that favors applying this law to your client. When stating the core question, choose a subject and verb that suggest the justice of the answer you want. When stating the facts, minimize unfavorable facts and emphasize favorable ones, ones that support the outcome you desire. Careful emphasis of your winning logic and support, more than strong wording, will produce a successful persuasive issue.

The logic and support that will persuade successfully depends on your audience, your situation, and your role in that situation.[8] For example, persuading the legal reader differs greatly from persuading the consumer. In advertising, the problem is to persuade consumers to purchase a product, but consumers often make purchases without a great deal of deliberation.[9] Consumers do not think too much about which bar of soap to use, for example, so appeals to basic emotions and pleasant associations may be effective persuasive choices.

With a legal brief, however, your audience is prepared to deliberate. Indeed the audience's job is to deliberate. Although the judge will want to be efficient, he or she will not make a decision without reflection and

---

8. O'Keefe, *supra* note 6, at 215–40 (1990).

9. *Id.* at 105–07.

careful reasoning. Because of this standard, appeals that cannot stand close logical scrutiny will not be persuasive.[10]

Nevertheless, objective and persuasive writing have much in common. For example, much of the same content is needed in both situations. Whether you are informing a senior attorney or persuading a judge, you will still need to explain the relevant law accurately, clearly, and concisely.[11] In both cases, you will need to explain why and how the fact situation before you falls into the category covered by the law, and what the effect of the law is on the outcome.[12] Similarly, you will have to address unfavorable precedent, although the issues you address may vary as you move through the court system. Your need to present your case objectively will also not change, because readers are more readily persuaded by information that seems fair.[13]

Nor will your focus on the reader change. Whether you are informing or persuading, you need to think about what questions the reader will be considering and address them.[14] The information and the structure should lead the reader to ask those questions. The reader of objective writing evaluates the strength of available options to decide whether to proceed; the reader of persuasive writing evaluates the merits of the position taken by the writer. Both situations require the reader to evaluate the reasoning, the sufficiency of the support, and the relevance of the content discussed within the reader's own framework for making the decision.

Finally, your desire to establish and maintain credibility will not change when you shift from objective to persuasive writing, although your reasons for wanting that credibility may shift. For example, you may want to impress the senior attorney with your credibility so he or she will see you as capable and trustworthy. In contrast, you may want to appear credible to the judge in order to be more persuasive and win your case.[15] In both circumstances, however, you are communicating specialized knowledge about a legal question to a skilled reader who has

10. "In legal argument, it can be fatal to assume that the judge agrees with your assumptions. If, after inquiry into the hidden assumptions of your position or those of your opponent, you decide that agreement is problematic, you should reckon with those assumptions. Do not presume that if you hide them, the judge or your opponent will remain in blissful ignorance. Just as assumptions are frequently hidden, so implications of deductive arguments are rarely discussed in briefs. While you may choose to forget about the implications of your argument, the judge never does. Because implications are critical to judicial decision-making, failure to examine all important implications fully may doom your argument." Judith A. Finn, *Writing Briefs for Federal Litigation: The Province of the Elect*, 22 Tulsa L.J. 127, 132 (1986).

11. "Persuasive writing is reader-oriented. This means your briefs should be judge-oriented." Edward J. Devitt and James A. Barnum, *10 Tips for Preparing Better Briefs*, 22 Trial 75 (Oct.1986).

12. Rolf Sandell, *Linguistic Style and Persuasion* 96 (1977).

13. *Id.* at 163.

14. Gerald R. Miller, *Persuasion* in *Handbook of Communication Science* 146 (C. Berger and S. Chaffee, eds., 1987). "Lawyers who write judge-oriented briefs tend to win more frequently than those who write lawyer-centered briefs." Finn, *supra* note 10, at 128.

15. "Communicators are more successful at persuading if they are viewed as competent and trustworthy." Miller, *supra* note 14, at 464.

general knowledge but not detailed understanding, and who must make a decision about the question based largely on the information you provide. To do this, the reader must perceive you as a reliable reporter of the information.

What does change from objective to persuasive writing is the question your reader must answer and the context in which your writing appears. For example, the reader of a memo is considering how to proceed on behalf of the client and may have many options, including doing nothing, negotiation and settlement, or litigation. The reader of a brief faces a narrower question; he or she must decide who prevails in the case and for what reason. This reader is generally limited to considering the relief requested by the plaintiff and the defenses offered by the defense. So the question a brief addresses might be quite different than the question addressed by an earlier memo on the same facts. Because of this, the content of the brief may differ greatly from the memo; in comparison, the changes created solely because of the brief being persuasive rather than objective are not as profound.

Although the judge addresses a narrow question, he or she must consider a broader context. The judge has documents from both parties, so your brief will be reviewed in the context of the opposition's brief. Additionally, the judge may consider the broader context of precedent, mandatory authority, and public policy, whether or not the attorneys addressed those concerns in their briefs. For example, a trial judge may consider whether a decision would be appealed, even though the question is not addressed directly in the briefs. A state court of final review might consider what signals its ruling will send to the state bar, even though that issue might not be addressed in the briefs.

If you focus on the reader and his or her needs, you will be able to adjust naturally from objective to persuasive writing without focusing on persuasive techniques per se. You will first choose the aspects of the law and the facts that will lead to a decision in your favor; then you can use the following persuasive writing techniques to communicate your vision of the issue effectively.

EMPLOYING SPECIFIC PERSUASIVE TECHNIQUES

Begin by crafting your persuasive issue just as you would the objective issue, developing and refining the three essential parts and fusing them into a unified question. When you have shaped the issue to address the question that will lead to your side prevailing, you have already done much to make the issue persuasive. After you have structured your issue logically, you can use any of the five following techniques to emphasize and underscore your logic. These techniques help you place the emphasis on your content to help the reader see the significance of points central to your argument. The techniques include

- incorporating favorable and relevant aspects of the applicable law in your explanation;

- adjusting the focus and level of specificity in the core question to establish your position;

- stating significant and favorable facts in detail and unfavorable ones more generally;

- suggesting the logical relationship of facts with skillful use of signals; and

- using words with subtle connotations that steer the reader toward your opinion.

Incorporating Favorable Aspects of the Law

If your argument centers on the point that the law you are applying is limited or broad, you can suggest this in your description of the law component. For example, if you were arguing that your client is not liable, you might begin with the following.

Under Ill. Stat. § 48.01, which *limits* liability to . . . ,

If you were arguing that your opponent is liable, you might begin with the following.

Under Ill. Stat. § 48.01, which *extends* liability to . . . ,

Similarly, you may quote phrases from the law that support your interpretation of that law.

Under Ill. Stat. § 48.01, which extends liability to *"all drivers,"*

If, however, the legislative history favors you more than the statute's language, you may choose to emphasize that aspect of the statute.

Under Ill. Stat. § 48.01, which *was intended to apply to operators of commercial vehicles,*

Although you must take great pains to be accurate in your description of the law, you may still use this description to remind the court of the point you are making.

Adjusting the Core Question to Establish Your Position

When structuring the core question in objective issues, you focused on presenting the question precisely. When writing persuasively, maintain that focus. Nevertheless, you may state the core question in slightly more general terms to make the application of the relevant law to the significant facts suggest the result you want. For example, if you were representing a city arguing that it has immunity, you might prefer the following more general core question.

does governmental immunity *prevent*

In contrast, if you were arguing that the city was liable, your core might focus on the city's responsibility.

does the city's duty to repair its public thoroughfares *extend* to

If you wanted to counter the opposition's argument directly, you might focus the core more specifically on the interaction of your legal position with the opposition's, that is, which law governs rather than how one law governs.

> does governmental immunity *excuse* a municipality from its *duty* to

The words you choose to be the subject and verb of your issue will have a substantial impact on the focus of the whole issue, just as the subject and verb affect the emphasis of any sentence. This step is often difficult, but its benefits are substantial, because it makes the issue both clearer and more persuasive.

Stating Significant and Favorable Facts in More Detail and Unfavorable Ones More Generally

Although you need to include significant facts whether favorable or not, you can change the way you state those facts. For example, if you are representing a plaintiff who was harmed when a neighbor's pet skunk escaped from its pen, you might emphasize the significant unpleasantness your client experienced by explaining it in memorable detail.

> when the plaintiff, unaware of the skunk's presence, started the car's engine, thus killing the skunk and spreading its odor throughout the car and when the plaintiff then had to spend two days removing traces of the animal from the fan, carburetor, battery, and other engine surfaces?

If, however, you were representing the defendant in this situation, you might not dwell on these details, but instead emphasize other facts relevant to the question.

> when the animal's death resulted from its unprecedented action of climbing under the hood of a car?

In summary, use detail and generality in conjunction to focus your reader on the facts you choose, even though you are including other facts as well.

Suggesting the Logical Relationship of Facts

This technique involves the connecting signals you use to join the pieces of the issue, usually the facts. These signals tell the reader how to organize the information he or she is reading, and they also signal the relative importance of those pieces of information. For example, within the fact section, you may want to emphasize one fact over another. If so, you might join the facts as follows.

> he drove over the speed limit *despite* the narrowness of the road.

If you want to suggest that the facts as a group counter the opposition's claim, you may follow a core question with a signal introducing the supporting facts.

> Under . . . , is a municipality immune *even though* . . . .

In this situation, you are developing a question you want the reader to answer "no," something traditionally avoided. Occasionally, however, that structure may be more persuasive than a blander version that can be answered "yes," especially if the "yes" version does not sharply show the sense of the rightness that the "no" version creates.

Using Words That Steer the Reader Toward Your Opinion

This technique, using slanted language, is often the first one writers turn to when seeking to make an issue more persuasive. It comes last in this list, however, because it is probably best to exercise this option only after the other alternatives have been explored. This option, if misused, can actually detract from the effectiveness of your issue. Slanted language is effective only when it does not destroy the credibility of the question as a fair statement; if it seems to overstate the case, the reader can readily dismiss the issue as dramatic posturing and neglect to see the merits otherwise present. Strong language also has a tendency to overshadow other aspects of writing, especially when it creates a negative response, so use it with care.

Nevertheless, moderate slanting can be effective. For example, the slight emotional charge in the facts below adds clarity and force without seeming unfair.

when, terrified by the noise of the explosion, the thoroughbred crashed into the stable wall, shattered its right front ankle, and subsequently had to be destroyed

In contrast, the following version seems somewhat uncaring.

when the explosion startled the horse, causing it to run into the stable wall and sustain a critical fracture of an ankle

But the next version is overdone and unconvincing.

when the explosion shattered the air in the stable, it caused the racehorse to fear for its life so much that it strove in vain to escape, shattering its delicate foreleg against the hardwood wall, ending its possibility to survive and thus needlessly shattering the life of this fine contender, this elegant thoroughbred

Slanted language can be very effective as long as it maintains accuracy and creates a more vivid picture of the facts themselves, rather than drawing attention to the writer's judgments or literary elaborations about the situation.

In summary, writing a persuasive issue first requires you to focus on the critical content, just as you did with the objective issue. It then requires you to adjust wording and order in many small ways to underscore your point.

CONCLUSION

Writing excellent issues requires an effort that is disproportionate in relation to their length, but not disproportionate to their importance. An effective issue will benefit you throughout the document by making it easier for you to choose content, organization, and even wording throughout your discussion. It will also benefit your image in the eyes of your reader. Senior attorneys and judges commonly bemoan the absence of useful issues in the memos and briefs they read. With an excellent issue, your document can stand above the rest, an oasis of clarity in the vast desert of words your reader must cross.

Exercise 1

Write objective issues using the following law and facts. Then write persuasive issues for each side based on the objective issues you just created.

Anystate Statutes 999.01 Criminal Recklessness

Criminal Recklessness exists when "the actor creates an unreasonable and substantial risk of death or great bodily harm to another human being and the actor is aware of that risk."

List of Facts

A bus driver, Samuel Johnson, has 10 years of experience driving for Charter Busline.

Charter Busline specializes in chartered short trips for retired citizens to concerts, nearby cities, and other cultural events.

Sam went to a nearby mall, North Towne Mall, to have coffee and wait until time to pick up his tour group after they finished attending a Medieval Christmas Dinner and Tournament. At 9:25 p.m., Sam realized he was running late; he was supposed to pick up a group at a location 2 miles away at 9:30.

Sam ran to his bus, started it, and drove the bus at 45 miles per hour through the mall parking lot.

The pavement was dry, but it was evening and thus dark. It was 10 days before Christmas.

Sam drove past the mall entrance nearest the movie theater entrance without slowing down. The parking spots were 80% full near this mall entrance.

Scores of moviegoers were entering and exiting the mall at this time. Approximately 15 moviegoers had to run to get out of the path of the oncoming bus.

One moviegoer fell while running, hitting his head on the pavement. The blow left him unconscious.

Sam stopped the bus after he saw the pedestrian fall and ran back to offer help.

The pedestrian, Mr. Boswell, suffered a severe concussion that required surgery to remove a blot clot on his brain. Mr. Boswell will recover fully within six months.

Exercise 2

Read the following persuasive issues, written by opposing sides, and then write an objective issue for each situation. You may assume that all the facts and law included are accurately stated. The attorney representing the buyer of a keyboard wrote the following issue.

> Under an implied warranty of fitness for purpose, is the manufacturer of an acoustical keyboard liable to a purchaser who bought a keyboard from a street vendor when the keyboard exploded the first time the purchaser plugged it in to a power source?

The attorney representing the manufacturer of the keyboard wrote the following issue.

> Does an implied warranty of fitness for a purpose apply to an acoustical keyboard when the buyer purchased the keyboard in pieces from an unlicensed street vendor and was injured when he attempted to assemble the pieces despite the warning engraved on the top of the keyboard, which stated in 24 point letters, "Do Not Open or Attempt to Repair This Product. Serious Injury May Result."?

Assignment 1

You practice with a small firm in Murfreesboro, Tennessee. You have been contacted by Jamie Blottner, a microbiology graduate student, who was recently injured. Jamie told you the following story and asked you to see if he has a possible claim. You are looking at a statutory claim under Tenn. Code Ann. § 471.20. The only likely defendant in this case is Dana Newton (she owns 120 acres of land and is a successful farmer); ignore any other defendants and any other causes of action (common law claims, etc.). Your task is to draft the issues you would use in a memo about Jamie's possible law suits. Also draft persuasive versions of the issues.

Facts

On April 3 of this year, Jamie went for an evening walk along the outskirts of Murfreesboro. As he was passing an area of new home construction, he decided to take a closer look at a particular house under construction. Although he realized that he was probably trespassing, Jamie stepped into the partially finished house and began looking around. The house had been framed and there was plywood flooring in most areas.

Jamie became fascinated with figuring out the floor plan of the house, and even decided to go up to the second floor. As he was gazing out of what was likely to be a second floor window, Jamie heard a low growl behind him. He turned to find a large mixed-breed dog running toward him. The dog, which probably weighed at least a hundred pounds, stopped five feet in front of him, but continued to growl and bare his teeth at Jamie while slowly moving toward Jamie.

Jamie tried saying "nice doggy" a few times but in his fright he stepped backwards, away from the dog. The dog continued toward him, and Jamie stepped off the floor and fell. Unfortunately, the area where he had been standing was above the first floor and a walkout basement, so Jamie fell approximately 30 feet to the gravel below. The dog, which never touched Jamie, left shortly afterward.

Jamie broke his leg in two places, broke two fingers on his left hand, and suffered numerous cuts and contusions. His glasses shattered and shards of glass become embedded in both his eyes and his cheeks. Jamie had to undergo surgery to set the broken leg bones and to remove the glass shards from his eyes and face. Jamie was unable to attend school for two months, he had to withdraw from the three graduate classes he was taking (with no refund of his tuition), and his research was interrupted for five months. Jamie continues to suffer headaches and eye strain as residual results of his fall. His out-of-pocket costs include medical costs, costs for replacement of his glasses and clothing, and lost tuition. He would also like to recover for his continuing pain and the lost time in his research. He now fears that he will not be prepared for his preliminary examinations in school.

The construction company was unable to identify the dog, but Jamie began interviewing neighbors and has discovered that the dog belongs to Billy Smathers, a hired hand on the farm of Dana Newton. Newton's farm is approximately 3/4 of a mile from the construction site. Smathers, who appears to be judgment proof, lives in the back room of Newton's house (although there is a separate entrance into the room). It appears that the dog, whose name is "Scout," essentially runs free; at night Scout sleeps in the back room with Smathers. Jamie has heard from neighbors that Newton occasionally gives dog food to Scout from her own dogs' supply, and that she also gives Scout and the other dogs scraps when she butchers pigs or cattle.

Jamie lives at 433 N. Locust St. in Murfreesboro. Dana's farm is located at N14587 County Road P, in the township of Roxbury. Both addresses are in Portland County, Tennessee.

Tenn.Code Ann. § 471.20 Owner's liability.[16]

The owner or keeper of any dog which has injured or caused the injury of any person or property or killed, wounded or worried any horses, cattle, sheep, ranch mink or lambs shall be liable to the person so injured and the owner of such animals for all damages so done, without proving notice to the owner or keeper of such dog or knowledge by him that his dog was mischievous or disposed to kill, wound or worry horses, cattle, sheep, ranch mink or lambs; but when ranch mink are killed, wounded or worried, it shall be proven that the dog forcibly entered the enclosure in which they were kept.

This statute was first passed in 1873 and has never been amended.

---

16. All citations are hypothetical.

Simon v. Colas, 117 Tenn. 132, 121 S.W. 51 (1911).

Colas owned a dog that bit Simon on the left leg, injuring Simon and ruining the pants Simon was wearing. Simon sued Colas under Tenn. Stat. § 471.20, claiming $15.00 damages for his injury, great pain and fright, and the value of his pants. The case was tried before a judge, who rendered judgment for Simon and awarded him $8 damages.

Colas appealed the judgment on the grounds that the damages were excessive and that under the statute no damages could be awarded for the value of Simon's pants.

The Tennessee Supreme Court examined the record from the trial court and found that the amount of the damages was not excessive. Even if the damages were given only for the injury to Simon and not for the value of his pants, the record supported the $8 amount. The court also said it did not think section 471.20 should be narrowly construed to allow damages only for injuries to the person. The court believed the liability of dog owners included not only damage to the body of the injured person, but also to the clothes he was wearing at the time of the injury.

Harnett v. Mirr, 175 Tenn. 455, 187 S.W. 871 (1956).

Mr. Mirr owned a three-story building in Knoxville. The first floor of the building was a restaurant, and the second and third floors were a hotel. Mr. Mirr's brother-in-law and sister, Mr. and Mrs. Ritter, rented two rooms on the third floor of the building. Mrs. Ritter owned three bulldogs that lived with her and her husband. Mrs. Ritter worked as a cook in the restaurant.

On May 20, 1955, the three bulldogs attacked and bit Mrs. Harnett as she was entering the funeral parlor located next door to Mr. Mirr's restaurant. Mrs. Harnett sued Mr. Mirr and Mr. and Mrs. Ritter, alleging that they were keepers of the dogs and therefore liable for her injuries under Tenn.Stat. § 471.20.

The jury found that Mr. Mirr was the keeper of the dogs and Mr. and Mrs. Ritter were not. The trial court rendered judgment against Mr. Mirr and awarded damages to Mrs. Harnett. Mr. Mirr appealed, arguing that he was not the keeper of the dogs.

The Tennessee Supreme Court reversed the trial court and held as a matter law that Mr. Mirr was not the keeper of the dogs. The court said that, to be a keeper of the dogs, Mr. Mirr must have exercised control over the animals and must have harbored the animals, providing them with shelter, protection, or food. The court found nothing in the record that showed that Mr. Mirr had done anything to qualify as the keeper of the dogs. The court also said:

Where a child is the owner of a dog kept on the premises of the father, who supplies it with food and furnishes it with shelter upon his premises, the father is deemed to be a keeper of the dog. Also, where a dog belonging to a servant is kept upon the premises of the master, with his knowledge and consent, the latter is the keeper. However, where a servant or tenant occupies a distinct portion of the premises of the master, where the dogs are kept, the master is not the keeper.

Severson v. Keating, 182 Tenn. 549, 201 S.W. 417 (1968).

The Keatings were farmers who owned several dogs that ran loose on their farm. One of the dogs attempted to cross a road in front of Severson's car. Severson ran into the dog and lost control of his car. Severson suffered very severe injuries and the dog died.

Severson sued the Keatings, alleging that they were liable for their dog's actions. The case was tried before a jury. At the end of the trial, the judge instructed the jury about the elements of negligence, but did not mention Tenn.Stat. § 471.20. The jury found that the Keatings did not fail to exercise ordinary care in controlling their dog, and therefore were not negligent. Severson appealed, arguing that although the Keatings were not found to be negligent, they should have been found liable under section 471.20.

The Tennessee Supreme Court upheld the judgment dismissing the complaint. In the opinion, the court discussed the application of section 471.20 at length. The court said that at common law a dog owner was not liable for damages resulting from the vicious act of his dog unless he had prior knowledge of the dog's vicious propensities. Because the statute dispensed with scienter, it was no longer necessary to a *prima facie* case to show the defendant's previous knowledge of his dog's vicious character. The statute, however, does not fix absolute liability on the owner for damages caused by the innocent acts of his dog, but only for its vicious or mischievous act. The record did not show that the Keatings' dog had been vicious or mischievous at any time before the accident, nor that it was behaving viciously or mischievously at the time of the accident. Therefore, the court found that statute was inapplicable to the case and the only possible basis for the Keatings' liability was negligence. Because the jury found that the Keatings did not fail to exercise ordinary care, there was no basis for holding them liable.

King v. Cotter, 115 Tenn.2d 50, 62 S.W.2d 526 (1969).

Mr. Cotter's adult daughter, Betty, lived at his home as a member of his family and received all of her support from him. Betty owned a collie that lived with her in her father's home and received its food in the home. Betty took her dog to a park and unleashed it. The dog ran around the park and ran toward Mrs. King. Mrs. King backed away from the dog, and fell to the ground, permanently injuring her back.

Mrs. King sued Betty and Mr. Cotter under Tenn.Stat. § 471.20. At the close of the trial, the judge granted a directed verdict in favor of Mr. Cotter. Therefore, the jury considered only the question of Betty's liability; it found Betty liable for Mrs. King's injuries. Mrs. King appealed the granting of the directed verdict in Mr. Cotter's favor.

The Tennessee Supreme Court held that Mr. Cotter was keeper of the dog, but because the dog was not behaving viciously or mischievously, section 471.20 did not apply to the case. Even though he did not care for or control the dog, Mr. Cotter was the dog's keeper because he allowed it to be kept in his home and fed scraps from his table. Mr. Cotter was not liable for the dog's actions, however, because the dog was not behaving viciously or mischievously when the accident occurred. Mere running, which is all the dog did, is neither vicious nor mischievous, and therefore the court held that section 471.20 did not apply to the case. The court affirmed the decision of the trial judge.

Assignment 2

You are a junior attorney in a New York boutique firm whose clients are business people in various artistic fields. You receive the following memos from a colleague, Simon. Write the issues requested

Memo from Simon

2/10/20__

New York City

Hey Pal!

Remember when I did you that favor two months ago and covered for you on that research project? Well, now I need a favor. I just won a trip for two to Paris for this weekend—one of those Valentine's Day promotions! The catch is that I have to leave tomorrow morning, and I have to get this research project to the boss by Monday at 5, because he's meeting with the client for dinner. But if you can draft the preliminary issues for me, I can review them Monday morning, polish them up, and whip up the rest Monday when I return.

It won't be too bad, really. I've done the research and the facts—but I haven't zeroed in exactly on the preliminary issues, and you know how the boss likes a good issue statement! There are a bunch of possible issues that I think we need to hammer out, but I've explained that in my memo first draft.

OK, so the case does involve admiralty law, and I know that's not your specialty. But nobody at the firm specializes in that area, so you're as good as anyone. I've isolated the relevant passages of law and the few cases that have the best language on the issues—you can do it!

Here's the stuff—I knew I could count on you!! I'll bring you a bottle of wine, or perfume, or some cheese or something! See you Monday!

Attached Information from Simon

Facts

Our client is Cliff Claussen, the fashion designer. Cliff is famous for his understated-but-always-elegant designs. He is 6'4'' tall and quite slim, and always immaculately dressed, so his personal appearance is just as stylish and almost as famous. Cliff was injured in an accident on a weekend tour with Eco–Getaways, and he wants to sue.

His friend, Celeste DeLonge, is a guide with Eco–Getaways. She called him on Wednesday night, October 11, and said that they had one opening left for the following weekend on an eco-tour of the Hudson Marshes, and she could get him a good deal. Cliff decided to come along.

The tour was on a small ship, the Sandpiper, and was limited to 6 tourists on the trip. The ship had private sleeping compartments for the tourists, and they spent Friday and Saturday night on the boat. Simple meals were served, and the tourists spent the whole weekend either on the boat or hiking in the wilderness preserves. The crew and tourists got to know each other pretty well, joking around, teasing each other about mistaken wildlife sightings, and talking into the night.

The tours generally offered more adventure than, say, a regular cruise ship. Passengers sometimes had to use steep or slippery trails in order to see the wildlife and explore the marsh areas and beyond. Passengers were told to bring sturdy hiking shoes and the literature for the tours says that only experienced hikers should inquire. Celeste told Cliff this information when she invited him to join the tour.

The Sandpiper cruised around the edges of the marsh areas, up inlets that were large enough, and moored at specified trailheads so they could get off the boat and take nature hikes for an hour or two. They climbed on and off the boat to hike by way of a rather narrow gangplank with ropes on each side for handrails. During orientation, Cliff and the other passengers had been warned by Celeste and other crew to be careful when using the gangplank. He had embarked and disembarked using the gangplank twice without incident, but when he was leaving for the third hike on Saturday afternoon, he wasn't so lucky.

On Saturday afternoon, the ship moored in about 3 ½ feet of water (it was specially designed for negotiating shallow water areas). The tide was out during the afternoon, so the gangplank had to extend about 40 feet to reach the shore. The water extended only 15 feet from the ship, but beyond that was 25 feet of muddy shore. The gangplank was extended over the shore so the passengers would not disturb the environment and so they would not have to deal with wading through foot deep mud. The gangplank was especially designed to handle a variety of situations, with telescoping metal planks that could extend 40 feet, although they became gradually narrower as each panel extended from within the previous one. The final panel was only 1 foot wide. The rope railings, however, were 30 inches apart for the length of the gangplank, so by the end of the extension the ropes were quite a bit farther out than the gangplank itself.

The passengers had to wait while one of the crew first went down the gangplank. Then, as usual, the passengers were reminded to be careful and watch their step as they disembarked. By this time, however, they were getting relaxed about the routine and were busy joking with the crew and with each other. As he was walking down the plank and just about 3 feet from the end, Cliff turned to respond to a teasing comment from the passenger behind him. As he did so, he continued walking but missed the plank. He hit his ankle on the side of the plank, cracking the bone, and fell into the mud. The pain was substantial, and he rolled to his side, curling into a ball, as a reflex, and then rolled back to the other side.

For a moment everyone stared in stunned silence. Then they laughed. Apparently the sight of the dapper designer rolling in the mud was so surprising that the whole group, as soon as they realized that Cliff was not seriously hurt, was overcome with the humor of the situation. They began guffawing, many doubled over with laughter, and two passengers making a show of swan diving into the mud to join him. They soon helped Cliff up and with some difficulty carried him to the ship's deck. The crew and passengers took good care with Cliff, and did not add to his physical injury. They could not, however, stop laughing. Cliff was not amused. They followed emergency injury procedures and took Cliff to the nearest hospital, but the passengers and crew could not help joking about the injury. After Cliff returned to the boat, they all lavished care on him, but persisted in teasing him about the event. For example, they referred to the "Cliffhanger" and called him "Dipstick," referring to his slim frame being covered in grime. They also joked frequently about him taking up mud wrestling, warning him about watching out for those modeling runways, and saying they couldn't wait until they got back to tell the story to the local columnists. No story ever appeared, though.

Eco–Getaways offered to pay for his medical bills, but accepts no liability and balks at paying for anything else. They say all tours of this type use this kind of gangplank, and so they weren't negligent or at fault in any way. I've found out that this is true; all the small ship eco-tours in this area do use this kind of gangplank. But new boats have a different kind of gangplank, which avoids this problem, and when a ship is remodeled or upgraded generally, then the telescoping gangplank is usually replaced. I also found one safety rule book, *Safety Guidelines for Adventure Tours*, that advised against using telescoping gangplanks because of the danger of this kind of accident. It's a book published by the American Association of Eco and Adventure Tours. Here's the key quote: "Telescoping gangplanks, although commonly used, are not recommended by AA EAT. The gradually narrowing dimensions invite passengers to misstep, especially when disembarking, and so they add an unnecessary opportunity for liability. To keep insurance and injuries to a minimum, AA EAT recommends using overlapping panels when extended gangplanks are needed, using metal joints to avoid the risk of passengers stumbling over the overlapping edges. . . . If telescoping gangplanks are used, be sure your passengers are careful when using the gangplanks. Take extra pains to warn them with each use of the gangplank, and to reduce problems allow only one person per 8 feet of gangplank at a time. This reduces distractions from conversation and avoids having one passenger jostle another." But I have no evidence that Eco–Getaways ever saw this book, and it's not regulatory in any way, just informational. It's a stretch to get that established as the industry standard.

But Cliff is really angry and wants to sue the company for emotional harm and anything else we can find. His ankle is healing normally and, although it's inconvenient, he hasn't lost any income or suffered other tangible damages. But his design company is a big client of the firm, so we have to do what we can. I've looked at negligence mainly, but there are some preliminary legal issues we'll need to win before we can even deal with the fact questions. I've researched the law pretty extensively and found the general areas that will present the main challenges. I've also isolated a few cases that we can rely on, since they are accepted law in our jurisdiction.

One issue regards whether the case would be subject to admiralty jurisdiction. Admiralty law might be more favorable, because then it may be easier to show Eco has a duty here. The best sources on whether admiralty jurisdiction exists for any specific case are *O'Hara v. Bayliner*, 679 N.E.2d 1049 (N.Y. 1997), and *Foremost Insurance Co. v. Richardson*, 457 U.S. 668 (1982).

Then, we'll definitely have an issue of this kind of gangplank. We'll have a battle of the experts eventually. So I need you to frame an issue about the foreseeability of there being a fall with this kind of gangplank. I haven't been able to find any records of lawsuits over injuries caused by these gangplanks. The foreseeability issue would follow general New York negligence law, so look at the cases of *Dunbar v. NMM Glens Falls Associates*, 693 N.Y.S.2d 746 (N.Y. App. Div. 1999), and *Blye v. Manhattan and Bronx Surface Transit Operating Authority*, 511 N.Y.S.2d 612 (Ct. App. 1987) on this issue. A related issue is whether Cliff could use the Safety Guidelines for Adventure Tours book as evidence that Eco was acting negligently in using this type of gangplank. A good case for this issue is *McComish v. DeSoi*, 200 A.2d 116 (N.J. 1964). (There are no reported New York cases on this question.)

One defense Eco is sure to raise is assumption of the risk, arguing that Cliff assumed the risk because he consented to encounter the known danger inherent in adventure tours. We may want to argue that the risk of falling on a gangplank is not a risk inherent in these tours. A good recent case laying out the law on this issue is *Morgan v. State of New York, et al*, 685 N.E.2d 202 (N.Y. 1997).

Ultimately, there will be the problem of proving the damages, even if we get through all these preliminary issues. Cause would be iffy, and there's no proof that he suffered any monetary harm anyway, and little pain and suffering. It's just not worth messing with, really, but what can we do?

The statutes you need are in those cases, too, by the way. You don't really have to look them up, because the relevant language is quoted there, sometimes in footnotes.

See you Monday—now I'll owe you, I guess!

Simon

BIBLIOGRAPHY

Beasley, Mary Beth, *A Practical Guide to Appellate Advocacy*. New York: Aspen Law & Business, 2002.

Berger, Charles R. and Steven H. Chaffee, eds., *Handbook of Communication Science*. Newbury Park, CA: Sage Publications, 1987.

Charrow, Veda R., Myra K. Erhardt, and Robert P. Charrow, *Clear and Effective Legal Writing*. New York: Aspen Law & Business, 3d ed. 2001.

Cooper, Frank E., *Writing in Law Practice*. Indianapolis: Bobbs–Merrill Co., 2d ed. 1963.

Crowhurst, Marion, *Interrelationships Between Reading and Writing Persuasive Discourse*, 25 (3) *Research in the Teaching of English* 314 (Oct. 1991).

Dernbach, John C. and Richard V. Singleton, II. *A Practical Guide to Legal Writing and Legal Methods*. Littleton, CO: F. B. Rothman, 2d ed. 1994.

Devitt, Edward J. and James A. Barnum, *10 Tips for Preparing Better Briefs*, 22 Trial 75 (Oct. 1986).

Finn, Judith A., *Writing Briefs for Federal Litigation: The Province of the Elect*, 22 Tulsa L.J. 127 (Winter 1986).

Murphy, Peter W., *Teaching Evidence, Proof, and Facts: Providing a Background in Factual Analysis and Case Evaluation*, 51 (4) J. Leg. Ed. 568 (Dec. 2001).

O'Keefe, Daniel J., *Persuasion: Theory and Research*. Newbury Park, CA: Sage Publications, 2d ed. 2002.

Peck, Girvan, *Writing Persuasive Briefs*. Boston: Little, Brown, & Co., 1984.

Pratt, Diane V., *Legal Writing: A Systematic Approach*. St. Paul: West Group, 3d ed. 1999.

Sandell, Rolf, *Linguistic Style and Persuasion*. San Francisco, CA: Academic Press, 1977.

Schauble, Leona and Robert Glaser, eds., *Innovations in Learning: New Environments for Education*. Mahwah, NJ: Lawrence Erlbaum Associates, 1996.

Schultz, Nancy L., *Introduction to Legal Writing and Oral Advocacy*. New York: Matthew Bender, 2d ed. 1993.

Shapo, Helene C., Marilyn R. Walter, and Elizabeth Fajans, *Writing and Analysis in the Law.* Westbury, NY: Foundation Press, 4th ed. 1999.

Spears, Franklin, *Presenting An Effective Appeal,* 21 Trial 95 (Nov. 1985).

Statsky, William P. and R. John Wernet, Jr., *Case Analysis and Fundamentals of Legal Writing.* St. Paul: West Group, 4th ed. 1995.

Tepley, Larry L., *Legal Writing, Analysis, and Oral Argument.* St. Paul: West Group, 1990.

Weihofen, Henry, *Legal Writing Style.* St. Paul: West Group, 2d ed. 1980.

Chapter 7

OBJECTIVE STATEMENTS OF FACT

Unlike the issues or the discussion section of an objective memo, the fact section requires a different focus. When you write an issue, your focus is on condensing the big picture into one sentence; when you write the discussion, your focus is on thoroughly explaining the logic of your answer. In contrast, when you write the objective statement of facts, your focus is on telling a story. Like a reporter, then, tell the story accurately, clearly, and simply.

> [C]onvey [your] meaning to the Reader with the least possible difference between the effect produced and that intended, and also with the least possible wear and tear on the Reader's capacity and goodwill.[1]

Also like a reporter, you need to be efficient, simply because neither the client nor the firm can afford for you to do otherwise. Be concise. Your reader wants to make sense of the who, what, when, where, why, and how of the facts as quickly as possible before proceeding to the legal issue. Despite these time and space limitations, the statement of facts offers some interesting opportunities for the advanced legal writer to develop his or her own style.

This chapter addresses both these limitations and opportunities while guiding you through the basic tasks involved in writing a fact statement:

- determining which facts to include,
- determining how to organize those facts, and
- writing the facts so they are accurate and clear.

The section about writing, however, includes only a beginning list of techniques for accuracy and clarity. The next chapter, on persuasive statements of fact, delves into the wording and sentence structures that affect the way the reader understands your content.

---

1. Vernon Lee, *The Handling of Words,*   40–41 (1992).
and Other Studies in Literary Psychology

DETERMINING WHICH FACTS TO INCLUDE

Although choosing which facts to include is one of the first questions you consider when drafting your facts, you cannot completely answer this question at first. Instead, you will return to this question during revision and throughout the writing process if the question of whether to include a fact is particularly difficult to resolve. When choosing facts, you must focus not on whether the fact is favorable, but on whether it is needed. To help you determine whether a fact is needed, consider three categories of facts: legally significant facts, background facts, and emotional facts.

Legally Significant Facts

Your primary obligation in the statement of facts is to communicate the legally significant facts: those facts that, if changed, would change the answer to the issue. For example, you would include all of the italicized facts in the statement of facts of a memo that addressed the following issue.

> Under Wis.Stat. sec. 346.11, passing or meeting a frightened animal, did a motorcyclist stop as promptly as she safely could when *the motorcyclist was driving around a curve on a wet gravel road at 40 miles per hour and might have lost control of the motorcycle if she had stopped more quickly?*

If, for example, the motorcyclist had been driving at 20 miles per hour or the road had been dry, the answer you reach in the memo would be different. These are the legally significant facts you should include. To make sure you have included all of these facts, revise your fact statement after drafting your issue and discussion, watching in particular for any omissions of facts that you included in those sections.

Background Facts

Include any background facts that clarify the story. Names and other details make the picture of what happened more concrete and easier to understand. For example, the second of the following two examples presents a clearer picture.

> When the balcony floor tipped, Karen fell.

> **When the accident occurred, Karen was standing on the wooden balcony, leaning on the railing. The area below the railing was not enclosed. When one of the supports under the porch broke, the right side of the balcony dropped suddenly, tilting the floor. Karen lost her balance, slid under the railing, and fell fifteen feet to the sidewalk below.**

Even though the first example includes legally significant facts, it does not give the reader a clear picture of the accident it describes.

Fact statements should be clear first, then concise. When you are deciding whether a background fact adds clarity or not, ask yourself the following questions. If your answer to any one of the questions is "yes," omit the background fact. If your answers are all "no," include it.

- Does the added fact confuse more than it clarifies?

- Does it clarify a point of no concern to the legal reader?

- Does including it make some irrelevant point seem relevant?

Length alone does not indicate wordiness. Wordiness is often caused by wordy phrasing of needed information. If you need to include background facts for clarity, do so. Then, when you have decided what needs to be included, revise your fact statement to be as concise as possible.

Emotion-laden Facts

One decision that can prove difficult is when to include background facts that carry emotional weight. Dealing with emotion-laden facts is even more troubling when, in a fair world, they would not be significant. This subsection guides you through the process of deciding how to handle these difficult facts ethically.

Judgmental labels stating your opinion about the facts must be omitted from your fact statement. For example, you would not use the following.

The *poorly maintained* balcony collapsed *without warning,* sending *young* Karen plunging to the *unforgiving* concrete below.

Instead, you would state the facts that show that the balcony was poorly maintained and that there was no warning of the coming collapse. You might include Karen's age or the details of her injuries. But you leave judgments about those facts to the reader and to your discussion of the legal issues. Do not introduce your own judgmental labels in the facts, although in some situations you may need to quote someone else who used judgmental labels because their use is legally significant.

Discussions about some emotion-laden facts are more problematic, however, when they are not legal significant but nevertheless important. For example, the handling of a case might be influenced by your client's history of mental disorders that led to violent episodes, even when that fact has no direct legal significance to the question involved. These facts may also be related to societal attitudes toward age, income, education, sexual orientation, sex, race, national heritage, religion or the absence of religion, appearance, weight, height, and so forth.

To determine whether an emotional fact should be included, first explain to yourself why this fact may deserve inclusion. This is a hard question, but it is better that you ask it of yourself in private and learn where you stand. You do not want to include the fact without recognizing your reasons and risk having to address this question in front of someone else. If, after careful consideration, you think an emotional fact will affect the decisions to be made in the case, state the fact objectively, using techniques discussed later in this chapter.

One example of a situation that might require this reflection and evaluation might be whether to include, in a memo addressing whether your client will be liable for damage resulting from a collision, the fact that the plaintiff, the driver of the other car, has a congenitally deformed right hand. This fact might not be legally significant to the issue of liability because no evidence suggests that the condition of the hand affected the plaintiff's driving. It may not be significant to any issue of damages because no injury to the hand is claimed. But would a jury be more sympathetic to this person, so that the deformity might affect the outcome of a trial if the case reaches that point? If so, perhaps the fact should be included for your reader's information, as part of your evaluation of the strength of the case. Alternatively, if you thought the fact could raise a question about the plaintiff's control of his car, you might decide to include it, even though it may disturb you to do so.

You may be able to convey the emotion-laden fact orally in some situations, communicating it to your reader without having to put it in writing. But beware of the easy answer. This approach is often tempting, but always consider any ethical obligations you have. It is better to make a decision about whether to include the fact in writing, making a decision you can live with, than to avoid the decision and allow yourself to slide into unprofessional or unethical behavior.

In summary, include emotion-laden facts when they are likely to affect the handling of the case. Do not, however, include your own emotions about those facts. Add these facts to the legally significant facts and needed background facts, and you are ready to organize your statement of facts.

ORGANIZING THE FACTS

As you move into advanced techniques for organizing the statement of facts, you have an opportunity to add another dimension to your writing of fact statements, your own story-telling style. Often the constraints of the legal writing task, especially the needs of the client and the reader, force you to set aside your own writing preferences. In the statement of facts, however, you have at least one choice that can be determined by your own style: the way you begin your statement.

This addition of your personal story-telling style may make the task not only more pleasant, but also more efficient. Because memos are in-house documents, your writing is not defined by legal rules or traditions, but rather by common sense, an awareness of house rules, and your reader's preferences. In particular, your own process can influence your approach to the organization of the facts.

Legal writers often organize facts chronologically. This order seems natural for telling a story. The reader can watch the story unfold, seeing how one event leads to another without having to reconstruct the chronology mentally. Chronology simplifies the reader's task in moving through the paragraphs just as active voice moves the reader through a sentence smoothly.

> At 7:30 a.m. on July 12, Kathryn Archer was waiting at a bus stop on Washington Avenue. While she was waiting, ...

But useful variations exist. For example, you might begin by stating the legal situation or the procedural history of the case, if there is one, before returning to the chronology.

> Our client, Kathryn Archer, is seeking to invalidate a document she signed. The document may waive her right to sue for damages for an injury she suffered while waiting at a bus stop.

This structure reveals the significance of the facts by clarifying their legal context. For example, when writing a memo on a *Miranda* issue, you may want to explain the procedural posture first so the reader sees how this issue arises from the facts. Alternatively, the procedural facts might be placed at the end of the facts, which allows the procedure to follow within the overall chronology when legal events were the last to occur.

> Another possibility is to begin with a sentence summarizing the facts on which the case turns. This structure is particularly useful when the chronology is complex and when, without that overview, the reader might wonder where the facts were leading.

> In return for a payment of $5,000, Kathryn Archer agreed to refrain from suing the City of Pleasantview for any additional damages arising from the injury she suffered while waiting at a city bus stop.

It is also useful when the facts initially suggest some legal question other than the one that will ultimately arise.

Facts may be divided into logical subgroups. When facts occurred at several separate locations or at different times, you may use those locations or times to divide the paragraphs, much as a scriptwriter organizes a film into scenes. This organization is useful when the sequence of facts is confusing; it is also useful when groups of facts go to different legal theories, incidents, or consequences.

Some other variations of the opening may be particularly useful for certain readers. One staff attorney for an appellate court opened her facts with a quick, concrete statement orienting the judges and providing a refreshing start.

> This is the Wilfred Bank Case come back to haunt us yet again.

This quick snapshot helped her judges keep the facts of various cases separate in their minds. She could refer to the quick reference in future conferences with the judges, helping them communicate quickly over the course of deciding a case. Although all readers might not appreciate this approach, her readers found it convenient and useful.

As you try new openings and organizations, much depends on your reader's preferences, and those preferences must supersede your own. When you write a research memo, you are summarizing and providing information to save your reader's time. No matter how clever your openings and organizations are, they will be effective only if they aid your reader. Within this boundary of clarity, you have a little room to allow your own style to influence the way you open and organize the facts.

WRITING STATEMENTS OF FACT

Whatever choices you make in your openings and organization, you must always maintain accuracy and clarity within the fact statement. You need not, however, focus on these goals in your first draft. In your first draft, focus on choosing and organizing your facts effectively. After you have settled on your organization and content, revise for accuracy and clarity by employing the following techniques:

- state key points specifically and concretely, even if they are unfavorable;
- keep labels minimal and consistent;
- substitute names for pronouns where needed; and
- state emotion-laden facts objectively and neutrally.

State Key Points Specifically and Concretely

You must state key points clearly in the memo's statement of facts. Although you may want to state an unfavorable fact abstractly to minimize it in a brief, you do not want to do this in an office memo. At this point in the legal process, minimizing the seriousness of a fact could be disastrous. State what happened specifically and concretely.

While driving approximately 45 m.p.h. through a school zone with a speed limit of 25 m.p.h., Mr. Protzsky saw a crossing guard step off the curb. He immediately applied his brakes, which caused his car to spin counterclockwise and jump the curb.

rather than

While driving through the school zone, Mr. Protzsky .... When he applied his brakes, the speed of his car caused ....

One way to make the facts more specific is to minimize use of the passive voice, which can obscure the cause of an action. If your client drove into a parked car, you need to say so in a research memo. While you will not state it so bluntly in your brief, clarity and accuracy are your current priorities, not tact. If concerns about subsequent discovery exist, you might convey some information to the senior attorney orally rather than in writing. But make sure the attorney somehow receives any information critical to his or her handling of the case.

In a similar vein, avoid using euphemisms. For example, do not say "failed to recollect" if the facts indicate "forgot," "overlooked," or "did not remember to ...." The reader must comprehend your meaning with a minimum of effort, and euphemisms make the reader work harder to understand your point.

Keep Labels Minimal and Consistent

If you have read anything by Tolstoy, you have experienced the struggle of keeping straight a cast of characters, each of whom has several names, nicknames, and titles. To be sure the actors in your facts are clear, choose one name for each person and use that name throughout your facts. You may refer to other roles in some situations, but always accompany any reference with the one consistent label you are using.

> Our client, Evelyn Post, ... Ms. Post .... As a teacher, Ms. Post .... When describing his colleague, Ms. Post, James Lassler said, "Evelyn has always ...."

Even though you might be tempted to substitute "the teacher" or "Evelyn" for variety throughout this passage, that change would be more likely to increase the work your reader must do than reduce his or her boredom. Similarly, make a habit of using the same noun for the same idea, the same verb for the same action. This can help your reader keep all the references clear in a complex story.

Substitute Names for Pronouns

If you have several "he's" or several "she's" in the facts, clarify the identity of each actor by using names more frequently. Also insert names instead of pronouns when the story shifts the focus to a different actor.

> Carl and Floyd had been working together on this boat for several years. *Carl* had modified the design to suit them better. He also purchased all necessary supplies and equipment and kept the financial records. *Floyd* invested more time in the actual construction of the boat, spending many of his weekends finishing the wooden deck and fixtures. He gave *Carl* an account of the hours he spent working on the boat, but *Carl* did not keep such an account of his hours.

Substitute the names when the scene changes, whether the change is marked by a change in time or location.

> Before they drove the boat out of the garage, Carl checked the hitch to make sure it was properly engaged and checked to see that the safety chains were attached. He did not, however, put any weight on the hitch or in any way check the framing attached to the truck to hold the hitch.
>
> After *Carl* climbed into the truck, he began studying the owner's manual for the outboard motor they had installed, and so he did not notice that the trailer was swaying back and forth as Floyd drove the truck down the street.

This inclusion of names helps the reader focus on the story without having to sort out who is doing what.

State Emotion-laden Facts Objectively and Neutrally

When describing an emotion-laden event, state the observable facts that establish the emotion. This approach for handling emotional facts is based on research into what makes a writer credible[2] and based on general principles of good storytelling. An effective storyteller will write

He clenched his fists and moved forward, yelling, "I've taken all I plan to from you!"

rather than

He shouted angrily.

You must give your reader enough factual information to reach an independent judgment about what those facts show. You must not force the reader to trust your judgment any more than necessary: "Credibility is just as fragile for a writer as for a President."[3]

When organizing the facts, position the emotional fact so it is read in meaningful context. For example, if the fact would be important only because it suggests possible intent, put it with the others that suggest possible intent. If the fact would be important only at trial, state it in the context of the other facts relevant to a trial.

> Mr. Yeats has asked us to prepare to take this issue to court rather than agreeing to settlement. He believes that the plaintiff's congenitally malformed right hand is evidence that the plaintiff did not have control over his automobile, even though the plaintiff was driving a vehicle with an automatic transmission, which is the only restriction listed on his valid Arkansas driver's license.

To add further clarity, communicate to the reader how that fact may be important, just as you do other significant facts in the discussion section. By stating important facts specifically, using consistent labels and clear pronouns, and stating emotional facts neutrally, you can tell a story that your reader can trust. Your statement of facts can clarify the situation for your reader, preparing that reader to understand the legal question and how it arose.

USING VISUAL AIDS

Consider using visual aids (charts, tables, maps, and so forth) when the facts are so complex that the reader needs the extra clarity the visual aid can provide.[4] When creating a visual aid, choose a structure that accurately conveys your meaning. Thus you would use a map to show locations in relation to each other, but use a picture to show how a scene appeared to an observer. You might refer to a video tape from a security

2. Research indicates that the reader judges the credibility of the writer based on the reader's sense of the writer's competence in the area addressed and on his or her sense of whether that writer can be trusted to represent the situation fairly.

Daniel J. O'Keefe, *Persuasion: Theory and Research* 184–85 (2d ed. 2002).

3. William Zinsser, *On Writing Well* 78 (25th anniversary ed. 2001).

4. *See* Kristin R. Woolever, *Untangling the Law: Strategies for Legal Writers* (1987).

camera, telling the reader what to watch for and then referring to the portion of the tape that contains the relevant information.

Each graphic form is suited for particular purposes. Your choice of which form to use depends on what comparison you want the reader to see. In memos, you are most likely to use some form of graph or table to organize and communicate a group of data.

When comparing amounts, use a pie chart when you want to communicate that all amounts are parts of a whole.

Pie Chart Comparing Parts of a Whole

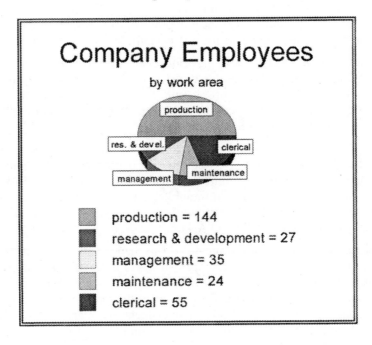

Use a bar graph to communicate changes in those amounts over time.

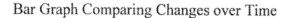

Bar Graph Comparing Changes over Time

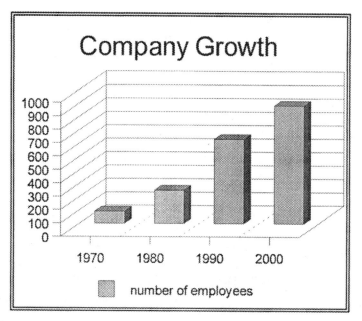

When comparing relative quantities over time, use a multiple bar graph.

Multi-Bar Graph Comparing Relative Amounts Over Time

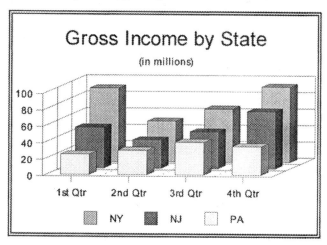

Tables are ideal for presenting information that needs to be compared or available for easy reference. When structuring a table, design it to be read from top to bottom, left to right. Although visual aids are not limited to the same sequential order as English text, the reader who spends more time with text than graphics will bring reading habits when studying the table, scanning it from the top left across, as with a page of text. If you work against these habits, you slow the reader. If you work with them, you help the reader move through the information correctly. For example, the first version of the following table is concise and clear, but its organization makes it hard for a taxpayer to see when to use which form because it is organized based on the form, which is not where this reader begins.

Table Organized Around Tax Forms

Form	Document Received	Item
1040	W-2 W-2G 1098 1099-INT	wages, tips, salaries gambling winnings refund of overpaid interest interest income interest on US savings bonds
Schedule C	1099-MISC 1099-PATR	non-employee compensation patronage dividends distributions from a co-op
Schedule D	1099-B	sale of stocks, bonds, etc.
Schedule E	1099-MISC	royalties, rents
Schedule F	1099-G	agriculture payments

In contrast, the following table begins with the information the reader knows, and moves to the information the reader needs.

Table Organized for Taxpayer's Use

Income source	Document You Received	Form to Use for Reporting
wages, tips, salaries	W-2	1040
gambling winnings	W-2G	1040
interest income	1099-INT	1040
interest on US savings bonds	1099-INT	1040
refund of overpaid interest	1098	1040
sale of stocks, bonds, etc.	1099-B	Schedule D
non-employee compensation	1099-MISC	Schedule C
distributions from a co-op	1099-PATR	Schedule C
royalties	1099-MISC	Schedule E
rent	1099-MISC	Schedule E
agriculture payments	1099-G	Schedule F

As a final step, eliminate information that is unnecessary to communicate your point. For example, the following graphic form is likely to confuse the legal reader.[5]

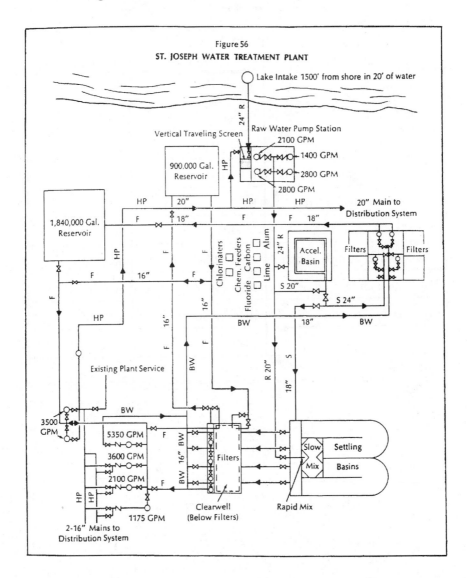

5. J.C. Mathes and Dwight W. Stevenson, *Designing Technical Report: Writing for Audiences in Organizations* 177 (1976).

The next graphic form, in contrast, is a simplified version of the same diagram, providing enough information to leave the reader adequately informed about the relevant point, not distracted or confused with unneeded data. As an extra benefit, it will be easier to understand and produce.[6]

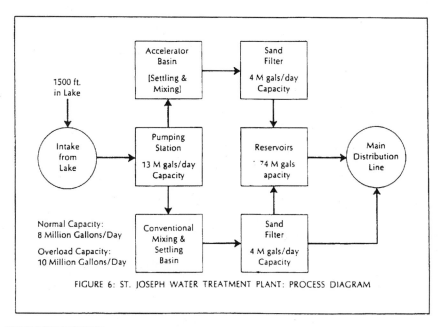

FIGURE 6: ST. JOSEPH WATER TREATMENT PLANT: PROCESS DIAGRAM

CONCLUSION

Rather than covering all the writing skills needed when drafting an objective facts section, this chapter has given you a general overview of the tasks you need to fulfill and some ways to address the most common or troubling questions that can arise. To these skills, add the basic writing concerns of conciseness and readability which you have studied in previous chapters. Together, these skills will round out your expertise when drafting fact statements. Integrate these skills into your own writing process. To develop your process, study the following sample checklist, which incorporates the techniques and questions discussed in this chapter into an overall checklist. Try this process on the following exercise. Then revise it, adapting the checklist to fit more closely to your natural writing process.

CHECKLIST FOR DRAFTING STATEMENTS OF FACT

1. Include all needed facts.
    a. Legally significant facts
        (1) Facts that will be used in the discussion section
        (2) Facts that show any elements of the causes of action or defenses
        (3) Facts that will be used in the other side's legal argument

---

6. *Id.* at 176.

        (4) Procedural facts

   b. Needed background facts

        (1) Dates needed to show events

        (2) Names needed to avoid confusion

   c. Emotional facts you have determined should be included

2. Organize those facts.

   a. Choose the most effective opening.

   b. Divide into subsections if needed.

   c. Organize each section or subsection chronologically.

   d. Divide facts into paragraphs that group the facts logically.

   e. Use visual aids if appropriate. When using visual aids,

        (1) use the form that accurately conveys your meaning,

        (2) structure tables to be read from left to right, and

        (3) remove distracting and unneeded details.

3. Draft the facts to be accurate and clear.

   a. State even unfavorable points specifically and concretely.

   b. Keep labels minimal and consistent.

   c. Substitute names for pronouns where needed.

4. After drafting the discussion, revise the facts.

   a. Include all legally significant facts.

   b. Delete unneeded background and emotional facts. Delete any details

        (1) that confuse more than clarify, or

        (2) that clarify irrelevant points, or

        (3) that signal to the reader that an irrelevant point may be relevant.

   c. Revise sentence structure for readability.

   d. Reword phrases that are ambiguous or unclear.

   e. Eliminate wordy phrases.

Exercise 1

    You are a law clerk for the District Attorney. Write a statement of facts for a memo using the facts in the Samuel Johnson case, Exercise #1 at the end of Chapter 6, applying all the techniques listed above.

Exercise 2

    You are an attorney in the firm representing the keyboard manufacturer in the situation described in Exercise 2 at the end of Chapter 6. Write a portion of an objective statement of facts for a memo to your senior partner, using the facts given in Chapter 6 and the issue you created for that exercise.

Assignment 1

Write the Statement of Facts for a memo about Jamie Blottner's situation. For the relevant facts and law, see Assignment 1 in Chapter 6.

Assignment 2

You are the junior attorney in the firm representing Cliff Claussen, whose situation is described in Assignment 2 at the end of Chapter 6. You have now received the following memo from Mr. Yu, your senior partner. Draft the fact section only for the memo your senior partner requested.

Memo from Mr. Yu

TO: Associate Andre Delavan

FROM: Kok Peng Yu, Senior Partner

DATE: February 11, 2003

RE: Cliff Claussen's injury on EcoGetaways–Tour

Since you have taken over the research and writing on this matter, and have not flown off to Paris and left a client hanging, I would like you to go ahead and draft a memo on these issues. I'm not sure there's any possible case here, but I want to be sure. Cliff is the kind of client who likes to see things in writing and he is willing to pay for them.

Since the damages for the sprained ankle would be minimal, Cliff's only theory for substantial recovery would be negligent infliction of emotional distress. He does have an accompanying physical injury, so that hurdle is behind us, but there are definite problems showing the damages and cause. For one thing, Cliff did see a psychiatrist after the incident, but he has seen therapists off and on over the years for various things. Additionally, Cliff was worried about whether he would be able to do a spring show, but the show did come off and there's no way to prove he lost money because of his injury; his sales may not have been as successful as some other years' shows, but there are too many factors, especially given the economy and events of this year, to pin any money loss specifically on his mental state.

BIBLIOGRAPHY

Acuna, Frank R., Daniel E. Casa, Claire P. McGreal, John Ossiff, and Roger M. Rosen, *Handbook of Appellate Advocacy*. St. Paul: West Group, 1986.

Brennan, Lawrence, *Handbook of Appellate Advocacy*. St. Paul: West Group, 3d ed. 1993.

Dernbach, John C. and Richard V. Singleton, II, *A Practical Guide to Legal Writing and Legal Method*. Littleton, CO: Fred B. Rothman and Co., 2d ed. 1994.

Lee, Vernon, *The Handling of Words and Other Studies in Literary Psychology*. Lewiston: E. Mellen Press, 1992 (originally published in 1923).

Mathes, J.C. and Dwight W. Stevenson, *Designing Technical Reports: Writing for Audiences in Organizations*. New York: Macmillan, 2d ed. 1991.

O'Keefe Daniel J., *Persuasion: Theory and Research*. Thousand Oaks, CA: Sage Publications, 2d ed. 2002.

Pearsall, Thomas E. and Kenneth W. Houp, *Reporting Technical Information*. Ft. Worth: Harcourt Brace Jovanovich College Publishers, 5th ed. 1994.

Pratt, Diane V., *Legal Writing: A Systematic Approach*. St. Paul: West Group, 3d ed. 1999.

Schultz, Nancy L., *Introduction to Legal Writing and Oral Advocacy*. New York: Matthew Bender, 2d ed. 1993.

Shapo, Helene C., Marilyn R. Walter, and Elizabeth Fajans, *Writing and Analysis in the Law*. New York: Foundation Press, 4th ed., 1999.

Weihofen, Henry, *Legal Writing Style*. St. Paul: West Group, 2d ed. 1980.

Woolever, Kristin R., *Untangling the Law: Strategies for Legal Writers*. Belmont, CA: Wadsworth Publishing Co., 1987.

Zinsser, William, *On Writing Well*. New York: Quill, 25th anniversary ed. 2001.

Chapter 8

PERSUASIVE STATEMENTS OF FACT

If briefs[1] to the court were gymnastics events, their statements of fact would be performed on the balance beam. Writing a persuasive statement is accomplished not by following one set of rules, but by balancing your use of various techniques to maintain credibility while achieving the stance needed to highlight favorable facts. It does not require the brute force of emphatic language so much as a subtle blend of strength and control of structure and detail. It involves much thought, consideration of alternatives, and monitoring the interactions of various techniques.[2] Yet an excellent statement of facts looks natural and effortless, just like a complex routine looks easy when performed by a skilled gymnast.

The statement of facts is critical to the brief.[3] It tells the story that makes the fairness of your client's position evident. Judges want to make a decision that is legally valid, but they also want to make a decision that is fair. Therefore, telling the facts well can make the judge more willing to accept your argument. This situation is congruent with that of persuasion generally: a reader is more fully persuaded if both head and heart are convinced.[4]

The fact section is the part of a brief most likely to help the reader develop a general opinion about which party ought to prevail. It provides the specific, concrete facts the reader needs to understand the legal situation. Many practitioners even claim the fact statement is the most important part of a brief, eclipsing even the argument in its ability to persuade the court.[5]

---

1. Briefs to the court are often called Memoranda of Points and Authorities, but for simplicity we are using the term "briefs" in these chapters. Similarly, a persuasive document's statement of facts may be called a "statement of the case."

2. See the discussion of studies by Thistlewait (1955) and Sharp and McClung (1966) in Rolf Sandell, *Linguistic Style and Persuasion* 79 (1977).

3. Irving M. Mehler, *Effective Legal Communication* 96 (1975).

4. Gerald R. Miller, *Persuasion* in *Handbook of Communication Science* 454 (C. Berger and S. Chaffee, eds. 1987).

5. For example, "[t]he statement of facts is the most important part of any appellate brief, for no matter how much substantive law the judge may know, he or she knows nothing about the facts of the

Writing a persuasive statement of facts requires a unique focus. Like a short story, a good statement of facts tells a story, complete with plot, characters, and setting. As a result, many of the techniques discussed in this chapter are drawn from the skills of the storyteller. But when writing the statement of facts, you are not free to create fiction. Your discretion rests in how you tell the story, how you select, word, and organize the facts. This chapter gives you general guidelines for making these decisions.

If you are tired of following rules in your writing, stating the facts persuasively offers a fascinating opportunity to balance competing concerns, try different techniques, and make judgment calls. If you enjoy the security that comes from rules, writing a persuasive fact statement presents some frustration and uncertainty. For most writers, it presents a little of both.

GUIDELINES FOR MAKING CHOICES

When looking at all the ways you can shape the facts to favor your client's position, remember both what you can and cannot do. The following rhyme incorporates those constraints, offering some guidelines for making effective choices and avoiding ineffective ones.

When news is bad, frame it.

If it's not true, don't claim it.

When news is good, be bold.

When it's too much, break the mold.

State essentials, every one.

But please stop writing when you're done.

These guidelines will help you use, and not misuse, the many specific techniques for emphasis and de-emphasis discussed in this chapter.

When news is bad, frame it

You cannot ignore unfavorable facts. To do so would be to allow the other side's presentation of those unfavorable facts to stand unchallenged. You also cannot avoid discussing unfavorable information with a judge who may be apprised of it by your opposition. Furthermore, including unfavorable facts will probably increase your credibility with the judicial reader.[6] Research in persuasion has found that a "both-sided" approach has greater success persuading listeners who were initially undecided or in opposition, were better educated, and were later exposed to counter-arguments.[7]

---

case before reading the appellant's brief." Thomas R. Newman, *Writing Briefs—Statement of Facts*, 200 N.Y.L.J. 3 (1988).

6. Communicators are more successful at persuading when viewed as competent and trustworthy. Miller, *supra* note 4, at 454.

7. Carl I. Hovland, Irving L. Janis, and Harold H. Kelley, *Communication and Persuasion: Psychological Studies of Opinion Change* 105–11 (1953).

Instead of excluding unfavorable facts, employ one of the de-emphasizing techniques discussed later in this chapter to place the unfavorable fact in a context that is less detrimental to your position. You may put the unfavorable fact in a dependent clause so the reader sees the fact in the context of more favorable information. You frame the bad news just as a storyteller frames the setting for a story to create the appropriate mood.

If it's not true, don't claim it

You cannot lie. This ban includes misinterpreting the record, stating an opinion not supported by the evidence, and presenting a disputed fact as undisputed. The ethical reasons for this guideline are obvious.[8] Even if there were no code of professional responsibility, misrepresenting the facts would be ineffective for many pragmatic reasons. "We rely on our images, caring about our image not for an immediate purpose, but like money in the bank to use when needed."[9]

A misrepresentation, even a small one, would most likely be caught by the opposing attorney, the court's law clerks, or the judges themselves. One such lapse could call all of your statements into question, not only in this brief but in your future submissions to that court.[10] Neither you nor your client can afford such a threat to your credibility, so state your facts persuasively but with circumspection. Aim for a fact statement the court could use in its opinion if it finds in your favor.

When news is good, be bold

Use the writing techniques described later in this chapter to highlight those facts the reader must not miss. Remember that your reader, although dedicated and conscientious, has many briefs to read. Make the main facts stand out memorably, then let the reader move ahead.

When it's too much, break the mold

Avoid depending on only one or two techniques for emphasis. Any technique, if overdone, loses its effectiveness. If too obvious, it draws attention away from the content. This in turn reduces persuasiveness by reducing the reader's acceptance of the message.[11] Develop your favorite techniques, but then develop the discretion to avoid overusing them. For example, you may repeat a key word for emphasis, but avoid repeating it too much. Try other techniques instead, such as putting a word to be

8. Model Rules of Professional Conduct Rule 7.1(a).

9. Herbert W. Simons, *Persuasion: Understanding, Practice, and Analysis* 77 (1986).

10. For example, one opinion censuring counsel for misrepresenting facts states, "A brief of this character, instead of being an aid to the court in determining the questions involved, furnishes no aid whatever, because suspicion must naturally rest upon every statement asserted as a fact in it and little reliance be placed upon a brief so made, and the counsel submitting it is deserving of the severest censure." *Ryan v. Courtland Carriage Goods Co.,* 118 N.Y.S. 56, 58 (N.Y. App. Div. 1909).

11. Sandell, *supra* note 2, at 163.

emphasized at the beginning or end of a sentence. Break the mold before it distracts from the content.

State essentials, every one

Provide all the information your reader needs to understand the story; you cannot expect the reader to fill in the gaps in your presentation. Most of us have occasion to say, "you know what I mean"; a statement of facts, however, is not one of those occasions. If you use a fact in your argument, include it in the fact statement. If the previous record documents a fact, cite the record. If you need a fact to clarify the overall situation, even though it is not essential to the legal argument, include it. Also include what you need for persuasiveness. Do not let a blanket concern for conciseness lead to bland, ineffective fact statements. Just as with objective facts, where you included enough specifics to be clear, here include enough detail to be interesting. Especially include the detail needed to convey the fairness of your client's position.

Please stop writing when you're done

You cannot claim an unlimited amount of the reader's time. State everything that is needed and state it clearly. But minimize repetition of content. When repetition is not creating effective emphasis, it can make you appear uncertain and the story appear boring.

Avoid unnecessary embellishment. Clearly biased words draw more attention to the writing than the content. You want the reader to focus sympathetically on the reasonableness of your client's position. This elimination of unneeded repetition and embellishment will make the statement sound confident and will get your brief off to an assertive start. It will also make your fact statement more concise, for which the reader will be grateful.

> [A]ll depends on what you can set the Reader[s] to do; if you confuse [their] ideas or waste [their] energy, you can no longer do anything with [them].[12]

SPECIFIC TECHNIQUES

Keeping these six guidelines in mind, you can use the following writing techniques to present the content so it has the desired effect on the reader. To choose the best writing technique to emphasize a fact, you must be aware of your options; this portion of the chapter provides you with that information.

Although the options for emphasizing any given facts are almost endless, all options involve only three variables: how you group the information, how you order it, and how you word it. Grouping and ordering are choices you make when organizing the whole statement, when organizing paragraphs, and when structuring sentences. As you

---

12. Vernon Lee, *The Handling of Words and Other Studies* in *Literary Psychology* 10 (1992).

study the following list of techniques, you will see they are all variations of these options. The techniques involve four areas of writing:

- overall organization of the statement of facts (large-scale organization),

- organization of individual paragraphs (small-scale organization),

- structure of sentences, and

- word choice.

Techniques Involving Overall Organization

You can emphasize facts when you set up the overall organization of your fact statement. You may be able to put a fact you want to emphasize in the opening paragraph, when you explain the nature of the case. To do this successfully, you must have a fact that can logically fit in the opening statement: it must be a fact that is central, either legally or emotionally, to the question the case presents.

> The defendant is charged with second-degree sexual assault upon an eleven-year-old girl who was going home from school.

Making that fact part of the reader's first impression of the case ensures the reader will notice the fact.

> The defendant, a sixty-five-year-old widower, is charged with second degree sexual assault.

Inserting a fact that is emotionally but not legally significant would not be as effective.

> The defendant, a sixty-five-year-old widower, pled no contest to a charge of driving while under the influence.

Similarly, you can reprise the fact in the summarizing paragraph to drive the importance of the point home.

> The defendant now argues his rights were violated during the course of the trial at which he was found guilty of sexually assaulting the child.

Make sure that repeating this fact underscores the point without boring or irritating the reader. If the statement of facts is only two pages long, for example, repeating a fact at the end might seem more redundant than emphatic.

To de-emphasize a point through organization, place the point one-half to two-thirds of the way through the fact section, if it is possible to do so without confusing the chronology. The beginning of a section gets attention because the reader is working to understand the situation, to become oriented to the story. By the time he or she has reached the middle of the fact narrative, the content is more familiar and the reader is more likely to skim information quickly. Thus, putting a point in the middle puts it in a position that encourages the reader to skim the point quickly, with less involvement.

Techniques Involving Paragraph Organization

To emphasize a fact that cannot begin the statement of facts, you may state it in the opening of a paragraph. Each time the reader starts a new paragraph, the slight pause and the white space around the new paragraph give the reader a break. The reader comes to the new paragraph slightly refreshed, as one is slightly refreshed after taking a breath. Additionally, some readers skim information by noting only the opening of each paragraph, and you can use this habit to provide the reader with an outline of your main points. By placing your main point in the first sentence of the paragraph, you communicate it even to a reader who is skimming. You can maximize this technique's effectiveness by putting the key words in the first half of the first line.

You can also put a point to be emphasized in the final phrase of a paragraph, although in legal writing this does not get quite as much emphasis as the paragraph's beginning sentence. You can combine these two techniques with particular effectiveness. You can introduce an important concept at the end of a paragraph and then address the fact in the next paragraph, giving the fact the emphasis of both positions. This technique not only provides you with a strong, smooth emphasis on the point, but it also provides a smooth transition between the paragraphs.

One final organizational technique for emphasis is to place a fact in a separate paragraph. Although it is often useful in the argument section, this is less frequently useful in fact statements because few facts make sense without the surrounding context. To write a one-sentence paragraph, you need to use a fact that suggests its legal significance even when standing alone. Usually, rather than a one-sentence paragraph, you will want to state a point and then support it with specific facts. A strong opening to a paragraph supporting the fact will probably be more effective.

Techniques Involving Sentence Structure

Sentence structure is a versatile and useful tool, and it provides more options than organization. Sentence structure, more than word choice, also influences how most people read a text, and how much of the text they read.[13] This section shows you how to use short sentences, choice of subjects and verbs, active voice, placement of dependent clauses, and unusual order of sentence parts to create emphasis or de-emphasis.

Short Sentences

At a general level, there are only three positions in a sentence: the subject of the main clause, the predicate of the main clause, and the dependent clauses or other phrases that add detail. Every sentence has to have a main clause, which is usually the main point of the sentence. If

---

13. V.H. Yngve, *A Model and an Hypothesis for Language Structure*, 104 Proc.   Am.Phil.Soc'y 444–66 (1960).

the clause is set off by itself, with no distractions, it gets all the attention, like a musician playing a solo.

> He followed her instructions.

You give the content all of the reader's attention, by making that content all there is to the sentence.

Short is strong.

rather than

> A sentence is much stronger when it is written so that its length is relatively short.

This longer sentence dilutes its point with more words. Therefore, if you want to play down a point, do not use a short sentence. This is the rare place where you may be intentionally wordy.

> One drawback of the short sentence is has no room for detail. If the short sentence is temporarily misleading, so your reader misunderstands the point, then your credibility might be at risk. Therefore, make sure the point is clear within the sentence or within the sentences around it.

> Short sentences are strong sentences.

or

> In sentences, length does have an impact on emphasis. Short is strong.

A word of caution: avoid overusing short sentences. You do not want to fall into the pattern described in the following dialogue.

> Cleander: I find his style convenient for short Lungs; and, methinks, of all things, you cannot complain his Periods put you out of breath.

> Eudoxus: They seem indeed to be generally made in favour of Readers that are troubled with an Asthma; and I fear, his are as much too short as those others are too long.[14]

Subjects and Verbs

One technique you can use frequently is to use the main subject and verb to carry the main point. The basis of the sentence's structure is the subject and verb, so it should express your main point.

> subject   verb

> Blackie had bitten another child one year before this incident and under similar circumstances.

This technique increases clarity and often adds conciseness by eliminating empty words, as in the following example.

---

14. John Constable, *Reflections upon Accuracy of Style* 7 (1731).

subject   verb

Blackie had bitten another child one year before this incident.

rather than

> There was a previous incident in which Blackie had bitten another child one year earlier.

Focused subjects and verbs also add natural variety and emphasis to your fact statement. This focus may lead you to repeat a central concept, thus adding emphasis.

> Blackie *attacked* a smaller dog owned by neighbors across the road. Several years earlier, Blackie's *attack* on a large stray dog had resulted in that dog's death.

Similarly, as the important concepts vary, your subjects and verbs also vary, so you avoid unintended emphasis.

> **The Anderson's *German shepard,* Blackie, attacked a smaller *dog* owned by neighbors across the road. Several years earlier, Blackie had bitten a large *stray* so severely that it eventually died.**

rather than

> The Anderson's dog attacked a smaller dog owned by neighbors across the road. Several years earlier, the Anderson's dog had bitten a large stray dog so severely that the dog eventually died.

Active Voice

Another structural technique for emphasis is stating the verb in the active voice.[15] Using active voice emphasizes the action by making the sentence more interesting and easier to read.

> **According to Helmsley, Acker offered to sell a small amount of marijuana for $40.**

rather than

> According to Helmsley, an offer was made by Acker to sell a small amount of marijuana for $40.

Active voice is useful for emphasizing a sympathetic action by your client. Because the subject of the sentence is the natural focus, the reader is likely to focus on your client when he or she is the subject of the sentence. The reader's position of emphasis structurally becomes the point of view of the sentence.

> Because he believed drug trafficking presented a serious problem in the neighborhood, Helmsley agreed to help the police by working as an informant.

---

15. Active voice is the use of the verb form that allows the subject to act, "He sold the car." In contrast, passive voice reverses the order of the nouns so that the subject becomes the thing acted upon, as in "The car was sold by him." Passive voice thus allows the actor to be left unidentified until after the verb, and even to be left unidentified in the sentence, as in "The car was sold."

Active voice can emphasize an unfavorable action by the opponent.

> According to Helmsley, Acker had boasted frequently that he could provide a variety of drugs.

In contrast, the passive voice can remove attention from the actor.

> The exchange was made later that evening.

The effectiveness of this technique is limited. Because it is so frequent in bureaucratic language, readers assume it is a way to avoid naming the responsible party.

> A decision has been made that your services are no longer needed.

Sophisticated readers can readily see the passive structure as an attempt to avoid responsibility, and the ploy may be ineffective if used too often or too obviously.

Placement of Dependent Clauses

After you have determined what information belongs in the main clause, you can relegate a less important point to a dependent clause to de-emphasize it. This structure puts that point structurally in the background and encourages the reader to focus on the point stated in the main subject and predicate. This placement is particularly useful when you are explaining away an unfavorable fact.

> Blackie had never bitten a person before this incident, *although she had gotten into fights with other dogs.* In fact, one of Blackie's attacks on another dog occurred because she was defending her master against the large stray.

This technique is the converse of setting a point in a separate sentence for emphasis, and it structurally de-emphasizes the point. To adapt a quotation from Vernon Lee, "If you want a person to seem less a villain, put a bigger villain by his side."[16]

The next decision is where to put the dependent clauses, because placement also affects emphasis. There are three possible places: the beginning, the middle, and the end. It sounds simple, but is not simple in practice. The parts of the sentence interact, and sentence structure interacts with word choice and other elements in the sentence. To guide you through these interactions, this section discusses the placement of clauses in detail, noting how you can use clauses for emphasis or de-emphasis as needed.

The principle that the beginning gets more attention than the middle applies to sentences as well as paragraphs. A dependent clause at the beginning of a sentence will get some emphasis, even though it is not the main clause. Following an introductory phrase by a main clause creates a sentence with two opportunities for emphasis: the set-up and the punch line. This structure is especially effective if the introductory

---

16. Lee, *supra* note 12, at 7.

phrase is slightly long, creating suspense, and the main clause following it is rather short.

> **Clifford had not yet been trained to operate the stamping machine when his supervisor, Morris, asked him to fill in at the machine.** *But, anxious to make a good impression on his first day at the job, Clifford agreed.*

rather than

> Clifford had not yet been trained to operate the stamping machine when his supervisor, Morris, asked him to fill in at the machine. But Clifford agreed because he was anxious to make a good impression on his first day at the job.

This structure has many uses. You can use it to set up a contrast.

> *Unlike the defendant,* the plaintiff had little experience operating tractors.

Use it to establish the context of an event.

> *Because there was no commingling of funds or sharing of proceeds,* the defendant believed no conflict of interest existed.

> *Soon after beginning this medication,* Ms. Rodriquez began suffering frequent headaches.

Use it to dismiss an opponent's point.

> *Although the defendant was advised of his Miranda rights,* he was not in a position to understand the advice. At the time, he was bleeding from a cut above his left eye and was in substantial pain caused by a broken arm.

Use it to build a stronger emotion.

> *Even after these warnings,* two employees became ill while working. *After other employees had complained of dizziness,* the management still took no action to notify employees of the danger.

You will not add emphasis, however, when you use a short introductory phrase as a transition. The emphasis of the beginning is muted when the introduction is short and rather commonplace.

> *In the morning,* Stacy left the breakfast table early.

> *For example,* Harrison called Valencia three times earlier in the day.

Here the emphasis is overridden by other techniques, such as putting the main point in the subject and verb and using more arresting word choice. The break in the ordinary pattern is also overcome by the familiarity of the wording and the fact that the reader moves quickly to the subject.

Another place to put a dependent clause is in the middle of the main clause, where it will be an interruption, or an intrusive phrase. Even though it comes in the middle, an intrusive phrase can create emphasis: it claims a share of the attention from the main point, as a child does when interrupting a parent who is talking.

The defendant, *unlike her predecessor,* did not review the daily balances.

This technique may seem to contradict other techniques, such as putting the point to be emphasized in the beginning or end of a sentence. But an intrusive phrase claims attention because it is out of the ordinary, like an unexpected interlude within a piece of music. This unusualness, when combined with important content, outweighs the disadvantage of being in the middle of the sentence.

The patch of ice, *shaded by the overhanging tree,* was not seen by the driver.

Like a short sentence within a group of longer sentences, an interruption can stand out in a crowd of phrases. A short, rather routine interruption will not stand out too much.

An intrusive phrase of more than a few words, however, puts a burden on the reader. It asks the reader to stop what he or she is doing and do something else. This burden can quickly become overwhelming and the reader can rebel, so avoid long interruptions.

At approximately 9:00 a.m., the defendant was taken from her cell and, *without an opportunity to consult an attorney,* **was again interrogated. She was not advised of her Miranda rights even during this second interrogation**.

rather than

At approximately 9:00 a.m., the defendant was taken from her cell and, *without an opportunity to consult an attorney as she had requested earlier and without being advised by any officer of her Miranda rights,* was again interrogated.

The burden on the reader can also be overwhelming if the sentence as a whole is long or complex.

In connection with his wholesale bedding and potted plant business, Mr. Gray purchased pre-cut, pre-drilled and shaped metal tubing from out-of-state retailers.

rather than

Mr. Gray *in connection with his wholesale bedding and potted plant business* purchased pre-cut, pre-drilled and shaped metal tubing from out-of-state retailers.

For this reason, the usefulness of intrusive phrases is somewhat limited. You can use them, however, to point up an irony.

The dealer, *despite his promise,* did not order the needed replacements.

They can also add an important explanation.

The defendant, *believing the prison term would be shorter,* agreed to plead guilty to this charge.

Using intrusive phrases makes the tone somewhat more formal because it requires coordinating two thoughts at once. It is associated with prepared statements, such as a written speech or other document. Intrusive phrases are hard to use well and easy to use poorly. Use them infrequently, not as the dominant technique in your repertoire.

> [I]f for instance, you have had to introduce a mysterious stranger but do not wish anything to come of his mysteriousness, be sure you strip off his mystery as prosaically as you can, before leaving him in the Reader's charge.[17]

In contrast to intrusive phrases, dependent clauses added to the end of the sentence are easy to read and more likely to create a relaxed tone. This effect may be desirable if you want the reader to see the situation you are describing as routine and not requiring heightened sentiments.

> The preliminary examination was held before Hon. Hillary Anderson, of the Wold County Circuit Court, on October 1, 2002, at the close of which the court found "reasonable grounds to believe the offense charged in the complaint was committed and was committed by this defendant." (R. 33–40)

The end of the sentence may therefore be the best place for information you want to play down or present as support. Using a dependent clause at the end of the sentence signals that the content is detail that fills out the picture once you have established the main point.

> **Garrison shoved Wagner into the car** *after Wagner told him that he did not have a driver's license.*

In this example, the point is made and the framework established in the reader's mind. The phrase at the end then adds detail. Notice how much more emphasis the point would get in an introductory phrase.

> *After Wagner told Garrison that he did not have a driver's license,* Garrison shoved Wagner into the car.

It would also gain more emphasis in an intrusive phrase.

> Garrison, *after hearing that Wagner did not have a driver's license,* shoved Wagner into the car.

One interesting combination of several techniques is to put a fact to be de-emphasized in the middle of a list within a sentence.[18] In the following example, the italicized fact is de-emphasized because it is placed in the middle of a list that is itself a dependent clause.

> Kevin Wagner testified that he was 16 years old, was a freshman at Central High School, *had been drinking that night,* and was walking home when Garrison offered him a ride.

As your routine sentence structure, use this structure with added information in a dependent clause at the end. Emphasis techniques can

---

17. *Id.* at 7–8.

18. Clear structuring of lists was discussed in the chapter on jury instructions earlier. This use adapts and builds on the skill you developed earlier.

work only when they contrast with the text around them. If each sentence had a dramatic structure, all the information competes for attention. Instead, choose the facts you want to emphasize, put those facts in specially crafted sentences, and then use this workhorse sentence structure for most of the other information.

One exception to this use of de-emphasis is the last sentence in a paragraph or section. In this case, the end receives the emphasis of the climax. The end of the last sentence is a place for emphasis.

Unusual Order

Another sentence structure technique is to put the elements of the sentence in an unusual order. Because something different tends to get the reader's attention, this technique will draw attention to the content of the sentence. For example, you might put the predicate, or some phrase from the last part of the sentence, before the verb.

> *Embracing,* the couple was observed by many witnesses as they stood by the entrance to the lounge.

One unusual order is multiple introductory phrases.

> *At 5:00 p.m. on Friday, June 2, as they had done on many previous Fridays,* the complaining witness and the defendant left work together and walked to the Backroom Tap.

Another somewhat unusual structure is to place multiple phrases at the end of the sentence.

> At the trial, Ms. Harrison testified the defendant forced her to the floor, forced her to remove her clothes, forced her to have intercourse.

You may use a longer, looser structure to vary from the usual.

> They stayed at the Backroom Tap until approximately 7:00 p.m., drinking several alcoholic drinks each and laughing with other patrons over some suggestive jokes told by the complaining witness.

You might even omit some needed words, as long as they are clearly implied by the structure of the sentence.

> The complaining witness was the defendant's secretary, eighteen, a high school graduate. The defendant was wealthy, forty-two, an attorney.

These unusual structures are dramatic and complex to construct, so use them with restraint. Structure an unusual sentence well and choose content that is easy to follow. The reader must not be overburdened or confused by the structure. Nevertheless, when used well, the unusual structures can make a fact memorable and interesting in the reader's mind.

Techniques Involving Word Choice

When legal writers first attempt persuasive writing, they often change their word choice, and with good reason. English offers a wealth of words. "[O]ne [person's] bandwagon is another [person's] reasoned consensus."[19] A senator who refused to change her vote even after some political arm-twisting might be labelled by various camps as "loyal," "unwavering," "resolute," "unchanged," "resistant," "rigid," "stubborn," or "pig-headed." Word choice is the way speakers or writers commonly reveal their biases.

> Senator, do you plan to persist with this plan despite the President's request that you reconsider?

or

> Senator, to what do you attribute your impressive ability to resist White House pressure in this situation?

Therein lies the main limitation of word choice: it easily projects the writer's bias, and obvious bias lessens the legal writer's effectiveness.[20]

> Semantic argument tries to make a persuasive point not by presenting or arranging evidence, but by using impressive language. It should convince no one.[21]

For maximum effectiveness, restraint is essential. The challenge of effective word choice lies in its multidimensional aspects.[22] Words vary not only in meaning (denotation), but also in emotional association (connotation), degree of detail (specific or general), terms of address (concrete or abstract), unusual wording (familiar or unfamiliar), repetition, and rhythm.[23] Each of these dimensions can affect the persuasive impact of the word, and each factors into the writer's choices. Words have an additive effect; one word's impact is colored by the words around it, so word choice often creates repetition and rhythm. No wonder legal writers find those techniques difficult to master. But not impossible. By considering each of these dimensions, you can build your understanding so that interrelating the various dimensions is easier.

Emotional Association

Stirring the reader's emotions will increase the likelihood that the reader will remember the fact generating the emotion.[24] Yet you want that memory to be appropriate to your goal, and the content must be what is remembered, not that you tried to create a feeling. Emotional association can be effective when managed well. To avoid showing bias, avoid words with strong connotations, either positive or negative.[25]

19. Wayne C. Booth, *Modern Dogma and the Rhetoric of Assent* 146 (1974).

20. Sandell, *supra* note 2, at 163.

21. Larry W. Burton and Daniel McDonald, *The Language of Argument* 128 (10th ed. 2001).

22. Lyle E. Bourne, Jr., *Human Conceptual Behavior* 22 (1966).

23. For more on the dimensions of word choice, *see* Theophil Spoerri, *Style of Distance, Style of Nearness* in *Essays in Stylistic Analysis* 62–78 (H. Babb ed. 1972).

24. Dean Hewes and Sally Planalp, *The Individual's Place in Communication Science* in *Handbook of Communication Science* 164 (C. Berger and S. Chaffee, eds. 1987).

25. Euphemisms are words with positive emotional loading; pejoratives are words with negative loading. For a rhetorician's discussion of emotionally loaded words, *see* Simons, *supra* note 9, at 314.

Instead, choose a word that is slightly positive or negative. For example, to describe a push you might use "shove" for a negative slant or "nudge" for a positive one, but you would use stronger terms only if the facts supported the label.

Another useful technique is to put the emotional association in the verb, rather than as adjectives or adverbs, because the verb has more impact. For example, "the group's leader shoved the woman into the car" is stronger than "the group's leader roughly pushed the woman into the car."

Degree of Detail

A technique related to both organization and word choice is to explain favorable facts in greater detail, less favorable ones in less detail. A more specific picture makes the fact more memorable and more persuasive.[26] For example, the following sentence creates a clear picture.

> The plaintiff, who is 6′ 3″ and weighs 210 pounds, strode toward the defendant, who is 5′ 10″ and weighs 160 pounds.

A more general statement would render the fact less memorable.

> The plaintiff, who is larger than the defendant, moved toward him.

One of the reasons specific language is more effective is that it gives the reader more information, so the reader knows more clearly what the writer had in mind. For example, "tree" could refer to a white pine, a cypress, or a dogwood. Because "tree" is so general, the reader has to think either of a specific kind of tree, which may or may not be the one the writer meant, or maintain the general idea of tree by keeping various possibilities open. Applying this principle, if the defendant's fear was the favorable fact, you might word it as follows.

> When he heard the defendant's question, the plaintiff did not answer. Instead he grasped the iron handle of the jack he was using and wrenched it loose. Still saying nothing, the plaintiff, who is 6′ 3″ and weighs 210 pounds, strode toward the defendant's car. The defendant rolled up the window and fumbled with his keys, meaning to start the engine. In his nervousness, he removed his foot from the clutch. His only thought was to secure his escape.

The abrupt release of the clutch caused the defendant's car to lurch forward unexpectedly, ...

If the fear was a fact to be minimized, the description of the situation might be much more general. Instead focus the passage as follows.

> When the plaintiff approached the defendant's car, the defendant attempted to drive away as quickly as possible. In his hurry, he

---

26. "[T]he example seems to be a particularly powerful form of information, especially when compared to information in statistical summary form." Daniel J. O'Keefe, *Persuasion: Theory and Research* 218 (2d ed. 2002).

released the clutch abruptly, causing the car to lurch forward unexpectedly.

Terms of Address

To make the reader feel closer to the people involved in the facts, you can use their names (Ms. Milkowski, Adam) or meaningful labels (mother, child, etc.). To move the reader away emotionally, use more abstract terms (plaintiff, relative). Just as a film director can pull the camera back to show the audience the larger view, more abstract terms of address pull the reader back from the individuals involved by suggesting the larger view. If you want the reader to focus on a ruling's effect on future cases, for example, it is logical and natural to use the label for the larger conceptual group.

Appellant was stopped by the Wold County Deputy Sheriff at approximately 8:30 p.m. after the officer observed a defective headlamp, but no erratic driving.

rather than

Jessica Birdsong was stopped by Deputy Sheriff Frank Buschman at approximately 8:30 p.m. after Officer Buschman observed a defective headlamp, although he did not observe Ms. Birdsong driving erratically.

If the sympathy of the situation runs in your favor, focus the reader by using names of the parties.

While struggling with Roger Green over a loaded gun Green was using to threaten Evans' sister, Will Evans was shot. Mr. Evans died from the resulting loss of blood.

rather than

The victim was shot while struggling with the defendant over a loaded gun the defendant was using to threaten the victim's sister. The victim subsequently died from loss of blood.

Unusual Wording

A word slightly out of the ordinary can add emphasis, but only if it is understandable. For example, the wording of the following sentence is unusual and eye-catching, but its meaning is likely to elude the reader.

To adumbrate a rhetoric of assent butters no parsnips.

When choosing unusual words, also pay attention to the word's level of formality; it must also be appropriate to the situation.

Although Mr. Green carried a loaded gun into the trailer, he said, "I didn't mean to hurt anyone!"

If it is not, the result will be awkward, and sometimes humorous.

Although Mr. Green was bearing arms as he entered the mobile home, he opined, "I didn't mean to hurt anyone!"

You can use this humor to belittle a fact.

The dog was not startled by the child. The dog ran up to the child while she was playing with a ball. He came. He saw. He bit.

Use care when incorporating humor in persuasive writing, however, because it can backfire.[27]

Informal language, or slang, is generally out of place in an attorney's language. Therefore, its presence in a fact statement is unusual and somewhat startling. In a brief's context, quoting a witness's description that includes slang would add effective emphasis.

Mr. Jones denied being drunk and denied hitting his wife, stating, "I'd remember if I'd whacked her."

Slang has a stronger emotional impact, so use it only when that emotion works in your client's favor. When the emotion does not need to be heightened, use a more formal description.

Mr. Jones denied being intoxicated and denied striking his wife.

Repetition

Repetition is obvious in concept but subtle in mastery. It requires a faithful ear, a sense of the level of drama and formality appropriate to the situation, and a balance of courage and restraint. Repetition creates a sense of heightened drama, an increased formality elevating the value of the content repeated. When using repetition, make sure the item repeated deserves emphasis. If the point repeated is minor, repetition can be distracting. You can repeat many elements. The most obvious are words. Also effective is the repetition of a phrase's structure.

During preliminary questioning, the defendant admitted that he had used marijuana in the past. *During the trial*, he denied this.

You can also repeat larger structures, such as those of whole sentences, paragraphs, or paragraph blocks. Repetition can be subtle, as in the following example.

The dealer *promised* to have the brakes tested on the car, but this *promise* was not kept.

Or it can be bold.

The clerk, Jerry Vance, fumbled with the cash drawer and coins clattered on the floor. *Silent*, the defendant pointed the gun at him. *Silent*, he pulled the trigger. *Silent*, he turned from the slumping body to gaze at the customers huddled behind the shelving.

Be vigilant against repeating once to often. One repetition too many can lead the reader to snicker or become irritated, either of which is a distraction from the content at hand.

---

27. Humor can increase the reader's liking for the writer, but does not increase the reader's estimation of the writer's competence. Humor can also decrease the reader's liking for the writer. *Id.* at 190–91.

Rhythm

Rhythm, a combination of structure and word choice, focuses on controlling the pace and vocal emphasis in the text, as the pace and intensity of music varies. In prose this is a subtle force; nevertheless, it can be useful to convey a certain mood while describing a set of facts.

> Later in the evening, while walking along the still, calm, lighted pathway, Mr. Hill heard a small cry. He stopped to listen. Hearing another cry, he moved in the direction of the sound. Pushing aside the heavy underbrush, he found the victim. The boy moaned again. Hill knelt beside him.

This sample slows the reader by placing three stressed syllables together "still, calm, light" which creates a touch of anticipation just before stating the event of hearing the small cry. When Hill stops, the reader is stopped by the rhythm of the short sentence, "He stopped to listen." The pace then increases with the faster, galloping rhythm of a series of phrases "hearing another cry," "in the direction," "of the sound," and "pushing aside the heavy underbrush." The reader can sense the rush here, and then is brought up suddenly by a short phrase with more stressed syllables: "he found the victim." The reader is held at this slower pace with two more short sentences that have more stressed than unstressed syllables. The reader reads slowly, quickly, then slowly again, lingering on the passages of greatest emotional impact.

To use rhythm effectively, it is important not to be too heavy-handed. A rhythm that is too strong can draw the mind away from the content to the writing, and in this circumstance the writing is likely to look rather silly. The use of rhythm is more art than science, and your ability will develop through experiment, experience, and evaluation.[28]

Word choice can sharpen the focus of your presentation when used effectively, but can distort it if used without skill or restraint. Be interesting, but always be accurate and thorough. Use emotional association, degree of detail, terms of address, unusual wording, repetition, and rhythm not solely to sound persuasive, but to emphasize the facts that are themselves persuasive.

The following table summarizes the persuasive techniques discussed in this chapter.

Techniques for Persuasive Statements of Fact		
Writing Aspect	To Emphasize	To De-emphasize
Overall Organization	• Begin with the fact.	• Put the fact in the middle or two-thirds of the way through the fact statement.

28. Metaphor may be the best way to explain the workings of rhythm in English: "[T]he movement is neither a rise nor a fall, but an easy progress, a punctuated comfortable swing, in which there is a combination of both [a rise and fall of stress]. The orchestra leader, who beats time exag- gerating greatly the force of stress, and the motion of the sea waves are in some ways better parallels to musical rhythm than the thrusts of a piston rod." J. Max Patrick and Robert O. Evans, ed, *Style, Rhetoric, and Rhythm: Essays by Morris W. Croll* 371 (1989).

Techniques for Persuasive Statements of Fact		
Writing Aspect	**To Emphasize**	**To De-emphasize**
	• Reprise the fact at the end.	• Include less detail on the fact.
Paragraph Organization	• Put the fact at the beginning of the first sentence. • Put the fact at the end of a paragraph. • Set the fact off in a separate paragraph.	• Place the fact within a paragraph on a more favorable point. • Place the fact with other facts that establish a mitigating background.
Sentence Structure	• Put the fact in a short sentence. • Put the fact in the subject and verb. • Use active voice to state the action. • Put the fact in the first few words of a sentence. • Put the fact in an intrusive phrase. • Put the fact in an unusual structure.	• Put the fact in a longer sentence. • Use a linking verb to move the fact out of the main subject and verb. • Use passive voice to state the action. • Put the fact in a dependent clause, usually at the end of a sentence. • Put the fact in the middle of a list at the end of a sentence. • Put the fact in a sentence with very routine structure.
Word Choice	• Use a word with a favorable connotation. • Describe the fact in detail. • Repeat a key word. • Characterize parties in sympathetic roles. • Use personal names or roles for the parties.	• Use a word with an unfavorable connotation. • Describe the fact in general terms. • Use synonyms if needed to avoid repeating a word. • Characterize parties in unsympathetic roles, but not insulting or inaccurate • Use legal terms or abstract terms for the parties.
	• When a legal concept is favorable, use the legal terms to describe the parties. • When the relationship of the parties is significant and favorable, use the significant relationship as a label. • Use a slightly unusual word. • Use slightly more informal wording.	• When the legal concept is not particularly favorable, describe your situation as unusual, not fitting in the general mold. • When the relationship of the parties is an unfavorable fact, avoid using the relationship as a label. • Use ordinary words. • Use slightly more formal words

Incorporating These Techniques Into the Writing Process

Although the previous summary of techniques helps organize options for you, you still must work these techniques into your larger writing process. To accomplish this, focus on a few tasks at once. Because of the complexity of large-scale and small-scale organization, sentence structure, and word choice, you cannot constantly consider each of these dimensions while writing a statement of facts. Instead, concentrate first on the concerns discussed in the chapter on objective fact statements: choosing your facts, organizing them, and writing your story clearly and accurately. Later, as you rewrite the section, identify the fact you want to emphasize or de-emphasize. Then turn to persuasive techniques and choose the ones that best suit your purpose. After you have rewritten the text for emphasis, you can revise it further for conciseness, omitting unneeded phrases and wordy structures.

Making a fact statement persuasive may be best attempted in the middle of the legal writing process, rather than shifting to a completely different process. The following checklist illustrates how you can add this persuasive step by mimicking the checklist for objective statements of facts, but adding the steps needed to state the facts persuasively.

Checklist for Drafting Persuasive Statements of Fact

1. Include all needed facts.

    a. Legally significant facts

        (1) Facts that will be used in the argument section.

        (2) Facts that show that the elements of the cause of action or defenses are met

        (3) Facts that will be used in the other side's legal argument

        (4) Procedural facts

    b. Needed background facts

        (1) Dates needed to show events

        (2) Names needed to avoid confusion

    c. Emotional facts you have determined to be helpful to your case

2. Organize those facts.

    a. Choose most effective opening for this fact statement.

    b. Divide into subsections if needed.

    c. Organize each section or subsection chronologically.

    d. Divide facts into paragraphs that group the facts logically.

    e. Use visual aids if they help your case. When using visual aids

     (1) use the form that accurately conveys your meaning,

     (2) structure tables to be read from left to right, and

     (3) remove distracting and unneeded details.

3.   Draft the facts to be accurate and clear.

    a. State necessary unfavorable key points specifically but not concretely.

    b. Keep labels minimal and consistent.

    c. Substitute names for pronouns where needed or where they add sympathy for your client.

4.   Either before or after drafting your argument, review the facts to determine which specific facts should be emphasized.

5.   Experiment with different techniques until you create the emphasis you want. (Refer to the previous table for a list of these techniques.)

6.   Rewrite the rest of the fact statement to frame your emphasized points effectively.

7.   Revise the facts for clarity and conciseness. Ask yourself the following questions.

    a. Are all legally significant facts included?

    b. Are all unneeded and unfavorable background and emotional facts deleted?

    c. Should any detail be deleted?

       (1) facts that may confuse more than clarify,

       (2) facts that clarify points that will not concern the legal reader, or

       (3) facts that signal to the reader that an irrelevant point may indeed be relevant.

    d. Are sentences readable?

    e. Is each word unambiguous and clear?

    f. Are all wordy phrases eliminated?

Exercise 1

Using the facts and law in Exercise #1 at the end of Chapter 6, write a persuasive statement of facts on behalf of the State, who has charged Samuel Johnson.

Exercise 2

The following excerpts from two statements of the case show you how two attorneys presented facts related to a case contesting the validity of a will. The plaintiff, James Hart, argues the will signed by Julia Hart, his stepmother, was invalid. The defendant John, Julia's son, argues the will was valid. The excerpts included show how each party described (1) Julia's health, (2) her medications, and (3) some unusual circumstances surrounding the signing of the will. Both excerpts make good use of various persuasive writing techniques, but neither is perfect.

Read the following statements of fact and locate examples of the writer's use of persuasive writing techniques. Then determine whether you think each technique is used effectively. Rewrite the passages, discussing the pluses and minuses of each revision. Also note other places where the writer could have used persuasive techniques to handle a point better.

Plaintiff–Appellant's Facts

As the picture from the Colonel's 1996 birthday party shows, time and chronic illness had ravaged Julia's health, so that Julia was prematurely old eighteen years before she died.

In 20__, Julia's health was terrible. She had always suffered from excruciating tension headaches (R. 925, 928–53) and in her late seventies and early eighties suffered from increasing cardiovascular problems, cataracts, arteriosclerosis, and many other problems (R. 928–53). So bad was Julia's health that, even though he was battling cancer at the time, Colonel Hart insisted that Julia never be left alone (R. 484, 710, 889). Julia was surrounded by many servants during the day (R. 454) and was watched by a baby-sitter at night (R. 484, 710, 889).

Julia was also on a large and complex daily regimen of drugs (R. 454). Daily she took three kinds of barbiturates—Tuinal (R. 1115–16), Fiornal (R. 113), and Fiornal with Codeine (R. 1113–14)—one of which included an opium derivative (R. 115). In addition to these drugs, she took greater-than-normal daily dosages (R. 1114–15) of Triavil, a specialized compound tranquilizer formulated and normally prescribed for mental depression (R. 1148–49).

Triavil was misprescribed for Julia. Dr. Desmond, Julia's personal physician in Adams, continued the prescription from one given to Julia by a Dr. Simmons, whom she had seen while on vacation in Florida (R. 454). Dr. Desmond continued the use of strong dosages of Triavil four times daily for Julia's tension headaches, which he had long feared would drive both Julia and himself out of their minds (R. 925). Dr. Desmond, in attempting to explain Julia's heavy medication, said that he later forgot that he had continued the use of Triavil for his patient. (R. 954–58).

Triavil offered no treatment or cure for tension headaches, as testified by Dr. Paul Wyles (R. 1149), a psychiatrist and former anesthesiologist with great knowledge of drugs used for both tension headaches and mental disorders (R. 1130, 1109–10). The Physician's Desk Reference 1083 (40th Ed.20__) concurs that Triavil is not used for headaches.

The only effect Triavil could have had on Julia's headaches, however, lay in its powerful tranquilizing effects (R. 113). Dr. Wyles testified in detail that, solely by reason of the drugs she took, Julia was susceptible to influence. He also testified that he normally prescribes taking Triavil only before retiring, so that the person taking it will be alert and functional during the day (R. 1117).

On November 1, 20__, five months before she died, Julia signed a new will in the presence of John Hart, Jr. (her sole heir under the new will), Sidney Green (the attorney John had urged her to hire), and Bill Wilson (Sidney Green's law partner) (R. 525, 630). The will, distributing over $8 million and allegedly taking three weeks to draft, was just three pages long. Despite its abolition of her estate plan of over twenty years, and despite the fact that it appointed a marital trust worth $6 million in addition to disposition of her own $2 million estate, a copy of the new will was never sent to Julia for her review and consideration.

Julia did not see the will until one-half hour before she signed it (R. 835). On November 1, Sidney Green and his partner arrived at Julia's home and read and summarily discussed the new will for twenty to thirty minutes (R. 836–37).

But Julia did not sign the will until John arrived. After John arrived, she signed the will within ten minutes. Sidney Green and his partner then departed immediately. This document not only reversed her twenty-year estate plan to the detriment of James and his sisters; it also disinherited Julia's own grandchildren from the $2.5 million trust that had been provided for them. . . .

Defendant–Appellee's Facts

Julia was uniformly described by all the witnesses who had personally known her as a strong-willed, positive, and independent woman who knew her own mind (R. 710, 719–20, 917–18). James Hart himself characterized Julia as an "independent and abrupt person" (R. 994).

Many witnesses who knew Julia for years and who observed her both before and after her husband's death testified that her personality and character were unchanged. They also testified that her mental faculties were unimpaired at the time of the execution of her last will, except that she was understandably sad over Colonel Hart Sr.'s recent death. Ms. Meyer stated that Julia's composure was "wonderful" at her husband's funeral (R. 1091). Dean Higgins, the family chauffeur and handyman for 27 years, testified that following John Sr.'s death "she was practically her old self" (R. 903).

Before his death, John Sr. had insisted on having someone present in the house when he was out of town because he was concerned about Julia's eyesight and was afraid she might fall (R. 746–47). As a result, since May 20__, Julia had aide-companions who stayed with her at night (R. 484). Dr. Desmond, Julia's personal physician, testified that the companions were traditionally used by wealthy persons in the community as aides, and that their presence therefore did not imply that Julia was incapable of caring for herself (R. 977).

Dr. Desmond and others have testified that Julia's medication had not affected her alertness (R. 918, 974, 984–87). Her doctor's opinion, based on his observations of Julia over the years, was that she was not susceptible to being influenced (R. 973–74). Because Julia had a history of osteoarthritis, tension headaches, thyroid deficiency, and cardiovascular disease (R. 984–85), she was and had been for many years taking a variety of medications. Nevertheless, no direct testimony from any witness shows that this schedule of medication affected Julia's mental alertness, independence, or forcefulness.

Shortly before executing her new will, Julia met twice with her attorney, visited the family office in the First National Bank of Adams building, and appeared at social functions. Angie Miller, who saw Julia frequently during this period and who accompanied her to Florida earlier, testified that during the period around November 1, 20__ (when Julia executed her last will), Julia was "remarkably peppy and alert" (R. 707).

Julia and her attorney, Sidney Green, had arranged for her to execute her will on the morning of November 1, 20__. Because of a conflict, however, Mr. Green asked Julia if they could meet in the afternoon, and Julia suggested that they meet at 5:00 p.m.

Attorneys Sidney Green and Bill Wilson drove to Julia's home together a little before 5:00. Julia greeted them at the door (R. 832). After they retired to the living room, Mr. Green briefly reviewed Julia's assets and then presented copies of the will for himself and attorney Wilson (R. 883, 638–39). Mr. Green then read through the will provision by provision (R. 471, 639). When they came to the language exercising the power of appointment over the marital trust established under Colonel Hart's will, Mr. Wilson explained the power of appointment to Julia. He made clear that, through the exercise of her power, all of the assets of the marital trust would be distributed to John Jr. (R. 639–40). At this point, Julia expressed her satisfaction with the provisions being read or explained to her (R. 639–41).

During the reading and discussion of the will, John Jr. arrived for his customary evening visit at his mother's home (R. 834, 630). He asked if he should come into the living room, and Julia indicated that he could (R. 1052). When he did so, he sat on the opposite side of the room until the attorneys completed their reading and discussion with Julia. Julia and the two attorneys then signed in the presence of each other (R. 446, 641–42). Both attorneys testified that in their opinion Julia was competent to execute the will at the time she did so (R. 466, 643–44).

Assignment 1

Your firm has filed a complaint on behalf of Jamie Blottner against Ms. Newton, and her attorney has filed a motion to dismiss. Write the statement of facts for a brief to the court arguing that the complaint should be dismissed, using the information in Assignment 1 in Chapter 6.

Assignment 2

Your firm still represents Jim and Kate Putnam, whose situation is described in Assignment 2 at the end of Chapter 4. At the trial level, your firm won your case and the Putnams recovered. City General Hospital appealed, however, on several issues, and one has survived to the point that it is now going before the Florida State Supreme Court. You must now write the statement of the case for the appellate brief on one issue, which is whether, as a matter of law, City General had a legal or contractual duty to preserve the vaporizer as evidence. City General is arguing that it did not. You must argue that City General did have this duty as a matter of law. This is a technical legal argument, and you know that this court as a reputation for being impatient with irrelevant information; thus you need to watch out for digressing on points not relevant to this particular appellate issue. Nevertheless, you do not want the court to forget the human tragedy in this situation, so you need to weave that sense of sympathy and justice into the brief as you can, without seeming obvious.

The hospital is arguing that it had no duty to the Putnams to preserve the vaporizer because

- 21 U.S.C.A. 360 does not create any duty toward private citizens;

- the Putnams' cause of action should be against the manufacturer, not the hospital;

- allowing this cause of action will open the floodgates to endless litigation

You need to argue that the duty exists under the law. To do this, use the following sources only; do not do any other research.

- Florida statute 395.0197 [Use as a reference, but don't try to quote the language—it doesn't help. This statutes requires a hospital to file a report to the state within 15 days of a patient's death, which they did. We need to say saving that writing that report logically leads to a duty to preserve the vaporizer until they are sure if it caused the death.]

- 21 U.S.C. 360i(b)(1)(A) and (D) [Here, too, you may use this as a reference but don't try to quote it. It creates a duty for hospitals to report to the Food and Drug Administration any equipment suspected of causing a patient's death and to secure the suspected equipment, but it doesn't create any duty to a private citizen.]

- *Grove Fresh Distrib., Inc. v. Flavor Fresh Foods, Inc.*, 720 F. Supp. 714 (N.D. Ill. 1989) [This case helps explain how a federal regulation can create a rebuttable presumption of negligence in a state tort action, which we can analogize to create a duty to the Putnams to secure the suspected equipment], and

- *Bondu v. Gurvich*, 473 So 2d 1307 (Fla. Ct. App. 1984) *cert. denied*, 484 So. 2d 7 (Fla. 1986) [This case establishes that a plaintiff can raise a separate tort claim against "the defendant which stands to benefit," which helps show we can sue the hospital separately from the manufacturer. You'll need to deal with the dissent's concern, though, if you use this case.]

BIBLIOGRAPHY

Babb, Howard S., *Essays in Stylistic Analysis*. New York: Harcourt Brace Javanovich, Inc., 1972.

Berger, Charles R. and Steven H. Chaffee, eds., *Handbook of Communication Science*. Newbury Park, CA: Sage Publications, 1987.

Bereiter, Carl and Marlene Scardamalia, *The Psychology of Written Composition*. Hillsdale, NJ: Lawrence Erlbaum Associates, 1987.

Booth, Wayne C., *Modern Dogma and the Rhetoric of Assent*. South Bend, IN: University of Notre Dame Press, 1974.

Bourne, Lyle E., Jr., *Human Conceptual Behavior*. Boston: Allyn and Bacon, 1966.

Burton, Larry and Daniel McDonald, *The Language of Argument*. New York: Longman, 10th ed. 2001.

Constable, John, *Reflections upon Accuracy of Style*. New York: Garland Publishing Co., 1970 (facsimile edition of original printed in 1731).

Corbett, Edward P.J. and Robert J. Connors, *Classical Rhetoric for the Modern Student*. New York: Oxford University Press, 4th ed. 1999.

Fowler, Roger, *Essays on Style and Language: Linguistic and Critical Approaches to Literary Style*. London: Routledge and Kegan Paul, 1966.

Hovland, Carl I., Irving L. Janis, and Harold H. Kelley, *Communication and Persuasion*. New Haven: Yale University Press, 1953.

Kirsch, Gesa, *Writing Up and Down the Social Ladder: A Study of Experienced Writers Composing or Contrasting Audiences*, 25 (1) Research in Teaching of English 33 (Feb. 1991).

Lee, Vernon, *The Handling of Words, and Other Studies in Literary Psychology*. Lewiston: E. Mellen Press, 1992 (originally published in 1923).

Mehler, Irving M, *Effective Legal Communication*. Denver: Philgor Publishing Co., 1975.

Murphy, Peter W., *Teaching Evidence, Proof, and Facts: Providing a Background in Factual Analysis and Case Evaluation*, 51(4) J. Legal Educ. 568 (Dec. 2001).

Thomas R. Newman, *Writing Briefs—Statement of Facts*, 200 N.Y.L.J. 3 (1988).

O'Keefe, Daniel J., *Persuasion: Theory and Research*. Newbury Park, CA: Sage Publications, 2d ed. 2002.

Patrick, J. and Robert O. Evans, eds., *Style, Rhetoric, and Rhythm: Essays by Morris W. Croll*. Woodbridge, CT: Ox Bow Press, 1989.

Rieke, R.D. and M.O. Sillars, *Argumentation and the Decision Making Process.* Glenview, IL: Scott, Foresman and Co., 1984.

Rybacki, Karyn C. and Donald J. Rybacki, *Advocacy and Opposition: An Introduction to Argumentation.* Englewood Cliff, NJ: Prentice–Hall, 2d ed. 1991.

Sandell, Rolf. *Linguistic Style and Persuasion.* San Francisco: Academic Press, 1977.

Sebeok, Thomas A., ed., *Style in Language.* Cambridge, MA: M.I.T. Press, 1960.

Simons, Herbert W., *Persuasion: Understanding, Practice, and Analysis.* New York: Random House, 2d ed. 1986.

Yngve, V.H., *A Model and an Hypothesis for Language Structure,* 104 Proc.Am.Phil.Soc'y 444 (1960).

Chapter 9

DISCUSSION SECTIONS OF RESEARCH MEMOS

Most beginning legal writers learn to follow a basic format for writing office memos, including a format for organizing the discussion section.[1] This format helps the writer achieve a standardized quality, conforming to what is recognized as acceptable work. This approach provides a sound foundation for writing memos.

In this chapter, however, you will build on that foundation for organization. You will explore a variety of specialized approaches to accomplishing these tasks. Just as getting the basics involved learning some standard patterns of organization, building on those basics will involve learning a broader variety of organization patterns. In all these patterns, the goal is to communicate your point clearly.[2]

Organizing is a process of grouping and sequencing information so the reader can, while reading, re-assemble those pieces of information into the construction you want. Organization was the process that made it possible for engineers to disassemble the London Bridge into individual bricks, ship it halfway across the world, and re-assemble it in Arizona. Personnel in England labeled each brick and grouped the bricks so others could accurately re-assemble the bridge, brick by brick.

Similarly, organization is the process that enables you to divide and organize your reasoning into individual words, lay out those words sequentially, and have your reader re-assemble your words to understand your reasoning as he or she reads. Organization makes a huge difference in the speed and ease with which the reader can comprehend the content.

---

1. One format, IRAC, which stands for issue, rule, analysis or application, and conclusion, is often taught in first year legal writing courses. We have no objection to the IRAC method, but this chapter moves beyond that format.

2. Dean E. Hewes and Sally Planalp, *The Individual's Place in Communication Science* in *Handbook of Communication Science* 147 (C. Berger and S. Chaffee, eds. 1987).

In a case of bad construction the single items might be valuable, but the Reader was obliged to rearrange them.... It is like good food badly cooked.[3]

As this quotation suggests, poor organization often forces the reader to read a document several times, thinking about the information and recombining it in his or her mind until the logical connection of the individual points becomes clear. This consumes too much of the reader's time and energy, which is why poor large-scale organization is one of the most serious flaws a discussion section can have.[4] In contrast, logical organization increases readability by increasing clarity and conciseness. Readers can read and comprehend information much more readily when you organize it in a way that makes sense to them.[5]

Comprehension is also increased by using the readability techniques you have studied in earlier chapters, such as using clear sentence structures, crafting sentences of reasonable length, using familiar words, and handling lists carefully. When you write a discussion section, employ all the skills you have mastered in these areas.

To enhance your organizational skills, you will need to build your ability in several areas. First, you need to learn how to use various tools more effectively to organize your content logically. Next, you need to understand a few common organizational patterns that may help you organize more quickly. Third, you need to learn how to incorporate your reader's needs as you adapt your organization. Finally, you need to learn how to use writing techniques to communicate your organization effectively to your reader.

ORGANIZATION TOOLS AND THEIR USES

Organizing a complex body of material can feel overwhelming. Most writers, therefore, use organizational tools to help them experiment with different organizations, rather than writing multiple complete drafts, to see which organization is best. Two common tools are outlines and a combination of rough drafts and thesis sentences. Although other visual forms of organization are also possible, all these tools share a common purpose: helping the writer see the forest beyond each individual tree of information.

Outlines

Outlining is one organization tool you can use. Outlines at their most effective reveal four aspects of the content:

- the groups into which your content logically falls,
- how those groups are relevant to the main point of your document,

3. Vernon Lee, *The Handling of Words, and Other Studies in Literary Psychology* 11 (1992).

4. William L. Rivers, *Writing: Craft and Art* 15 (1975); Carl Bereiter and Marlene Scardamalia, *The Psychology of Written Composition* 156 (1987).

5. Hewes and Planalp, *supra* note 2, at 160.

- how each piece of information is relevant to one of those groups, and

- the best order to use when sequencing those groups.

To outline efficiently, avoid initially worrying about the order of your points. For example, do not use your word processor's automatic outline format on the first draft. Instead, begin writing your outline by listing the points you want to make, perhaps in a bullet point list. Adding numbers initially requires you to know the best order for the points before you have clarified what all those points will be; that is too much to reasonably expect from your first draft of the outline. Instead, focus initially on stating each point you need to support your answer. Focus on including everything needed.

After you have listed all the points you need to make, look at the length of the list you have created. If you have listed four or fewer points, then you have probably focused on your major points.

- duty

- breach

- harm

- proximate cause

Your next step is to fill out the support for each of those points, so that you have not glossed over essential steps in your reasoning.

duty

- general duty of due care

- duty to invitee

- foreseeable harm

If you have listed many details, usually eight or more, then you have probably focused on some specific supporting detail in your list.

- duty of due care to all

- duty to invitee applies to grocery stands

- foreseeable harm to slippery floor

- failed to clean up spilled vegetable oil

- average person knows oil makes surfaces slippery

- problem with plaintiff wearing high heels at the time

- farmer's market was there to sell food products

- sprained ankle not an unusual injury

- proximate cause

When you have listed many points, your next step is to check to see which points logically fit together because they address one larger issue. Group those points together, and then fill out more supporting points as needed.

duty

- general duty of care
- foreseeable harm caused by vegetable oil spill
- duty to invitee because selling vegetables on sidewalk

If you have listed five to seven points, you may have listed your major points, your supporting points, or a combination of both. You next need to check for logical groupings of the listed points and check to fill out needed supporting points, but you can complete these checks in either order with equal efficiency.

After you have listed and grouped the points you need to make, consider the order that will be most logical. Sometimes this will be apparent, and you can simply add numbers to the list you already created. Often, however, the law is more complex and multiple orders are possible. Nevertheless, you will be able to see the possibilities and choose one more quickly and accurately now that you have the overall content displayed on the page before you.

Outlines do not make organization automatic, only more apparent. Creating a successful outline will require many of the components of your general writing process: initial drafts, rewriting, and revision. The outline will not flow naturally from your brain to the paper, any more than the document itself would.

Rough Drafts and Thesis Sentences

If outlining does not work well for you, consider writing a rough draft first, and then identifying your main points and organizing the information you have drafted. Thesis sentences provide useful tools for doing this. After you have written out your thoughts completely in a rough draft, you can find potential thesis sentences by reading through your draft and highlighting sentences that state conclusions about how the content supports your conclusion. Pull out those statements and revise them enough to be sure they state the point you want to make. Then study the sentences, contemplating how those conclusions relate to each other logically. As you do this, you will begin grouping the thesis sentences, and discovering the logical order of sentences within each group. You will also discover the order of those larger groups within the whole.

As you read through your thesis sentences, determine which conclusions are logically parallel. For example, if a legal test has four elements, then your statement about those elements and your conclusions on the elements are logically parallel. Each parallel thesis sentence contributes equally to the same larger point: meeting all the elements of the test. Do not be confused by the fact that some of those elements are met much more easily than others. That is often true, and it simply means that you will spend less space discussing the easily met elements. Ease of proof does not, however, change the logical relationship of the points itself.

In your organization, points that are logically parallel should be expressed in some form of parallel structure. This allows the grammatical structure to reflect and clarify the substantive structure of your discussion. For example, if many of the elements of a cause of action are complex, you may list the elements of a rule in your overview paragraph and create a subheading for each element. You can then synthesize and present the law for each element and apply it in turn. If some policy or other overall issues needs to be discussed separately, you may group the claim into one large section, with each element as a subsection, and then cover the policy issue in a separate large section. If the elements can be handled more simply, their parallel importance may be reflected in parallel structure at a smaller scale, such as parallel sentence or phrase structure.

Also determine if any of the conclusions stated in your thesis sentences logically must precede others. For example, any issues about jurisdiction logically precede issues about substance. There is no reason to discuss how a court might rule on an issue before determining whether the court would even reach that issue. Within a cause of action, sometimes one element must logically proceed another. Thus in a tort action you would need to address whether a harm occurred before addressing whether the defendant's behavior caused that harm, because causation would be a moot point if no legally recognized harm occurred. Similarly, within an element, one aspect sometimes logically must precede another. Thus you would logically address the general rule related to an element before discussing whether your situation falls within an exception to that rule.

When one point logically precedes another, you must employ that logical order in your document. If you do not, the reader will be forced to read a complete paragraph or paragraph block wondering "What about ... ?" or "Why does this matter?" Or even "Why am I reading this?" These are not questions you want your busy legal reader to ask.

You may, however, cover logically precedent points quickly when it is possible to do so. Sometimes they can even be addressed and resolved in your overview paragraph. Often they can be addressed in one short paragraph, while more complex points will require longer paragraph blocks.

When your thesis sentences are neither logically parallel nor logically precedent to others, consider beginning with the points that explain your answer to the memo's question. Place sentences that dismiss unsuccessful theories, speculative arguments, and supplemental supporting theories later, after the determinative information is covered. When reading a discussion section, the legal reader wants to understand the support for your answer first. Then, after your position is supported, the reader may be interested in your reasons for not choosing alternative lines of reasoning, alternative legal theories, and other possibilities. Include this information when you believe that your reader would ask, "But what about ... ?" or "Why doesn't ... work?"

When you discuss legal points that you will ultimately dismiss, do not hide the ball. Let you reader know, by the wording of your thesis sentence, that you will ultimately find this legal approach unsuccessful.

> Although possible, a claim under the theory of intentional infliction of emotional harm would be more difficult to prove.

This early signal of your conclusion allows the reader to see where you are headed as he or she is reading the discussion. Then fully support your position by stating the legal test and explaining your analysis thoroughly, giving the reader all the information he or she needs to determine whether your position is valid.

Webs and Other Visual Tools

In contrast to outlines, which lay out content in a sequence, many newer organizational techniques lay out the content to show interrelationships without sequence. Different visual techniques allow you to begin by focusing on particular interrelationships between ideas. When using a Web, you draw lines between ideas that are logically connected, then study the connections to see how you may organize. Logic trees show how each piece of content is a subpart of other, larger pieces, but again sequence is not required.

These techniques can provide a useful starting point. They encourage flexibility and make it easier for you to start organizing. They can promote flexibility by helping you envision multiple connections, each of which might provide a different organization. They can make it easier to start writing because they do not require you to decide initially about the order, subordination, or other interrelationships you decide to use.

These tools, however, will not completely resolve all your organization questions. For example, at some point you must determine the order of your points because reading is ultimately linear. English readers read from left to right, top to bottom, phrase by phrase, through a document. Thus, you ultimately must funnel all your organizational decisions into one mix that determines the order of points in your documents. Similarly, you must communicate the logical relationship of your ideas through words, rather than pictures. You must therefore substitute transitions for the relationships communicated in your visual tool.

Organization helps you as well as your readers. As you determine your organization of the document, you are likely to find any existing errors in your logic. It is almost impossible to organize incorrect reasoning clearly. As you organize your discussion section, you check your logic. This self-checking mechanism can help you be more confident that your answer is correct. After all, your employer and your client are going to rely on your answer when making decisions about how to proceed. Providing them with a well-organized discussion section will make it easier to make those decisions.

COMMON PATTERNS FOR PRESENTING CONTENT

The tools discussed previously help you discover the organization that is innately logical for your content. Those tools help you see how sub-points relate to major points and help you determine what order is best for your content. Still, when you begin rewriting your rough draft, or writing a first draft from an outline, you may be unsure how to communicate your organization within the constraints of sentences and paragraphs. Fortunately, other tools come to your rescue at this point.

Your organization probably falls into one of the common patterns discussed below. Patterns help reduce stress and increase efficiency, and many experienced writers have one or two patterns they regularly use. But when one pattern does not suit the task at hand, be prepared to use another more appropriate pattern. Understanding the following patterns provides you with the resources to do this. The challenge for the advanced writer of discussion sections, then, is to choose the logically appropriate pattern, in light of its strengths and limitations.

Five common patterns are discussed below: the trial format, the analytical pattern, the bifurcated analysis, the educational approach, and weighing possibilities. Choose the one that seems clearest to you and use that as your usual pattern. But also review the other patterns, so you have options for organizing when your favorite pattern does not work.

Trial Pattern

In the trial pattern, the writer explains one party's position, then the other's, and then weighs the two to reach a result. This pattern, organized around the two sides, is often a natural choice for bench memos because it provides the reader with the foundation of both parties' arguments before moving into the writer's analysis. Because it does not organize around the abstract ideas of the law, it may seem simpler.

> *A possible defense is the argument that* Tommy should have known, even at his age, that ... because ....

> *The plaintiff, however, could respond that* this expectation is not reasonable because ....

> In conclusion, *a California court will probably decide that* Tommy's injuries were foreseeable because ....

The trial pattern has limitations that can create problems with more complex subjects. First, it can lengthen the presentation. If you present one position, you may need to refer to it when presenting the other side's position. This tends to add explanatory phrases that would be unneeded if the two positions were combined into one description of the law.

A more serious problem is that the comparison of the two positions, which in essence answers the issue, does not appear until after much preliminary information, so the reader gets the answer relatively late in the memo. This is not a problem when the comparison comes after one focused, brief description, as in the previous example. But if each position takes several paragraphs or pages to explain, a reader can get impatient or confused.

If you decide to use the trial format, you need to offset some of these disadvantages. First, add topic sentences to communicate the main points. Then organize the issues so the reader gets to the conclusion as soon as possible. Finally, add an overview paragraph at the beginning of the discussion to show the reader the larger picture of the differences between the two sides and to foreshadow the conclusion you will ultimately reach.

> The first question here is whether the corporation is entitled to a Class One or a Class Two hearing. If it is entitled to a Class One hearing, then the request for a hearing is premature. If, however, it is entitled to a Class Two hearing, then .... In this situation, a Class Two hearing is probably required because ....[6]

Alternatively, consider using one of the following organization patterns.

Analytical Pattern

A second possible pattern is the analytical one, which means organizing by subissue. This is often useful if the issue has clear elements. In this pattern, begin by identifying the subissues in an overview, which usually contains a list. Then discuss each subissue in turn. If several cases are needed to explain a listed item, organize them to work together to make a point, rather than organizing around the separate supporting cases or statutes. Similarly, if one case develops several of those listed points, split your presentation of the case, using the relevant parts of the case in each place needed.

The analytical pattern allows you to divide information into discrete points that can each be handled in a page or so, which means that the reader does not have to juggle many pieces of information at one time. In general, this is a readable and concise organization. It is helpful in situations that include disjunctive and conjunctive elements. For example, there may be three required elements, but two of them could be met in either of several ways. Dividing the text by elements permits you to address each element in relative isolation, so you can apply each element without worrying that the reader does not know where he or she is in the analysis.

The following example illustrates the use of organizing by elements in a more complex situation, where there are elements within elements, some disjunctive and some conjunctive. It also shows how to organize one case to support several points. The memo discusses how a group of nonprofit organizations can argue that a house in a single-family residential area should be rezoned to provide group housing for the Children with AIDS Project (CAP). The group reasons that this is an allowable use of spot zoning (rezoning one parcel of land without changing the

6. To help you focus on the organization structure, this chapter's remaining exam-   ples omit much of the specific context.

zoning of the surrounding area). The segment begins in the middle of the memo, after the writer has established that spot zoning is the applicable theory.

Introductory Paragraph

Spot zoning is legal in Missouri if it is in the public interest and is not solely for the property owner's benefit. *Ballenger* .... In addition, spot zoning may be legal if it satisfies one of the following three criteria. First, spot zoning may be legal if it .... *Howard* .... Second, spot zoning may be legal if .... *Eggebeen* .... Third, spot zoning may be legal if .... *Ballenger* .... The CAP spot zoning is legal because ... , ... , and ....

Thesis Sentences for Synthesis of First Point of Law

Spot zoning is legal if it is done in the public interest and is not solely for the benefit of the property owner. *Ballenger* ....

Spot zoning is legal if it is in the public interest, even if .... *Howard* ....

Spot zoning has been found illegal, however, when it is solely for the benefit of the property owner. *Cushman* .... In *Cushman,* ....

Thesis Sentences for Application of First Point of Law

Under this law, CAP's zoning is in the public interest. CAP sought to rezone to ....

CAP can argue that its rezoning request will benefit the public by ....

Interim Overview of Next Point of Law, With Its Three Subpoints

Spot zoning also may be judged legal if one of the following three criteria are met: (1) ... , (2) ... , and (3) ....

Thesis Sentences for Synthesis and Application of First Subpoint of Law

Applying the first criterion, the court stated that .... *Howard* ....

Under this criterion, spot zoning is illegal if it does not ... , even if rezoning .... *Cushman* .... In *Cushman,* .... The court held this was illegal spot zoning because ....

Zoning for CAP meets this criterion because it is consistent with ....

Thesis Sentences for Synthesis and Application of Second Subpoint of Law

The second of the three criteria by which spot zoning may be judged legal is whether .... *Eggebeen* ....

Under this criteria, CAP ....

Thesis Sentences for Synthesis and Application of Third Subpoint of Law

> The third additional criterion by which spot zoning may be judged legal is whether . . . . *Ballenger* . . . .

> As in *Ballenger,* CAP's zoning is legal because . . . .

The analytical pattern has its limitations as well. It can be cumbersome when several elements need little discussion, because the structure may require too many transitions to make the organization clear. It may also be cumbersome when one case is being used for several elements, leading you to repeat the same facts or holdings too much. In this situation, you might be self-conscious about restating all the information just stated for a previous element; yet you know omitting it would delete logically necessary steps unless the previous use is close by and the reader can likely remember the needed details. Additionally, this pattern may not help when several elements overlap or when your question concerns which set of criteria should be applied.

In short, you may find yourself facing an organizational dilemma: a choice between a boring and awkward structure, or a structure that provides inadequate support. At that point, consider other possible patterns.

Bifurcated Pattern

A third organizational option, the bifurcated pattern, combines the trial pattern and the analytical pattern, and can be useful for more complex discussions that the previous two patterns cannot handle well. This pattern divides the discussion of the issue into parts (elements, subquestions, etc.), then for each part discusses first one side, then the other, and finally weighs the two. In essence, this pattern inserts the trial pattern within a looser version of the analytic pattern.

Bifurcated analysis lets the reader focus on one task at a time, while still allowing the integration of a complex set of ideas. In this approach, first organize the larger issue into subissues and explain in an overview how the subissues fit together.

> The test for superseding cause has two prongs, each focusing on a different aspect of foreseeability: (1) . . . and (2). . . . The first prong of the test focuses on . . . . The second prong. . . .

After this overview, focus on each subissue separately, discussing each subissue individually as in the trial format. Throughout the explanation of the law, use transitions and interim summaries to remind the reader where he or she is in the larger analytical framework.

> The test for superseding cause has two prongs, each focusing on a different aspect of foreseeability: (1) . . . and (2) . . . .

> The first prong of the test focuses on the foreseeability of the intervening act. An intervening act that is . . . satisfies this prong.

> The plaintiff could argue that the District should have foreseen
> . . . .
>
> The defendant, however, can argue that . . . .
>
> In conclusion, the court will probably decide . . . .
>
> The second prong of the superseding cause test . . . .
>
> The plaintiff can meet this prong by . . . .
>
> The defendant may respond that . . . .
>
> The plaintiff, however, could overcome this argument because
> . . . .
>
> In conclusion, the court will probably decide . . . .

Step by step, the reader moves through an organization that is sufficiently complex to communicate the logic of the analysis and yet sufficiently clear to be understood quickly. This organization can be presented without the sometimes tedious references to "plaintiff" and "defendant" for a more concise discussion that focuses on the law, rather than who is making which argument.

Educational Pattern

In the educational pattern, you begin by explaining to the reader that a broader understanding of the law is necessary to understand how that law will be applied. After you have convinced the reader that this education is necessary, you explain your law, whether it involves the development of a legal theory or a rule through a line of cases. You then apply that law to the current issue.

This pattern can be useful when the historical development is central to the reasoning you are presenting. It can also teach the reader the basics of a specialized area of law that is unfamiliar to the reader.

The following example comes from an unusually complicated research question that required a lengthy answer. To answer the question, the writer applied a sophisticated analysis to various interpretations of a "termination liability provision" within one title of a complicated body of law, the Employee Retirement Income Security Act (ERISA). But first, the writer showed the reader where this provision fit in the larger context of the law, because that larger context was critical to the later analysis.

> The court's answer to this issue will depend on its interpretation of the meaning of a "termination liability provision" in Title IV of the Employee Retirement Income Security Act (ERISA). When interpreting that provision, the court will look to the goals the Act was intended to fulfill.
>
> ERISA's primary goals are twofold: (1) . . . and (2) . . . . ERISA contains four titles; each is designed to correct problems that had previously resulted in . . . . Title I established . . . . Title II established . . . . Title III imposed . . . . Title IV . . . .

To encourage pension plan growth, ERISA . . . . Implicit in the statutory scheme of Titles I through III is . . . . Employee interests are protected by the requirements in Titles I through III, and as part of . . . .

Although ERISA's statutory language does not directly address . . . , Title IV of ERISA does . . . .

This organization is not useful, however, if this full development is unneeded, because the reader does not want to learn a lot of unneeded law. Many beginning legal writers mistakenly include this background information, even when it is unneeded, because they want to share all their research or knowledge with the reader. Their reader, however, is only concerned with how the law applies to a specific set of facts. But if a historical overview or explanation is needed to help the reader understand that application, this organization is effective.

Weighing Possibilities Pattern

A final organizing pattern, weighing possibilities, is useful when the heart of the issue is how two large bodies of information as a whole interact, rather than how they compare on particular points. This may occur when the issue will be resolved based on broad policy issues, rather than specific applications of the law. It is also likely to arise when the question is neither whether nor how the law applies, but rather which law applies. This pattern is complex, but that very complexity facilitates understanding when simpler patterns are inadequate.

Begin with an overview of the problem explaining why the issue boils down to how two bodies of information or theories interact. This may seem unusual because you are explaining the why before the what. Yet the order is logical because the reader needs to know why presenting this law is necessary. At this point, let the reader know what position you think will prevail and perhaps hint at your ultimate reasons, but do not go into those reasons in detail. By using this structure, you are signaling that the reader cannot fully understand the reasoning without the background, so it would be futile to present it.

After introducing the content and structure of your analysis, discuss one of the possible theories or policies and explain the result if that theory or policy prevails. Then take the other and play that one out. Sometimes one of your possibilities blends several theories or policies. If so, explain that blend and its result. After you have presented each possibility separately, you are ready to begin weighing them.

To do this, you will compare options, often organizing in ways similar to those you use when comparing cases. As part of your comparison, explain thoroughly the reasoning that led you, step by step, to your conclusion. If you weighed one policy against another, state that and then explain how you reached your conclusion. Finally, summarize your comparison section. You return, naturally, to restating the point you made in the overview, but stating it with more detail and elaboration now that the reader understands the context. This becomes a natural conclusion for the issue, and the organization, even though protracted and complex, seems intuitively clear.

These five patterns provide you with organizational tools for planning the large-scale organization of your discussion section. You are likely to develop one or two favorite patterns that you use most frequently. The remaining patterns can be reserve ideas that you can use when your favorite patterns do not work. Use these patterns as tools, rather than rules, adjusting the patterns as the logic of your law dictates, until you find an organization that is clear and understandable to your reader, yet accurately reflects the logic of the law you are presenting.

ADAPTING YOUR CONTENT FOR YOUR READER

When choosing what content to include, you begin by thinking about the information needed to resolve the question, and your organization is based on your research and your understanding of that information. During this process, you first will use one or more of the organizational tools discussed earlier, and then will use one of the organizational patterns previously discussed.

Nevertheless, some organizational questions will remain. Your answer to these final questions will be determined by the reader's needs or preferences, rather than the content itself. Two common questions that you will resolve by considering your reader are "how thorough should the explanation of the reasoning be?" and "should you raise other issues not initially included in your project?" You will determine these questions by contemplating your reader's needs, rather than focusing solely on your research.

When researching a question for a senior partner or for a judge, you usually feel two contradictory pressures: one for doing a thorough job and one for getting done in the allotted time. The pressure for thoroughness comes from your desire to impress the boss and do a good job. The pressure for efficiency is also immediate. Conflict is likely. Fortunately, some of the thinking necessary to resolve this conflict may be done once in general, rather than done for each research assignment. Because you will often write more than once for the same reader, you can develop a default model for memos to that reader, varying the model only as the situation warrants.[7] These specialized models for memo discussion sections function like the form clauses you developed for contracts because you will also use them repeatedly when writing memos. You can also adapt the writing system you have been developing since Chapter 2 to create a helpful routine for organizing.

Central to your development of this default model is the question of what your reader wants from the memo.[8] All readers have an optimum

7. Just as a computer program has a default setting that it chooses unless told to do otherwise, you can have a default pattern of organization that you choose unless circumstances dictate a change.

8. Joseph N. Cappella, *Interpersonal Communication: Definitions and Fundamental Questions* in *Handbook of Communication Science* 212 (C. Berger and S. Chaffee, eds. 1987).

amount of information they find desirable,[9] but what that amount is varies from one reader to another. For example, some attorneys value conciseness greatly and want a memo to state the points generally, not dwelling on specifics or supporting details. Others want more detail and more support. After considering these preferences, you will be able to choose the amount of detail and support that each attorney wants without compromising the quality of the conclusions you reach. The following paragraphs sketch other common preferences legal readers have and outline ways you can organize to provide those readers with effective discussion sections.

Some attorneys prefer for clerks or associates to write a cut-and-paste memo, which means including long passages quoted from the cases and statutes they have found to be relevant. This sometimes happens because the attorney may not fully trust the analysis to the clerk or associate and may prefer to analyze the law personally. This approach may not reflect a negative view of the writer's personal abilities, but rather how the attorney likes to work. This attorney wants the writer to complete the research and organize it, but leave the task of making conclusions to him or her.

For this attorney, your main writing task will be to provide clear, concise signals that show the purpose of each inserted quotation. One way to do this is to explain why the quotation is included. For example, if a case has been reversed but is quoted to develop some needed history about the issue, let the reader know that. Alternatively, if the case is the one most applicable to the client's situation, state that. These signals, which you can communicate in one sentence, are a tremendous help to the reader, who can then adjust his or her reading to obtain the information most efficiently. Readers who want cut-and-paste memos may want to see the extended quotation, but may not need to read all of it.

Other attorneys have the opposite view, looking with disgust at pages with long passages of single-spaced, indented text. These readers view the major function of the memo to be analysis and application of the research, and they do not expect to do this work themselves. For these attorneys, include quotations only when the particular language is central to your point or when it is so well stated that it will be pleasant reading for your reader. One way to determine when to include a quotation in this circumstance is to consider whether you would quote it in a brief. If so, you probably should include it in the memo. If not, you probably should paraphrase it and include a pinpoint citation instead.

---

9. Their response can be analogized to that of consumers in general. One study in consumer research found that, when the amount of information about a product increases, the consumer will increase the time spent studying that information, but only up to a point. After that point, the consumer's response to more information is to spend less time studying the information, not more. (Jacoby, Speloler, and Knon, 1974). Scott Ward, *Consumer Behavior* in *Handbook of Communication Science* 659 (C. Berger and S. Chaffee, eds. 1987).

Most attorneys fall between these extremes. In addition to wanting the writer to analyze and apply the law, these attorneys want the writer to communicate the answer quickly, stating it up front followed by a quick, clear explanation of the reasoning behind it. The attorney does not want to be instructed on the law, nor does he or she want long quotes. The attorney wants an answer that provides a clear framework for the memo, so he or she can evaluate the following support. This attorney does not want to read the history behind the law unless and until it is relevant. He or she does not want to follow the complexities of a cited case unless and until the need to understand those complexities is apparent.

For this attorney, boil down the information. This means conciseness, but it also means focus. Rather than leading your reader through each step of your research or analysis, digest the research for the reader and present your findings as clearly and directly as possible. State the point of each section and paragraph as quickly as possible.

Also consider whether your reader will question you about other alternatives beyond those covered in the memo. The reader wants a concise memo focused on the issues most likely to arise, but he or she expects you to be prepared to address other possibilities if asked. In this situation, you may want to note your thoughts on those possibilities in a separate memo to your file. You can then discuss the matters intelligently if they do arise. For example, as you eliminate unworkable theories, jot down your reasons for the theory not working and keep these notes in your file. Specifically, if you wrote a memo determining that settlement should be pursued because litigation would not be worth the expense, list the possible theories for litigation but explain why settlement is preferable.

In your own notes, prepare to explain each possible approach to litigation. This way you can develop these approaches without too much work if a senior partner asks you to pursue them. In contrast, if you determine that a theory will not succeed but you expect that the answer will surprise the reader, include the theory in your discussion and explain your conclusion to the reader.

Also consider tone. Some readers prefer a down-to-earth tone, and a straightforward opening can sharpen the clarity of the whole memo for these readers. For example, consider the following opening sentence from a memo.

This case is far less complicated than the size of the complaint would indicate.

These sentences may build on the style you developed for your objective statement of facts.

Develop a default model adapted to your reader. If you have different readers, develop different models. As soon as you start a job, begin working out these default models for memos, and refine them as you receive feedback from each reader.

PRESENTING YOUR ORGANIZED CONTENT

After you have chosen and organized your overall discussion, revise your draft to be sure that you have communicated your organization and content clearly. This organization occurs at multiple levels:

- large-scale organization of the whole discussion section and the content under each sub-heading;

- mid-scale organization of the presentation of the law (often called synthesis), the application of that law, and the presentation of individual cases; and

- small-scale organization of each paragraph and each sentence.

Large-Scale Organization of the Discussion Section

After you have determined your organization and after you have written a complete draft, you need to check to be sure you have communicated your organization clearly. You now understand your content, but you need to see how a reader, approaching the content without that background, will read your discussion. Assessing organizational clarity can be surprisingly difficult when you are so familiar with the content.

A few technical checks, however, can help you see the document afresh. First, read the headings in your discussion separately. They should be parallel in logic, grammar, and format.

I. Duty to Prevent Foreseeable Injury

II. Duty to Exercise Due Care

rather than

I. Duty to Prevent Foreseeable Injury

II. Due Care

or

I. Preventing Foreseeable Injury

II. Duty for Due Care

The headings, if read aloud, should communicate not only the nature of your discussion section's largest divisions, but also how those divisions fit together into the whole. After checking headings, you need to check the flow of the document from point to point under those headings.

A useful technique for checking this is to print up a copy of the document and highlight the first line of every paragraph. Then read those lines aloud, one after the other. If the document flows well, you will hear the logic flowing from paragraph to paragraph, even when reading only the first line of each paragraph. Often a key term from the previous paragraph will re-appear in the opening sentence of the following paragraph. Introductory phrases at the beginning of a paragraph will summarize the previous paragraph's point, while the subject and verb following that introductory phrase will introduce the new point to be supported in this paragraph. Two paragraphs containing logically parallel points will be phrased in parallel structure. In short, the structure of each paragraph's opening sentence will communicate how that paragraph fits into the larger structure of the document. Like street signs at every corner, these consistent references help the reader remember where he or she is.

Mid–Scale Organization of the Law and Application

Just as a staircase provides the structure to lead a person up from the foundation to the next level by a series of steps, mid-scale organization provides the structure for your reader to move from your legal support to your conclusion by a series of logical steps. To provide this structure for each legal rule or element you need, you must construct three elements:

- the legal *foundation* for your point,

- the logical *steps* in your reasoning that arise from the foundation, and

- the *landing* leading from that point to the next point to be developed.[10]

The Legal Foundation

Presenting the legal foundation is basically a task in expository writing,[11] explaining the law that you will use to resolve the question at hand. It includes (1) a statement of the legal principle or rule that you will apply later and a citation to that rule, (2) the facts that are critical for interpreting that rule, (3) a statement of how courts have used the rule to resolve this issue in the past, and (4) an explanation of the reasoning the court used when applying the rule. Sometimes, the logical foundation is rather straightforward, as in the following example.

> The Wisconsin Court of Appeals held that "highways" as used in the Wisconsin highway defects statute included sidewalks. *Bystery* .... In *Bystery,* the plaintiff was injured when .... The court decided that a village could be liable ... if the facts established .... The court reasoned that it was legislative policy that ....

Sometimes, however, the rule cannot be stated so succinctly.

> The third requirement to obtain a temporary injunction is that the plaintiff must show .... When the damages are ... , the courts will not grant a temporary injunction. *Werner v. Grootemaat* .... In

---

10. Some of you have used the IRAC formula (Issue, Rule, Application, and Conclusion) for organization at this level. This way of looking at the organization does not contradict that formula, but presents an alternative way to view what is basically the same logical process. Similarly, this is an alternative approach to the Toulmin model, which is used by Karyn C. Rybacki and Donald J. Rybacki in *Advocacy and Opposition: An Introduction to Argumentation* (1991).

11. In other words, it presents and explains ideas, rather than telling a story (narrative).

Werner, the plaintiffs were . . . . The court denied the injunction because . . . .

Conversely, when an action for damages would not afford the plaintiff relief from the injury, there is no adequate remedy at law. *American Mutual Liability Insurance Co. v. Fisher* . . . . In *American Mutual,* the appellant-defendants were trying to terminate a permanent injunction. The appellants argued that . . . . The Court, however, reasoned that . . . . Therefore, the court affirmed the injunction because . . . .

In a bench memo written for a judge about a case to be reviewed, often the foundation is actually the arguments made by the parties.

Patient and Doctor Service (PDS) is arguing that Stat. 636.10(1) does not apply to them. The statute requires . . . . But PDS argues that . . . .

Your reasoning rests on this foundation, so it must be solid. Common errors here are for writers to omit needed reasoning or to include unneeded detail that obscures the main point. To avoid these problems, keep the focus on the issue at hand. For example, if the focus of your issue was the point stated in the topic sentence of the following paragraph, you would focus on that aspect of the case. The following paragraph illustrates this by focusing on the concept of "subjective intent."

> **The recreational status of an activity, and therefore whether immunity attaches, is not based upon subjective intent.** *Bystery* **.... In that case, Ann Bystery was bicycling on a Sauk City sidewalk and suffered injuries when her bike overturned. Although Bystery's travel was recreational, the court reasoned that the legislature did not intend for immunity to be determined by the specific motivation for the activity. If it had so intended, liability would turn solely on the subjective intent of the actor.** *Id.* **Instead, the court reasoned that bicycling is generally recreational, and for that reason Bystery's activity was recreational.**

Avoid rambling to related-but-distinct points, as in the following, less focused version.

The recreational status of an activity is based on the nature of the activity rather than the actor's subjective intent. *Bystery* . . . . Ann Bystery was bicycling on a Sauk City sidewalk and suffered injuries when her bike overturned. The court reasoned that the legislature did not intend for immunity to apply whenever the activity was recreational, for liability would then turn solely on the subjective intent of the actor. *Id. The legislature created the immunity statute to promote the recreational use of property by encouraging owners to permit access without fear of liability. Id.* at 613. Bicycling is generally recreational and, therefore, Bystery's activity was recreational. The court held that Bystery's activity was recreational, regardless of her subjective intent.

Sometimes it is easier to determine how much detail to include about a case after you have written the application of that case to your facts. What you include in your presentation of the case depends on what you plan to do with that case later. If you are using reasoning from the precedent case to resolve your question, then your presentation of that case must explain that reasoning and show how it was applied by the precedent court. If you have compared or distinguished specific facts of your case to facts of the precedent case, then you must explain why those facts are important when initially presenting the precedent case. If you are applying policy from the precedent case, then you must establish that this policy was a deciding factor for the court in the precedent case.

When presenting any precedent or supporting law, give the reader enough information to convince him or her that your understanding of the precedent, the understanding you will later apply to your issue, is in fact correct. Your goal is not to teach the reader about the case itself, but to teach the reader about the common law you will be using. Thus one presentation of a case may include few facts but many sentences about the court's reasoning when you are using the broader reasoning later. Another presentation may include procedural details because you will distinguish your case based on procedural differences. If you remain focused on your point about the law, rather than on the precedent case itself, you will find it easier to determine what information you need to include.

The foundation gives the reader the information he or she needs to understand the reasoning that follows and to have confidence in its reliability. For this part of your presentation, focus on giving the reader all the important information and omit information unrelated to the point being made here.

The Logical Steps That Explain Your Reasoning

The second part of your discussion involves taking the reader through your reasoning step by step. At this stage, apply the rule stated in the foundation to the facts of your case and lead your reader through its application. The rhetorical stance of this paragraph is somewhat different from the preceding legal foundation, and this portion usually begins in a new paragraph.

[the foundation]

The Wisconsin Court of Appeals held that "highways," as used in the Wisconsin highway defects statute, included sidewalks. *Bystery* .... In *Bystery,* the plaintiff was injured when the bicycle she was riding overturned when it struck an uneven portion of a sidewalk. The court decided that the village may be liable for her injury under the Wisconsin highway defects statute. The court reasoned that it has been legislative policy that "municipalities are to keep their highways and sidewalks in repair and are liable for injuries caused by want of repair and dangerous conditions." *Id.*

[the steps]

In our case, pedestrians routinely used the footpath to travel between a large residential area and a small commercial district. Therefore, the footpath performed the function of a sidewalk and should be included in the definition of a highway, just as the concrete sidewalk in *Bystery* was included. Given the policy of encouraging cities to keep sidewalks in repair and free of dangerous conditions, the court should decide that it would be appropriate for the city to be liable for any dangerous conditions allowed to exist on the footpath.

You must discern the essential logical steps and include all of them. For example, the following paragraph omits a logical step that the revision includes.

Just as a homeowner's electrocution was the precise injury foreseeable due to SPG & E's negligence, a child being hit by a car while walking home from school was the precise injury foreseeable from the District's negligence in not informing parents of the school's early closing. Tommy's being hit by a car then is the type of injury that could be foreseen as a result of the District's negligence.

In contrast, the following revision includes the needed logical steps without adding unnecessary information.

Just as a homeowner's electrocution was the precise injury foreseeable due to SPG & E's negligence, a child being hit by a car while walking home from school was the precise injury foreseeable from the District's negligence in not informing parents of the school's early closing. *Three miles is a long way for a child to walk, especially when alone and for the first time.* **A child being hit by a car then is the type of injury that could be foreseen as a result of the District's negligence.**

When writing the logical steps leading from your legal foundation to your conclusion, focus on including each step and stating it clearly. One way to clarify these steps is to use transitions ("thus," "as a result,"), but a subtler technique is to repeat sentence structure or key words, or both. These techniques allow you to show how the logical progression arises from the content itself.

The Landing

The landing, or the concluding statement, states how the law applies to your fact situation. This statement is also the platform leading to the next point. This element tells the reader the significance of the logic concerning the broader issue you are addressing in that section of the memo. It answers the question, "So what?" that appears in the reader's mind after he or she has made the effort to follow your reasoning. For example, the final sentence of the following example finishes the reasoning.

> A child being hit by a car then is the type of injury that could be foreseen as a result of the District's negligence. *Thus the District is liable for Tommy's injuries.*

You may find it useful to use the image of foundation, steps, and landing to make sure that you have included all the necessary logical steps when explaining your reasoning. Having made sure that your reasoning moves logically, you can now focus on the organization of individual paragraphs and sentences.

Small-Scale Organization: Paragraphs and Sentences

Within each paragraph, your organization needs to be unified in two ways. First, all the sentences in the paragraph need to contribute information that supports the point of the paragraph, as it is expressed in your thesis sentence. Second, each sentence needs to logically follow the preceding sentence and lead to the subsequent sentence. When each of these qualities is attained, you will achieve the smooth logical flow that communicates clearly how the paragraph works together as a unit.

This unity is probably best achieved during revision, after you have clarified and ordered your thesis sentences. At this stage of the writing process, you can focus on one paragraph at a time without fear of losing the overall focus of the document. In an earlier review, you read the first line of each of your paragraphs to check the overall logical flow. In this review, you will compare those same first lines with the text in the paragraph following each line. Just as you looked for important terms to be repeated from one opening sentence to the next, you now look for important terms from the previous sentence to reappear in the beginning of the next sentence.

> Recently, courts have *interpreted* this statute to exclude general threats made between individuals during an argument. This broader *interpretation* stems from the courts' understanding of the legislative *purpose*. That *purpose* was *not to prosecute* people for threatening *statements* they made in a moment of anger, *but to prosecute* people for *statements* made when planning acts of terrorism, even when they have not succeeded in carrying out those acts.

Like Tarzan swinging through the jungle from vine to vine, your logic swings from idea to idea, advancing with each swing toward your conclusion.

Sentence structure itself helps the reader understand the unity and logical flow of your paragraphs. You can make use of sentence structure by phrasing your sentences so the subject and verb carry important meaning; this puts the important meaning of the sentence in the grammatically important part of the sentence. For example, consider the subjects, verbs, and objects in the previous example. These words themselves read almost like a syllogism, communicating the logical progression at the heart of the paragraph.

courts have *interpreted* statute

interpretation stems from *purpose*

purpose was not to prosecute ... but to prosecute

As you discern the logical connections between sentences and use key words to communicate that connection, you can also help your reader glide from connection to connection by careful use of transitions. Transitions make it easier for the reader to follow your logical path by signaling the nature of the next logical step you are taking. For example, "not ... but" signals a key contrast in the previous example. Other common examples include "however," which signals the introduction of a counter point, and "furthermore," which signals that the point to come is perhaps more persuasive than the one just completed. "If," one of the smallest words in the language, sends a precise and complex signal when it begins a sentence; "If" at the beginning of a sentence signals that the logical consequence of a situation will be stated after that particular situation has been described. In light of this word's efficient and precise meaning, it is no wonder that "if" is used so frequently in legal writing.

The small-scale tools used in paragraph and sentence organization are more powerful than most legal writers realize. These tools often seem trite to adult writers; thesis sentences, transitions, and grammatically complete sentences are the concepts taught in middle school. Taught, perhaps, but not mastered. Mastery comes not through memorizing the techniques explained in this chapter, but through practice and understanding. But it is worth the effort. When you understand how English sentences and paragraphs affect your reader's understanding of content, you understand how to communicate your ideas in writing.

CONCLUSION

Organization is the driving force behind a great discussion section, governing choices you make in choice of supporting content, overall organization, headings, and every aspect of writing down to the construction of a sentence. This chapter has provided you with guidance on how to improve your organization at all those levels.

The guidelines for organization in this chapter are not, however, provided to set out rules for every organizational step, however. Instead, they provide you with a wide range of tools you can use when organization decisions become difficult, or when the expression of your organization is less than clear. Keep this information as a resource, and consult it when you have organization questions. Over time, many of the techniques will become second nature to you, and organization will become a more natural, comfortable process.

Exercise 1

Compare the organization of the discussion sections of several research memos written by yourself or another. Determine which organizational patterns the memos use. Choosing one of those examples, sketch out an organization of the same content using two different patterns. Compare the different patterns, then determine which works best, and why it works.

Exercise 2

The following statute includes topics in an illogical order. To practice applying your general organization skills, re-group the statute's topics logically, determining which points are logical subpoints of others. Then choose a logical order for your groups. Sketch out the organization you think would be more logical, and then compare your organization with those of two other students.

Anystate Statutes

Chapter 80 on Laying Highways.

Section

80.01.   Creation, Alteration and Validation of Highways.
80.02.   Town Highways; Petition to Lay, Alter or Discontinue.
80.02.5 Highways Abutted by State Park Lands; Discontinuance or Relocation.
80.03.   Restrictions on Condemning for Town Highways.
80.04.   When Supervisor Disqualified; Vacancies.
80.05.   Notice of Meeting; Service and Publication.
80.06.   Proceedings After Notice.
80.07.   Order; Survey; Award; Recording; Presumptions.
80.08.   Width of Highways.
80.09.   Damages; Agreement, Award.
80.10.   Considerations Affecting Damages.
80.11.   Highways On and Across Town Lines.
80.12.   Highways On and Across Town and Municipal Boundaries.
80.12.5 Highways and Bridges on State Boundaries.
80.13.   Land Excluded From Highway.
80.14.   Highway From Shut–Off Land Through Adjoining Town.
80.15.   Highway to Islands in Mississippi River.
80.16.   Shut–Off School Buildings; How Laid.
80.17.   Appeal From Highway Order.
80.18.   Bonds; Service of Notice.
80.19.   Commissioners, How Selected.
80.20.   Commissioners; Fees; Papers Where Filed.
80.21.   Proceedings on Reversal.
80.22.   Determination Final for a Year Unless Appealed.
80.23.   Removal of Fences From Highway; Notice.
80.24.   Appeal From Award of Damages by Owner.
80.25.   Taxpayer May Appeal; Service of Notice.

Section

Assignment 1

Write the rest of the research memo about Jamie Blottner's situation. For the relevant facts and law, see Assignment 1 in Chapter 6.

Assignment 2

Your senior partner, Mr. Yu, has asked you to write the rest of the research memo in Cliff Claussen's situation. See Assignment 2 in Chapter 6 and Assignment 2 in Chapter 7 for the relevant information.

BIBLIOGRAPHY

Beardsley, Monroe C., *Thinking Straight: Principles of Reasoning for Readers and Writers.* Englewood Cliffs, NJ: Prentice–Hall, Inc., 4th ed. 1975.

Bereiter, Carl and Marlene Scardamalia, *The Psychology of Written Composition.* Mahwah, NJ: Lawrence Erlbaum Associates, 1987.

Berger, Charles R. and Steven H. Chaffee, eds., *Handbook of Communication Science.* Newbury Park, CA: Sage Publications, 1987.

Brannon, Lil, Melinda Knight, and Vara Neverow–Turk, *Writers Writing.* Montclair, NJ: Boynton/Cook Publishers, Inc., 1982.

Eisenberg, Anne, *Effective Technical Communication.* New York: McGraw–Hill, 2d ed. 1992.

Houp, Kenneth W., and Thomas E. Pearsall, *Reporting Technical Information.* New York: Oxford University Press, 10th ed. 2002.

Lannon, John M., *Technical Writing.* New York: Longman, 8th ed. 2000.

Lee, Vernon, *The Handling of Words, and Other Studies in Literary Psychology*. Lewiston: E Mellon Press, 1992 (originally published in 1923).

Rivers, William L., *Writing: Craft and Art*. Englewood Cliff, NJ: Prentice–Hall, Inc., 1975.

Rybacki, Karyn C. and Donald J. Rybacki, *Advocacy and Oppositions: An Introduction to Argumentation*. Englewood Cliff, NJ: Prentice–Hall, 2d ed. 1991.

Chapter 10

ARGUMENT SECTIONS

When many legal writers think of writing a brief,[1] they think of presenting their adversarial position to defeat the opponent's logic. They organize their argument as they would for a debate[2] and treat the brief as different from a memo. They also view the reader's role as passive, more like an audience than a participant. But the changes from writing an objective memo to writing a persuasive brief are subtler than this.

For this reason, this chapter focuses on the many smaller adjustments made when moving from objective to persuasive writing. It does not address new aspects of writing, but instead explains additions and changes you can make to the techniques you learned in the previous chapters.

PURPOSE AND FOCUS

The purpose of a brief, like that of a memo, is helping a busy reader decide how to resolve a problem. Your reader is a judge who, like the attorney reading your memo, has a job to do. The reader is actively involved[3] and has a question he or she must answer. The purpose of the argument section is to explain why the answer you propose is the correct one under the law. You are not writing as the judge's adversary, and you are not writing to debate with the opposing attorney, as you might do in a hearing before the judge.

To fulfill this purpose, focus on your role as that of an advisor or expert helping the judge solve this problem, rather than focusing on the adversarial role.[4] Think about the questions that judge will address as he

---

1. This book uses "brief" to include what is called in some states "memorandum of points and authorities."

2. "Students or young lawyers may have the impression from their own experience that an oral or written argument is a kind of verbal combat, whereas it is in fact an exercise in artful salesmanship." Girvan Peck, *Writing Persuasive Briefs* xv (1984).

3. Daniel O'Keefe, *Persuasion: Theory and Research* (2d ed. 2002).

4. "Unless you settle first the questions that are on your readers' minds, they won't listen to a thing you want to say." Eugene R. Hammond, *Critical Thinking, Thoughtful Writing* 80 (2d ed. 1989) (quoting Herbert Miller of the Nuclear Regulatory Commission). *See also,* Rolf Sandell, *Linguistic Style and Persuasion* 229–36 (1977).

or she decides the case. As you write a brief, remember this focus when choosing what content to include, what arguments to make, and how to order the arguments you do make. Consider how to help your reader and in the process help your client.[5]

When you focus on helping the reader make a decision, you will begin making subtle shifts in your organization, and your thesis sentences will reflect these shifts. For example, the following series of thesis sentences gives the reader the information he or she needs to decide the issue. The thesis sentences sound similar to those of a discussion section, but they communicate confidence in the correctness of the writer's position.

> **The test for determining whether a document is subject to the qualified immunity from discovery under the work product rule is whether** . . . .

> **This document meets this test** . . . . **Thus** . . . .

> **To compel production of material subject to qualified immunity, defendant debtors must at least make a showing of** . . . .

> **Production of this document is not, therefore, compulsory.**

In contrast, the following passage organizes around the writer's debate with another attorney. This creates a defensive tone, rather than a confident one. It also makes the organization of the writer's own line of reasoning more obscure. The reader has to infer the plaintiff's opinion from the response to the defendant's position.

> The defendant argues that the documents are discoverable.

> Despite their extensive arguments, the defendant has failed to show the necessity of obtaining the requested documents.

> The defendant has not shown that the documents requested do not meet the test for determining qualified immunity, so the documents should not be discoverable.

> The defendant thus failed again to meet the required standard.

In these thesis sentences, the plaintiff has yielded the stage to the defendant. This is not desirable.

The writer's awareness of the purpose of the argument above is apparent in the subjects and verbs the writer uses in the thesis sentences.

Advisory Purpose	Adversarial Purpose
the test is	defendant's attorneys argue
this document meets the test	defendant's attorneys have failed to show

---

5. For discussion of individual persuasion processes and the way they are affected by the style of the persuasive message, *see id.* at 110–43.

to compel production, debtors must make a showing of production is not, therefore, compulsory	defendant has not shown defendant thus failed again

The focus in the more effective version is primarily on persuading the reader that the writer's position is valid. Although doing this often entails explaining why the opposition's position is invalid, the writer must maintain a focus on the merit of his or her position, not on the weakness of the opposition's.

CONTEXT

The context of a brief is more public than that of a memo. A memo is an in-house document, read by a few; a brief is a public document read by not only the judge, but also the judge's clerks, the opposition, the appellate courts, and sometimes even the press.

This public context leads most writers to use a more formal tone, although the argument should never cross the line to stuffiness or pedantry. An appropriate level of formality conveys respect for the court and for the legal system in general. Respect for the court precludes personal attacks on the opposing attorney. Even when the opposition has behaved unprofessionally or disrespectfully, leave judgment of the opposition's behavior to the court. Berating the opposition is not the purpose of an argument, and indulging in that activity will only make you look less professional in the eyes of the court.

The public context also requires careful observance of any court rules and citation rules, and an awareness of common conventions used in briefs in your jurisdiction. Just as you would not slouch or slur your words when speaking to a court, you should not be careless about the details of your written presentation to the court. To find out what the court rules are, contact the clerk of the court, who is usually happy to see an attorney making an effort to follow the rules. If writing for a jurisdiction with which you are unfamiliar, such as a federal circuit or the U.S. Supreme Court, also consult practitioners' guides in law libraries.[6]

The brief also communicates in the context of other documents. In contrast, a research memo is the main document upon which the reader will depend when making his or her decision about how to proceed, so it needs to communicate the pros and cons of any position so the reader is adequately informed. But a persuasive brief will be read in the context of previously filed legal documents and the opposition's brief. This context provides a framework that can simplify the requirement of a brief. For example, you do not need to communicate the opposition's position fully; the opposition will do that for you. Instead, you can focus more tightly

6. For example, one useful source is　(2002).
Robert Stern, *Supreme Court Practice*

on the one legal position you are advocating, explaining why it is superior to the opposition's position without stopping to explain their position. This can make the large-scale organization of a brief appear more unified and straightforward to the reader, although it is not always simple for the writer to achieve this organization. This context can also provide opportunities for new options in organization, particularly in a reply brief, where your purpose often becomes following the opposition's structure as you correct errors in the position.

Always remember the purpose, focus, and context of your argument section. As you study and then employ the persuasive writing techniques explained in the rest of this chapter, think about how you can use these techniques to serve these larger concepts. Focusing on your purpose, which is to explain respectfully how your client's objectives are congruent with the court's, is central to persuasive writing. This focus is more important than all the persuasive techniques you learned in the earlier chapters. As you learn to employ the writing techniques explained below to create a balanced and unified presentation, this focus on your purpose will make you a formidable adversary in litigation.

TECHNIQUES FOR PERSUASIVE ARGUMENT SECTIONS

Persuasive techniques are useful in all aspects of your argument: large-scale organization, paragraph organization, sentence structure, wording, and overall balance.

Large-Scale Organization

Organization is particularly critical for persuasive writing. So consider your persuasive goals when

- choosing content appropriate to your reader's role,
- choosing content that resolves the issue,
- determining how to handle emotional facts, and
- grouping and ordering the content into paragraphs and sections.

In each of these tasks, the choices you make will depend upon the court you are addressing and the issues that court must resolve.

Choosing Content Appropriate to Your Reader's Role

Choose the content that will lead the reader to take the action you request. Consider what kind of authority will meet this reader's needs and what legal criteria this reader is obliged to apply.

When writing for a trial judge, choose the mandatory authority that leads to a favorable ruling for your client. A trial judge cannot change the law if mandatory authority exists resolving the issue; he or she must follow this authority. For this reason, you are less likely to use persuasive authority that contradicts mandatory authority. Use sufficient authority, but do not burden the court unnecessarily with research. The trial judge may not have a clerk to assist in checking research; do not place the judge in the position of checking each of your citations, only to discover that the extra cases add nothing to your argument. String cites often add no persuasion. Concurring persuasive authority may also be extraneous. Use persuasive authority only when it is needed to support your position, as when no mandatory authority exists to support your case. Attach copies of any out-of-state cases used and include pinpoint cites. These two considerations can save the judge much work, which can never hurt your case.

Choose content that addresses the issue at hand. The trial judge probably had a specific purpose in mind when requesting the brief, or will have a particular issue to determine when your brief is in support of a motion. As you address that issue, also address any procedural or substantive criteria the court must apply to resolve your motion. For example, if requesting that a pleading be dismissed for failure to state a claim, focus on how the facts cannot establish each element of the cause of action claimed, rather than on what the facts are.

If the question involves deciding which legal standard the court should apply to an issue, include the standard that you believe should be used and explain why it applies. For example, if the question were whether in-home child care providers are covered by either the zoning ordinances for day care centers or by those for single family dwellings, you would focus on the criteria the court should consider, which might include the governing definitions of day care centers and family dwellings, the intent behind the zoning ordinances, or other criteria. In summary, when choosing content for a trial brief, include all that is needed to support the action you want, but omit extraneous cases or arguments that may support your position generally but are not relevant to the trial judge's criteria for deciding the immediate issue.[7]

Like the trial court, the appellate court has specific criteria for deciding the issues it faces, but these criteria sometimes differ from those used by the trial court. Look first to the standard of review the court must apply. An error correcting court will not retry the case on the facts, but will review the case to see if the trial judge exercised his or her discretion appropriately and if the judge applied the right law. Whether arguing for appellant or respondent, you must focus on those criteria, although you will probably emphasize different aspects of them.

When writing the appellant's brief, you may focus on the standard of review as it relates to making sure justice is served. To win reversal, you must show that the trial judge made an error and that the error made a difference in the outcome. Do not include every harmless error, because that will have the same negative impression as criticizing the opposing attorney. Instead, show that the trial court made errors and show how those errors are substantial enough to justify reversal, modification, retrial, or the other relief you are requesting. Explain how the error has prevented justice from being served.

7. For a source for developing and focusing your arguments other than books focused on legal writing, see Paul Bergman, *Trial Advocacy in a Nutshell* (3d ed. 1997).

When writing a respondent's brief, explain the standard of review in terms of its limited scope. In a respondent's brief, you are more likely to develop the idea that the appellant court does not and should not retry the case. If possible, argue that the trial court made no errors. If you cannot argue that point successfully, argue that any errors made are harmless. Explain how the error has not created an injustice. Often larger questions about use of legal appeals can be important. Policy arguments about "opening the floodgates" and potentially inefficient use of the court system may be useful choices.

Expect to write the appellate brief from scratch. Because the appellate court is essentially reviewing the events of the preceding legal action rather than the original conflict between the parties, you face different issues. Those new issues require fresh research and new choices of governing cases and statutes, facts, and reasoning.

Your appellate brief will omit much information needed in a trial brief, and will include much information unneeded in that trial brief. For example, if you were arguing that the trial court abused its discretion when granting a judgment because the judgment was based on an error of law, you might state the following supporting assertions.

The trial court erred by grounding its decision on an erroneous view of the law of unjust enrichment.

The trial court granted judgment based upon the theory of unjust enrichment.

Unjust enrichment requires a showing of a benefit being conferred by the party making the claim.

Here the party making the claim did not confer the benefit, but rather a third party did.

Thus the party has not established all the needed elements.

The judgment is therefore based on an erroneous view of the elements of unjust enrichment.

An error-correcting court is constrained in what it can and cannot consider, so you must not waste the court's time arguing points it does not have the discretion to resolve. Challenge the court's factual findings on appeal only when those findings are not supported by the great weight and clear preponderance of the evidence.[8] Do not challenge those decisions where the court weighed the evidence in the record and made a finding against your client that is supported by the evidence.

If your reader is the supreme court in your jurisdiction, the court that reviews constitutional issues and other broad questions,[9] consider

---

8. *See, e.g., Cogswell v. Robertshaw Controls Co.,* 274 N.W.2d 647, 650 (Wis. 1979).

9. Not all the highest courts are called "supreme" courts. For example, New York's highest court is called the Court of

Appeals. The court we are referring to here is the court of last resort in your jurisdiction, but for simplicity we will use the term "supreme court" throughout.

what issues your case presents that are worth the court's time. You know that this court will be looking at the policy concerns and the development of the law beyond your case. You also know that this court will consider how trial courts and appellate courts will use this decision to resolve future cases.

When writing to a supreme court requesting review, consider the grounds upon which the court will review a case and choose the grounds appropriate to your situation. When choosing content, you must first include why the case you present merits review. Is it a wrong that cries out to be rectified? Is it a case that provides an opportunity to address something the court wants to address? Is it an opportunity to address a common societal problem and therefore provide a tool to resolve future cases? For example, if its decision in a custody case will resolve an unsettled aspect of the standard of "best interests of the child," include that point. Find the main reason the court should consider this case and include it. Choose also to address the larger picture of the development of the law and explain how this case will address some issue you think the court would like to address. If it addresses an issue the court would like to avoid, show why justice compels this review. Focus your argument on why this court needs to review this case.

If you are writing for an administrative law judge who decides administrative issues, learn how the agency makes decisions and what your administrative judge can and cannot decide. Learn what the agency's criteria are for determining the issue that exists in your case.

Each agency has its own rules and legal guidelines, and even within an agency there can be variety from department to department. Some agencies want you to spell out the relevant law in your argument, although others may not require this when the relevant law is clearly prescribed and the range of issues decided is narrow. Research these criteria carefully; they are often quite specific. For example, if you were arguing that a firing was discriminatory, you might need to show that the firing was based on illegal criteria. Even if the judge personally disapproved of the employer's practices, he or she must decide the case based on whether the evidence meets the criteria for illegal discrimination. Sometimes administrative law judges have broader guidelines, so you have more latitude. For example, if you were writing a brief to a public service commission arguing that a rate increase was not in the public interest, you would probably be able to use a wider variety of relevant legal criteria, including economic issues, general public interest, and the policies behind regulation.

Whether your argument is broad or narrow, keep the argument organized around the issues you need to address. As you address those issues, show how the result you request is fair. Generally, agency law judges, like trial judges, see the people involved and the results of their decisions, and can see the human side of the case more readily.

When writing for a specialized court, such as a bankruptcy or admiralty court, you will probably be addressing a judge who is well aware of the law you are applying. You can often focus on how the law applies to your case without a lengthy description of the law. If, however, you are arguing for a new interpretation of the law, you may need to set out the history or theory supporting your interpretation.

When writing to a federal court, begin by establishing that this court has jurisdiction.

> A. THE DISTRICT COURT HAS JURISDICTION TO HEAR AN ACTION REQUESTING A DECLARATION OF THE RIGHTS OF MENTALLY RETARDED ADULTS CONCERNING THE EXERCISE OF PROCREATIVE DECISIONS BECAUSE THIS DECISION AFFECTS THEIR FEDERAL CONSTITUTIONAL RIGHT TO PRIVACY.

If you have exhausted other possible areas of relief, explain that to the court. Address the preliminary argument addressed first. Then move to the issue you want the court to resolve.

With all courts, avoid dwelling on distracting points. Was the other side's brief filled with grammatical errors that destroyed its credibility and made it an insult to the court? No need to comment on it; if the court noticed the errors, the other side has already lost credibility. Let the court initiate any sense of irritation or outrage if it so chooses. If the court has not noticed the errors until you comment on them, the court will either (1) feel slightly embarrassed at failing to notice it first or (2) be displeased that you are wasting its time on a factor unrelated to the issues at hand. Does natural sympathy favor your client? Do not waste the court's time with impassioned pleas that are unrelated to the issue. Instead, weave the emotionally favorable points into your argument where appropriate, so the court is aware of them without being forced to address whether they are relevant. By weaving the facts into your legal argument, you can use them to support your position while maintaining your focus on the legal issues that will form the basis for the court's resolution.

Choosing Content That Resolves the Issue

Three particular questions frequently arise when deciding what content to include in your brief. The first two are whether to include authority unfavorable to your position and whether to anticipate and counter the other side's arguments. A third is how to include supporting information.

First, you must include authority, whether helpful or not, if it is mandatory authority directly addressing the issue. You may need to include the case if it is an essential link to another point. But when you cite unfavorable precedent, distinguish the case from yours and explain why the unfavorable authority should not control this decision. For example, use language such as "While the defense argues that this case resolves the issue in favor of her client, a closer reading reveals that the facts of the two cases differ in significant ways . . . ."

Second, you may also want to include your answer to an issue if you believe the other side will focus on it. Some writers argue that this may be dangerous because (1) you may give the other side the idea for an argument it overlooked or (2) you will reveal your answer too early and give the other side a chance to counter it.[10] These concerns are valid, but they are countered by other factors. People are more resistant to subsequent counter-arguments if they have been exposed to answers to those arguments previously.[11] Furthermore, the reader's opinion of the advocate's competence and trustworthiness will be enhanced by its inclusion.[12]

The best solution may lie in the middle. If an issue is so obvious that you are sure the opposition will discuss it and if your counter for the issue is strong, offer your alternative reasoning in the initial brief. Showing that your position is strong is seldom a disadvantage in litigation or negotiation. Do not, however, address an issue that would be harder to defeat or that is not obvious. Save that battle for the reply brief. Be realistic in deciding to address the issue. If the issue must be resolved to decide the case, address it regardless of the strength of your argument.

Third, include the best cases supporting your arguments, but do not include all possible supporting cases or cases that duplicate a point already made. "Two or three decisions directly on point are worth a dozen which are not, or in most cases, a dozen which are."[13]

Handling Emotional Facts

Another organizational question is when and how to include emotional arguments that do not go specifically to legal questions. When determining when and how to include emotional aspects of the case, try to include favorable aspects, but you must handle them carefully. Courts not only want to apply the law properly; they also want to do justice.

> Counsel should hesitate to rest [a] case on mere technicalities, however strongly they may be embedded in earlier decisions. [Counsel] should never feel safe unless he [or she] can and does demonstrate the reasonableness and utility of the rule .... [14]

An impassioned plea alone, however, is not convincing. What is convincing is when the heart and mind unite behind the same conclusion. Therefore, through the cloth of your argument, weave the golden threads of common human fairness.[15] Make the reader want to see the legal

---

10. Peck, *supra* note 2, at 169.

11. Both-sided approaches to persuasion have greater success with listeners who were initially undecided or in opposition, who were better educated, and who were later exposed to counter arguments. Herbert Simons, *Persuasion: Understanding, Practice, and Analysis* 67–68 (2d ed. 1986); O'Keefe, *supra* note 3.

12. A communicator whom the receiver perceives as having only biased knowledge will presumably be viewed as less competent. Simons, *supra* note 11, at 133.

13. Herbert Goodrich, *A Case on Appeal* 17 (4th ed. 1967).

14. Peck, *supra* note 2, at 80 (quoting Chief Justice Vanderbilt of the New Jersey Supreme Court).

15. O'Keefe, *supra* note 3, at 158–61.

strength of your argument and want to find in your client's favor. Avoid setting up a separate section within your organization to deal with the emotions of your claim.

Grouping and Sequencing Content

Generally, your issues will determine how you group your cases and other authorities, and your grouping will not differ from that of a memo. Start with your strongest argument unless logic requires you to modify this approach. Although some research suggests that readers remember the point most recently read,[16] this advantage pales in this situation, because you have no assurance that the reader will read your document just before making the decision. You cannot be sure that recency will occur just because an argument comes at the end of your brief.

When sequencing those issues, however, your choice may differ from the one you would put first in a memo. In a memo, you may have started with the argument that would gain the largest award for your client, with the argument suggested by your senior partner, or with some other point. But in an argument, you want to start with your strongest point because you are making an important initial impression about the merit of your argument. Starting with the strongest point is supported by research in persuasion.[17]

Do not, however, violate the logical order of your argument. If you must address an issue regarding standards of review, for example, address it before moving to the merits of your case. In general, always follow the pattern the court will need to follow to resolve the question.[18] Choose the stronger of two points only when the court may address either of several issues first.

When you have chosen the best logical organization for your argument, convey the organization in clear headings that communicate your assertions. This will help the reader understand your logical development and your point. Also consider dividing larger sections with subheadings. Subheadings give the eye a respite and the mind a map, and they encourage the reader to continue reading the document. When subdividing, moderation is the key. Avoid headings that fragment, rather than organize, your text.[19]

Guide your reader through your logical organization step by step, showing how the logic of the law leads to the result you want. Include all the information needed to answer the reader's questions, but exclude

---

16. Some research suggests that listeners remember the last point because it is the most recent, but results on this are divided, and readers are in a different situation than listeners, in that readers may reread if they choose. Simons, *supra* note 11, at 140–48.

17. *Id.* at 151–57.

18. The writer not only determines what the reader thinks, but also how. Vernon Lee, *The Handling of Words, and Other Studies in Literary Psychology* 190 (1968).

19. "[A] great number of divisions, far from rendering a work more solid, destroys its coherence. To the eye the book seems clearer; but the author's design remains obscure." Georges Louis LeClerc, Comte de Buffon, *Discourse on Style: An Address Delivered Before the French Academy* in *Essays in Stylistic Analysis* 14 (H. Babb, ed. 1972).

irrelevant information. Then mark the path clearly for your reader, using an order that seems natural and headings that communicate the progression of your argument.

You can communicate this logical organization through the wording you choose for the first line of each paragraph. As you revise your thesis sentences, for example, think about the logical connection between this paragraph and the previous one, and express that connection in the beginning of the sentence. Taking time to do this helps you communicate the overall logical flow of your argument, as in the following revision of an example used earlier in this chapter. The italicized words are terms repeated from the previous thesis sentence.

> A document is subject to the qualified immunity from discovery whenever it falls under the work product rule.

> This *document qualifies as work product.*

> Discovery of these *work product documents* may not be compelled unless . . . .

> *Discovery* of this *document* is thus not required.

This repetition, which occurs naturally as you develop your argument, also helps the reader remember the point of the previous paragraph and connect it quickly to the current one.

Small-Scale Organization

For small-scale organization, your focus remains on choosing and ordering information to guide the reader. You simply move your attention from the choice of issues to a choice of sentences, from which cases to use to what amount of explanation is needed, and from ordering sections to ordering sentences.

Maintaining Focus

Keep the reader focused on your point.[20] To do this, begin each paragraph block or paragraph with an affirmative statement of your position.[21] For example, write

> **A parolee's reasonable expectation of privacy is less than that of other citizens.**

rather than

> Generally a citizen has a reasonable expectation of privacy in his or her home. Jason Harrow's reasonable expectation, however, is lower because he is a parolee.

The affirmative opening states your topic and shows your reader how you intend to develop your reasoning. For example, if sympathy runs in your client's favor, you may add a sentence mentioning the point.

---

20. Persuaders need to let the audience know what it is they will be discussing and why, not leaving it to the end. O'Keefe, *supra* note 3, at 160.

21. *Id.* at 150.

Furthermore, Officer Washington's warrantless search was essential to determining if Harrow was again selling drugs to high school students.

But more likely you will use language throughout your paragraph that suggests sympathy.

To perform his or her duties, a parole officer needs to be able to conduct a warrantless search of a parolee's apartment. [citation] So it was that Officer Washington needed to search Harrow's apartment to determine if Harrow was indeed violating parole by again selling drugs. The parole system is designed to help the parolee reintegrate into society while preventing further anti-social behavior. [citation]

Officer Washington was furthering this prevention when he conducted the warrantless search in response to information that Harrow was using his home as a base for selling drugs at a nearby high school.

Weave themes through your argument, but do not allow them to draw you away from your main focus.

Answering Opposing Arguments

Generally, if you decide to address the opposition's arguments, you may refer to them while stating your position. But do not focus on them. For example, state the other side's position in the middle of the paragraph, not at the beginning. Keep the focus on your affirmative position, using the other side's argument as a backdrop for your reasoning, rather than presenting its argument and putting yourself in a defensive position. Arrange your phrases and choose your language carefully. You might refer to your opponent's position in a dependent clause, rather than giving it a sentence of its own. For example, compare the following two versions of the same argument. The first takes an affirmative stance, so the writer confidently presents an argument while dismissing the other side's position. The second version focuses on the opponent's position, creating a defensive tone rather than a clear statement of the writer's position.

The standard of reasonable cause is the appropriate standard by which to evaluate warrantless searches by parole officers. Because they have a special relationship with the parolees they supervise and because of the special circumstances of parole, the standard should be "flexible enough to give the parolee meaningful protection and to preserve the functions of parole."[citation] Thus the reasonable cause standard, rather than a stricter standard, is necessary for and consistent with the purposes of parole. Although a later case did require a warrant before a search by a parole officer, that court did not clearly define what showing of cause would justify that warrant. [citation] Indeed, the court concluded that the strong governmental

interests in maintaining a viable parole system require a standard not as rigorous as that applied in an ordinary case. [citation]. Thus ....

rather than

Opposed to the *Latta* rule is the view that a warrantless search by a parole officer is acceptable only when it falls under a judicially recognized exception to the warrant requirement. [citation] Proponents of this position contend that a warrant requirement for parole officers would not hinder the rehabilitative and law enforcement process of the parole system. [citation] They fear that parole officers may be tempted to abuse their discretion in conducting a search if they are not first required to obtain a warrant. [citation].

To the contrary, a warrant requirement would be destructive to the goals of the parole system and particularly to the special relationship between the parole officer and his client. Officer Washington was a professional. He was uniquely qualified to determine when to conduct a search of his client's home. Parole officers need the latitude to conduct warrantless searches and to do so spontaneously if necessary. The reasonable cause criterion for searches by parole officers is consistent with the purposes of parole.

These small-scale changes accumulate throughout the passage affecting the focus and tenor of the whole passage.

In a reply brief, you may organize around your opponent's argument if doing so shows the strength of your position. But if your position counters the opposition on a broader scale, such as on the relative importance of issues, use your own organization and refer to the opposing argument only when needed to explain your point.

To attack the opposing argument, you must find an error in its position. By explaining how the opposing argument is faulty, you can interrupt its progress, so it cannot lead to the outcome your opponent desires. Perhaps you can assert that their argument is based on cases not applicable to this situation because they turn on facts not analogous to this situation. Even if the facts are similar, you may state that the issue in this case is not the same. Or you may state that the reasoning used in a previous case does not apply to this situation. Perhaps the case is not mandatory, and need not be considered. Perhaps another equally relevant case states a position favorable to you, which may let you establish that the law is not clearly running against your position. Moreover, it may be that the law is stated correctly, but the logical steps flowing from that statement are flawed. Perhaps the opponent states logically inconsistent points, overgeneralizes, or misapplies the law so it works against the original purpose for which the law was promulgated.

If you must concede a point, do so by saying that it is not important to the case, that it is overshadowed by some other point, or that it is countered in some other way. Rather than conceding a point in a separate sentence, concede it in a dependent clause that brushes the reader's mind away from the concession and right into another point you present as more important.

> Although other jurisdictions have broadened their interpretation of this phrase, Idaho has not. As recently as ..., the Idaho Supreme Court has held that ....

The position that "other jurisdictions have broadened" is never given full focus, but is overshadowed by "although," signalling to the reader that the forthcoming counterargument is the main focus.

Blending Policy into Reasoning

Beginning legal writers often include policy in a separate paragraph, after the case law has been reasoned to its conclusion. But this structure treats the policy as an extra. For example, in the following passage, the policy is introduced in a separate paragraph after the logical progression through the case law is completed.

> The rule from these two cases is that sexual conduct must be shown to affect the child adversely before it can be considered relevant to a child custody determination. [citation] There must be a demonstrable nexus between the conduct and the best interest of the child. [citation] In the present situation, the trial court presumed Devon's sexual conduct would adversely affect Erica absent any evidence in the record. This is contrary to the precedent of *Gould* and *Schwantes*. [citations]
>
> The trial court's presumption against lesbians in child custody cases is also against Wisconsin policy toward homosexuality ....

If the policy is introduced within the reasoning as a broader level of support, it can appear integral to the precedent itself.

> **These two cases establish that sexual conduct must be shown to affect the child adversely before it can be considered relevant to a child custody determination. [citation] There must be a demonstrable nexus between the conduct and the best interest of the child, just as there must always be demonstrable relevance before a person's sexual conduct can be a factor in any legal decision. [citation] Without this nexus, the law would become a club used to maintain prejudice rather than a yardstick to determine when children need protection. [citation] In the present situation, the trial court presumed Devon's sexual conduct would adversely affect Erica absent any evidence in the record. [citation] The court abandoned its legal yardstick, contrary to mandatory precedent. [citation]**

In this example, policy appears as it applies throughout the reasoning, rather than as a concept apart from the law itself. By explaining how policy also supports the reasoning, you underscore the reader's sense that your position is congruent with the law on many levels. The position appears not only legal, but also just.

Effective small-scale organization is often a matter of maintaining your logical progression and focus. Address the opposing arguments, the emotions of the situation, and other facets of the case that come into play, but keep the reader's eye fixed on the logical path you have blazed to your conclusion.

Sentence Structure

Because persuasive sentence structures are discussed at length in the chapter on persuasive fact statements, refer to that chapter for techniques to use here. This section presents some general aspects of sentence structure that are particularly useful in arguments and ways to combine and extend them.

Using Sentence Structure to Enhance Arguments

In general, identify points you want to emphasize and use structural techniques to draw attention to those points. Then identify points you want to minimize and structure those to achieve your goal. Beyond emphasizing and de-emphasizing points, use sentence structure throughout your argument to signal how your points fit together. Most writers have learned the importance of transitions, but may not realize that structure, as much as transition words, is also useful. For example, the structure of the following two topic sentences subtly suggests a logical relationship between the two.

> In *Eberhardy,* the supreme court carefully specified the limits of its jurisdictional holding in each of the four places in the opinion where it defined the issues . . . .

> Here, the supreme court's jurisdictional holding is therefore limited to . . . .

The first sentence focuses on the court's action by making the subject and verb "the supreme court . . . specified." But the second topic sentence uses passive voice when discussing the current case ("holding is . . . limited"), suggesting that the decision has already been made by the previous action.

Repeating a structure alerts the reader to logically parallel points and makes them easier to remember.

> Language serves three functions. The first is to communicate ideas. The second is to conceal ideas. The third is to conceal the absence of ideas.[22]

The following example uses parallel structure to emphasize each fact and show how together they support the same conclusion.

> Jane performed academically at the second or third grade level. When asked a question, she could respond in short, articulate sentences, but her communication skills were substantially below normal. Jane could feed herself, but could not cut her own food. She

22. Richard Hatch, *Business Communication: Theory and Technique* 1 (1983).

could bathe herself, but could not regulate the temperature of the bath water. She could put on a dress, but could not button it.

Finally, structure can be used to emphasize a word within a sentence that provides a critical link between ideas.

> The defendants both expected the plaintiff to disagree on this point, *an expectation that* ....

Combining and Extending Structural Techniques

As you refine your sentence structure to emphasize points in your argument, you need not employ one technique in isolation. You can combine several techniques to get a particular effect. The following examples show four ways to word the same point with differing levels of emphasis. The example used introduces a distinction between the precedent and the current facts. These variations use structural repetition, short sentences, and careful placement of phrases. They also apply wording techniques such as using concrete and abstract terms and stronger verbs. By combining these techniques in different ways, the sentences achieve noticeably different effects.

Emphasis employed	Version of same sentence
• none	There is no "right to be let alone" in a customs search at a nation's borders, which is very different from a police search through a private library.
• short first sentence • strong parallel structure for comparison in second sentence • emphasis dampened by use of prepositional phrases, wordy modifiers, somewhat abstract descriptions, and a weak verb in second sentence	**Revision #1** The "right to be let alone" does not apply to this situation. A customs search at a border is very different from a police search through a private library.
• short first sentence • active verbs • more concise sentences • emphasis dampened by use of plural, general nouns in the description	**Revision #2** The "right to be let alone" does not apply here. A customs search of one's baggage does not equal a police search of one's library.
• concrete, specific images • strong parallels • emphasis dampened by prepositional phrase in first sentence so second sentence sounds stronger in comparison, like a punch line	**Revision #3** The "right to be let alone" does not apply to these facts. Suitcases are not like books, and international borders are not like private libraries.
• slightly formal language • unusual structure in second sentence. • emphasis dampened by prepositional phrase in first sentence so second sentence sounds stronger in comparison	**Revision #4** The "right to be let alone," however, does not fit this body of facts. International borders are not private libraries, nor are suitcases books.

As you read these examples, you probably found you preferred some, disliked others. Balancing the interplay of emphasis techniques and the subtlety or boldness of their use involves personal judgment.

In summary, sentence structure is a tool with many possible uses in the argument section, as in the persuasive statement of facts. To master sentence structure, experiment and reflect on the results of your experiments, combining and recombining phrases until you arrive at a sentence with just the effect you want. Then, when you craft an effective sentence, study it so you know how to replicate its structure when you need a similar effect. Bit by bit, you will build your expertise and expand your capacity to control not only the content of your argument, but even the way the reader will remember it and the way your reader will feel about it.

Word Choice

Content and clarity should anchor your argument, but an effectively worded presentation is also important. Although the judge wants to make a just decision regardless of how well the advocates plead their cases, it is immensely helpful if the advocates make this job more pleasant. A well-written brief will stand out in the judge's memory of the day's readings. To help your brief stand out, you can use the techniques discussed in Chapter 8 on persuasive facts. You may also use some other techniques not available within the constraints of the fact statement, which are discussed next.

Using Imagery

Metaphor, simile, and other figures of speech can enliven your argument, especially in introductions or conclusions.[23] For example, the following sentence promises a text that will be fun to read, and yet not be frivolous.

Precedent has reached, but not grasped, this question.

Careful selection of imagery can also introduce the emotional aspect of your message.

The writer seems to be bludgeoning a butterfly.[24]

Although the way imagery enhances persuasion is not clear, it does enhance an argument.[25] Imagery creates a more concrete picture in the reader's mind, and concreteness increases memory.[26] Additionally, because you are dealing with an educated reader, these rhetorical devices may be appreciated as adding grace to your writing.

---

23. For some useful examples and further discussion of figure of speech, *see*, Simons, *supra* note 11, at 223–24.

24. William L. Rivers, *Writing: Craft and Art* 81 (1975).

25. Sandell, *supra* note 4, at 75.

26. *Id.* at 182.

Because imagery is an attention-getting and an emotion-inducing device, make sure you use it on worthwhile points. Drama for its own sake can be distracting rather than emphatic,[27] or embarrassing rather than impressive. You do not want to be remembered by the judge as the following speaker was remembered by a fellow member of the House of Lords.

> The late Duke of Argyle, though the weakest reasoner, was the most pleasing speaker I ever knew in my life. He charmed, he warmed, he forcibly ravished the audience; not by his matter certainly, but by his manner of delivering it .... I was captivated like others; but when I came home, and coolly considered what he had said, stripped of all those ornaments in which he had dressed it, I often found the matter flimsy, the arguments weak .... [28]

As with any technique, you also need to guard against overuse.

> If a writer will seem to observe no decorum at all, nor pass how he [or she] fashions [the] tale to [the] matter, who could doubt but he [or she] may in the lightest cause speak like a Pope, and in the gravest matters like a parrot, and find words and phrases enough to serve both turns, and neither of them commendably.[29]

Describing Concisely

Although conciseness is considered a virtue in itself, it can also serve other purposes, especially in argument. A short sentence, combined with effective wording, can drive a point home with unusual force.

Discretion was not abused; it was exercised.

A sentence using an active, strong verb instead of longer prepositional phrases can add energy to a whole paragraph.

The beam plummeted to the pavement.

When the verb also packs an appropriate emotional punch, you can again weave equity into your logical argument.

He *assumed* he could handle the large machine without further training, and in so doing he *assumed* the risk.

The conclusion is an excellent place to be concise because the groundwork for your points has already been laid. But be concise throughout your argument. If you can present your side more effectively in forty pages than the opposition can in fifty, your position will be stronger.[30] If you can do it in thirty, you will gain the court's admiration.

27. "Nothing is more inimical to this warmth [of effective style] than the desire to be everywhere striking; nothing is more contrary to the light which should be at the center of a work, and which should be diffused uniformly in any composition, than those sparks which are struck only at the cost of a violent collision between words, and which dazzle us for a moment or two, only to leave us in subsequent darkness." LeClerc, *supra* note 19, at 15.

28. *Classics in Composition* 100 (D. Hayden, ed. 1969) (from a letter from Lord Chesterfield to his son in 1749).

29. *Id.* at 41 (quoting George Puttenham's "Of Stile").

30. Albert Tate, Jr., *The Art of Brief Writing: What a Judge Wants to Read*, 4 Lit. 11, 12 (Winter 1978).

Injecting Humor

Humor is refreshing for a reader, but risky to use in persuasive writing. Humor may enhance the reader's liking for you, which can enhance trustworthiness, but it will not generally enhance the reader's view of your competence.[31] If you decide to use humor, make sure it is appropriate to the mood and message you are communicating, and make sure the reader will understand it. When you ask yourself if the humor is worth it, the most likely answer will be "no." If the answer is "yes," craft the humor carefully, test it on someone whose judgment you trust, and if he or she says delete it, take the advice.

Widening Vocabulary

Although a reader will usually be put off by being forced to consult a dictionary to read your brief,[32] correct and skillful use of a broader vocabulary may be a pleasant diversion. Variety is interesting. More important, using a varied vocabulary improves your chances of choosing the best word. Widening your vocabulary does not always mean using more multisyllabic words. As Justice Jackson said, a skillful advocate will "master the short Saxon word that pierces the mind like a spear and the simple figure that lights the understanding. He [or she] will never drive the judge to the dictionary."[33]

In wording, as in the use of sentence structure, expertise comes with practice, with balancing and combining different writing techniques until you get the effect you want.

Polishing Details

Improving the readability of the content will also be appreciated by your reader, so do all you can to make it appealing to the eye and easy to understand. Polishing aids persuasion by increasing the reader's comprehension of the point you are making.[34] Polishing reduces distractions.

> Readers see misspellings as oddities—like a troop of bald Boy Scouts—and must give their attention to them. Distracted by the oddities, readers find it impossible to follow the sense of the writing.[35]

It also helps by increasing your credibility.

> God does not much mind bad grammar, but God does not take any particular pleasure in it.[36]

Consider your audience when polishing. Observe any requirements the court has, making especially sure that forms, numbers in citations,

---

31. O'Keefe, *supra* note 3, at 190.

32. "Using language readers do not understand invites them to stop reading." Rivers, *supra* note 24, at 38.

33. Robert Jackson, *Advocacy Before the Supreme Court: Suggestions for Effective Case Presentations,* 37 A.B.A.J. 801, 863 (1951).

34. Comprehension in persuasion has been studied extensively. Sandell, *supra* note 4, at 82–101.

35. Rivers, *supra* note 24, at 7.

36. Hatch, *supra* note 22, at 135 (quoting Erasmus) (1983).

and other small mechanical details are correct. An error here may seem small, but it might loom quite large in the time it takes the judge to discern what you meant to do. In appellate briefs, cite to the page in the record that supports your point, use headings to help the reader refer to the part of the brief needed, and use the parties' names to help the reader understand the facts. In agency briefs, follow any specific form or content requirements of the agency. In short, take pains with the details of your brief, so your reader's job is painless.

ACHIEVING BALANCE AND UNITY

An effective persuasive message is greater than the sum of the techniques used. The most memorable and effective writing smooths the individual persuasive techniques into a flawless whole, so that the result you want the reader to reach seems logically inevitable. As with excellence in dancing, singing, and other performance arts, an excellent piece of persuasion seems natural and effortless, even though it is neither.

Every work of enduring literature is not so much a triumph of language as a victory over language; a sudden injection of life-giving perceptions into a vocabulary that is, but for the energy of the creative writer, perpetually on the verge of exhaustion.[37] Its craft is subtle, and best exercised with restraint. Consider, for example, the following two versions of a passage from Abraham Lincoln's second inaugural address. The first is the draft he was given by W.H. Seward for consideration.[38]

> I close. We are not, we must not be aliens or enemies but fellow-countrymen and brethren. Although passion has strained our bonds of affection too hardly, they must not, I am sure they will not be broken. The mystic chords which proceeding from so many battle fields and so many patriot graves pass through all the hearts and all the hearths in this broad continent of ours will yet again harmonize in their ancient music when breathed upon by the guardian angel of our nation.

Lincoln revised this, making a series of small changes. First, he lengthened the first sentence to "I am loath to close." This softened the strength of the sentence, reducing the focus on this transition and personal reference. At the same time, it added a note of personal emotion by changing the verb of the sentence from "close" to "am loath," focusing on regret instead of action. These simple changes made the paragraph open with a different feeling.

He then simplified the next sentence, eliminating the insistent tone of "we must not be" and the repetition of "aliens or enemies" and "fellow-countrymen and brethren." Instead of repeating words, he chose the simple "enemies" and substituted the logical and simple opposite, "friends": "We are not enemies, but friends." This simpler wording strengthened the sentence, making it shorter and clarifying the contrast.

---

37. J. Middleton Murry, *The Problem of Style* 85 (1980).

38. Henry Weihofen, *Legal Writing Style* 324 (2d ed. 1980).

But the revisions also warmed the tone of the sentence, maintaining the feeling established in the opening sentence.

Then Lincoln repeated the idea, "We must not be enemies," thus using several short sentences for emphasis, unlike the original, which added more words to one sentence. He also used the insistent "must," but only after the personal tone had been established. This made "must" seem more a personal request, less an edict.

He simplified the next sentence, omitting modifiers ("too hardly") and putting the sentence in parallel structure: "Though passion may have strained, it must not break our bonds of affection." He also created some syntactical suspense by stopping the introductory phrase with "strained," and leaving the reader waiting for the completion of the phrase until the end of the sentence when the object of "strained" ("our bonds of affection") appeared, at that point also the object of the verb "break." It is a streamlined sentence, with each word, each omission of a word, and each structure communicating a part of his meaning.

The final sentence of the paragraph, although still long, moves smoothly to its conclusion. The subject was simplified; "the mystic chords which proceeding from so many battle fields and so many patriot graves pass through all the hearts and all the hearths in this broad continent of ours" became "the mystic chords of memory," with modifying information put in a supporting phrase set off with commas. The predicate, "will yet again harmonize in their ancient music" was changed to "will yet swell the chorus," becoming a concrete image stated more concisely. The intervening phrase also became more concrete, so the reader could see more clearly the picture Lincoln was painting. For example, "proceeding from" was replaced by "stretching from" and the plural "battlefields" became the singular and more concrete "battle-field." "Breathed" became the more physical "touched." Finally, he revised "the guardian angel of our nation" to "the angels of our nature," choosing the more personal image over the nationalistic one.

Each change was small. Each was a detail many writers would have been tempted to overlook. And yet the overall change was anything but small. To appreciate it, reread the original version aloud, and then read Lincoln's following revision.

> I am loath to close. We are not enemies, but friends. We must not be enemies. Though passion may have strained, it must not break our bonds of affection. The mystic chords of memory, stretching from every battlefield and patriot grave to every living heart and hearthstone, all over this broad land, will yet swell the chorus of the Union, when again touched, as surely they will be, by the angels of our nature.

Persuasive communication is an imprecise art, but that does not reduce its power. The cause you are advocating may not be as moving as that of President Lincoln, so the eloquence required may not be as great. Yet, having seen the potential that word choice and word order have to move the human spirit, you know what is possible. You can reach toward the goal as much as your abilities, time, and cause allow.

CONCLUSION

When moving from writing the memo to writing the argument, the needs of the reader remain central. Adjust for the differing demands placed on trial, appellate and supreme courts, on agencies, and on specialized courts. Then, throughout your writing, make the subtle changes required to advocate effectively. As you make these changes, pay attention to both the specific techniques and the general impression you want to create.

Practice. Expect to gain expertise through trial and error, then through trial and success. As you become comfortable with these techniques, you will reach for the right technique unconsciously. You will be able to see beyond the task of choosing the word and constructing the sentence or paragraph to the larger task of writing the brief.

Checklist for Writing the Argument Section

Large-Scale Organization

1. Choose content appropriate to your reader's role.

    a. Choose points within the court's discretion.

    b. Choose content that resolves the issues.

    - Choose points on which your objectives can be met while also meeting the court's concerns.

    - Choose legally compelling reasons why you should prevail.

    c. Include emotional facts only if they are relevant and help demonstrate a sense of justice that favors your side.

    d. Omit unneeded points.

    To determine when to exclude information, consider whether you must include it for any reasons:

    - if mandatory authority on the issue,

    - if the other side will definitely make it seem central, or

    - if it is an essential link to another point.

    If it is unfavorable and none of the above, exclude it.

2. Group and sequence content.

    a. Follow the pattern that the court will need to follow to resolve the question.

    b. If you have several options, start with your most persuasive point, or with the one in the reader's mind after reading issues.

Small–Scale Organization

1. Maintain the reader's focus on your point.

    a. Begin each paragraph with an affirmative statement of your point.

    b. Weave favorable emotional themes into paragraphs rather than stating them separately or allowing them to dominate the logic.

2. Answer the opposition's points, but do not organize around them. (In a reply brief, you may organize around the opposition, addressing each of their points in turn.)

3. Blend policy into your reasoning, rather than isolating it in a separate paragraph or section.

4. Phrase the opening of each paragraph to communicate the logical links between paragraphs.

Sentence Structure

1. Identify important points and restructure to emphasize, and use writing techniques described in Chapter 8 to emphasize them.

2. Identify unfavorable points and restructure to minimize, and use writing techniques described in Chapter 8 to de-emphasize them.

3. Use parallel structure or repetition of key words to show links between points.

4. Combine and extend techniques to create the effect and style you want.

Wording

1. Use wording to increase interest as well as clarity, including the following possible techniques:

    a. imagery,

    b. concise wording,

    c. humor, and

    d. broader vocabulary.

Polishing Details

1. Make sure all cites are accurate and in proper form.

2. Observe all court rules.

3. Eliminate grammatical, spelling, and other mechanical errors.

Exercise 1

Read and compare the following two versions of an excerpt from an argument section in which the writer is arguing that the plaintiff should be able to recover the full cost of producing a made-to-order carpet. The first version takes a defensive position by dwelling on a point that does not favor the plaintiff's position. In contrast, the second version does a better job of handling the weak point while retaining a focus on the point that favors the plaintiff. Identify and discuss the errors made in the first version and the effective techniques used in the second version. For conciseness, the citations have been omitted from these excerpts.

First, Less Effective Version

In *Colorado Carpet*, the plaintiff was not allowed to recover expectation damages when the carpet ordered by the defendant was not purchased. [Citation] The court reasoned that the carpet was a stock item that did not meet the statutory exemption established by that court. [Citation.] The court interpreted this statute as applying to goods when the difficulty in selling the goods is related to the special manufacturing of those goods. [Citation.] When the goods conform to the special needs of a particular buyer and are not suitable for sale to others, the court reasoned that the exemption exists. [Citation.]

Colorado Carpet does not apply to this situation. These drapes were made to mimic originals in the buyer's historic hotel. They included a medallion design that was the logo for the hotel itself. Unlike ..., these drapes .... Thus these drapes do meet the requirements of the exemption.

The statutory exemption should not be withheld from this plaintiff. It would be unfair to burden the plaintiff with the cost of these drapes. The plaintiff will have to raise prices from drapes, which will hurt customers and might drive the plaintiff out of business if it can no longer compete with custom drapery manufacturers from other states. Such rank injustice cannot be foisted upon the honest business people of Colorado. Doing so would go against the very spirit of the exemption itself, thus frustrating the purpose of the legislation itself.

Second, More Effective Version

This court has interpreted this statutory exemption to apply to goods when the difficulty in selling the goods is related to the special manufacturing of those goods. [Citation] When the goods conform to the special needs of a particular buyer, and as a result the goods are not suitable for sale to others, then the court reasoned that it would be unfair to burden the seller with the goods [Citation.] In *Colorado Carpet*, the carpet in question was a stock item that was suitable for sale to others. [Citation.] Therefore the carpet did not meet the exemption. [Citation.]

The drapery ordered by the plaintiff in this case does meet the requirements of the statutory exemption. The drapes were not a stock item. They were manufactured specifically to conform to the buyer's need to reproduce the originals in the buyer's historic hotel.

The drapes incorporated a medallion design that was the logo for the hotel, making the drapes unsuitable for sale to others....

Applying the statutory exemption in this case would prevent placing an unfair burden on the plaintiff as the seller. It would be unfair to burden the plaintiff with the cost of drapes that are historical reproductions of the drapes of a specific hotel. Furthermore, placing this burden on the plaintiff would spread the burden to the shoulders of all Colorado manufacturers of custom products. Without the contractual assurance that buyers would indeed purchase the items they ordered, Colorado manufacturers would have to increase prices substantially to cover their potential loss. Customers would suffer from the higher prices, and the Colorado custom manufacturing industry would have difficulty remaining competitive nationally and internationally.

Exercise 2

The following excerpt from an appellate brief includes a clear point heading and explains the law clearly. Sometimes, however, the text takes a defensive posture rather than focusing on the points that are strong for the client's position. Read the first excerpt to understand the brief's position generally. Then read the second excerpt to identify the points that favor the writer's client and that should be emphasized. Choose two of those points, then rewrite two paragraphs so the paragraphs will emphasize those points.

First Excerpt from an Appellate Brief

I. A DEPENDENT CHILD HAS A RIGHT TO RECOVER FOR THE WRONGFUL DEATH OF HER MOTHER WHEN THE RECOVERING HUSBAND HAS TAKEN NO RESPONSIBILITY FOR THE CARE OF THE CHILD; THEREFORE THE COURT OF APPEALS ERRED IN REVERSING THE TRIAL COURT'S RECOGNITION OF THIS CAUSE OF ACTION.

A. Existence Of A Cause Of Action Is A Question Of Law, And Is Therefore Entitled To Independent Review By This Court.

The existence of a cause of action, whether based on the common law or statutory interpretation, where the facts are undisputed, is a question of law. *State v. Williams*, 310 N.W.2d 601 (Wis.1981). Plaintiff–Petitioner does not dispute any factual determinations made by the trial court. Plaintiff–Petitioner asserts only her right to recover for the wrongful death of her mother under the state's wrongful death statute or, alternatively, under the common law. The Supreme Court must decide questions of law independently, without deferring to the Court of Appeals, if it is to fulfill its function as a developer of principles of common law and statutory interpretation. *Ball v. District No. 4, Area Bd. of Vocational, Technical and Adult Ed.*, 345 N.W.2d 389 (Wis. 1984), *Levy v. Levy*, 388 N.W.2d 170 (Wis. 1986).

Second Excerpt from the Same Brief

B.   When A Statute Is Ambiguous, The Ambiguity Must Be Interpreted To Avoid Unreasonable Results; Therefore, The Court Must Interpret The Wrongful Death Statute To Allow Recovery By A Dependent Child When The Surviving Spouse Has Not Taken Responsibility For The Care Of The Surviving Child, And When The Child Has No Other Means Of Recovery.

Twenty years ago, the Supreme Court interpreted the Wisconsin wrongful death statute, secs. 895.01–895.04, Stats., to bar recovery for surviving children when the decedent is survived by a spouse who will support the child. *Cogger v. Trudell,* 151 N.W.2d 146 (Wis. 1967). In *Cogger,* plaintiffs, Ronald Cogger and September Trudell brought suit for the wrongful death of their mother, Darla Trudell. Darla had been killed when their car, driven by her husband, Joseph Trudell, collided with a car driven by Paul Jensen. Defendants included Paul Jensen, the insurance company, and the plaintiff's father, Joseph Trudell. The court held that the Wisconsin wrongful death statute did not give Ronald Cogger and September Trudell a cause of action for the wrongful death of their mother, because their mother was survived by her husband, Joseph Trudell.

The *Cogger* court began its analysis with the statutory language prior to the 1961 amendment. In 1940, the court had interpreted the pre–1961 statute as creating a series of priorities regarding the ownership of a cause of action for wrongful death. Under this priority scheme, surviving children had no cause of action if a spouse survived. *Lasecki v. Kabara,* 294 N.W. 33 (Wis. 1940). Although the statute was amended in 1961 to provide increased protection to minors, the *Cogger* court determined that the amendment did not intend to modify the pre–1961 priority scheme. Therefore, the *Cogger* court held that a dependent child did not have a cause of action for the wrongful death of a parent when the decedent was survived by a spouse.

Despite the important factual distinction between *Cogger* and the case before this Court, the Court of Appeals rigidly held that the *Cogger* decision was controlling. Whereas the surviving spouse in *Cogger* was also the natural parent of the surviving children, Hans Nelson is not the natural parent of Amanda. This distinction is crucial because it bears directly on the policy behind the 1961 amendment of the wrongful death statute: protection of minor children. While it can be assumed that the natural parent of the surviving child will provide adequate care for the child, this assumption is unreasonable when the surviving spouse is not the child's parent and has never assumed any responsibility for the child's care.

Because the facts of this case are significantly different from *Cogger,* the analysis in *Cogger* must be reconsidered to take into account the peculiar facts of this case. Although reference to prior statutory language, used in *Cogger,* is often a legitimate method of statutory interpretation, courts must also construe statutes to avoid unreasonable results.

Keithley v. Keithley, 289 N.W.2d 368 (Wis.Ct.App. 1980). Denying Amanda a cause of action would be unreasonable because it would vitiate the policy of protecting dependent minors explicit in the 1961 amendment and would result in an outcome which the legislature could not have intended.

A rigid application of *Cogger* is especially unreasonable in light of *O'Leary v. Porter,* 167 N.W.2d 193 (Wis. 1969). The court in *O'Leary* ruled that children of divorced parents have a cause of action for the wrongful death of the supporting parent, even if the decedent is survived by the ex-spouse. In *O'Leary,* the surviving child, Kevin O'Leary, was allowed a cause of action for the wrongful death of his mother, Janice O'Leary, even though Mrs. O'Leary was survived by her ex-husband. The court held that Kevin did have a cause of action for the wrongful death of his mother. In reaching its decision, the *O'Leary* court stressed that past support of the mother was sufficient proof of actual pecuniary loss by the child.

Our case is more factually analogous to *O'Leary* than *Cogger.* Just as Kevin O'Leary was dependent on his mother for support, Amanda was dependent on her mother. Furthermore, just as the surviving ex-spouse, Patrick O'Leary, has assumed no responsibility to care for Kevin, Hans Nelson has not assumed any responsibility to care for Amanda. Our case is distinguishable from *O'Leary* only by the remarriage of the supporting parent prior to the accident. Unlike the differences between *Cogger* and our case, which are important because of their close relation to the policy of protecting minor children, the distinction between our case and *O'Leary* rests only on the parent's marital status, which in this case bears no relation to the policy goals advanced by the statute.

It is unreasonable to deny Amanda recovery simply because Amanda's mother and Hans Nelson chose to marry. Had Karen and Hans Nelson merely lived together, Amanda would have had a cause of action for wrongful death under *O'Leary.* In both cases, the legal relationship between Amanda and Hans Nelson is the same. Therefore, it is unreasonable to interpret the wrongful death statute to forbid Amanda recovery.

Because this Court has a duty to interpret statutes to avoid unreasonable results, the *Cogger* decision must be modified to permit recovery where the surviving spouse has not assumed any responsibility to care for a surviving child. This is necessary to realize the legislative purpose of the post–1961 wrongful death statute: the protection of dependent minors.

Assignment 1

Write the brief supporting a motion to dismiss Jamie Blottner's case. See Assignment 1 in Chapter 6 and in Chapter 12 for details.

Assignment 2

Write the rest of the appellate brief for the Putnams' case, described in Assignment 2 at the end of Chapter 4 and Assignment 2 at the end of Chapter 8.

BIBLIOGRAPHY

Babb, Howard S., *Essays in Stylistic Analysis*. New York: Harcourt Brace Jovanovich, Inc., 1972.

Beasley, Mary Beth, *A Practical Guide to Appellate Advocacy*. New York: Aspen Law & Business, 2002.

Benson, Robert W. and Joan B. Kersken, *Legalese v. Plain English: An Empirical Study of Persuasion and Credibility in Appellate Brief Writing*, 20 Loy.L.A.L.Rev. 301 (Jan. 1987).

Bergman, Paul, *Trial Advocacy in a Nutshell*. St. Paul: West Group, 3d ed. 1997.

Board of Student Advisers, Harvard Law School, *Introduction to Advocacy*. Mineola, NY: Foundation Press, 7th ed. 2002.

Cooper, Frank E., *Writing in Law Practice*. Indianapolis: Bobbs–Merrill, 2d ed. 1963.

Crowhurst, Marion. *Interrelationships Between Reading and Writing Persuasive Discourse*. Vol. 25, no. 3, p. 314 (Oct. 1991).

Dernbach, John L. and Richard V. Singleton, III, *A Practical Guide to Legal Writing and Legal Method*. Littleton, Co: Fred B. Rothman, 2d ed. 1994.

Eble, Timothy E. and Mary M. Molloy, *Ten Commandments of Appellate Advocacy*, Case & Comment 16 (Jan.-Feb. 1986).

Goodrich, Herbert Funk, *A Case on Appeal: A Judge's View*. Philadelphia: Joint Committee on Continuing Legal Education of the American Law Institute and the American Bar Association, 4th ed. 1967.

Grey, Lawrence, *Writing a Good Appellate Brief*, 57 N.Y.B.J. 24 (Feb. 1985).

Hammond, Eugene, *Critical Thinking, Thoughtful Writing*. New York: McGraw–Hill, 2d ed. 1989.

Hatch, Richard A. *Business Communication: Theory and Technique*. Chicago: Science Research Associates, 1983.

Hayden, Donald E. *Classics in Composition*. New York: Philosophical Library, 1989.

Jackson, Robert. *Advocacy Before the Supreme Court: Suggestions for Effective Case Presentations*, 37 A.B.A.J. 801 (1951).

Kaplan, Lueithe R., *Writing That Persuades: No Quick Fix for The Advocate*, 20 Trial 44 (June 1984).

Kirsch, Gesa, *Writing Up and Down the Social Ladder: A Study of Experienced Writers Composing or Contrasting Audiences*, 25 (1) Research in Teaching of English 33 (Feb. 1991).

Lee, Vernon. *The Handling of Words, and Other Studies in Literary Psychology*. Lewiston: E. Mellen Press, 1992 (originally published in 1923).

Murry, John Middleton, *The Problem of Style*. Westport, CT: Greenwood Press, 1980.

O'Keefe, Daniel J., *Persuasion: Theory and Research*. Thousand Oaks, CA: Sage Publications, 2d ed. 2002.

Peck, Girvan, *Writing Persuasive Briefs*. Boston: Little, Brown, & Co., 1984.

Pittoni, Mario, *Brief Writing and Argumentation*. Brooklyn: The Foundation Press, Inc., 3d ed. 1967.

Re, Edward D., *Effective Legal Writing and the Appellate Brief*, 89 Case & Comment 9 (July–Aug. 1984).

Rivers, William L., *Writing: Craft and Art*. Englewood Cliff, NJ: Prentice–Hall, Inc., 1975.

Sandell, Rolf, *Linguistic Style and Persuasion*. San Francisco, CA: Academic Press, 1977.

Schauble, Leona and Robert Glaser, *Innovations in Learning: New Environments for Education*. Mahwah, NJ: Lawrence Erlbaum Associates, 1996.

Schultz, Nancy L., *Introduction to Legal Writing and Oral Advocacy*. New York: Matthew Bender, 2d ed. 1993.

Simons, Herbert G., *Persuasion: Understanding, Practice, and Analysis*. New York: Random House, 2d ed. 1986.

Spears, Franklin, *Presenting An Effective Appeal,* 21 Trial 95 (Nov. 1985).

Stark, Steven D., *Writing to Win*. New York: Doubleday, 2000.

Stern, Robert, *Supreme Court Practice*. Washington, DC: Bureau of National Affairs, 8th ed. 2002.

Tate, Albert Jr., *The Art of Brief Writing: What a Judge Wants to Read*, 4 Lit. 11 (Winter 1978).

Villanueva, Victor, Jr., ed., *Cross-Talk in Comp Theory: A Reader*. Urbana, IL: National Council of Teachers of English, 1997.

Weihofen, Henry, *Legal Writing Style*. St. Paul: West Group, 2d ed. 1990.

Wydick, Richard, *Plain English for Lawyers*. Durham, NC: Carolina Academic Press, 4th ed. 1998.

Chapter 11

PLEADINGS

———

Many new associates in law firms are dismayed when asked, often within the first month of practice, to draft pleadings. They have had little or no practice drafting them during law school. In addition, they quickly learn that pleadings can be difficult to write because of the analytical, tactical, and writing concerns they raise. But drafting pleadings is an integral part of the practice of law. Although most attorneys do not have a litigation practice or even try cases, virtually all draft pleadings during their careers.

Pleadings are the documents that initiate a lawsuit and, although ninety-five percent of cases settle before trial,[1] all cases filed in court start with pleadings. In the complaint, the plaintiff alleges the actions by the defendant that are the basis of the plaintiff's claims. The complaint describes the damages the plaintiff has incurred and states the remedies desired. In the answer, the defendant responds to the allegations contained in the complaint.[2] The answer states which of the plaintiff's allegations the defendant admits are true and which he or she denies. The answer also raises affirmative defenses to the plaintiff's claims and can raise counterclaims against the plaintiff as well. This chapter discusses the drafting of both of these pleadings, after discussing the general writing concerns that come into play with both complaints and answers, and the process needed to address those concerns.

GENERAL CONCERNS

Pleadings have many purposes. Filing the complaint commences the

---

1. William W. Schwarzer, *The Federal Rules, The Adversary Process, and Discovery Reform*, 50 U.Pitt.L.Rev. 703, 707–08 (1989)(for civil cases filed in federal courts). Percentages in state courts may vary. For example, in California, 98% of all civil cases settle before trial. *Senate Bill Curbing Secrecy Agreements in Insurance Bad Suits*, 13 (No. 5) Cal.Ins.L. & Reg.Rep. 75 (2001).

2. Before answering the complaint, the defendant must decide whether to bring any motions challenging the complaint.

Fed.R.Civ.P. 12(b). (Due to the numerous differences between the states in their procedural practices, most references in this chapter are to the Federal Rules of Civil Procedure. However, even these rules are subject to variation under the Local Rules of each district. Always check the rules controlling your jurisdiction before drafting these documents.) For a fuller discussion of the role motions play, see Chapter 12, Notices of Motion, Motions, and Orders.

action.[3] It gives the other party notice of the claim pending against him or her.[4] Once filed or served, it stops the running of the statute of limitations. Together, the complaint and the answer focus the disputed facts and issues between the parties. The answer prevents the plaintiff from seeking a default judgment. Either document can encourage the opposing side to settle and may establish a dollar amount for settlement negotiations.[5] Both documents also provide notice of the facts underlying each side's arguments and the legal theories on which they rely.

When you consider the important role pleadings play in most attorneys' daily practice, it is surprising how little time most attorneys spend writing a particular pleading. Many simply copy language from form books or sample pleadings found in the office, making only those changes required by the different fact situations. These documents, however, deserve careful preparation. Much valuable attorney and court time can be saved when these documents are drafted with more attention.

Because the pleadings establish the substance of the lawsuit, you must be thorough and precise. Thoroughness is necessary to present your client's cause of action fully. You must include all causes of action you want to raise, including all elements in those causes of action and alleging the facts necessary to establish each element. You must allege the facts establishing a particular element even if they appear undisputed because, without them, you will fail to support every element of the cause of action. If you do not include every element of each cause of action, the complaint is vulnerable to a challenge for failure to state a claim upon which relief can be granted, and may be dismissed with or without leave to amend.[6]

Precision is necessary when stating both the allegations in the complaint and the admissions or denials in the answer. You will be unable to narrow the issues for trial if these documents are not precise. By precisely stating the allegations of each cause of action, you tell your opponent exactly what your view of the facts is, and you force your opponent to answer your allegations specifically. If your allegations are precise, your opponent must admit those that are true, which reduces the facts you must prove at trial and strengthens your case for settle-

---

3. Fed.R.Civ.P. 3.

4. Fed.R.Civ.P. 8(a). This rule states that the complaint should be "a short and plain statement of the claim showing that the pleader is entitled to relief." Additionally, in federal court, the complaint must state the basis for the court's jurisdiction and a demand for judgment for the relief sought. *Id.*

5. The federal rules do not require that specific dollar amounts be pleaded and Rule 54(c) states that the final judgment should grant the relief to which the party is entitled, even if that specific relief was not demanded in the pleadings. However, Rule 54(c) only permits relief in the amount requested in the demand for judgment in the

case of default judgments, thus encouraging specific dollar amounts to be included in case of default. Some state rules forbid specific dollar amounts to be pleaded in some instances. For example, Cal.Civ.Pro. § 425.10(b) provides that you may not allege a specific dollar amount in a personal injury complaint, and Cal.Civ. § 3295(e) provides that you may not allege the amount of punitive damages sought.

6. In the federal courts, this challenge would be brought as a motion under Fed. R.Civ.P. 12(b)(6). Some states refer to this challenge as a demurrer to the complaint, but the result is the same: if the challenge is granted, your complaint is dismissed.

ment. The same holds true for the answer: if your responses are precise, you can eliminate undisputed issues and focus on defending your client on the issues that are in dispute.

PROCESS FOR ACHIEVING THOROUGHNESS AND PRECISION

The need for thoroughness and precision begins even before you begin drafting. Just as you must research before writing a memo or a brief, you must also obtain the information you need to write pleadings. You will interview your client and investigate the facts, research the procedural and substantive law, and make many tactical decisions. Only after completing these initial steps will you be prepared to begin drafting, a process also requiring several steps.

Interview Your Client and Investigate the Facts

The basis for writing a thorough pleading comes from knowledge of the client's situation, so the interview is the usual place to begin. In the interview, obtain as much information as possible with an eye toward framing the cause(s) of action. Although your client may know that he or she wants to bring a lawsuit, you must determine what cause(s) of action to pursue. A good framework for beginning the interview is to use interviewing techniques that "encourage clients to express the full range of their concerns."[7] During this initial interview, remember to ask reporter's questions: who, what, when, where, why, and how. Elicit the dates, times, places, parties, documents, events, and any other relevant information. Be sure to ask the hard questions: those questions that may challenge the client's version of what happened or that may put the client in a harsh light. For example, if your client is describing a traffic accident, ask whether he or she was driving over the speed limit or broke any other traffic rules. While you need to ask these questions with tact and understanding, you do need to ask them.[8]

After completing the interview, verify the information you have and obtain any other needed information. For example, rather than assuming that your client was correct in her statement that the president of the company refused to provide the contracted-for items, you may want to contact the company and verify who the president is and whether that person did, in fact, refuse to provide the items specified under the contract. This investigation may help you avoid bringing a breach of contract action because of an error in the shipping department.

As part of your verification, obtain relevant documents and witnesses' statements when possible. This additional information can help

---

7. *See* Gay Gelhorn, *Law and Language: An Empirically–Based Model for the Opening Moments of Client Interviews,* 4 Clinical L.Rev. 321, 358 (1998).

8. For additional information on interviewing techniques, *see* David A. Binder, Paul Bergman, and Susan C. Price, *Lawyers as Counselors: A Client–Centered Approach* (1991). For an empirical study establishing the importance of using certain techniques during the initial interview to elicit a complete statement of the client's concerns, *see* Gelhorn, *supra* note 7.

fill out the facts that you learned during the client interview and help you make decisions about how to proceed. For example, if your client told you he was injured in an automobile accident, you would contact the police department to obtain a copy of the police report and contact the insurance company to obtain a copy of the applicable policy. Then you might check with the witnesses listed on the police report and try to obtain a brief statement from each of them regarding their views of the accident. It is preferable to find out whether any of them considers the accident to be your client's fault before filing a negligence action against the defendant.

Research the Procedural and Substantive Law

After gaining a thorough understanding of the situation by interviewing your client and investigating the facts, the next step is to research the procedural and substantive law controlling lawsuits in your jurisdiction. Before you can draft a complaint or respond to one, you must understand the procedure that controls the lawsuit. You must also understand the underlying substantive law because pleadings are based on legal theories, even though those legal theories are not always explicitly stated within the pleading.

Start your research by determining the procedural requirements for your jurisdiction. Each jurisdiction has different rules controlling pleading practice, and each court within a given jurisdiction may have additional local rules controlling that practice. Usually the code of civil procedure for your jurisdiction will contain the general rules, and the clerk of court can provide the local rules.[9] These rules will control the appearance and content of your pleading.

These rules, for example, require you to use the correct caption for each document. Most courts have very specific rules regarding the format of the caption of your documents. Federal Rule of Civil Procedure 10(a) specifies that the caption must state the name of the court, the title of the action, the file number, and the name of the document.[10] While these details may seem insignificant, they are not. Many court clerks reject documents that do not conform to these rules.

These procedural rules also control the content of the document. For example, California rules state that a general denial may be used only for those complaints that are unverified or for verified complaints alleging less than $1,000 in damages.[11] When answering a verified

9. For a discussion of the challenges that these different local rules present for practitioners and of how to handle questions when the local rules conflict with the Federal Rules, *see* Walter W. Heiser, *A Critical Review of the Local Rules of the United States District Court for the Southern District of California*, 35 San Diego L.Rev. 555 (1996).

10. This rule requires that all the parties must be named in the complaint, but subsequent captions can simply include the first party on each side, with an indication that other parties exist. Fed.R.Civ.P. 10(a). Similar rules exist in most states. *See, e.g.,* Mass.Civ.P. 10(a); N.Y.C.C.P. 2101(c); Pa. R.C.P. 1018; Utah R.Civ.P. 10(a).

11. Verified complaints must be signed by the complaining party. Cal.Civ.Pro. § 431.30.

complaint alleging more than $1,000 in damages in California, you must use the special denial form and respond to each allegation of the complaint specifically, rather than use the general denial form that denies all the allegations of the complaint.[12]

In contrast, the Federal Rules of Civil Procedure virtually preclude the use of general denials, even though many states use them, because they require the person answering to deny specific allegations in the complaint, unless he or she intends "in good faith" to controvert all of them.[13] Thus, in federal court you must admit any of the allegations in the complaint that are true. A few states also require the answer to include "the substance of the matters on which the pleader will rely to support the denial."[14] In these jurisdictions, you would be required to state the factual basis for your denial.

The procedural rules also control some substantive aspects of pleading. For example, the federal rules state that, when pleading the performance or occurrence of conditions precedent, it is sufficient to allege generally that all the conditions precedent have been performed or have occurred.[15] The same rule requires that the denials in the answer of the performance or occurrence of conditions precedent "be made specifically and with particularity."[16] The federal rules also require that all affirmative defenses be set forth when responding to a preceding pleading.[17]

To draft a thorough and precise complaint, you must also understand the legal theories underlying the document. You cannot simply state the facts and expect the court to allow your pleading to withstand a demurrer motion or motion to dismiss for failure to state a claim.[18] To avoid such a motion, you must include every element necessary to every cause of action raised within your complaint, even if those facts are not disputed. Otherwise, your complaint will not withstand scrutiny. Some sources for determining the elements of specific causes of actions include cases decided in your state, your state's jury instructions, Restatements, form books containing sample complaints and counterclaims, encyclopedias and hornbooks, and statutes within your jurisdiction. You may want

---

12. Cal.Civ.Pro. § 431.40. A general denial to verified complaints is allowed in municipal court. Cal.Civ.Pro. § 431.30(d).

13. Fed.R.Civ.P. 8(b). Federal Rule 11 states that an attorney's signature at the bottom of a pleading indicates that the allegations have evidentiary support and the legal constructions are warranted by law and not imposed to cause unnecessary delay, harassment, or increase in litigation cost.

14. Michigan Court Rules 2.111(D)—Form of Denials. Irwin Alterman, *Plain and Accurate Style in Lawsuit Papers,* 2 Cooley L.Rev. 243, 281 (1981).

15. Fed.R.Civ.P. 9(c).

16. *Id.*

17. Fed.R.Civ.P. 8(c). These affirmative defenses include accord and satisfaction, duress, estoppel, laches, res judicata, and statute of limitations. The rule also states that when a party has "mistakenly designated a defense as a counterclaim or a counterclaim as a defense, the court, if justice so requires, shall treat the pleading as if there had been a proper designation." *Id.*

18. Different jurisdictions use different names to refer to their motions to dismiss for the legal insufficiency of the complaint. For example, in the federal system, this motion is controlled by Fed.R.Civ.P. 12(b)(6) and is called a motion to dismiss for failure to state a claim upon which relief can be granted. In California, the same challenge is raised by a demurrer motion. Cal.Civ.Pro. § 430.10(e).

to look specifically for cases that upheld the sufficiency of a complaint on the same cause of action.[19] By reading several cases that analyze the causes of action you plan to include in the complaint, you can ensure that you understand which facts the judge will be looking for when analyzing the complaint's sufficiency.[20]

Before drafting the answer, you must complete the same research. You must be thorough, because most jurisdictions require that all affirmative defenses be stated in the answer.[21] While you can amend your answer freely,[22] the better practice is to include all defenses within the original answer, so you need not spend the time and money filing an amended answer.

To help ensure that their pleadings include all possible causes of action or affirmative defenses, many attorneys use checklists. A sample checklist is included in the section below on drafting the body of the complaint. Although you cannot draft a checklist that will list everything needed for every pleading, you can draft one that includes the standard causes of action arising in your area of practice and the usual denials and affirmative defenses made in response to those causes of action. You can then compare your checklist to the facts involved in a particular case to determine which causes of action or defenses are available.

Consider Tactics When Drafting Pleadings

Many new associates move right from interviewing and researching into drafting. But if they do this, they skip an important step taken by more experienced attorneys. That step is considering tactics when drafting pleadings. When associates ask for advice from other attorneys in their firm, they find that most of those attorneys have definite opinions about how pleadings should be written based on tactical considerations. Experienced attorneys often cannot take the time to discuss these considerations, so the associates are left to struggle on their own. By reviewing the tactical considerations discussed in this section, you will be better prepared to draft your own pleadings with a more advanced approach.

Several tactical considerations arise when drafting the complaint. The first is who should be named as defendants and what claims should be joined. After you have interviewed your client and completed your factual and legal research, you must analyze this information to determine the possible defendants and causes of action. Then consider which of these defendants your client should sue and which claims to join. You may want to include all defendants in your complaint and join all

---

19. Jan Armon, *A Method for Writing Factual Complaints*, 1998 Det. C.L.Mich.S.U.L.Rev. 109, 140.

20. *Id.* at 124.

21. Fed.R.Civ.P. 8(c), Tex.T.R.C.P. 94, Cal.Civ.Pro. 431.30, Mich.C.P. 2.111(F)(3).

22. Fed.R.Civ.P. 15(a) allows you to amend a pleading once as a matter of course any time before the responsive pleading is served, or if no responsive pleading is required, within twenty days after the pleading is served. Otherwise, you may only amend the pleading with leave of the court, which is to be "freely given when justice so requires."

possible claims. Other tactical considerations, however, may militate against this. For example, the presence of remote defendants might irritate the jury. Extensive briefings on sophisticated jurisdictional issues relating to another defendant might not be worth the aggravation. Difficulty of proof might render another cause of action virtually useless. Or you might want helpful testimony from someone who would not be friendly if named as a defendant. Now is the time to decide whom to sue and for what.[23]

The second tactical consideration involves deciding what legal theories to allege. Consider which legal theories will be easiest to prove, which will best provide the relief desired, and which will reach the defendants who have the most resources to contribute. Also consider what theories your evidence will support. Many attorneys allege different causes of action to ensure that at least one will be established by the evidence that is admitted by the court and presented by the witnesses. If your complaint supports several causes of action, then your client may achieve the desired result even if the evidence does not support the main theory you expected to advance when the lawsuit began. But do not include causes of actions that are clearly outside the facts or that have no chance for success.

The third tactical consideration concerns where to file your complaint. Jurisdiction and venue requirements will significantly affect your decision in this matter. But you may have some choices. For example, you may have the choice to bring your action either where the defendant resides or where the accident occurred.[24] When you have such a choice, you should carefully consider what location will be most favorable for obtaining your client's desired result. For example, consider the situation of conflicting federal court of appeals decisions, some of which support your legal theory, some of which destroy it. Your research indicates that the court of appeals where the defendant resides has decided a case contrary to the argument you must make, while the court of appeals where the accident occurred has not decided any cases on this particular issue. You may decide to bring the action where the accident occurred to avoid direct case law against you, depending on other considerations, such as ease of movement for yourself, the plaintiff, and your witnesses; local court rules; and jury considerations.

The fourth tactical consideration involves how much information to provide in your complaint if notice pleading is allowed in your jurisdiction. The federal rules state that a pleading need only include "a short and plain statement of the claim showing that the pleader is entitled to relief."[25] This is known as "notice pleading" and requires only that the complaint give the defendant enough information to provide notice of the claim against him or her.[26] A majority of the states also allow notice

---

23. Karla Wright, *A Seven Step Process for Preparing Non–Routine Complaints,* 77 Ill.Bar J. 662, 663 (August 1989).

24. 28 U.S.C. § 1391.

25. Fed.R.Civ.P. 8(a).

26. Many commentators dislike use of this term and prefer "modern pleading" or "simplified pleading" due to concerns that

pleading.[27] You may decide to provide only the minimum information required by the rules, so you can avoid informing your opponent of your strategy or assisting him or her in discovery. On the other hand, providing additional information establishing a strong case for your client at the outset can induce settlement negotiations and may require the defendant to admit or deny information that will assist you with discovery.

The fifth tactical consideration involves what types of relief to request and what amount of damages to allege. Many attorneys try to include as many types of relief as possible so that, once trial has been completed, the judge or jury will have as many options as possible in granting relief. Additionally, including multiple claims for relief may make the incentive for settlement stronger.

One final tactical consideration concerns whether to rebut anticipated affirmative defenses. Under the federal rules, no pleading is required beyond a complaint and an answer.[28] Thus you have no opportunity to reply to an answer. While the court may order a reply to a third-party answer, do not assume that permission will be granted to respond to a standard answer.[29] If you do not anticipate affirmative defenses, you may be precluded from responding to them until the motions are filed or the case goes to trial. But it can be dangerous to state your responses to anticipated defenses because, without your assistance, your opponent might not have raised those defenses.

Different tactical considerations arise when drafting the answer. The first is whether the answer is the best response to the complaint. Before answering to the complaint, you may want to raise defenses to the plaintiff's claims for relief.[30] In federal court, the defenses that may be raised by motion before answering include

- lack of subject matter jurisdiction,
- lack of personal jurisdiction,
- improper venue,
- insufficient process,
- insufficient service of process,
- failure to state a claim upon which relief can be granted, or

---

pleadings that, in fact, merely provide notice that a suit was filed and damages alleged are insufficient to meet the requirements of either federal or state rules. Jack H. Friedenthal, Mary Kay Kane, and Arthur R. Miller, *Civil Procedure* § 5.7 (3d ed. 1999).

27. *Id.* at § 5.1 n.14. *See, e.g.,* Mass. Rule of Civ.Pro. 8(a), Wis.Stats. § 802.02(1), Ill.Comp. Stat. 5/2–603. A number of states still use code pleading. Drafting code pleadings is more difficult than drafting notice pleadings because of controversies that arise concerning what

constitutes a "cause of action," and an "ultimate fact" as compared to evidentiary facts or conclusions of law. For further discussion of these problems, *see,* Friedenthal, *supra* note 26, at §§ 5.4–5.7.

28. Fed.R.Civ.P. 7(a). Rule 7(a) also permits a reply to a counterclaim, an answer to a cross-claim, and a third-party complaint and answer.

29. *Id.*

30. Fed.R.Civ.P. 12(b). See Chapter 12: Notices of Motion, Motions, and Orders for a fuller discussion.

● failure to join a party under Rule 19.[31]

Although you can also raise these defenses in your answer, you may decide to raise them by pre-answer motion. Then you do not need to admit or deny your opponent's allegations while raising defenses that may eliminate the lawsuit completely. You will waive some of these defenses if you do not raise them either in a pre-answer motion or in your answer.[32]

The second consideration is whether to raise any affirmative defenses and whether to present any counterclaims. You must make these decisions when preparing your answer or you may be precluded from doing so. Federal Rule 8(c) requires you to raise all the affirmative defenses you have when answering,[33] or you may waive them and have them excluded from the case.[34] Although the list in Rule 8(c) is not exhaustive, it can help remind you of defenses you might otherwise have overlooked.[35] Similarly, you will waive any compulsory counterclaims if they are not raised in the answer; these counterclaims arise out of the same transaction or occurrence as the main claim and do not include third parties outside the court's jurisdiction.[36] You may also include permissive counterclaims against any opposing party; these counterclaims do not arise out of the same transaction or occurrence on which the complaint is based.[37] If you forget to include a permissive counterclaim, however, you may amend the pleading to raise it.[38]

After gaining some experience with these tactical considerations, most attorneys develop strong opinions about what should and should not be included in pleadings. The attorneys you work with will likely have their own views, and you must learn these preferences when drafting pleadings for them. Talk with other attorneys about their

---

31. Fed.R.Civ.P.12(b).

32. Fed.R.Civ.P. 12(g)-(h). Those waived are defenses of lack of personal jurisdiction, improper venue, insufficient process, or insufficient service of process. Fed.R.Civ.P. 12(h)(1). The defenses of failure to state a claim upon which relief can be granted, to join an indispensable party under Rule 19, or to state a legal defense to a claim may be made up to the trial. Fed.R.Civ.P. 12(h)(2).

33. Fed.R.Civ.P. 8(c) states that a party must set forth any matter constituting an avoidance or affirmative defense in the answer to the complaint.

34. 5 Charles A. Wright and Arthur R. Miller, *Federal Practice and Procedure* § 1278 (1990). *See also, Dole v. Williams Enterprises, Inc.,* 876 F.2d 186, 189 (D.C.Cir.1989); *Mooney v. City of New York,* 219 F.3d 123, 127 n.2 (2nd Cir. 2000); *Red Deer v. Cherokee County, Iowa,* 183 F.R.D. 642, 650 (N.D. Iowa 1999). Several exceptions to this rule do exist. Wright and Miller, at § 1278. If you neglect to include an

affirmative defense, move to amend your answer under Fed.R.Civ.P. 15(a).

35. Irwin Alterman, *Plain and Accurate Style in Court Papers* § 5.05 (1987).

36. Fed.R.Civ.P. 13(a). These counterclaims do not need to be presented if (1) at the time the action was commenced, the claim was the subject of another pending action, or (2) the opposing party brought suit upon the claim by attachment or other process by which the court did not acquire jurisdiction to render a personal judgment on that claim and the pleader is not stating any counterclaim under Rule 13. *Id.*

37. Fed.R.Civ.P. 13(b). But you must also have an independent basis of jurisdiction for any permissive counterclaim. Joseph W. Glannon, *Civil Procedure: Examples and Explanations* 281–83, 287 (4th ed. 2001).

38. Fed.R.Civ.P. 13(f). Amendment is allowed when the counterclaim is excluded through oversight, inadvertence, excusable neglect, or when justice requires.

tactics in drafting pleadings and vary your pleading practice accordingly. With experience, you will develop your own preferences and this will save you time. Be careful, though, to avoid becoming too set in your ways; analyze each situation anew.

DRAFTING THE COMPLAINT

Having completed your factual and legal research and having considered your tactics, now draft the complaint. As you do, maintain your focus on thoroughness and precision. A complaint usually has six main parts:

- the caption,
- the commencement,
- the body or charging part,
- the prayer or demand for judgment,
- the signature, and
- the verification.

This section discusses each of these parts, including drafting considerations that apply to each part and to the complaint in general.

The Caption

The caption includes the jurisdiction, the name of the court, the venue, the title of the case including the names of the parties and their positions, the case number, the file or docket number, and the name of the document.

STATE OF KENTUCKY CIRCUIT COURT FAYETTE COUNTY

Branch 11

SUSAN G. BLACK and DAVID R. BLACK,		
	Plaintiffs,	COMPLAINT
vs.		
STEWART PROPERTIES, INC.,		Case No. 20___ CV 10
	Defendant.	

This caption is repeated on all the documents filed with the court; the only change is in the name of the document. Many rules also require the first pleading to include the names of all parties, while subsequent pleadings can simply state the first party for each side and an indication, such as "et al.," that other parties exist.[39] Although it may seem arbitrary and a bother, this form and repetition serves a useful function. The caption's information insures correct filing, and the record of the

---

39. Fed.R.Civ.P. 10(a).

case proceedings shows that the proper legal procedure was followed. To insure clarity, consider naming each document even if your jurisdiction does not require it.

The Commencement

The commencement follows the caption and introduces the complaint, but is set off from the body of the complaint. Most form complaints include legalese, which indicates to the court that additional legalese will likely follow. For example, the following commencements are often found in form books.

> Now comes Mollie Anderson by her attorney Henry Frank and alleges as follows:

Or

> Comes now the plaintiff Mollie Anderson and for cause of action and complaint against the defendant herein alleges:

Many users of form books feel compelled to include this legalese as magical "fairy dust" because they are afraid that, without this language, the judge may reject their complaints as incorrect. That fear, however, reveals a lack of sure knowledge about what is and is not required in the document. The judge will more likely applaud your decision to eliminate this legalese.

In addition to including legalese in the commencement, most attorneys also err by punctuating the commencement with a colon at the end.

> NOW COMES Mollie Anderson, by her attorney Henry Frank:

By ending the commencement with a colon, the attorney must either state each allegation as an incomplete sentence or misuse the colon.[40] Stating each allegation as an incomplete sentence makes the complaint difficult to read. Instead, rewrite your commencement as a complete sentence and, while rewriting it, eliminate the legalese.

> **Plaintiff, Mollie Anderson, represented by her attorney Henry Frank, states the following as a cause of action against defendant, John Hopkins.**

Or

> **Mollie Anderson, plaintiff, by her attorney Henry Frank, complains against John Hopkins, defendant, and asserts the following in support of her claim.**

These commencements include the same information as the traditional ones above, but are much more readable.

The Body or Charging Portion

This is the main portion of the complaint and consists of a series of numbered paragraphs. The paragraphs comprising this part must be

---

40. Mary Barnard Ray and Jill J. Ramsfield, *Legal Writing: Getting It Right and* *Getting It Written* 77–78 (3d ed. 2000).

broad enough to give you flexibility in proving your case at trial. They must also be sufficiently precise to give notice of the claims against your opponent. They must be thorough by including all the elements of the cause of action you are alleging. Remember that the opposing counsel, before answering, will consider whether to bring a demurrer or motion to dismiss for failure to state a claim. You must write your complaint with a view toward preventing or surviving that demurrer or motion.

Developing templates for each individual cause of action that you frequently encounter in your practice and overall checklists to use when drafting complaints, defensive motions, and answers is often helpful. To improve precision in the body of the complaint, some attorneys develop templates for each cause of action. As you research the law, you can organize the elements of the cause of action into a template and state categories of facts in ways that add up to state the cause of action.[41] Then, in the future, you can draft other complaints using that template, revising and updating it as the law changes or develops.[42] When you state your facts in language that was successful in previous cases, you help convince the judge that your complaint fits in with that successful line of cases.[43]

Additionally, using a checklist for each pleading or document that includes procedural and substantive elements is most useful for thoroughness because it reminds you of both procedural concerns and substantive causes of action that may be raised. How general or specific the checklist will be depends on the variety of cases you handle in your practice. The following excerpt shows the checklist's usefulness.

Complaint Checklist[44]

Related documents and questions

- Required statement and cover sheet
- Court fee
- Service fee
- Proper jurisdiction
- Proper venue
- All *proper* plaintiffs named (Name individuals in partnership or fictitious entity. Name guardians, if necessary.)
- Proper defendants and all defendants
- Proper service on all defendants
- Right courts (federal/state)

---

41. Armon, *supra* note 19, at 112.

42. *Id.*

43. *Id.* at 173.

44. The complete checklist is contained in Nancy Schleifer, *Complaint and Defensive Checklists*, 61 Fla.Bar J. 23 (July–Aug. 1987).

- Demand for jury trial

Allegations
- Jurisdiction over each defendant and capacity and jurisdictional amount or other basis of jurisdiction. Is corporation "in good standing"?
- Conformity of allegations to general rules of pleading
- Sufficient ultimate facts to show each type of relief sought
- All elements of each type of relief sought
- Separate statements—single set of circumstances per paragraph

Consider Causes of Action
- Negligence
- Breach of contract
- Breach of warranty

Special Damages—allege specifically in addition to compensatory damages. (Some of these may go in body of complaint rather than in plea for damages or costs.)
- Pain and suffering
- Consequential damages limited by contract?
- Loss of use
- Rental Value
- Punitives/trebles
- Cost of cover
- Lost profits
- Cost of collection (in contract?)
- Cost of receiver (in contract?)
- Costs of accounting (in contract?)
- Costs of investigation (in contract?)
- Prejudgment/postjudgment interest
- Attorney's fees
- Emotional damages (impact rule)

Developing a checklist will take time, but it may save time in the long run. It should be specifically annotated to include your local procedural rules and should include as much information as possible concerning potential causes of action and defenses. Having a checklist will help you feel more assured that you have considered the available options when drafting complaints or answers.

You must be careful, however, not to become overly dependent on your checklist; you might overlook other options available to your client. One way to avoid this lapse in thoroughness may be to have the last item or section of your checklist refer to brainstorming or researching other possible causes of action or defenses. Or your last item may refer to discussing these matters with your colleagues to help you recognize other options.

When you start drafting, the first paragraphs of the complaint's charging part identify the parties. If there are only two parties, paragraph one identifies the plaintiff and paragraph two identifies the defendant.

1. Mollie Anderson, the plaintiff, is an adult residing at 1234 Happy Valley Lane, Smalltown, Goodland County, Washington 98072.

2. John Hopkins, the defendant, is an adult residing at 5678 Mountain View Avenue, Village, Goodland County, Washington 98147.

Include a separate paragraph for each additional plaintiff or defendant. These paragraphs should state each individual's name and address, whether he or she is an adult or minor, and perhaps the person's occupation. If needed for indicating venue, include other information such as the county. If a party is a business, state the type of business (sole proprietorship, partnership, or corporation) and its principal business address. For corporations, consider including the state law under which it is incorporated. If you do not know the names of all the defendants, many state and federal courts allow you to allege them fictitiously using the name "Doe 1" or "John Doe."[45]

After identifying the parties, you will state the allegations that support your cause of action. Depending on your tactical decisions, you may include all or only some of the causes of action arising under the facts that concern the defendants named in the complaint. You will probably include most of the possible causes of action, because those not raised when an incident is being litigated may be precluded by res judicata.[46] Many attorneys start with the cause of action that is factually most comprehensive or the one that may be most familiar to the judicial reader. If you have several counts arising under each cause of action, organize each one separately with headings that specify the cause of action and then state Count I, Count II, and so on under each.[47] Because

---

45. *See e.g.,* Mass.Gen.Laws Ann. ch. 223, § 19.

46. Res judicata or claim preclusion means that a final judgment on the merits of a cause of action is conclusive on the parties' rights and has binding effect on all subsequent lawsuits arising from the same cause of action. How "cause of action" is defined determines whether subsequent lawsuits arising from the same incident can be litigated. The federal rules broadly de-fine cause of action and allow for liberal joinder of claims, so that all claims arising from one incident should be litigated in the same lawsuit. If joinder of claims is restricted, then the cause of action is restricted, and the judgment may not be res judicata on other claims. Friedenthal, *supra* note 26 at § 14.4.

47. Armon, *supra* note 19, at 153. Then, in later Counts, you can refer to the relevant facts in the earlier counts. Simply

the allegations may add up to more than one cause of action, some attorneys shy away from naming the specific cause of action in the headings and, instead, use headings that state Claim I, Claim II, and so forth. Doing this is fine as long as you make sure that you have stated all the elements of each cause of action you intended to raise.

While you must include factual allegations for every element of each cause of action, how much you include is a tactical decision for you to make. For example, you may withhold some favorable facts for some tactical advantage later. Or you may include these favorable facts if you believe they demonstrate the strength of your case to the defendant and increase the possibility of obtaining a good settlement. Just be sure to include enough facts to survive a motion to dismiss.

Controversy exists on whether the code pleading distinctions between evidentiary facts, ultimate facts, and conclusions of law should continue to matter to those drafting complaints. But some code pleading jurisdictions continue to maintain these requirements.[48] Even if the courts in your jurisdiction no longer make these distinctions, understanding each will help ensure that you have adequately included the needed allegations in your complaint. The following example explains the differences between each type of information. Evidentiary facts are those facts that tell the story of the incident. An ultimate fact is a fact that, if proven, would establish one element of your cause of action. A conclusion of law is a statement of an actual legal element of the cause of action that results from the ultimate fact.

For each element of the cause of action, you must allege enough evidentiary facts to establish the ultimate fact. You may want to allege that Fred was driving faster than the posted speed limit of twenty-five miles per hour, that the roads were icy, that snow was falling, and that the wind was blowing. You probably do not need to allege that Fred was driving a red car, unless the allegation is needed for identification. You must plead the ultimate fact that Fred was driving too fast for conditions because this is the factual basis supporting your allegation that Fred breached his duty of care to Sally, a required element to prove a cause of action for negligence. Although courts used to ignore conclusions of law and treat them as "nonexistent allegations" in your pleadings, most no longer do so,[49] and including them may help ensure that you have stated all elements of your cause of action.

state "The allegations in paragraphs X through Y are adopted" without including "by reference" to eliminate redundancy. *Id.*

48. *See* Friedenthal, *supra* note 26, at § 5.1 n.15 (referring to statutes in California and Nebraska requiring "fact" pleading), § 5.5 and § 5.8. For further discussion, *see also* § 5.5 on the "Uncertain Meaning of 'Facts' in the Code Pleading Section"; Armon, *supra* note 19, at 174, indicating that the question of what is an ultimate fact "has refused to go away." Both Florida and Oregon statutorily refer to including ultimate facts. *Id.* at 174 n.169.

49. Friedenthal, *supra* note 26, at § 5.5.

Sample Interrelationship of Facts and Law

Evidentiary Facts Discovered During Investigation	Ultimate Fact You Are Trying to Establish	Conclusion of Law This Would Support
Joan saw Fred driving very fast down the street. Joan wrote down the car's license plate number. Fred was driving a red car. The posted speed limit was 25 m.p.h. Snow was falling and the wind was blowing. The roads were icy. Fred hit Sally while she was crossing the street.	Fred was driving too fast for conditions.	Fred breached his duty of care to Sally

In your complaint, write separate paragraphs for your factual allegations and your conclusions of law. Defendants routinely deny conclusions of law, even if they admit some or all of the facts supporting the conclusion. By separating facts from conclusions, you prevent the defendant from denying the existence of a fact simply because it is contained in the same allegation as a conclusion of law. For example, do not state your allegations as follows.

7.　Snow was falling, the wind was blowing, and the roads were icy. Fred was driving too fast for conditions and thus breached his duty of care to Sally.

Instead, rewrite your allegations to separate evidentiary facts from ultimate facts from legal conclusions.

7.　Snow was falling, the wind was blowing, and the roads were icy.

8.　Fred was driving too fast for conditions.

9.　By driving too fast for conditions, Fred breached his duty of care to Sally.

By separating the allegations, the defendant may have to admit allegation 7 if those facts are true.[50] The defendant will probably deny both the ultimate fact and the conclusion of law contained in allegations 8 and 9, but if you gain an admission of allegation 7, you do not have to prove those facts at trial. This can save time and money.

State your facts precisely and unemotionally. Hyperbole and generalities make it easy for the defendant to deny allegations containing them. If your allegations are precise and brief, the defendant may be forced to admit them. Being precise means using objective words, rather than coloring your evidentiary facts or ultimate facts. Saying that Fred drove "recklessly" or "carelessly" would probably result in a denial by

---

50.　However, the defendant may try to file a general denial to the complaint in this situation, if allowed under the procedural rules, so that he or she does not have to admit any allegations. Fed.R.Civ.P. 8(b) seems to preclude this practice if the defendant knows that some facts are true.

the defendant. In contrast, it would be harder to deny that Fred drove "faster than the speed limit."

Use verbs to make it clear how the defendant acted wrongfully. "Every cause of action is a verb transformed into the name for a wrongful act."[51] For example, in a complaint against a municipality for wrongful exclusionary zoning, you might allege "The Town's zoning ordinance in effect excludes the proposed use for plaintiff's land."[52]

Finally, do not allege more than you actually know. In the example above, it would be easy to allege that Fred drove "his" car too fast for conditions. However, you probably do not know whether it was his car or not. By using "a" car, you avoid letting Fred deny the allegation solely because it was not his car. In the same way, do not allege that a defendant "owned, operated, controlled, and managed" the restaurant. If the defendant simply managed it, then he or she will be able to deny the allegation because three-quarters of your allegation is incorrect. The need to state facts precisely underscores the importance of investigating the facts after interviewing your client. Good investigation allows you to draft your allegations precisely and thus obtain the defendant's admissions.

Similarly, be precise about the dates, amounts, facts, and circumstances you do include. Oftentimes, attorneys answering complaints are able to deny allegations that otherwise would have to be admitted because a date or amount is incorrect. This denial by the defendant may lead you to believe that the substance of the allegation is being challenged when, in fact, the allegation was denied because of imprecise facts. If the primary factual basis for your complaint is found in a document (contract, letter, etc.), you can attach the document and incorporate it by reference. For example, you could state: "attached as exhibit A and incorporated in its entirety into this complaint."

The last paragraph of the body or charging portion of the complaint describes the plaintiff's injuries and damages. In jurisdictions where you can plead the amount of damages, the charging portion may end with an "ad damnum" clause, which means "to the damage."[53] This clause states "all to his [her] damage in the sum of $_____." But many attorneys prefer not to include a specific statement of the amount of damages unless that amount can be readily computed because the stated amount may cap the amount the plaintiff receives. Stating a specific amount may also cause the defendant to request that you itemize and explain each item of damage leading to the amount, or if the amount claimed is large and unsubstantiated, the ad damnum clause makes it appear that the plaintiff is inflating his or her demand.

The Prayer or Demand for Judgment

The federal rules require you to include a demand for judgment of the relief desired but allow you to demand several different types of

51. Armon, *supra* note 19, at 125.

52. *Id*. at 120 and 125.

53. *Black's Law Dictionary* 38 (7th ed. 1999).

relief.[54] This demand is not numbered. It usually starts with "Wherefore," which indicates that the demand follows from the allegations stated in the complaint's body, although "wherefore" can be eliminated. Here the plaintiff lists all the types of relief he or she believes are appropriate. Different types of relief include equitable relief, consequential or special damages, punitive damages, or specific performance. Here is a sample demand for judgment.

Plaintiff requests that the court:

(1) declare the defendant has tortiously interfered with plaintiff's contract;

(2) permanently enjoin the defendant from tortiously interfering with plaintiff's contract;

(3) award plaintiff the entitled amount of damages plus interest;

(4) award plaintiff its costs and attorney fees; and

(5) grant plaintiff any other relief the court considers equitable and just.

Notice the demand for judgment usually ends with the catchall phrase "any other relief the court considers equitable and just." The federal rules do not require this additional phrase in most situations; Rule 54(c) states that final judgments should include the relief to which the winning party is entitled, even if the party did not request that relief in the pleadings.[55] This phrase is important, however, in default judgment situations because default judgments may not be different in kind or exceed the amount requested in the demand for judgment.[56] Thus your demand for judgment limits the relief granted in default situations. In anticipation of those situations, adding "any other relief the court considers equitable and just" may allow the court to provide relief beyond that explicitly requested in your demand.

In the demand for judgment, also request interest and costs, and request attorney's fees if there is some basis for doing so. Some statutory causes of action (such as Title VII) provide for attorneys' fees for the successful complainant.[57] Most causes of action for frivolous suits or for frivolous motions also provide for attorneys' fees. Many contract actions involve a request for attorneys' fees, if the contract provides for them. You should include these requests if you want your fees included as part of the damages awarded to the plaintiff, but remember that usually each side pays its own attorneys' fees.

Some attorneys place the demand for judgment at the end of the complaint, after all the causes of action have been stated. Others make a demand for relief at the end of each cause of action. This approach is best when each cause of action requires different types of relief, and when separating them will clarify matters.

---

54. Fed.R.Civ.P. 8(a)(3).

55. Fed.R.Civ.P. 54(c).

56. *Id.*

57. *See, e.g.,* 42 U.S.C. § 2000(e)(5)(k).

Signature and Address

The final required section of the complaint is the seemingly formalistic requirement that the attorney who prepared the pleadings must sign them, or the plaintiff must sign them if he or she does not have an attorney.[58] Include your business address with your signature.

HANRAHAN & HOWARD, P.C.

BY: _____
       Jude Hanrahan

AND: _____
       Dara Howard
       Attorneys for Plaintiff
       210 Main Street
       Lexington, Kentucky 40511

While it seems formalistic, your signature has a substantive component as well. For example, your signature at the bottom of any document filed in the federal courts indicates that you have read it, that the legal claims are warranted by existing law or by establishing new law, that the factual allegations have evidentiary support, and that it is not filed for any improper purpose.[59] If you sign the pleading in violation of the rule, then the court may impose sanctions, including the expenses and attorney's fees that the opposing party incurred because of the document.[60] Even if your jurisdiction does not place a substantive restriction on your signature, treat your signature as if it did. This will help you ensure that you are not wasting your client's or the court's time in presenting documents that are unsubstantial or frivolous.

Verification

The verification states that the client verifies that the stated facts are true. Under the federal rules, complaints need to be verified only when specifically required under the rule or statute upon which the complaint is based.[61] States vary on whether they require verification. Some attorneys prefer to include a verification by their clients, regardless of whether it is required, to impress upon their clients the seriousness of the step they are taking.

---

58. Fed.R.Civ.P. 11.

59. *Id.* A large amount of controversy has surrounded Rule 11 since it was amended in 1983 and again in 1999. For a fuller discussion of this controversy, *see* Arthur Miller, *The New Certification Standard under Rule 11,* 130 F.R.D. 479 (1990); *Developments in the Law–Lawyers' Responsibilities and Lawyers' Responses,* 107 Harv. L.Rev. 1547, 1629–51 (1994); Maureen N. Armour, *Practice Makes Perfect: Judicial*

Discretion and the 1993 Amendments to Rule 11, 24 Hofstra L.Rev. 677 (1996).

60. Fed.R.Civ.P. 11(b)(2). Sanctions are limited to what is needed to deter repetition.

61. *Id.* Among those that must be verified are derivative actions by shareholders under Fed.R.Civ.P. 23.1, depositions taken before an action under Fed.R.Civ.P. 27(a)(1), and requests for temporary restraining orders under Fed.R.Civ.P. 65.

In summary, carefully draft each aspect of the complaint so you will not waste time and money pursuing fruitless claims or defending your complaint from challenges by your opponent. The time spent on this careful drafting is minimal compared to the time it takes to respond to motions raised by your opponent or to bring motions to amend defects in your complaint.

DRAFTING THE ANSWER

An answer is a response to the complaint, and it simply indicates which of the complaint's allegations the defendant admits, denies, or is unable to answer because of insufficient information. Answers help narrow the issues for trial. If the defendant admits some things, they can be stipulated to and do not need to be established at trial.

The format of an answer is quite simple. If you are making a general denial, you need only state: "The Defendant denies each allegation contained in plaintiff's complaint." If you are making a special denial, you should indicate which paragraphs you admit and which ones you deny. If you do not have enough information to admit or deny an allegation, state your lack of information, which acts as a denial.

(1) Defendant admits the allegations in paragraphs 1, 2, 3, 4, and 8 and admits the allegations in paragraph 10 except to state (or to deny . . .).

(2) Defendant denies the allegations in paragraphs 5, 6, 7, and 9 (or denies paragraph 9 except that portion that states . . .).

(3) Defendant is without sufficient information or facts to admit or deny the allegations in paragraphs 11, 12, 13, and 14 and puts plaintiff to his (or her) proof on these matters.

One question that arises in answering a complaint is when an allegation must be admitted or when it can be denied. The federal rules require the attorney responding to admit that portion of the allegation that is true.[62] Many attorneys believe that the answer must admit any portion of an allegation that is true.

Complaint:

(5) Defendants wrongfully entered the Happy Trails Convention Center on June 25, 20__, by misrepresenting themselves as authorized to enter and videotape the workshop.

Answer:

(5) Denies paragraph 5, except admits that defendants entered Happy Trails Convention Center on June 25, 20__.

Other attorneys deny any allegation that is untrue in any part, however small. They would interpret the federal rule to allow them to deny the entire preceding allegation because part of it can be denied as untrue.[63]

62. Fed.R.Civ.P. 8(b). Alterman, *supra* note 35 at § 5.03.　　**63.** *Id.*

But the federal rules state that the pleader will be responding "in good faith," so, if you know that the defendants did enter the convention center on June 25th, you would be obliged to admit that information.

One way you can prevent this ambiguity when you draft a complaint is to separate the evidentiary facts from the ultimate facts. The above example could be redrafted as follows.

5. **The defendants entered the Happy Trails Convention Center on June 25, 20—, and videotaped the workshop.**

6. **The defendants entered the Convention Center on June 25, 20—, by representing themselves as authorized to videotape the workshop.**

These allegations require different responses from the attorney drafting the answer. The allegations of paragraph 5 are factual in nature and, if the attorney knows that they are true, he or she must admit them. The answer will presumably deny paragraph 6 because the dispute probably revolves around whether the defendants were misrepresenting their authority. But the complaint drafter will have obtained admissions on two important points: the defendants did enter the center and they did videotape the workshop. These admissions have thus eliminated plaintiff's need to prove these facts at trial and have focused the litigation on the issue of misrepresentation, not on the factual question of whether the event was videotaped by defendants.

Once you are finished responding to the complaint, you should include any affirmative defenses or counterclaims that you need to raise. Allegations in counterclaims resemble the allegations in the complaint. Provide the same amount of specificity in stating defenses or counterclaims that you would provide in the complaint.[64]

CONCLUSION

Drafting excellent pleadings requires concentration on thoroughness and precision. Thoroughness requires considering (1) all the possible causes of actions, affirmative defenses, and counterclaims and (2) all the allegations needed to establish each element of the causes of actions, defenses, or counterclaims you raise. Precision requires drafting the documents so they comport with the procedural and substantive rules of your jurisdiction and are most helpful to your client.

Exercise 1

The following complaint was written by another associate in your firm. The firm's senior partner is unhappy with the overly long and complex allegations and the language that associate used in the complaint. He has given it to you to revise, by dividing up the allegations so that each one will be more difficult for the defendant to deny and by revising the language to make each allegation clear and straight-forward.

64. *Id.*

Martin Larsen,
          Plaintiff,

v.

Shaft Insurance Company, and
DOES 1–X, Inclusive,
          Defendants.

Case No. 20＿–1234

Complaint for Damages
For Breach of Contract

Comes now the plaintiff Martin Larsen and for cause of action and complaint against the defendants herein alleges:

(1) At all times herein mentioned below, plaintiff, Martin Larsen, was, and now is, a single man and at all times relevant to this action was a resident of the State of Compulsion and the owner of an insured residence known as 1331 Terrace Drive, in the City of Hawshua, County of Hawshua, State of Compulsion.

(2) Defendant Shaft Insurance Company is, and at all times herein below mentioned was, a corporation organized and existing under the laws of the State of Compulsion, with its principal place of business in this state situated in the City of Hawshua, Hawshua County, and authorized by the State of Compulsion Insurance Commissioner to transact, and transacting business, in this state as a homeowners' liability insurer.

(3) Plaintiff is informed, believes, and thereon alleges that defendant, Shaft Insurance Company, is, and at all times herein mentioned was, engaged in the business of writing homeowners' insurance policies insuring against losses by reason of liability imposed on him by law for damages, among other things, because of bodily injury or property damage during the term of the policy. Such policies provided for payment of the amount fixed therein in the events of losses described and covered by the aforementioned policies.

(4) Plaintiff is ignorant of the true names and capacities of defendants sued herein as DOES 1–X inclusive, and therefore sues these defendants by such fictitious names. Plaintiff will amend the complaint herein stated to allege the true names and capacities of the above-mentioned DOE defendants when ascertained. Plaintiff is informed and believes and thereon alleges that each of the above-mentioned fictitiously named defendants is responsible in some manner for the occurrences herein alleged below, and that the plaintiff's damages as herein alleged below were proximately caused by their conduct.

(5) Plaintiff's homeowners insurance policy with Shaft Insurance Company was in full force and effect on May 16, 20＿.

(6) Plaintiff's policy, number 54321, hereinafter referred to below as "the policy" in and by which defendant insured plaintiff against losses and damages, was in full force and effect when the plaintiff

was sued for assault and battery and intentional infliction of emotional distress in the Superior Court of Hawshua County, State of Compulsion, in May 20__, said lawsuit resulting from the incident on May 16, 20__, where plaintiff shot at what he thought was the devil and injured a Mr. Allen Hurt. The underlying action was commenced in the Superior Court of the State of Compulsion by, in, and for the County of Hawshua, the cases entitled *Hurt v. Larsen*, case number 310, in which Mr. Hurt sought to recover damages resulting from the shooting on May 16, 20__.

(7) While the policy was in full force and effect, and as a result of the incident herein described above, defendant insurance company defended the plaintiff during trial under a reservation of rights, but refused to pay and continues to refuse to pay the judgment against plaintiff in the amount of $650,000.00. Defendant insurance company defended its action by asserting that the injury to Mr. Hurt was not the kind covered by Mr. Larsen's policy. Exclusionary Clause E of the policy excludes from coverage injury done intentionally by or at the direction of the insured. The clause excludes "bodily injury or property damage which is intended from the standpoint of the insured." Shaft Insurance Company asserted that intentionally referred to the intent to do the act that caused the injury.

(8) At the time of the incident, plaintiff was occupying the insured dwelling as his home. Plaintiff had no intention to injure Mr. Hurt. His act of shooting the gun was to shoot the devil. Plaintiff had been taking a new anti-depressant medication, GoodStuff, for two weeks preceding the shooting incident which plaintiff is informed and believes and thereon alleges caused plaintiff to feel angry, aggressive, and agitated, and to believe he was seeing the devil at the window. Plaintiff has demanded of defendant payment of the sums hereinbefore alleged, but defendant has failed and refused, and continues to fail and refuse, to pay these sums or any part of them.

(9) As a proximate result of defendant's failure and refusal as hereinbefore alleged, plaintiff has been damaged in the sum of $650,000.00 together with interest thereon at the legal rate from the date the judgment was entered and continuing until the date it is paid. Notwithstanding plaintiff's request, defendant has denied all liability under said policy and has refused to pay said judgment.

WHEREFORE, plaintiff prays for judgment against defendants, and each of them, as follows:

(1) For the sum of $650,000.00 together with interest thereon at the legal rate from April 15, 20__ until paid;

(2) For emotional distress and emotional injury in the sum of $200,000.00;

(3) For exemplary damages in the amount of $1,000,000.00;

(4) For costs of the suit incurred herein;

(5) For such other and further relief as the court may deem proper.

Dated June 1, 20___

Hanrahan and Howard

By_____
Dara Howard

Exercise 2

Using the complaint above, review the allegations as the attorney for Shaft Insurance Company. Determine which allegations you could deny, because of the length, complexity, and legal assertions or conclusions contained in them knowing nothing more than the facts presented in the complaint and assuming them to be true for purposes of this exercise. Then, draft an answer denying those allegations that you believe the insurance company could deny, admitting those that they would have to admit, and stating that you lack information or knowledge sufficient to admit or deny the others.

Assignment 1

You represent Jamie Blottner, whose situation is described in Assignment 1 in Chapter 6. Jamie has decided to sue Ms. Newton. Your job is to draft a complaint on Jamie's behalf for a statutory claim under Tenn. Code Ann. § 471.20, which is also included in Assignment 1 in Chapter 6. Ignore any other defendants and any other causes of action (common law claims, etc.). Make sure that you allege all necessary elements under the statute (hint: one of them does not appear overtly) and that you allege facts in support of those elements.

Assignment 2

Your firm represents Jim and Kate Putnam, parents of the deceased Heather Putnam. The facts and law are in Assignment 2 in Chapter 4, and in Assignment 2 in Chapter 8. Your clients are now suing City General Hospital for negligence and spoliation of evidence under Florida law, and your supervisor has asked you to draft the part of the complaint for the spoliation cause of action. There are six required elements to the cause of action. Be sure to include all six elements in your complaint.

BIBLIOGRAPHY

Alterman, Irwin, *Plain and Accurate Court Papers*. Philadelphia, PA: American Law Institute, 1987.

Alterman, Irwin, *Plain and Accurate Style in Lawsuit Papers,* 2 Cooley L.Rev. 243 (1981).

Armon, Jan, *A Method for Writing Factual Complaints*, 1998 Det. C.L.Mich.S.U.L.Rev. 109.

Armour, Maureen N., *Practice Makes Perfect: Judicial Discretion and the 1993 Amendments to Rule 11*, 24 Hofstra L.Rev. 677 (1996).

Binder, David A., Paul Bergman, and Susan C. Price, *Lawyers as Counselors: A Client–Centered Approach*. St. Paul: West Group, 1991.

Black, Henry Campbell, *Black's Law Dictionary*. St. Paul: West Group, 7th ed. 1999.

Developments in the Law–Lawyers' Responsibilities and Lawyers' Responses, 107 Harv.L.Rev. 1547 (1994).

Friedenthal, Jack H., Mary Kay Kane, and Arthur R. Miller, *Civil Procedure*. St. Paul: West Group, 3d ed. 1999.

Glannon, Joseph W., *Civil Procedure: Examples and Explanations*. New York: Aspen Law & Business, 4th ed. 2001.

Gelhorn, Gay, *Law and Language: An Empirically–Based Model for the Opening Moments of Client Interviews*, 4 Clinical L.Rev. 321 (1998).

Heiser, Walter W., *A Critical Review of the Local Rules of the United States District Court for the Southern District of California*, 35 San Diego L.Rev. 555 (1996).

Miller, Arthur R., *The New Certification Standard Under Rule 11*, 130 F.R.D. 479 (1990).

Neubauer, Mark A., *Check-The–Box Pleadings*, 11 Litigation 28 (Winter 1985).

Owens, William Brownlee, *California Forms and Procedure*. Los Angeles: Parker & Son Publications, Inc., 1990.

Ray, Mary Barnard, and Jill J. Ramsfield, *Legal Writing: Getting It Right and Getting It Written*. St. Paul: West Group, 3d ed. 2000.

Schleifer, Nancy, *Complaint and Defensive Checklists*, 61 Fla.Bar.J. 23 (July–August 1987).

Schwarzer, William W., *The Federal Rules, The Adversary Process, and Discovery Reform*, 50 U.Pitt.L.Rev. 703 (1989).

Schwarzer, William W., *Rule 11 Revisited*, 101 Harv.L.Rev. 1013 (1988).

Wright, Charles Alan, and Arthur R. Miller, *Federal Practice and Procedure*. St. Paul: West Group, 2d ed. 1990.

Wright, Karla, *A Seven Step Process for Preparing Non–Routine Complaints*, 77 Ill.Bar J. 662 (August 1989).

Chapter 12

NOTICES OF MOTION, MOTIONS, AND ORDERS

Like pleadings, motions play a central part in many attorneys' practices. Although many law students anticipate exciting jury trials and rousing closing arguments, upon joining a law firm, they soon realize that most litigation practice is completed long before the case reaches trial. Thus your opportunity to persuade a court to rule favorably for your client may occur most frequently during the "law and motion" practice at your local courthouse. Even before the pleading stage of the lawsuit is completed, you may have to decide whether to raise certain motions before answering because you will be precluded from raising them after you have served the answer.[1] You may also make other motions after answering and before trial. These may include motions to compel discovery, motions for a continuance, motions in limine[2] to exclude specific testimony from trial, and other pretrial motions. Thus, learning to draft these motions will help you throughout your practice and will provide you with many opportunities to help your client.

Motions are requests for assistance from the court. If the judge grants your request, he or she will issue an order explaining the assistance being granted. Before a judge can issue the order in most cases, however, due process concerns within our legal system require that your opponent be given an opportunity to respond.[3] To meet these

---

1. Fed.R.Civ.P. 12(h)(1) lists the motions that must be raised before answering or when answering, or the right to raise these motions is waived. The next section of this chapter describes these motions in detail.

2. Lawyers are raising these motions more frequently than they have in the past, primarily due to the importance of avoiding jury exposure to harmful evidence or offers of proof. Robert E. Bacharach, *Motions in Limine in Oklahoma State and Federal Courts,* 24 Okla. City U.L.Rev. 113, 114 (1999).

3. U.S. Const. amend. V and XIV. Additionally, Fed.R.Civ.P. 6(d) requires notice of all motions except ex parte ones, as do state statutes. *See, e.g.,* Cal.Civ.Pro. § 1005.5. Ex parte motions are those requesting orders in the absence of other interested parties and without notice of the hearing. An example of an ex parte order is a temporary restraining order granted when "great or irreparable injury" is established. 26 *Cal. Forms of Pleading and Practice Annotated* 17 (Matthew Bender 2002). Fed.R.Civ.P. 65(b) requires that, in addition to injury, the attorney must certify to the court the

due process requirements, the judge will hold a hearing on your motion, although it may be an informal conference in the judge's chambers or even via telephone.

For example, suppose that the trial in your client's personal injury accident case is set for October 16th and, one week before the trial, your chief witness calls and tells you that one of his parents has been hospitalized in critical condition and he needs to leave town. Your first step is to contact your opponent to see if he or she would agree to a continuance. In routine matters, always attempt to reach an informal agreement or stipulation with opposing counsel before proceeding into court to make formal motions to resolve the issue.[4] If your opponent agrees, then you simply call the judge's chambers, inform the clerk of the problem, indicate your opponent's agreement, and determine whether the judge has any objections.[5]

If your opponent opposes the continuance, perhaps because that is the only week his or her chief witness can be present, then you must apply to the judge for an order resetting the trial date. You call the judge's clerk and determine when the judge wants to hold a hearing on the matter. Next you send a Notice of Motion and Motion for Continuance to your opponent, stating the basis for your motion and requesting the desired relief. You might also attach an affidavit from your witness stating the need for the continuance and prepare the Order granting your motion, so the judge can simply sign the order if he or she decides to grant the motion.[6] At the hearing, both sides present their arguments for and against the continuance and the judge will issue an order granting or denying the motion.

This motion process can repeat itself before the trial, during the trial, and even after trial. Some motions are made orally during trial, such as motions to exclude evidence, and others are made after trial,

---

efforts made to provide notice and why notice should not be required. Ex parte motions are granted in extremely rare circumstances.

4. Besides saving valuable attorney and court time by not having to prepare or defend the motions and argue them in court, these conversations with opposing counsel increase communication between the parties. This communication may lead to informal resolution of nonroutine matters or to settlement. 1 *California Points and Authorities* § 1.03(1)(c) (1999).

5. The judge may very well object. In some jurisdictions, he or she may be virtually prohibited from granting a continuance in this type of situation. For example, regardless of the opposing party's problem of his or her witness's availability, Cal.Rules of Court 375(a) states that continuances are disfavored and the date set for trial is firm.

6. You might also consider sending a memorandum of points and authorities containing legal support for your motion, although the factual nature of the motion in this example might make legal argument unnecessary. These memoranda are known as trial briefs in some jurisdictions. Local court rules may require the filing of memoranda of points and authorities regardless of the motion's nature. *See* Cal. Rules of Court 313(a), which requires a party filing a notice of motion, except a motion for a new trial, to file a memorandum of points and authorities with the notice of motion. The court considers the absence of the memorandum to be an admission that the motion is not meritorious and thus cause for its denial.

such as motions for judgment as a matter of law[7] or for reconsideration.[8] Your litigation practice will return continuously to drafting, defending, and arguing motions.

The documents involved in motion practice are usually rather short and simple to draft. The writing concerns involved in these drafting tasks are being clear and eliminating legalese. Because the documents tend to be short, most attorneys choose to copy documents from form books or files within their law firm. This practice perpetuates overlong sentences and legalese, which makes these otherwise simple documents difficult to understand. Your goal is not to avoid using forms, but to revise or develop them to increase clarity and decrease legalese.

This chapter divides drafting these documents into two sections. The first section concerns the general rules governing motion practice, as well as the procedural, strategic, and ethical concerns of presenting motions to the court. The second section concerns the drafting requirements for notices of motion, motions, and orders. Together, these sections will prepare you to join the attorneys whose work revolves around the "motion calendar" at the local courthouse.

PROCEDURE, STRATEGY, AND ETHICS OF MOTION PRACTICE

This section addresses (1) the general procedural rules and timing requirements controlling motion practice and (2) the strategic and ethical considerations governing this aspect of practice. By becoming acquainted with these rules and considerations, you will more effectively achieve your client's desired goals.

Rules Controlling Motion Practice

Both the federal courts and the state courts have statutes regulating motion practice. Becoming familiar with these statutes will help you understand how your jurisdiction regulates motion practice. For example, Federal Rule 7(b) requires attorneys to file motions when requesting orders from a judge and requires most motions to be in writing; it also permits the notice of motion and motion to be made in the same document if the notice of motion states the legal grounds for the motion.[9] The substantive argument supporting the motion is contained in the brief or memorandum of points and authorities supporting your motion.[10]

---

7. This motion had been known as one for judgment notwithstanding the verdict. Amendments to the Federal Rules changed the name of it and the directed verdict to judgments as a matter of law. Fed.R.Civ.P. 50 (a) and (b). The procedure and purpose of both motions has not changed. Jack H. Friedenthal, Mary Kay Kane, and Arthur R. Miller, *Civil Procedure* § 12.3 n.6 (3d ed. 1999).

8. For a practical guide on federal post-trial motion practice, *see* David J. Healey, Robert B. Lytle, and Richard J. Lutton, *From Final Judgment to Notice of Appeal:* *An Overview of Post–Judgment Motions, Supersedeas and Stays Pending Appeal, and Notices of Appeal from Final Judgments in Federal Court,* 5 Fed.Cir.B.J. 1 (1995).

9. Fed.R.Civ.P. 7(b). These rules are the same in many states. For example, *see* Cal. Civ.Pro. § 1010; Fla.R.Civ.P. 1.100; Or. R.Civ.P. 14; Tex.R.Civ.P. 21.

10. This brief or memorandum of points and authorities is a persuasively written document that presents the legal argument that supports the court ruling in your favor.

These rules may also control substantive aspects of your documents. For example, Rule 7 also requires that motions include the particular grounds on which they are based.[11] Motions have been dismissed simply for failure to state the particular grounds for the motion.[12] When bringing a motion, you are asking the court for a specific remedy. Therefore, you must provide enough information for the court to understand your request, without presenting so much that you burden the court with unneeded information or outline your overall strategy for your opponent.[13]

These procedural rules may also control which motions you make. For example, the federal rules differentiate between a motion to dismiss for failure to state a claim upon which relief can be granted and a motion for summary judgment. If the motion is based on the pleadings alone, the federal rules will treat it as a motion to dismiss for failure to state a claim upon which relief can be granted under Rule 12.[14] On the other hand, if the motion is based on matters outside the pleadings, the federal rules will treat it as a motion for summary judgment under Rule 56.[15] Thus your understanding of the procedural rules controlling motion practice must extend to recognizing the interplay between the rules and the motions you make.

Similarly, local federal court rules control many aspects of motion practice.[16] These rules control numerous details, including (1) time limits, (2) page limits for memoranda of points and authorities,[17] (3) meet-and-confer rules requiring the attorney bringing a motion to meet with opposing counsel before filing the motion,[18] and (4) requirements for documents supporting the motion.[19] To be successful in your motion practice, you must become aware of and understand how your jurisdiction regulates these documents.

A full discussion of drafting these documents is contained in Chapter 6 on Persuasive Issue Statements, Chapter 8: Persuasive Statements of Fact, and Chapter 10: Argument Sections of Briefs.

11. Fed.R.Civ.P. 7(b)(1). Despite the clear language of this rule, the courts have never clearly articulated what degree of specificity is required to fulfill this rule. David F. Herr, Roger S. Haydock, and Jeffrey W. Stempel, *Motion Practice* § 3.03[B] (4th ed. 2001).

12. For example, *see, Lynn v. Smith,* 193 F.Supp. 887, 888 (W.D.Pa.1961).

13. In this regard, motions strategy is similar to pleadings strategy, such as when drafting a complaint, you may prefer to make your allegations as narrow as possible to avoid providing your opponent with your overall plan.

14. Fed.R.Civ.P. 12(b)(6).

15. Fed.R.Civ.P. 12(b).

16. *See,* Herr, *supra* note 11, at § 3.09.

17. *Id.* at § 3.09, n.62., listing some federal courts that have imposed page limits on memoranda of points and authorities supporting motions. For example, the Southern District of Mississippi imposes a thirty-page limit while the Northern District of Oklahoma imposes a fifteen-page limit. *Id.*

18. *Id.* at § 3.09. Fed.R.Civ.P. 37(a)(2)(A) requires a declaration of good faith efforts to confer prior to bringing motions to compel disclosure in discovery. In California, some local court rules require attorneys to file a declaration with their motions indicating what good faith efforts were undertaken to resolve substantive issues raised in the motion. *California Judges Benchbook: Civil Proceedings Before Trial* § 6.18 (1995).

19. Herr, *supra* note 11, at § 3.09.

Just as the federal rules and local court rules regulate federal court motion practice, state statutes and local court rules regulate state court motion practice. These state rules cover many of the same details covered by the federal rules, even regulating the organization of your documents. For example, the California Rules of Court require the opening paragraph of the notice of motion to state the nature of the order requested and the grounds supporting it.[20] Thus, in California, if you place the time, place, and location of the hearing in the first paragraph of your notice, you will have violated a court rule. This error probably will not result in the dismissal of your motion or sanctions being imposed against you. But organizing your motion in this way interferes with the judge's expectations, and the judge would have to take a few moments to determine how the organization of your motion differs from the others he or she is reading. While you want your motion to be noticed by the court, this is not the kind of attention you should seek.

As you learn these rules, also determine who handles motion practice in your jurisdiction. Some jurisdictions assign the entire responsibility for a case to one judge who addresses all matters arising in the case from the pleadings through the post-trial motions. If that is your situation, find out from the particular judge's clerk how motion practice is run by the judge. In contrast, other jurisdictions rotate judges into "law and motion" practice.[21] These judges hear all pending motions during a specific amount of time. If this is your situation, your motions must follow that judge's dictates in all your currently pending cases, and you will want to learn as much as possible about that judge's predilections.[22] Knowing his or her views on specific aspects of motion practice will help with your litigation strategy. For example, if the judge grants a continuance only when a party is hospitalized, you would be well advised to bring that motion only in that specific circumstance. To learn these predilections, talk to other attorneys or listen to the judge resolve several other motions and see whether you can determine any patterns the judge has. This may provide you with a clear advantage in deciding how your motion practice should proceed.

The timing of motions is also controlled by the statutes and local court rules in your jurisdiction. For example, Federal Rule 12 requires that a motion to strike be made by a party either before responding to the pleading or within twenty days after service of the pleading if no responsive pleading is permitted.[23] Rule 56 states that a claimant's motion for summary judgment may not be made until twenty days after beginning the action or after service of the adverse party's motion for summary judgment.[24] Rule 6 requires that notice of the hearing on a

---

20. Cal. Rules of Court 311(a).

21. *See* Cal. Rules of Court 307, which states that the presiding judge or a judge designated by him or her will hear all proceedings in law and motion.

22. 1 *California Points and Authorities*, *supra* note 4, at § 1.03(1)(b).

23. Fed.R.Civ.P. 12(f). The Rules also permit this motion at any time on the court's own initiative.

24. Fed.R.Civ.P. 56.

motion must be served no later than five days before the hearing, unless ex parte or otherwise specifically fixed by the court.[25] Successful motion practice thus requires knowing these timing rules and conforming to them.

When practicing in state court, consult state statutes and local court rules which regulate the timing of motions there. In California, for example, most motions and supporting papers must be served and filed twenty-one days before the hearing (with increased time limits for notices served by mail), and all opposing papers must be filed ten days before the hearing.[26] Additionally, the moving party must file a memorandum of points and authorities within ten days of filing a motion for a new trial.[27] If the memorandum is not filed within ten days, the court may deny the motion without a hearing on the merits.[28]

You can lose options for your client during litigation by not knowing the procedural rules governing motion practice; you can also be liable for malpractice.[29] As these restrictions on motion practice indicate, you must be aware of the procedural rules governing practice in your jurisdiction.

Ethical and Strategic Considerations of Motion Practice

Besides learning the rules regulating motion practice, also learn the ethical and strategic considerations involved in motion practice. Do not use motions to harass your opponents, delay the movement toward trial, or force the opposing side to expend resources. Ethical questions "include limitations on the nature, scope, and frequency of motions made; the authorities cited or not cited in support of any motion; and the underlying purpose of motions."[30] Related to these ethical concerns are the numerous strategic questions that arise during motion practice. These include decisions on using motions "to control the timing of various events in litigation, to shape the issues to be decided by the court, to dispose of claims and defenses that are not meritorious, and to seek specific relief."[31] Before you begin drafting your motions, consider these questions to ensure that you use motions to your client's best advantage.

Concerns about inappropriate motion practice led Congress to amend the Federal Rules. Rule 11 now requires that all pleadings, motions, and other papers be signed by the attorney of record, except when a party is unrepresented.[32] This signature certifies that the signer has read the pleading, motion, or other paper; and that, to the best of the signer's knowledge, information, and belief formed after reasonable inquiry, (1) the allegations have or likely will have evidentiary support;

---

25. Fed.R.Civ.P. 6.

26. Cal.Civ.Pro.Code § 1005(b). Summary judgment motions need to be filed 28 days before the hearing, although the time period is also increased if the notice is sent by mail. Cal.Civ.Pro. § 437(c).

27. Cal. Rules of Court 203.

28. *Id.*

29. The most significant exposure to malpractice relates to missing deadlines. Herr, *supra* note 11, at § 7.07.

30. *Id.* at § 7.01.

31. *Id.* at § 2.01.

32. Fed.R.Civ.P. 11. Then the party must sign all papers.

(2) the legal contentions are warranted by existing law or a nonfrivolous argument for the extension, modification, or reversal of existing law; and (3) the motion is not presented for any improper purpose, such as to harass, cause unnecessary delay, or needlessly increase the cost of litigation. If a pleading, motion, or other paper is not signed, the court will strike it unless it is signed promptly after the omission is called to the attorney's or client's attention.[33]

By submitting motions to the court, you are certifying that you are bringing them for valid purposes. This rule attempts to prevent attorneys from interposing numerous motions whose main purpose is to harass or delay.[34] If you sign a pleading, motion, or paper violating this rule, then Rule 11 permits the court to impose sanctions, which may include the costs incurred by the other side due to the improper filing of the document.[35]

The Model Rules of Professional Conduct, passed by the American Bar Association in 1983, also address the ethical issues arising during motion practice.[36] The most pertinent of these require you to raise only meritorious claims and defenses, to expedite litigation to the extent consistent with your client's needs, to treat the court with candor, and to treat the opposition fairly.[37] These rules recognize that motion practice can be the major cost of litigating and encourage you to make only those motions that will ultimately minimize the time spent by you and the court.[38] Your roles as an advocate for your client and as an officer of the court require you to spend time judiciously while pursuing a lawsuit.

Spending your time judiciously also requires you to make strategic decisions so you do not file motions at random. At the beginning of the lawsuit, before filing your complaint or responding to it, establish your litigation strategy. Consider the motions needed to implement your strategy and plan to file those. Anticipate the motions your opponent may raise and prepare for those. Remember, however, that all the motions your opponent files may not require opposition. Some may even help you achieve your goals, so do not immediately challenge them just because your opponent has filed them.[39]

Throughout the lawsuit, you can use motions strategically to inform the judge about numerous aspects of the case, including your theories of the case. For example, bringing a motion to strike irrelevant portions of the complaint tells the judge what you think are the actual issues in the suit. Bringing a motion for a protective order tells the judge that you

---

33. *Id.*

34. While this was never acceptable practice, the rule amendment indicates that the federal court system will no longer ignore this problem. For a fuller discussion of Rule 11 and the controversy surrounding its amendment, *see* note 60 in Chapter 11 on Pleadings.

35. Fed.R.Civ.P. 11. Sanctions are to be limited to those necessary "to deter repetition" of that conduct or similar conduct by others. Fed.R.Civ.P. 11(c)(2).

36. Herr, *supra* note 11, at § 7.02[B]. Chapter 7 of that book discusses these ethical aspects in depth and is highly recommended to all attorneys starting or involved in motion practice.

37. *Id.* at § 7.02[C](see Model Rules 3.1, 3.2, 3.3, and 3.4)

38. *California Points and Authorities 1, supra* note 4, at § 1.03(1)(a).

39. *Id.*

believe matters that could be raised in a deposition should be limited to avoid annoyance or embarrassment.[40] Bringing a motion in limine explains why you believe a particular witness's testimony needs to be restricted at trial. While you would not bring these or any other motions solely for educational purposes, the judge who resolves them will be better acquainted with the parties, the attorneys, and the issues in the pending suit than if he or she knew nothing more than what the pleadings stated. This increased knowledge about the case can work in your favor because informing the judge about your case may help you reach the result your client desires, especially if you are raising novel theories or require unusual evidentiary proceedings.[41] In contrast, the judge who must find time to hear and decide your motions will be unfavorably disposed toward you if your motions are questionable or frivolous. In summary, bring motions that will further your client's case and use them to educate the judge along the way. But avoid having the judge throw his or her hands up in dismay when yet another time-consuming motion related to your lawsuit crosses his or her desk.

Additionally, the rules controlling motion practice require you to use motions strategically to preserve your client's procedural rights.[42] For example, you must make (1) a motion showing good cause before the court can order an examination of a party whose physical or mental condition is in controversy,[43] (2) a motion for judgment as a matter of law at the end of your opponent's case in order to renew that motion after entry of the judgment,[44] and (3) a motion requesting particular jury instructions and a motion objecting to the judge's instructions in order to appeal issues arising from those instructions.[45] Knowing the rules is vital to protecting your client's options and must remain an integral part of your long-range strategy.

Considering the ethical concerns of motion practice will lead you to use motions to protect your client but not to harass your opponent or delay the movement toward trial. Considering the strategic concerns of motions practice will lead you to plan your litigation strategy and use motions as an integral part of that strategy. Having mastered these rules governing the procedure, timing, ethics, and strategy of motion practice, you will be ready to draft your notices, motions, and orders.

DRAFTING THE DOCUMENTS FOR MOTION PRACTICE

There are five main documents in motion practice: notices of motion, motions, affidavits or declarations, briefs (or memoranda of points

40. See Fed.R.Civ.P. 26(c).

41. For example, *see*, Elizabeth Schneider and Susan Jordan, *Representation of Women Who Defend Themselves in Response to Physical or Sexual Assault*, 4 Women's Rts.L.Rep. 149 (1978) where the authors discussed the importance of educating the judge and jury when raising "battered women's syndrome" as a defense in a murder trial. Due to this education, judges and jurors now better understand the seri-

ous harm that battered women suffer. *See* Elizabeth M. Schneider, *Particularity and Generality: Challenges of Feminist Theory and Practice in Work on Woman Abuse*, 67 N.Y.U.L.Rev. 520, 538–39 (1992).

42. Herr, *supra* note 11, at § 2.01.

43. Fed.R.Civ.P. 35.

44. Fed.R.Civ.P. 50.

45. Fed.R.Civ.P. 51.

and authorities), and orders.[46] The three documents discussed in this chapter are notices of motion, motions, and orders.

In drafting these documents, the primary writing techniques involve clarity and elimination of legalese. Law and motion practice at the local courthouse often resembles a cattle call, with your motion placed on the judge's calendar along with all the others currently pending. Keep in mind the judge's heavy workload. He or she will be moving from one pressing matter to another, trying to keep an overburdened court system running as smoothly as possible, and will be reading your motion and supporting documents between attending to other matters. Remember that you want your motion to be granted and you want the judge to be kindly disposed toward doing so. Therefore, you must do everything possible to help the judge understand your motion quickly so the relief you request will be granted.

Most documents for motion practice are short and straightforward. Unlike many of the other documents discussed in this book, they do not require a great deal of time to draft. But the judge will scrutinize your motion, so avoid making that scrutiny difficult. Do not simply turn to in-house forms or to form books, because these sources frequently provide examples full of legalese and obtuse sentence structure. Instead revise these forms to eliminate this legalese and clarify the sentence structure.

Many attorneys are hesitant to remove the legalese because they feel that the language is a magical "fairy dust." They are afraid that, by changing the language, they may eliminate some part of the document vital to its success. This belief simply underscores the problem with these forms: their meaning defies ready understanding.

Eliminating legalese and clarifying sentence structure does not require eliminating forms. Re-inventing the wheel is not required. Redesigning is. Once redrafted, you can use these forms repeatedly. Remember, however, to alter them to fit the particular facts of each case. For example, avoid filing a notice of motion that refers to a motion to dismiss and attaching to it a motion to strike irrelevant allegations from the complaint. The judge receiving these documents may believe that you do not take your work seriously or that you are not precise in your document production, assessments that may lead the judge to look unfavorably on your motions.

---

46. Techniques for drafting memoranda of points and authorities or briefs are discussed in Chapter 10: Argument Sections for Briefs. (Memoranda of points and authorities are the same as briefs and are actually persuasive documents despite their name.) Affidavits and declarations are sworn statements. The affidavit begins by stating "Wanda Witness, being sworn, states that ..." Then you write out the statement, which is based on an interview with the witness. The witness signs at the bottom, swearing that the statement is true. The person witnessing the signature notarizes the statement. Try to write the affidavit in language the affiant would use and avoid using identical language in multiple affidavits. Too much similarity may make the court skeptical about the information you are providing in the affidavit. *See, Visser v. Packer Engineering Associates, Inc.*, 924 F.2d 655, 659 (7th Cir. 1991)(en banc).

Notices of Motion

The notice of motion informs your opponent that you are bringing a motion before the court to request particular relief. The notice indicates the time, date, and place of the hearing (which you obtain from the clerk of the court); the substance of the motion; and references to any supporting documents. Parts of the notice include the caption, the name and address of the recipient, the body of the notice, the date, and your signature.

The caption indicates the court in which the motion is being heard, the parties to the lawsuit, the case number, and the name of the document. Altering the caption for each document to include the name of the document is central to the caption's usefulness and its role of increasing clarity for those reading it.

STATE OF KENTUCKY CIRCUIT COURT FAYETTE COUNTY

Branch 11

SUSAN G. BLACK and
DAVID R. BLACK,

                      Plaintiffs,   NOTICE OF MOTION TO
                                        DISMISS AND MEMORANDUM
             vs.   OF POINTS AND AUTHORI-
                                        TIES IN SUPPORT

STEWART PROPERTIES, INC.,
                      Defendant.   Case No. 2002 CV 10

Immediately following the caption, the notice names the person to whom the notice is directed. If the opposing party does not have an attorney, then the notice should be directed to the party.

TO: Juanita P. Martinez
Williams, Fox, and Smith
110 Main Street
Lexington, KY 40501

You may want to eliminate this step altogether because most procedural rules require only that the summons needs to be directed to the party.[47] Including this information will clarify your documents, however, because it ensures that everyone reading the documents knows to whom the document is addressed.

The notice next indicates the time, date, place, and matter being brought before the court. This is the substance of your notice, so this

---

47. Irwin Alterman, *Plain and Accurate*   F.R.C.P. 4(b).
Style in Court Papers 79 (1987), citing

should be where your language is as clear as possible. Yet this is the point where many attorneys resort to legalese. Rather than simply stating when the motion will be heard and the basis for the motion, they copy the archaic language from in-house forms or form books.

> PLEASE TAKE NOTICE that upon the affidavit of _____, sworn to the _____ day of _____, 20_____, a copy of which is hereto annexed, and upon the pleadings, papers and files herein, the affidavit of _____, sworn to on the _____ day of _____, 20_____, and served herewith, the undersigned will move this Court at the courthouse at _____, on Tuesday, the _____ day of _____, 20_____, at the hour of _____ o'clock in the (fore)noon of said day or as soon thereafter as counsel can be heard for an order (requiring _____ etc.), on the ground that (state grounds upon which the motions will be made) and for such other and further relief as to the Court may seem just and proper and for costs of this motion.

Numerous problems exist with this form. First, the purpose of the motion is stated at the end of the form after the time, place, and day of the hearing and the time, place, and date of the supporting affidavits. Placing smaller details before the main purpose makes the notice difficult to understand. Second, including the date the affidavits were made is unnecessary. The judge can easily determine those dates, if important, by looking at the affidavits.

Rather than simply copying this form, it could be rewritten to be clear and concise.

> **PLEASE TAKE NOTICE that plaintiff's counsel will make a motion to the Court for _____ on the ground that (state grounds with particularity)[48] and for any other relief that the Court may find appropriate.**
>
> **The hearing will be held on (month) (day) (year) at the courthouse (judge's chambers) at (time) or as soon as the matter can be heard. The motion will be based on the pleadings, papers and files of the case and on the affidavits of _____ and _____ which are attached to this Notice.**

Even the conventional "PLEASE TAKE NOTICE" language is unnecessary. The caption states that it is a notice of motion. This language is not a required part of the document. It would be just as valid, and shorter, to state "Plaintiff's counsel will make a motion to the Court" or "Plaintiff's counsel will move the Court." Either introduction helps clarify your documents and creates a form that you can use repeatedly.

It may also be unnecessary to indicate specifically where the motion will be heard. While this is sometimes important in urban areas where

---

48. Fed.R.Civ.P. 7(b)(1) states that all motions shall state the grounds for them with particularity. Although you do not need as much specificity in the notice, tell the reader the basis for the attached motion since this is the first document he or she will read.

more than one courthouse is used, some commentators believe that including this information is superfluous because both the judge and opposing counsel are well aware of the location of the judge's chambers.[49] It may be helpful, however, to indicate whether the motion will be heard in the judge's chambers or the courtroom, if you have this information. It may also be useful to indicate the place where the hearing will be held if your court has a rotating law and motion calendar, in which motions are made to judges who may not have ultimate control of the case.

It may also be unnecessary to identify the documents on which the motion is based. This will depend on the specificity you desire. If you want the court and opposing counsel to know that the motion is based on the pleadings and on attached or already filed affidavits, clarify that point by stating it in your notice or motion. Consider eliminating it, however, if you are simply going to use the generic language, "This motion is based on the record and files herein." Everything a court does will be based on those documents;[50] including the information does nothing more than require additional time to read it.[51] In developing your forms, consider these options and decide which you prefer. You may also decide to develop different forms, some with the language included and some without it, so you can simply select the appropriate form for each case.

Some notices include more legalese than clear language. For example, the following "Notice of Motion to Set for Trial" is twice as long as it needs to be.

_____, and _____, HIS ATTORNEY ARE HEREBY NOTIFIED THAT:

On _____, 20_____, plaintiff will move the above-entitled court in department (division) _____ thereof, located at _____, City of _____, Michigan, at _____M., to set the above-entitled action for trial on the ground(s) that said action is at issue, and (any further grounds). Said motion will be based upon the files and records of said case.

DATED: _____, 20_____.

This notice could be revised to simplify its language and save time whenever it is used.

     On _____, 20_____, at (time), plaintiff will move the Court to set this action for trial because issues of fact exist.

---

49. "If the other parties don't know where the courthouse is, they are in real trouble." Alterman, _supra_ note 47, at 79.

50. _Id._ at 77.

51. However, some jurisdictions may require you to state the documents on which your motion is based. For example, N.Y.Civ. Proc.Law and Rules § 2214 states that the notice of motion must specify the support-ing papers upon which the motion is based. It is questionable, however, whether the language "this motion is based on the record and files herein" gives the court any information at all. If you are in a jurisdiction that requires that the supporting documents be indicated, list them specifically, instead of using this general language.

As this revision shows, the motion can be clearer and easier to read if the unnecessary language in the original is eliminated.

In some jurisdictions, the notice of motion not only provides notice but also takes the place of a separate document entitled "Motion." Under the federal rules and many state rules, a specific document entitled "Motion" is unnecessary.[52] Check the rules of your jurisdiction to determine whether a separate document is required or whether the motion can be part of the notice of motion.

We encourage you to separate the motion from the notice of motion, however, because it streamlines both documents. Including all the necessary information in the notice of motion may force you to try to do too much at once. Besides providing notice and the date, time, and place of the hearing, you must also include the motion requested, the grounds for the request, and the relief desired. Also be especially careful to state the grounds for your request as specifically as possible because the notice will be the only document received by the judge and opposing counsel. The next section provides more information on drafting this part of your document.

When revising your forms, consider the judge who is receiving countless motions every day. Remember, that judge has significant discretion in whether to grant your motion and, because many of these are interlocutory matters, you probably cannot appeal his or her decision.[53] When taking the time to draft the notice, motions and supporting documents, also take the time to use language that will be easy to read and understand.

Motions

The motion is the document that actually requests the particular relief from the judge. Under the federal rules, the motion should be made in writing, state the grounds for making the motion with particularity, and state the relief or order requested.[54] Even if you practice in a jurisdiction that allows you to combine your notice of motion and motion and if you decide to combine these documents, you must still fulfill the requirements of the rules governing motions. Thus, in addition to the information referred to above, you would add the particular grounds underlying the motion and the relief requested.

If you do not state the grounds for your motion, the court may deny your motion simply because no basis for granting it exists on the face of the document. It is not enough to say that you are making a motion to dismiss the plaintiff's complaint; you need to explain the reasons why you believe the court should grant your motion.

---

52. Fed.R.Civ.P. 7(b)(1) states that "[t]he requirement of writing is fulfilled if the motion is stated in a written notice of the hearing of the motion." Many states also permit this practice. For example, *see* Minn.R.Civ.P. 7.02(a); Fla.R.Civ.P. 1.100(b); Colo.R.Civ.P. 7(b)(1).

53. Friedenthal, *supra* note 7, at § 13.1, citing 28 U.S.C. § 1291.

54. Fed.R.Civ.P. 7(b)(1).

Some states also require that a Memorandum of Points and Authorities accompany all motions.[55] If your jurisdiction does not require this support, you must decide whether to attach it. While doing so will increase the time necessary to pursue the motion, there is no point in pursuing the motion without the support needed to succeed.[56]

Your motion should be simple and straightforward. Remove legalese and clearly state why you are bringing the motion and what relief you are requesting. Do not allow your language to obscure the purpose of the motion, as the following example does.

> Defendant moves the Court to stay the taking of the deposition of (witness), by plaintiff, pursuant to the notice served on defendant by plaintiff on the _____ day of _____, 20_____, until _____, on the ground that examination of the witness has already been commenced and is now proceeding in an action pending in the _____ Court of the State of _____, entitled _____ vs. _____, which action involves the same issues as are involved in this action, as more particularly appears from the affidavit of _____, attached hereto, which defendant is informed and believes will come on for trial before the trial in this action, and the judgment in which will be dispositive of the issues in this action; defendant intends to move for summary judgment on the ground of _____ which if granted will make it unnecessary to take the deposition referred to herein.

This motion would be clarified by rewriting.

> **Defendant moves the court to stay the deposition of (witness) by plaintiff because the witness has been deposed in an action pending in the _____ Court of the State of _____, entitled _____ vs. _____, which involves the same issues that are involved in this action. The attached affidavit of _____ supports this motion.**
>
> **Defendant believes that action will be resolved before trial in this lawsuit and that it will dispose of all issues in this action. Defendant will then move for summary judgment on the ground of _____ which, if granted will make (witness') deposition unnecessary.**

Even motions that are not full of legalese can be difficult to read or unnecessarily lengthy.

> _____ (Name), plaintiff (or defendant) in the above-entitled cause, respectfully moves that this court grant a continuance of the cause, which was originally set for trial on _____, 20_____. The ground for this motion is that _____ (state specifically ground on which continuance requested).

---

55. For example, Cal. Rules of Court 313(a) requires a memorandum of points and authorities with all motions, and motions missing these documents may be dismissed by the court as not meritorious.

56. Chapter 10 discusses the drafting concerns for writing briefs or memoranda of points and authorities.

> This motion is based on records and files in this cause, including notice of motion and appended affidavit, the latter papers dated _____, 20_____.

This motion can be shortened and made more direct with some simple revisions.

> **Plaintiff (or defendant) requests that this court grant a continuance in this matter, which was set for trial on _____, 20_____ because (state specifically ground for continuance).**
>
> **This motion is based on the documents in this case, including the affidavit of _____, which is attached.**

Taking time to rewrite these motions will clarify them for the court and will increase the chances that the judge will understand what you are requesting. Additionally, your new forms will provide this same advantage in the future.

Orders

The requirements for an order vary with every judge in each court and with the statutes on which the order is based. Most orders, however, contain the following sections:

- the caption,
- the preamble (what happened up to this point that justifies the order),
- the order (the action the court is taking),
- the date of the order, and
- the signature of the judge or clerk issuing the order.

Depending on the order being made, findings of fact and conclusions of law may or may not be necessary.

The caption should clearly state that this document is the judge's order; you can simply name the document "Order." Following the caption is the preamble, which, in most forms, recites everything that has preceded the motion in one long unintelligible sentence.

> Defendant's motion for an order setting aside the default judgment heretofore entered herein came on for hearing before me this (date), (name) appearing as attorney for plaintiff and (name) appearing as attorney for defendant, and the Court being fully advised in the premises, and good cause appearing therefor, and it satisfactorily appearing from the declarations and proposed Answer on file herein that the said default judgment was rendered against said defendant by reason of his (mistake, etc.) and it further appearing that said defendant has a valid defense to the action upon the merits;

Too many attorneys draft the preamble as though it were the introductory phrase of a sentence whose main subject and verb do not occur until the order section. Treating the preamble as a phrase leaves it with little coherence because it includes no subjects and verbs of its own. Additionally, the preamble itself refers to several different subjects, each one properly the basis for a sentence. The preamble should be rewritten for clarity.

> **Defendant moved this Court for an order setting aside the default judgment entered in this action. [Name] appeared for plaintiff and [name] appeared for defendant. Based on the arguments of the parties and the documents filed in support of the motion, this Court finds good cause to grant defendant's motion because of his [her] [mistake, etc.] and his [her] valid defense on the merits.**

This revision makes it much easier to determine what has already occurred in the case and then states the basis for the order.

The next section actually orders the action the judge deems appropriate. In addition to structural problems, the problem of legalese frequently recurs here.

> IT IS HEREBY ORDERED that the judgment heretofore entered in this action against the said defendant (name) and in favor of the said plaintiff (name), in the sum of (amount) [or otherwise, according to the facts], said judgment having been entered in book _____ at page _____ on (date) is hereby vacated and set aside and defendant is permitted _____ days within which to plead or to file the answer accompanying his notice of motion.

This order could be improved easily.

> **IT IS ORDERED that the judgment entered in this action against defendant for (state amount of judgment), which was entered in book _____ at page _____ on (date) is vacated. Defendant is given _____ days to plead or file the answer accompanying his notice of motion.**

After the preamble and the order, include a line which allows the judge to fill in the date of the order. Also add a blank signature line (with the judge's name typed underneath the line) for the judge sign if he or she grants the motion.

Many states require the moving party to draft the order resulting from the motion. While most judges are too burdened to spend time cleaning up your orders, you can be assured that they will sign them with a certain distaste when they contain legalese and redundancies. Try to draft your motions so the judge will be comfortable signing his or her name.

CONCLUSION

Redrafting all these documents so they are simple and direct will make them seem like a fresh breeze when read by the judge. Most judges read impenetrable prose hour after hour, day after day. Additionally, many motions can go either way on the law, thus the advantage of clear motions is easily apparent. The judge may gain a favorable estimation of you based on your notices, motions, and orders, and may believe that anyone who attends to detail enough to rewrite forms to make them clear and effective will not be one to waste the court's time with meaningless motions. Take the time to help the judge form such an impression of you.

Exercise 1

Revise the following Notice of Motion to Extend Time to Respond to Interrogatories to eliminate legalese and obtuse sentence structure. Then draft the Motion to Extend Time and the Order by the Judge granting the Motion. The reason for the Motion is the need for more time to investigate the files of the corporation, some of which are only available from other countries.

Court of Anywhere

Jennifer Hancock,

Plaintiff,	Notice of Motion to Extend Time To Respond to Interrogatories
v.	
Perry International, Incorporated Defendant.	Case No. 999–999–9

TO: Mary Ellen Kerper
    Attorney for Jennifer Hancock
    227 Beech Street
    Anywhere, State 00101

PLEASE TAKE NOTICE that the undersigned will move this Court on Tuesday, the _____ day of _____, __ at the hour of _____ o'clock in the (fore)(after)noon of said day or as soon thereafter as the matter may be heard, in the courtroom of _____, at _____, City of _____, State, for an order extending the time which said defendant may serve and file answers or objections to the interrogatories by plaintiff under date of _____, 20__, to and including _____, 20__. This motion is based on this notice of motion, motion, and the declaration of _____ served and filed herewith and from which the need for the extension fully appears, the aforesaid interrogatories, and upon all the records and files in this case.

Dated this _____ day of _____, 20__.

Sigourney Etourny
Attorney for Defendant

Exercise 2

Using the following Order, draft the Notice of Motion and Motion that would have been presented to the court in support of this Order.

Make sure to eliminate legalese and obtuse sentence structure in all three documents.

Court of Anywhere

ABC Corporation,

               Plaintiff,   Order Granting Motion to

         v.   Dismiss Cause of Action

123 Incorporated,   Case No. 111–111–1

              Defendant.

Defendant's motion for an order dismissing the action for failure to state a claim upon which relief can be granted under Federal Rule of Civil Procedure 12(b)(6) came on for hearing before me this ___ of _____, 20___, _____ appearing as attorney for plaintiff and _____ appearing as attorney for defendant, and the Court being fully advised in the premises, and good cause appearing therefor, and it satisfactorily appearing from the motion, documents supporting the motion on file here, and arguments of counsel that plaintiff has not stated a claim against defendant that can survive the hereattached motion;

NOW THEREFORE IT IS HEREIN ORDERED that the cause of action heretofore filed by the said plaintiff against the said defendant shall be dismissed for failure to state a claim upon which relief can be granted because the plaintiff has not alleged facts sufficient to fulfill each and every element of said cause of action alleged.

    Signed this _____ day of _____, 2002

Judge Judy Johnson

Assignment 1

You are the attorney for Dana Newton, who is the defendant named in Jamie Blottner's complaint. The facts and law controlling her case are provided in Assignment 1 in Chapter 6 and Chapter 10. Prepare a Notice of Motion, Motion to Dismiss for failure to state a claim, and Order granting the motion. Check your jurisdiction's rules for any requirements concerning the caption and organization of these documents. Using those rules, write these documents. Remember that you need to provide the basis for the motion, so read the cases and make your statement in the motion conform with them.

Assignment 2

You are the attorney for City General Hospital, which has been sued by Jim and Kate Putnam for negligence and spoliation of evidence. The relevant law and facts are provided in Assignment 2 in Chapter 4. Prepare a Notice of Motion, a Motion to Dismiss for Failure to State a Claim, and an Order granting the motion. Check your jurisdiction's rules for any requirements concerning the caption and organization of these documents. Using those rules, write these documents. Remember that you need to provide the basis for the motion, so read the cases and statutes and make your statement in the motion conform with them.

BIBLIOGRAPHY

Alterman, Irwin, *Plain and Accurate Style in Court Papers*. Philadelphia, PA: American Law Institute, 1987.

Bacharach, Robert E., *Motions in Limine in Oklahoma State and Federal Courts*, 24 Okla. City U.L.Rev. 113 (1999).

26 *California Forms of Pleadings and Practice Annotated*. New York: Matthew Bender, 2002.

1 *California Points and Authorities*. New York: Matthew Bender, 1999.

California Judges Benchbook: *Civil Proceedings—Before Trial*. San Francisco, CA: Bancroft Whitney, 1995.

Fidel, Noel, *Some Do's and Don'ts of Motion Writing*, 19 Az.Bar J. 8 (Aug. 1983).

Friedenthal, Jack H., Mary Kay Kane, and Arthur R. Miller, *Civil Procedure*. St. Paul, MN: West Group, 3d. ed. 1999.

Healey, David J., Robert B. Lytle, and Richard J. Lutton, *From Final Judgment to Notice of Appeal: An Overview of Post–Judgment Motions, Supersedeas and Stays Pending Appeal, and Notices of Appeal from Final Judgments in Federal Court*, 5 Fed.Cir.B.J. 1 (1995).

Herr, David F., Roger S. Haydock, and Jeffrey Stempel, *Motion Practice*. New York: Aspen Law & Business, 4th ed. 2001.

Lankford, Jefferson L., *How to Write and Argue Motions*, 25 Az.Atty. 24 (March 1989).

Rombauer, Marjorie D., *Legal Problem Solving: Analysis, Research and Writing*. St. Paul: West Group, 5th ed. 1991.

Schneider, Elizabeth M., *Particularity and Generality: Challenges of Feminist Theory and Practice in Work on Woman Abuse*, 67 N.Y.U.L.Rev. 520 (1992).

Schneider, Elizabeth M. and Susan B. Jordan, *Representation of Women Who Defend Themselves in Response to Physical or Sexual Assault*, 4 Women's Rts.L.Rep. 149 (1978).

Chapter 13

INTERROGATORIES

Rule 33 of the Federal Rules of Civil Procedure and corresponding state rules[1] added the word "interrogatory" to the daily life of practicing attorneys. Although interrogatories are simply questions sent by one party to another party during discovery, which that party must answer under oath, in prior years practicing lawyers often viewed them as a creature from a horror movie, complete with fangs and claws, threatening to destroy the life of the attorney who received a packet of extremely broad interrogatories intended to bury him or her in a mountain of paperwork.[2]

Lawyers viewed interrogatories this way because Rule 33 did not impose any limits on the number of interrogatories propounded until 1993. This lack of restrictions led many attorneys to propound huge numbers of interrogatories, which were challenged for violating Rule 26(c).[3] For example, an Illinois court held that 209 interrogatories with 432 separate questions were oppressive and burdensome.[4] Even more

---

1. California rules differ substantially from the federal rules. For this reason, we use the California rules throughout this chapter to illustrate differences between federal and state interrogatory practice. For a comparison of state rules with Rule 33, *see,* 11 *Bender's Forms of Discovery* App. B–85 to B–96 (Oct. 2001 Supplement). The following states' rules also differ substantially from the federal rules: Alaska, Connecticut, Idaho, Illinois, Iowa, Maryland, Massachusetts, Michigan, Nevada, New Hampshire, New York, North Dakota, Pennsylvania, Rhode Island, South Carolina, and Texas. For a copy of those state rules, *see, id.* at App. C–1 to C–236.

2. In the 1950s, many attorneys had three objectives when using interrogatories: "(1) terrorize the [respondent] into dismissing the suit or settling under panic conditions; (2) request so much detail that it could never be assembled; and (3) obtain relevant information." Jacob A. Stein, *The*

Discovers, 15 Litigation 46, 46 (Fall 1988). *See also,* John D. Shugrue, *Identifying and Combating Discovery Abuse,* 23 (No. 2) Litig. 10 (1997).

3. Rule 26(c) permits the court managing the discovery process to protect a party from "annoyance, embarrassment, oppression, or undue burden or expense." When faced with an objection that interrogatories are burdensome or oppressive, courts consider whether the information sought is relevant and frequently weigh the burden on the interrogated party against the benefit to be received by the propounding party. *Pilling v. General Motors Corp.,* 45 F.R.D. 366 (D.Utah 1968).

4. *Boyden v. Troken,* 60 F.R.D. 625, 626 (N.D.Ill.1973) *See also, Zenith Radio Corp. v. Radio Corp. of America,* 106 F.Supp. 561 (D.Del.1952), where the court found that 166 pages of interrogatories with 419 questions containing 1185 subparts would ex-

extreme was a California case with 2,736 questions and subparts spread over 381 pages.[5]

Because of lawyers' tendencies to burden opposing parties with numerous interrogatories and the inadequacy of Rule 26 to resolve this problem, Rule 33 now limits the number of interrogatories that any party may serve on any other party to 25.[6] While this change means attorneys no longer enjoy wide-open interrogatory practice,[7] it also means attorneys are shrinking back in horror less often when a package of interrogatories arrives. As reforms control the use and number of interrogatories in lawsuits, however, these changes have altered the way interrogatories are drafted and changed the purposes for which interrogatories are used. But interrogatories remain an extremely useful discovery device when used correctly and with forethought.

Rather than beating one's opponent into submission, or worse, imbuing him or her with a desire to respond in kind, a well-drafted set of interrogatories provides information needed for case development, helps the parties accurately consider the strength of their case which may facilitate settlement, and even helps you discover your opponent's factual and legal basis for each cause of action or defense. It is particularly important for new attorneys to become familiar with discovery practice because it is both the biggest part of civil litigation and likely to be the focus of most of a new lawyer's time.[8]

There are three steps to drafting interrogatories effectively. First, research the procedural rules controlling discovery practice in your jurisdiction generally and the substantive law controlling the particular causes of actions and defenses in your lawsuit so that you know what information is required to win or defend your case. Second, determine how interrogatories will fit into your overall discovery plan. It may be that using depositions, requests for admissions, or other discovery devices instead will allow you to obtain information more efficiently. Third, draft interrogatories to ask precise questions that clearly request the

---

pand the case to require an amount of oppressive detail that courts should not allow, despite the fact that the propounding attorney asked them in good faith.

5. *In re U.S. Financial Securities Litigation,* 74 F.R.D. 497 (S.D.Cal.1975). The court struck the interrogatories, *sua sponte,* after determining that effective discovery could be accomplished with significantly less detail.

6. Fed.R.Civ.P. 33(a). Leave to serve additional interrogatories must be obtained by written stipulation from the party served with the interrogatories or from the court. *Id. See also, Bender's, supra* note 1, at § 3.01[6]. The Advisory Committee Notes accompanying the 2000 Amendments to Rule 26(b)(2) indicate that districts cannot alter the number of interrogatories by local rule or standing orders. Roger S. Haydock

and David F. Herr, *Discovery Practice* § 4.4.2 (2001). But courts will permit additional interrogatories under Rule 26(b)(2) so long as they do not make discovery unreasonably cumulative or duplicative and the information can not be obtained from another source more conveniently, less burdensomely, or less expensively. Fed.R.Civ.P. 26(b)(2).

7. *See* Morgan Cloud, *The 2000 Amendments to the Federal Discovery Rules and the Future of Adversarial Pretrial Litigation,* 74 Temple L.Rev. 27 (2001)(for a discussion arguing that these changes have made discovery less attorney-controlled and more judicially-managed).

8. Diane Cooley, *Modern Discovery Practice: Search for Truth or Means of Abuse?,* 41 N.Y.L.Sch.L.Rev. 459, 459 (1997).

needed information. This will ensure the best use of this discovery device for your client.

RESEARCH THE RULES AND THE LAW

This step has two stages: (1) researching the procedural rules that control interrogatory use and (2) researching the law that controls the causes of action, defenses, and counterclaims at issue in the lawsuit. Complete this research before considering how to use interrogatories within your overall discovery plan and how to draft your questions. After you have become familiar with the rules governing interrogatory use, you will not have to repeat this research.

Researching Procedural Rules

Start by reviewing the federal, state, and local court rules that control interrogatory practice in your jurisdiction.[9] If you have a federal action, Rule 33 of the Federal Rules of Civil Procedure will control. If you have a state action, find the corresponding rule in your state.[10] These federal and state rules specify how interrogatories are to be used and explain their function. They detail, among other things, that only parties, not witnesses, can be required to answer interrogatories[11] and that the party served must answer them.[12] Additionally, the rules state that the answer to each interrogatory must be separate, written, given under oath,[13] responsive, complete, and not evasive.[14]

Also learn how Rule 33 or the corresponding state rule fits with the other discovery rules. You need to understand, for example, that Rule 26(a)(1)-(3) requires initial disclosures between parties;[15] thus, the parties will disclose "much of the information previously obtained by this form of discovery, and there should be less occasion to use it."[16]

Although the disclosure rules obviate the need for some of the traditional uses for interrogatories (such as to determine the relevant individuals involved, which expert witnesses will be called, and whether

---

9. These changes in the discovery rules in federal court may impact state court defendants when deciding whether to seek removal to federal court. 28 U.S.C. § 1441. *See also* Conrad M. Shumadine, et al, *Discovery in Newsgathering and Libel Litigation 2000*, 604 PLI/Pat 15; Haydock and Herr, *supra* note 6, at§ 4.1.4.

10. For example, in California, the corresponding rule is Cal.Civ.Pro. § 2030 and in Wisconsin, it is Wis.Stat. sec. 804.08. For a list of interrogatory rules for all the states, *see,* Bender's, *supra* note 1, at App. B–85 to B–96.

11. Fed.R.Civ.Pro. 33(a). Interrogatories may also be served on third parties or on co-parties.

12. Fed.R.Civ.P. 33(a). Attorneys play a vital role in drafting the answers to inter-

rogatories, usually after receiving information from their clients and after the clients have reviewed those answers. Haydock and Herr, *supra* note 6, at § 4.6.4.

13. Fed.R.Civ.P. 33(b).

14. *Pilling v. General Motors Corp.*, 45 F.R.D. 366 (D.Utah 1968).

15. Fed.R.Civ.P. 26(a).

16. Haydock and Herr, *supra* note 6, at § 4.1, citing the Advisory Committee Notes. Attorneys faced with disclosure of material that they consider potentially damaging or confidential will have to use motions to dismiss or motions for summary judgment early in their litigation strategy to delay disclosure of that material unnecessarily. *See* Conrad M. Shumadine, et al, *Litigating Libel and Privacy Suits*, 446 PLI/Pat 17, 35 (1996).

insurance exists), they remain useful for other purposes.[17] They retain their traditional usefulness "to particularize and elaborate on the notice pleadings, to refine and narrow the eventual issues for trial, and to facilitate subsequent discovery."[18] Additionally, they are useful to discover organizational structures and business statistics.[19] In fact, they are particularly helpful when one party is a corporation or other complex institution because the answers "represent the collective knowledge of a responding party, its attorneys, and its agents, rather than being restricted to the knowledge of the one individual being deposed."[20] Additionally, interrogatories can be useful when detailed, complex, or technical information is sought which would be difficult to explain fully in a deposition.[21] Haydock and Herr provide an extensive list of information that is particularly susceptible to discovery by interrogatories.[22] Among these are facts obtained from witnesses no longer available, contracts or transactions before or after the events involved in the lawsuit which may be relevant to the lawsuit, financial data, government licenses, facts relating to a court's jurisdiction, and determining which individuals have given statements about the action.[23]

Even though the reason for using interrogatories may have changed with the changes to the Federal Rules, the need to prevent misuse of this discovery device convinced the federal courts to impose nationwide limits, in part because of the positive experiences of those federal district courts that had previously imposed limits on the number of interrogatories by local court rule and found the limits to be useful and manageable.[24] After the 1993 Amendments, the party requesting more than 25 interrogatories bears the burden of demonstrating that the greater number is required under the circumstances of the particular case.[25] As long as the additional interrogatories fulfill the requirements of Rule 26(b)(2), the limits are not to "prevent needed discovery, but to provide judicial scrutiny before parties make [extended] use of this discovery

---

17. Kenneth R. Berman had listed six areas as fruitful for interrogatory questions. Four of those are now required as initial disclosures: (1) insurance, (2) expert witnesses, (3) claimed damages, and (4) knowledgeable persons. Two other areas–contentions and technical or statistic data–are not included in the disclosure requirements, although Rule 26(a)(1)(B) does require disclosure of all documents and data compilations used to support the disclosing party's claims or defenses. *See* Kenneth R. Berman, *Q: Is This Any Way to Write an Interrogatory? A: You Bet It Is,* 19 (No. 4) Litig. 42 (1993). But remember that you may need to use interrogatories to follow-up on information that has been disclosed. For example, although initial disclosures will tell you whether any insurance policy may cover the events involved in the lawsuit, you may still want to use interrogatories to find out whether the insurer will be defending the lawsuit because this may affect how the plaintiff tailors the case. *Id.* at 44.

18. *Bender's, supra* note 1, at § 3.08[1][a].

19. *Id.*

20. This is particularly true when you use the instructions to remind the person answering that he or she is required to conduct an investigation before answering. *Id.*

21. *Id.*

22. Haydock and Herr, *supra* note 6, at § 4.2.1.

23. *Id.* Remember that documents prepared in anticipation of litigation will likely be subject to limited discovery under Rule 26(b)(3).

24. *Bender's, supra* note 1, at § 3.02[4], citing the Advisory Committee Notes.

25. *Id.* at § 3.03[3][b].

device."[26] Frequently, courts will find it appropriate to permit an increased number of interrogatories.[27]

Most states have also imposed limits.[28] The limits range from twenty-five to fifty questions, with thirty being the most common.[29] To obtain the fullest use of your interrogatories, determine how these rules affect your drafting. For example, some jurisdictions exempt certain questions from counting toward the limit.[30] Others state that some multi-part interrogatories will be counted as only one question.[31] Still others allow more interrogatories when the parties stipulate to do so or when leave of the court is obtained.[32]

Even though your jurisdiction likely limits the number of interrogatories, you may find that, in practice, these limits are not as harsh as the rules indicate. Part of your research may include talking to other attorneys in your jurisdiction to determine how strictly these rules will be enforced. Currently, many attorneys answer and do not object to reasonable interrogatories that exceed the limits.[33] Opposing counsel may also want to exceed the limit, and so may stipulate to allowing additional interrogatories.[34] Even if stipulation is not possible, many judges will grant leave to exceed the limit if you can convince them that the complexity or amount of discoverable material in your case necessitates the increase.[35] Rather than ignoring the rules, try to establish a practice of asking for, and granting in return, stipulations to exceed the limits when doing so will promote the proper use of this inexpensive discovery device.

These numerical limits have spawned many additional questions. One question is "exactly what is one interrogatory?" Does each numbered interrogatory count as one, regardless of the number of separate subparts, or does each subpart count as an interrogatory even though by itself it may not ask for more than a small piece of information? Rule 33 includes discrete subparts as counting against the limit of 25 interrogatories.[36] One California rule limits attorneys' drafting flexibility by requiring that "[e]ach interrogatory shall be full and complete in and of

---

26. *Id.*

27. *Id.*

28. *Id.* at App. C. (States that do not impose limits currently include Connecticut, Iowa, Michigan, New York, Pennsylvania, and Texas.)

29. *Id.* at App. B (listing each state's rules).

30. For example, Kentucky excludes interrogatories asking the name and address of the person answering or of witnesses, or whether the party will voluntarily supplement responses from being counted in the total. *Id.* at § 3.03[3][b] n.59.

31. Oklahoma counts questions on the existence, location and custody of documents and physical evidence as only one interrogatory. *Id.*

32. *Id.* at § 3.03[3][b]. Leave of the court is not necessarily given freely. *See Johnson v. United States*, 188 F.R.D. 692, 697 (N.D. Ga. 1999), *aff'd on other grounds* 214 F.3d 1357 (11th Cir. 2000)(court denied motion where counsel "mistakenly" served 146 interrogatories); *Archer Daniels Midland Co. v. Aon Risk Services*, 187 F.R.D. 578, 586–87 (D. Minn. 1999)(court denied motion). *Id.*

33. Haydock and Herr, *supra* note 6, at § 4.4.3.

34. *Id.*

35. *Id.*

36. Fed.R.Civ.P. 33(a).

itself" and "[n]o specially prepared interrogatory shall contain subparts, or a compound, conjunctive, or disjunctive question."[37] However, some courts have determined that interrogatories with subparts are treated as only one interrogatory if the "subparts ... are logically or factually subsumed within and necessarily related to the primary question."[38]

These numerical limitations may force you to draft interrogatories that violate some of the drafting suggestions given below. For example, we encourage you to use subparts to clarify the information you are requesting, writing branching interrogatories. If, however, each branch is counted as a separate question, you may have to use longer, less precise questions. Nevertheless, consider the suggestions given below and try to draft interrogatories that are as clear as possible, given the rule limitations.[39]

Researching the Substantive Law

One useful way to handle these restrictions is to pinpoint the information you need by understanding the requirements of the relevant substantive law. You must research the causes of action and defenses at issue in the lawsuit to determine what information you need to pursue the lawsuit successfully. If you are the plaintiff's attorney and propound the interrogatories with the complaint,[40] your research for drafting the complaint will also control your interrogatories.[41] If you propound the interrogatories after you receive your opponent's answer, you must also research any defenses or counterclaims raised in the answer. This research is required because, in order to prevail in court or during settlement negotiations, you must provide the factual information establishing each element of your client's causes of action. Thus, you must know the elements of the causes of action and defenses to use interrogatories to locate gaps or inconsistencies in your information.

You can also use interrogatories to obtain your opponent's opinions and contentions, which may form an important part of the lawsuit. One common example is, "Do you contend that plaintiff was contributorily

---

37. Cal.Civ.Code § 2030(c)(5). California limits the number of specially prepared interrogatories for each party to 35 but allows unlimited use of uniform interrogatories developed for specific kinds of lawsuits by the California Judicial Conference. *Bender's, supra* note 1, at § 3.03[3][b] n.61.

38. *H.N. Dang v. Gilbert Cross*, No. CV0013001GAF(RZX), 2002 WL 432197, at *3 (C.D. Ca. 2002)(citing *Safeco of America v. Rawstron*), 181 F.R.D. 441, 444 (C.D. Ca. 1998). In deciding whether subparts are sufficiently related to the primary interrogatory, courts ask whether "the subsequent question could stand alone." *Id.*

39. Many attorneys believe that these requirements impair the attorney who has carefully drafted his or her interrogatories. "The limitation on the number of interrog-

atories penalizes counsel who draft questions carefully and so reveal clearly each discrete subpart. The limitations thus encourage lengthy, difficult-to-answer questions." John Shepard and Carroll Seron, *Attorneys' Views of Local Rules Limiting Interrogatories* 21 (Federal Judicial Center Staff Paper 1986). For examples of redrafted interrogatories intended to lessen the number of interrogatories used, *see* Haydock and Herr, *supra* note 6, at § 4.4.2.

40. After the 1993 Amendments to the Federal Rules, attorneys may not serve any discovery requests until after they have established a discovery plan under Rule 26(f). But attorneys may stipulate to submit discovery requests at any time. *Id.* at § 4.1.4.

41. *See* Chapter 11, which discusses drafting complaints.

negligent regarding the accident" on April 22, 20__?[42] Asking for these contentions, which apply law to fact, is specifically allowed under Rule 33(c).[43] In contrast, interrogatories seeking purely legal conclusions unrelated to the facts are improper.[44] Thus, asking "Was defendant negligent regarding the accident on April 22, 20__?" would be improper. When questions arise concerning whether a particular interrogatory applies law to fact or asks for a legal conclusion, the courts resolve these questions case by case.[45]

In addition to asking contention interrogatories, you can ask for a list of all statutes, codes, and regulations that the other party claims your client has breached.[46] This information will enable you to determine the basis for the complaint or counterclaim against your client without asking for your opponent's legal conclusions. Be careful to leave this question open-ended, or you may suggest another legal basis for your opponent's claims against your client.[47]

After you have completed this introductory research, consider how and when to use interrogatories. The information you need will be clearer and your questions more focused if you take time to determine their place in your overall discovery plan.

LOCATE THE INTERROGATORIES WITHIN YOUR DISCOVERY PLAN

What interrogatories you prepare and when you send them will depend on your overall discovery plan; your use of them will vary as their function varies. Changes in the Federal Rules on both timing and initial disclosure impact the use of interrogatories in your discovery plan. You cannot seek discovery "before the parties have conferred . . ."[48] and the parties must confer "as soon as practical" and at least fourteen days before a Rule 16(b) scheduling conference is held or scheduling order is due.[49] The parties must discuss the substance of their claims and defenses, including whether settlement is possible, they must make or arrange for initial disclosures, and they must develop a proposed discovery plan.[50] Included in this plan are when and how the parties will

---

42. Haydock and Herr, *supra* note 6, at § 4.2.3.

43. This rule states that "an interrogatory otherwise proper is not necessarily objectionable merely because an answer to the interrogatory involves an opinion or contention that relates to fact or the application of law to fact, but the court may order that such an interrogatory need not be answered until after designated discovery has been completed or until a pre-trial conference or other later time." Fed.R.Civ.P. 33(c).

44. Haydock and Herr, *supra* note 6, at § 4.2.3.

45. *Id.*, and the cases cited therein. Often, courts will postpone answers to these questions until much or all of the discovery

process has been completed or until the pre-trial conference if the judge needs to resolve whether the question is objectionable. Therefore, while you may ask contention questions, you may not receive any answers until late in the discovery process.

46. Fred Setterberg, *The Artful Question*, 6 Cal.Law. 45, 46 (Feb. 1986).

47. *Id.*

48. Fed.R.Civ.P. 26(d). This is true except for certain types of proceedings exempted from the initial disclosure requirements under Rule 26(a)(1)(E) or when otherwise ordered.

49. Fed.R.Civ.P. 26(f).

50. *Id.*

conduct discovery and whether any limits, such as those contained in Rule 33, should be made or changed.

The timing of interrogatories also depends on your overall discovery plan. Use interrogatories early in the process when you want to force opposing counsel to investigate and obtain information while the information is fresh in the witnesses' minds.[51] Otherwise, wait until you have enough information to ask the precise questions that will force your opponent to answer specific factual contentions.[52] Given the strict limitations on the number of interrogatories permitted (unless enlarged by stipulation or court order), you may decide to submit them in sets: for example, asking some questions before depositions and some as later follow-up questions, or asking some follow-up questions after receiving the initial disclosures from the other side. This approach allows you to shape later questions in light of the answers you receive to earlier questions.

Each case requires a different discovery plan, and the use and timing of interrogatories will vary from case to case. Think through your discovery plan, the information you want, and the options you have to obtain it. Then use interrogatories to obtain the most information with the least cost for your client. Effective use depends on advanced planning.

DRAFT THE INTERROGATORIES

Having completed the initial steps stated above, review the client file, pleadings, and any other documents filed in the case to focus yourself on the lawsuit and the information you want to obtain before starting to draft your interrogatories. As suggested in other chapters, consider developing a checklist to use when drafting interrogatories.[53]

As when drafting jury instructions, complaints, and motions, most attorneys start with pattern or form interrogatories. Choose form interrogatories "drafted by experienced attorneys, accepted in the practice, and tested and approved by a bar committee or court."[54] From those forms, select the ones that are appropriate for your case. If your jurisdiction does not restrict specially drafted interrogatories, revise the form interrogatories to address your issues specifically and make sure that the questions are clear and precise. If, however, your jurisdiction restricts the use of specially drafted interrogatories, then use form

51. Richard A. Lavine and Margaret M. Morrow, *Creating and Implementing a Successful Discovery Plan* § 1.25 (Cal.C.E.B., Sept/Oct 1985).

52. *Id.*

53. Bender's provides an example checklist that you may want to review when developing your own. *See Bender's, supra* note 1, at § 3.08[1][b]. You may also want to develop interrogatory checklists for specific practice areas. An example of checklists for pleadings and discovery in employment termination cases in Illinois and Federal courts can be found at Michael T. Roumell, et al, *Pleadings, Discovery, and Settlement: Checklists and Forms*, ET IL–CLE 17–1 (Ill. Inst. for Continuing Education,1994).

54. Haydock and Herr, *supra* note 6, at § 4.4.4.

interrogatories to the fullest extent possible.[55] This will allow you to obtain information without expending your limited specially drafted interrogatories.

When using form interrogatories, focus on your particular lawsuit. First, choose which interrogatories fit your discovery needs. Sending all the form interrogatories for a given type of lawsuit, such as a personal injury case, is ineffective. For example, if you are a defendant's attorney in a personal injury case with a six-year-old plaintiff, it would be inappropriate to send this form interrogatory: "What was your occupation at the time of the incident referred to in the Complaint?" This error would indicate to your opponent that you are not giving the case careful consideration.

Having chosen your interrogatories, fit them to your client's situation so you can obtain the needed information. Interrogatories that are too general or all-inclusive need not be answered.[56] So, while form interrogatories allow you to reduce drafting time, they also require tailoring to fit the case.[57] Now you are ready to begin drafting the preface, the definitions, and the questions.

The Preface

In drafting the preface, bear in mind that some local court rules limit the use of prefaces or have style requirements. For example, California rules allow only prefaces or instructions that have been approved by the Judicial Council.[58] The preface usually states the statute or rule under which the interrogatories are propounded, the required duties of the parties, and the time limit for answering. Also consider stating that the interrogatories are continuing, because if they are, then the party must provide supplemental answers if any of the answers change while the lawsuit is pending.[59] Even if your jurisdiction does not

---

55. For example, California restricts the number of specially drafted interrogatories but does not restrict the use of official form interrogatories. Cal.Civ.Pro. § 2030.5 restricts specially-prepared interrogatories to thirty-five. Section 2033.5 authorizes the California Judicial Council to develop official form interrogatories and requests for admission for civil actions in state courts based on personal injury, property damages, wrongful death, unlawful detainer, breach of contract, family law, and fraud.

56. *In re Ashland Oil,* 1998 WL 351293, at *3 (Tex. Ct. App. 1998) citing *Dillard Dep't Stores Inc. v. Hall,* 909 S.W.2d 491, 492 (Tex. 1995).

57. Fred Setterberg notes that most lawyers use form questions incorrectly, ignoring the subtleties of the particular case and requiring other attorneys to spend valuable time researching answers to irrelevant questions. Setterberg, *supra* note 46, at 46.

58. Cal.Civ.Pro. §§ 2030(c)(5) and 2033.5.

59. Fed.R.Civ.P. 33 does not require supplemental answers, but Rule 26(e)(2) imposes a duty "seasonably to amend" a prior interrogatory or request for production or admission if the party learns that to some material extent the prior answer is incomplete or incorrect and the correct information has not already been given to the other party. Haydock and Herr recommend including an instruction that the interrogatories are continuing and updated information must be disclosed. They note that this instruction alone will not compel updating but it may encourage it. *See* Haydock and Herr, *supra* note 6, at § 4.3.2. However, under Cal.Civ.Pro. § 2030(c)(7), for example, questions are not continuing and attorneys cannot impose a duty to supplement an initially correct and complete answer, although they may serve supplemental questions asking for updating.

require supplemental answers, consider sending a final interrogatory just before the end of discovery to ask whether any of the previous answers has changed.[60]

When your jurisdiction permits, revise the preface to avoid legalese. For example, avoid statements such as:

> Plaintiff requires Defendants to answer the following Interrogatories under oath within thirty (30) days after the date of service hereof pursuant to Rule 33 of the Federal Rules of Civil Procedure.

Instead, use statements such as:

> **These interrogatories are sent to you under Rule 33 of the Federal Rules of Civil Procedure. You must answer them under oath within thirty (30) days of receiving them.**

Although opposing counsel will usually revise their client's answers before sending them to you, the client will initially answer the questions. For this reason, your preface should be clear, concise, and simply worded so the layperson will understand his or her responsibilities in answering the interrogatories. You may also need to explain how interrogatories work, including the responding party's duties under the Rules. For example, you might write the following.

> You are required to answer these interrogatories and to furnish any information available to you. This information includes information that can be obtained by conducting a reasonable investigation to answer these questions.[61] These interrogatories are continuing, and you are required to supplement your answers whenever you obtain information that is different from the information provided in your answers.[62]

Write your preface to provide clear instructions so the person answering the interrogatories will be able to understand how to respond. Do not assume that your opponent will provide instructions to his or her client clarifying your interrogatories. After you have developed a standard preface, you can use it repeatedly, making only those minor changes that may be necessary from case-to-case.

The Definitions

While your goal is to draft questions that "use simple language with plain meaning that cannot be evaded,"[63] it may be necessary to identify certain terms, documents, dates, or occurrences that you use in your interrogatories. Definitions may be the best way to do this. For example, definitions can explain your use of a word that may raise different connotations for different respondents.

60. Setterberg, *supra* note 46, at 46.

61. *Jackson v. Kroblin Refrigerated Xpress, Inc.,* 49 F.R.D. 134 (N.D.W.Va. 1970); *National Labor Relations Board v. Rockwell–Standard Corp.,* 410 F.2d 953 (6th Cir.1969).

62. See notes 59 and 60, *supra.*

63. U.S. Army Legal Services, *Interrogatories to Answer or not to Answer, That is the Question: a Practical Guide to Federal Rule of Civil Procedure 33,* 1997 Army Law 38, 39 (Aug. 1997).

Describe: This word means to specify in detail and to particularize the content of the answer to the question and not just to state the reply in summary or outline fashion.[64]

You may also use definitions to ensure that the person answering the questions uses a word in the legal context you intend. For example, although attorneys realize that "person" also refers to corporations, many laypeople do not. Thus you may want to define that term. Be careful to alter the definition with each case, however, to delete any irrelevant possibilities.

Person: This word means any individual, individual association, joint venture, partnership, public or municipal corporation, governmental entity or any other legal or business entity.[65]

You can use definitions to make interrogatories easier to understand if you place any long or frequently used definitions in a separate definition section rather than in the text of the interrogatories. To show which terms are defined, you may want to mark defined terms with italics or bold face type.[66]

State the name of any *person* who *you* know has information concerning this lawsuit.

You can also use definitions to help underscore the respondent's duty to answer the questions using all the information available to the party, not just the information available to that particular person. This is particularly true when the party answering is a corporation or other complex institution.

You or *your*: This word means the defendants, their predecessors or successors, if any, their employees, agents, attorneys and all other people acting or purporting to act on behalf of the defendants.

Avoid going overboard with definitions by defining words to include all possible interpretations. The following definition of "document," while probably including all possible variations, is so long and confusing that the respondent is likely to ignore the definition or not understand it.

Document shall mean the original and any copy of any written, typed, printed, recorded or graphic matter of any kind, however produced or reproduced, including, but not limited to, letters or other correspondence, telegrams, memorials of telephone conversations or of meetings, interoffice communications, memoranda, reports, summaries, tabulations, work papers, cost sheets, financial

64. Haydock and Herr, *supra* note 6, at § 4.3.3.

65. You would want to focus on only those possibilities that would arise in this particular set of interrogatories.

66. If you use definitions, be sure to check in your jurisdiction for rules that regulate their use. For example, some states require that, if definitions are used, the terms defined must be stated in boldface type or capitalized throughout the interrogatories. Cal.Civ.Pro. § 2030(c)(5). Even if your state does not impose this rule, you may want to follow this format because it will help the reader understand when terms used in the interrogatories are included in the definition section.

reports, photographs, advertisements, motion picture films, tape recordings, microfilms, other data compilations, including computer data, from which information can be obtained or translated into usable form.[67]

If a term is important enough to require a definition, write one that the person answering will be able to read and understand. Definitions should be as specific as possible and should clarify, not obscure, the information sought. It is possible to define "document" more simply and still inform the respondent that the broadest possible definition of the word is intended.

> **Document means the original and any copy of any writing of words or numbers, or films, recordings, or data compilations of any type from which information can be obtained or translated into usable form.**

You may also want to include definitions specific to the particular litigation. For example:

> *Accident* means the accident between the plaintiff and the defendant at the intersection of Fourth and Cedar Streets that occurred on November 13, 20___.

> *Employment manual* means the employment manual used at Defendant's factory from April 1, 1992, through March 30, 20___.

Using specific definitions helps ensure that the person responding cannot avoid answering by asserting that he or she is unclear about the question asked.

The Questions

The questions fall into three categories:

- preliminary questions, which request introductory material such as the name, address, occupation, and age of the responding party;

- substantive questions, which elicit the specific information desired; and

- concluding questions, which identify the people who helped answer the interrogatories, the people who may be called as witnesses, and the people who have relevant information or documents.[68]

Preliminary Questions

Preliminary questions ask for identification information about the person completing the interrogatories. Before limitations were imposed

---

67. When referring to an even longer definition of "document," Stein notes:

Such a definition does not, of course, spring up overnight. It represents a Darwinian adaption to the need for survival. When the simple definition of document—a writing—was used, it was evaded. The lawyer who was able to evade became suspicious that others would be just as unscrupulous as he, so he made additions to the definition. Thus the coral reef grew.

Stein, *supra* note 2, at 47.

68. *Bender's, supra* note 1, at § 3.08[1][b].

on the number of interrogatories asked, many identification questions were asked; as a result, most form books include many preliminary questions. But with current limitations on the number of interrogatories, you can no longer include any unnecessary preliminary questions, such as some of the following.

(1) State your full name, age, and place of birth.

(2) Have you ever used or been known by any other name?

    a. If so, state such name or names.

    b. State where and when you used or were known by such names.

    c. State whether your name has ever legally been changed and, if so, state when, where and through what procedure.

(3) State your present address and the period during which you have resided at said address.

Including all these preliminary questions in most cases is unnecessary. These questions need to be revised to obtain the information more efficiently and to eliminate legalese. A more efficient method of drafting these questions would be as follows:

(1) State your full name, present address, age, and place of birth.

(2) State whether you have been known by any other name and if so, when and where you were known by such names.

You may be able to avoid having these questions count against your limited supply of questions if they are contained in the pattern interrogatories included in some statutes or are included in the required initial disclosures. You may be able to eliminate most of these preliminary questions. For example, it may be unnecessary to ask for the former names of the party involved. After you have chosen the questions to ask, revise them to be as clear and specific as possible.

Whether you can use branching interrogatories may depend on the rules of your jurisdiction. If branching questions are allowed and each subpart is not counted against the total, use them because they clearly indicate what information is requested. Each branch relates to the main question and simply requests a finite piece of information. Each branch is short and easy to understand. Consider the following example:

"State whether the defendant is a corporation or a partnership. If a corporation, identify the members of the board of directors. If a partnership, identify all the partners."[69]

If you cannot use branching questions or if each subpart is included in your total count, avoid them. Simply use direct, declarative sentences and keep your subjects and verbs close together to make your questions clearer.

69. Haydock and Herr, *supra* note 6, at § 4.4.2.

Substantive Questions

Next, draft the substantive questions that will provide most of the desired information. In drafting these questions, even if your interrogatories are unlimited in number, remember that you will have to sift through the endless pages of responses. Ask only what you need to know. Draft questions clear and precise enough to obtain the needed information. Tailor interrogatories obtained from form books or from your office's files. If your questions are limited, each question asked prevents you from asking some other question. Choose wisely.

Revise any form questions to be precise and clear. Precision comes from asking for the specific pieces of information you need; clarity comes from asking the question in a way that makes it easy to understand. In the same way that at trial you "never ask a question to which you do not know the answer," never ask an interrogatory without being sure why you are asking it. Precisely what information do you hope to obtain from the answer? How will that information help you to reach your client's goals? Is it possible to ask the question in a way to ensure receiving the specific information you want, especially considering that another attorney will be reviewing all the answers?

A question that is general and not precise, while seemingly innocuous, can result in an answer harmful to your client. For example, one plaintiff in a personal injury case received interrogatories asking general background about her case. Her leg had been broken in a car accident and the defendant was attempting to find out whether this injury would significantly affect the way in which she lived her life. The defendant's interrogatory was general: "List all hobbies and forms of recreation in which you have participated in the past ten years."

In the past two or three years, this plaintiff had been a college student who engaged in little or no physical recreation or hobbies. While in middle and high school, however, the plaintiff had been extremely active in sports as a member of several school teams, had hiked extensively, ridden horses, and also played many sports informally with friends. Because the interrogatory was phrased so generally, she was able to answer it truthfully and include a long list of recreation and hobbies in which she had participated over the past ten years. As a result, the defendant's attorney did not receive information that would have helped limit the plaintiff's damages.

It may be more useful to ask for the specific information sought rather than to ask a general question in the hope of obtaining information without giving away your intended use for the information. Here the better choice may have been to focus on a more specific period of time. Thus, the question could have stated: "List all hobbies and forms of recreation in which you have participated in the past two years." This example also shows the dilemma that must be resolved when drafting interrogatories because, depending on the plaintiff, the defense attorney may have received just as harmful an answer with the revised question. In fact, some plaintiffs may have been significantly more active in the past two years than in the previous ten years. Nevertheless, the revised interrogatory would gain information more relevant to any damage claims than would the more general one. In contrast, the general question provided misleading information.

Clarity comes from drafting questions your reader can understand, so he or she can provide the information you are seeking. One of the best ways to make your questions clear is to make them direct and short. While limits on the number of interrogatories may force you to draft questions that are more complex than you prefer, those limitations do not excuse the use of vague or cumbersome questions. Ask questions that will require direct answers.

> Are you claiming that you suffered any property damage as a result of the November 13, 20__, accident?

Ask clear questions; they are difficult to evade.

> Please give the dates on which you were able to do the following for the first time after your injury:
>
> (1) sit up in bed,
>
> (2) remain out of bed for an entire day, and
>
> (3) leave your house for any reason.

Remember that, although your opponent will at some point review and revise the answers, the person who originally answers them will usually not be a lawyer. Write to communicate with that person, which increases the chance that you will receive useful answers.

The best use of interrogatories is for gathering facts. Focus your questions on who, what, when, where, and how.[70] Avoid asking "why" because you will usually receive a generalized, unsupported answer that requires follow-up questions you cannot ask.[71] Additionally, answering "why" usually requires subjective or interpretive responses which may affect the witness's demeanor and credibility. These questions are better asked at deposition.[72]

By carefully determining your questions, you not only determine the information your adversary possesses, but can also force him or her to examine important documents and records and thereby shoulder some of your research.[73] Remember that your questions will educate your opponent. "Opposing counsel might not have thought of asking his [or her] own client the careful question you have composed. Moreover, your set of questions frequently sets out your strategy like a road map."[74] For example, if you serve interrogatories before a deposition, you may

---

70. Lawrence S. Charfoos and David W. Christensen, *Interrogatories: How to Use Them Effectively in Personal Injury Cases*, 22 Trial 56, 56 (June 1986); Setterberg, *supra* note 46, at 46–47; and Patricia A. Seitz, *Get More Information and Less Indigestion Out of Your Interrogatories*, 71 A.B.A.J. 74, 77 (March 1985). For other helpful examples of the types of factual questions that are most susceptible to being asked through interrogatories, *see id.* at 75–76; Charfoos and Christensen at 56–59.

71. Setterberg, *supra* note 46, at 57.

72. Seitz, *supra* note 70, at 75.

73. Setterberg, *supra* note 46, at 45.

74. *Id.*

encounter a witness who has been prepared to avoid problems with the case because your interrogatories forced the witness and the attorney through an educational process.[75] If you want to surprise your opponent, you may save questions that could inform your opponent about your strategy for deposition.

Concluding Questions

Concluding interrogatories are somewhat similar to the introductory questions. They ask for information not necessarily related to the lawsuit's substance. The concluding questions ask for identification information about other people who may have helped answer or provided information for answering the interrogatories.

> Identify all documents related to and all persons with knowledge of the subject matter of these interrogatories.

One problem with this example is that, while it asks for the identity of each document, it does not ask for its location or its custodian, which is more helpful information. One way to solve this problem would be to define the term "identify" to include the name and location of documents and the name, address, and telephone number of the custodians.

> *Identify* means include the name and address of each person and include the name and location of each document, as well as the name, address, and telephone number of the document's custodian.

That definition may also allow you to obtain a significant amount of information without depleting your limited number of interrogatories.

The next example is frequently included as a catch-all question in personal injury cases.

> State in detailed narrative form your complete version of how the accident that is the subject of your complaint occurred, including (1) your observations; (2) all sounds, conversations, exclamations, or other things heard by you; and (3) all pertinent details you have obtained from other sources, including the name, address, and telephone number of each such source.

The person asking the question hopes to find out the respondent's "big picture" view of the accident and perhaps to obtain information about the legal theories that will be raised. Additionally, this question attempts to determine the names of potential witnesses and what information they may provide. You may find it useful to draft catch-all questions for the typical cases that you usually find in your practice.

CONCLUSION

Before sending your interrogatories to your opponent, consider whether they make fullest use of this important discovery device. Understanding the procedural rules and substantive law permits you to be sure how to use interrogatories and what information you need from the

---

75. Berman, *supra* note 17, at 42.

other party. Developing an overall discovery plan permits you to use interrogatories in combination with other discovery devices to obtain the best information you can. Drafting the interrogatories so they are clear and precise permits you to get the answer you are seeking.

Expect your opponent to try to avoid a direct answer and then frame your questions to force the direct answer you want. Think in the context of your discovery plan; think of why you want the information; think about how your opponent will try to avoid your question; think about preventing that. Then reread your interrogatories to determine whether they will obtain the information you desire. There are several ways to trouble-shoot your questions. You may play devil's advocate by asking the following questions.

- Can any interrogatory be made simpler, less complex, or more precise?

- How will the answer to each interrogatory provide you with information helpful to the case?

- Can any questions be eliminated or consolidated.

- Can the answer to any question be fudged? If so, then redraft the question.[76]

Or you may ask the following questions.

- Does the question advance my discovery plan?

- Does it pursue missing information that is valuable?

- What loopholes can the other side use to avoid answering the question in a useful way?

- Can I tighten the noose, and will the court allow it?

- Can any questions be eliminated?[77]

If you ask yourself these questions after drafting and answer them as honestly and completely as you expect your opponent to answer yours, then you will have ensured the best use possible of this discovery device. A carefully asked question requires a responsive answer.[78] Expect your opponent to try to avoid a direct answer and then frame your questions to force just the direct answer you want.

Exercise 1

Draft a standard preface to use when drafting interrogatories for future cases. You should include the following items in your preface:

---

76. Haydock and Herr, *supra* note 6, at § 4.4.1.

77. Setterberg, *supra* note 46, at 57.

78. Strategies for objecting to interrogatories and for answering them are beyond the scope of this chapter focusing on drafting concerns. For helpful information on these issues, *see*, Haydock and Herr, *supra* note 6, at §§ 4.5–4.6.12; and Bender's, *supra* note 1, at §§ 3.04–3.06[2] and 3.08[2]. For a discussion of the appropriate level of sanctions for courts to impose for failure to answer interrogatories, *see* Nathan T. Smith, *The D.C. Circuit Review–August 1996–July 1997: Civil Procedure*, 66 Geo. Wash.L.Rev. 804 (1998).

(1) a statement that explains to the answering party what interrogatories are and what role they play in civil litigation, including the civil procedure rule that controls interrogatory practice in your jurisdiction;

(2) a statement of when the interrogatories must be returned to your office;

(3) a statement that the interrogatories must be answered completely or as completely as possible and that the person should answer based on his or her personal knowledge, but that he or she should also make a good faith effort to obtain the information from other people in the same organization;

(4) a statement that any document referred to in answering an interrogatory should be attached and an indication given where in the document the answer can be found; and

(5) a statement indicating that the answers must be written, verified as being true and correct, dated, and signed.

Exercise 2

Revise the following interrogatories to make them clearer. Since the number you can send is limited and each subpart counts as one question against that limit, work on writing these as complete interrogatories. Most courts do not consider questions that ask for identification information to consist of subparts, even when you are asking for several pieces of information about each. Thus, you may ask for multiple pieces of identification information and have that question only count as one against your limit. Additionally, you may divide the interrogatories into separate questions, but do not exceed a total of six interrogatories. Also revise the language as needed to make the question clearer and more likely to obtain the answer you are seeking.

(1) As to all persons whose names are set forth heretofore in the answers to the preceding or following interrogatories, have you, your agents, investigators, or attorneys, or anyone acting on behalf of you, said agents, investigators, or attorneys, obtained statements of any kind, whether written, stenographic, recorded, reported, oral, or otherwise, from any of the persons heretofore named in the answers to said interrogatories? If so, please state separately for each: the name of the person who gave the statement, that person's address and phone number, and a brief summary of what the statement says.

(2) On the date of this accident, was there in effect any policy or policies of insurance, either automobile, homeowner's comprehensive liability, farm liability, so-called "umbrella" or excess policy, or any other type of liability policy or coinsurance coverage by or through which you were or may be insured or covered in any manner, or to any extent for any cause of action for the injuries or damages claimed against you in the above-entitled

action? If so, please state separately for each: the name of the company or companies issuing each of said policies of insurance; the name and type and number of each of said policies of insurance; the name or names of the insured under each of said policies of insurance; the limits of said insurance policy or policies; and the name, address, and employer of the present custodian of said insurance policy or policies.

(3) On the date of this accident, was there in effect one or more policies of insurance under which any question or controversy exists whether coverage is afforded thereunder to you for any cause of action for the injuries or damages claimed against you in the above-entitled action? If so, please state: the type and number of the policies on which there is question; the names of the insurance companies involved; the names of the insured involved; and the nature of the controversy.

Assignment 1

Draft interrogatories in the Jamie Blottner case, from the plaintiff to the defendant, Dana Newton. Limit yourself to twenty questions, asking for information that would indicate whether Newton was Scout's keeper. Use the facts and law stated in Assignment 1 in Chapter 6.

Assignment 2

Draft interrogatories in the Heather Putnam case, from the plaintiff to Fred Willis, risk manager of City General Hospital, defendant. Limit yourself to twenty questions, asking for information on (1) when risk management filed the "15 day report" required under Florida law after a death occurred while using equipment in a Florida hospital, and (2) why Willis, who knew of Putnam's death and the vaporizer's involvement in that death, did not tell Alpha not to disassemble the vaporizer. Use the facts and law stated in Assignment 2 in Chapter 4.

BIBLIOGRAPHY

11 *Bender's Forms of Discovery*. New York: Matthew Bender 1990 and 2001 Supplement.

Berman, Kenneth R., *Q: Is This Any Way to Write an Interrogatory? A: You Bet It Is*, 19 (No. 4) Litig. 42 (1993).

Charfoos, Lawrence S. and David W. Christensen, *Interrogatories: How to Use Them Effectively in Personal Injury Cases*, 22 Trial 56 (June 1986).

Cloud, Morgan, *The 2000 Amendments to the Federal Discovery Rules and the Future of Adversarial Pretrial Litigation*, 74 Temple L.Rev. 27 (2001).

Cooley, Diane, *Modern Discovery Practice: Search for Truth or Means of Abuse?*, 41 N.Y.L.Sch.L.Rev. 459 (1997).

Cooper, Allan B., and Mitchell L. Lathrop, *Use and Abuse of Interrogatories*. California Continuing Education of the Bar, October/November 1985.

Haydock, Roger S. and David F. Herr, *Discovery Practice*. Boston: Little, Brown and Co., 2001.

Lavine, Richard A. and Margaret M. Morrow, *Creating and Implementing a Successful Discovery Plan*. California Continuing Education of the Bar, September/October 1985.

LeSage, Bernard E. and Steven E. Smith, "Summary of Statutory and Case Law Relating to the Enforcement of Discovery" in *Compelling, Opposing, and Enforcing Discovery in State Courts*. California Continuing Education of the Bar, April 1988.

Roumell, Michael T., et al, *Pleadings, Discovery, and Settlement: Checklists and Forms*, ET IL–CLE 17–1 (Ill. Inst. for Continuing Education, 1994).

Seitz, Patricia A., *Get More Information and Less Indigestion Out of Your Interrogatories,* 71 A.B.A.J. 74 (March 1985).

Setterberg, Fred, *The Artful Question,* 6 Cal.Law. 45 (February 1986).

Shapard, John and Carroll Seron, *Attorneys' Views of Local Rules Limiting Interrogatories*. Federal Judicial Center Staff Paper, 1986.

Shugrue, John D., *Identifying & Combating Discovery Abuse*, 23 (No. 2) Litig. 10 (1997).

Shumadine, Conrad M., et al, *Discovery in Newsgathering and Libel Litigation 2000*, 604 PLI/Pat 15.

Shumadine, Conrad M., et al, *Litigating Libel and Privacy Suites*, 446 PLI/Pat 17, 35 (1996).

Smith, Nathan T., *The D.C. Circuit Review–August 1996–July 1997: Civil Procedure*, 66 Geo.Wash.L.Rev. 804 (1998).

Stein, Jacob A., *The Discovers*, 15 Litigation 46 (Fall 1988).

Sussman, Edna R., *Strategic Discovery,* 13 Litig. 37 (Fall 1986).

Thames, Lee David, *Discovery Strategy,* 28 For the Defense 12 (January 1986).

U.S. Army Legal Services, *Interrogatories to Answer or not to Answer, That is the Question: A Practical Guide to Federal Rule of Civil Procedure 33*, 1997 Army Law 38 (Aug. 1997).

Chapter 14

GENERAL CORRESPONDENCE

Great letter writing is an art. The right touch with tone, organization, and level of formality requires a clear eye and ear. Although the individual factors in a piece of correspondence are easily understood,[1] the interaction of those factors is so complex that the exact effect defies easy prediction.[2] Although good letter writing can be learned, great letter writing cannot be reduced to a dry set of rules.

You can learn to write good letters quickly and reliably, and that ability paves the way for you to develop your art at writing great letters. This chapter teaches you how to write good correspondence by explaining

- the priorities of correspondence,
- the components of correspondence,
- various format choices and their effects,
- various readers and how your relationship to them affects your correspondence,
- various correspondence tasks and ways to accomplish those tasks, and
- techniques that help you vary tone to create the impression you want.

Correspondence is one of the main opportunities an attorney has to establish the goodwill and trust that makes for a solid working relationship. Effective correspondence has helped many lawyers retain their clients and maintain a successful practice without needing to write many briefs.

1. Interpersonal communication science divides its research into the study of coherence, regulation, sequencing, preventatives, and repairs. Joseph N. Cappella, *Interpersonal Communication: Definitions and Fundamental Questions* in *Handbook of Communication Science* 212–13 (C. Berger and S. Chaffee, eds. 1987).

2. Behavior and attitudes are known to be related, but that relationship is complex, and changes in either area can affect the other. Herbert Simons, *Persuasion: Understanding, Practice, and Analysis* 72 (2d ed. 1986).

PRIORITIES

To write effective correspondence, focus on both content and tone. Correspondence communicates not only the writer's message, but also how the writer views the reader.[3] A letter is the written equivalent of a statement made in conversation, not of a speech to a group. A letter is structured as a communication from one person to another; a successful letter communicates the message within the context of the relationship between those people. Therefore, your success at legal correspondence depends not just on your knowledge of law, but also on your knowledge of people.[4]

The relationship between the writer and reader is important because the purpose of a business letter is usually to get the reader to do something. To accomplish this, the writer needs a reader who is willing to cooperate.[5] This cooperation is encouraged by goodwill, which in turn is encouraged by an appropriate tone.

Even the most routine letters establish this relationship. For example, the following two paragraphs from cover letters communicate quite different relationships, although the content is similar. The first communicates some sense of personableness, while the second does not.

> **I have enclosed the standard form contracts we discussed in our phone conversation yesterday. Please contact me if I can help further.**

> Enclosed please find standard form contracts per your phone request of yesterday. If further information is needed, advise accordingly.

The first version communicates courtesy and friendliness, and the reader is left with a positive feeling about the writer. The second version sounds unappealing with its use of bureaucratic phrases like "enclosed please find," "per your request," and "advise accordingly." Overall, the second version creates the impression that the writer wants distance from the reader. The tone distances the writer from the reader, which erodes trust,[6] which in turn can erode the writer's credibility.[7] The letter leaves the reader wanting to have nothing further to do with the writer. Assuming this is not what the writer wanted, the second version's tone contradicts its purpose.[8]

When writing business correspondence, a legal writer needs to be precise and clear, as in all other legal writing. But tone takes on equal

---

3. *Id.* at 32.

4. "Good writing [is] writing that gets ideas across. And that's much more a matter of paying attention to your reader than of paying attention to your English." *Id.* at 5.

5. Rolf Sandell, *Linguistic Style and Persuasion* 70–103 (1977).

6. Daniel J. O'Keefe, *Persuasion: Theory and Research* 190 (2d ed. 2002).

7. The combination of expertise and trustworthiness makes for more reliable communication. *Id.* Respect and trust are more significant factors in the receiver's response to the sender than is attraction. Simons, *supra* note 2, at 131–35.

8. "[M]ost readers respond favorably to a concerned and courteous spokesperson. Whatever your personal character, let your writing reflect a warm, human personality." Daniel McDonald, *The Language of Argument* 4 (3d ed. 1989).

importance. For this reason, tone is included both in a separate section and throughout other sections of this chapter.[9] This information should help you determine how to manage effectively the dual focus correspondence requires, a dual focus on your message and your attitude.

COMPONENTS

Regardless of its length or complexity, a good letter always needs three basic components:

- an opening, which orients the reader to the letter's purpose and the writer's tone;

- a middle, which delivers the content with needed support or explanation; and

- an ending, which closes politely while reaffirming the writer's original tone and purpose.

The Opening, Orienting the Reader

An effective letter opens by answering the reader's initial question. In the brief time before reading a letter—the time when the reader scans the return address, opens the envelope, and unfolds the letter—the reader usually forms some questions is his or her mind. Often those questions are

Why is this person writing to me?

What is this letter about?

Is this good news or bad news?

As a writer, you can often anticipate what those questions would be, and then your opening sentences can answer those questions. Thus a cover letter for a resume can begin by stating that the writer is applying for a job. A request for insurance information can start with the reason for the request. A letter answering the reader's question can start by reminding the reader of that question. The writer needs to take special care in crafting the opening when the reader's initial question is "Is this good news or bad?" and this will be discussed in a later section.

The Middle, Delivering the Content

As soon as the reader is oriented to the letter's purpose and tone, he or she is ready for the content. Delaying the delivery of that content further will only frustrate the reader. Thus the writer should deliver the main point by the beginning of the second paragraph, if not sooner. The writer can elaborate as needed, adding details, caveats, or further questions.

The reader will move through this information in detail or in cursory fashion, at his or her discretion. In either case, the reader will move through it with an understanding of the main point, rather than

---

9. For similar reasons, this chapter draws substantially from communication science, the psychology of persuasion, and business writing.

with confusion or frustration. The writer's goal in this part of the letter should be to answer the reader's questions and deliver needed information without causing the reader to wonder "Why do I need to read this?"

Clear presentation, rather than creation of a particular tone, is the main concern of this section of the letter. While tone is important in the opening and closing portions of the letter, it is not as noticeable a factor in the middle of the letter. Because this part of the letter includes details and explanation, it usually sounds neutral, having little affect on the overall tone.

The Ending, Closing Consistently and Politely

After the content has been delivered and explained, the writer needs to exit gracefully. This involves echoing the tone of the original paragraph; explaining the action the reader needs to take, if applicable; and telling the reader where to go with further questions, if needed. Thus a cover letter for a resume can thank the reader for his or her attention and explain how to reach the writer. A request for insurance information can thank the reader and give the phone number to call if questions remain. A letter answering the reader's question can offer more assistance if further questions exist.

The letter's closing paragraph, although short, is important to the overall tone. The closing should echo the tone and level of formality used in the letter's opening. This detail is important for creating a sense of the writer's sincerity. For example, if a letter is friendly in the opening but distant in the closing, the reader is left questioning the writer's true attitude.

This three part structure breaks letter writing into three manageable pieces that can be adapted to all sorts of correspondence structures, as the following table illustrates.

How the Three Part Structure Applies to Various Types of Letters

Kind of Letter	Orient the Reader	Deliver the Message	Close Consistently
Giving good news	State the news.	Elaborate as needed.	Close politely.
Answering a Request	Refer to request.	Answer and explain.	Say whom to contact with questions.
Making a Routine Request	Identify self and make request.	List what is needed.	Thank reader.
Making a Special Request	Explain why you need this.	Make request, with list as needed.	Thank reader and explain how to reach you if there are questions.
Giving Directions	Overview task.	Explain tasks step by step.	Explain what to do if the reader has problems.
Persuading to Take Action	Refer to background that puts writer in position to recommend.	State the recommendation and reasons.	Refer to recommendation and action it would require.
Cover Letter	Refer to project to which materials relate.	List what is enclosed.	Refer to project at which materials will be used.

Kind of Letter	Orient the Reader	Deliver the Message	Close Consistently
Answering a Complaint	Summarize the complaint.	Answer and explain.	Explain next step if appropriate and close politely.
Giving Bad News	Establish your role with reader.	State the news and explain.	Echo the role established in first paragraph.

Often, what a lawyer needs to do is write a good letter quickly rather than spend hours or days writing a great letter. For those times, the three part format presented above can help you create a good letter quickly and with minimal stress. And, when you want to write a great letter, this format can help you quickly reach the place where you can begin focusing on your art.

FORMATS

The first format choice you must make is whether your verbal[10] message should be communicated orally or in writing. Although often writers make this choice based on convenience, it is wise to consider other factors. If a written correspondence is inappropriately formal, you may want to communicate orally. If you do not want a message to be discoverable by another party, avoid writing it down. Conversely, if you do want a point established for the record, do write it down, even if it is written to the attorney in the next office, to create a paper trail.[11]

The next format choice is what form to use, such as electronic mail, a memo, or a letter. Beyond the superficial differences in these three written documents, each has its own connotations and uses.

Electronic Mail

E-mail, or electronically transmitted messaging, is convenient but not without risk. It is a relatively new genre of correspondence, and its uses are still evolving. Social conventions related to e-mail are still in flux, so it is hard for a writer to know and meet the reader's expectations for tone. Perhaps because of this newness and uncertainty, many writers ignore the reader's expectations and focus on their own inclinations. Some writers allow a surprising level of informality in e-mail, using abbreviations and ignoring spelling or grammar errors. Others always include the conventions of a standard letter, such as a salutation and closing. Still others try to convey a conversation as they write, interjecting humor, using capital letters for emphasis, and adding smiling faces. But writing, even in e-mail, is not the same as conversation.

When writing e-mail, focus on stating your main point as early as possible. Busy readers often will not scroll down to the end of an e-mail, so they may miss information placed late in the document. If the e-mail

---

10. If this sentence confuses you, it is probably because many writers use the term "verbal" incorrectly and have blurred its meaning in your mind. The term "verbal" means "in words," and contrasts with "nonverbal." "Oral" means spoken words, and contrasts with "written."

11. One example of this use of correspondence is detailed in Chapter 16 on Wills and Trusts.

contains many important points, include an enumerated summary near the top of the message, and then add headings throughout the e-mail so the reader can easily scroll down and find a particular point.

If you choose to use e-mail, do not expect it to be easier than writing a letter, and do not expect it to convey any nuance you could not communicate in a standard letter. Do not depend on smiley faces. Proofread your e-mails for tone, content, and form, especially watching for any phrasing that could be ambiguous. E-mail can be forwarded even more easily than a letter can be photocopied, so avoid writing anything that you would not want broadcast. You have probably heard stories about private, vitriolic descriptions of bosses being mistakenly forwarded to a whole office, or confidential information being leaked through an e-mail that had been forwarded one time too many. These stories are not all urban legends. Take special care to send e-mail only to the person you intended.

Memos

The memo format is often used for in-house correspondence when e-mail is not appropriate. Memos are useful for in-house communication, when frequent communication makes it unnecessary to signal how you view the reader. A memo's format focuses on content rather than on the reader. The salutation (Dear Joan,) is replaced by the subject line (RE: Discovery of In–House Statistical Summaries of Pons Corporation's Cash Flow). The closing is omitted, and initials next to the "From" line replace the personal signature. These changes in format also eliminate personal comments, such as the good wishes that often appear in the closing paragraph of a letter. A memo gets down to business and is the appropriate choice when conciseness and efficiency are the pre-eminent goal.[12]

Memo format is appropriate for detailing a research task to a subordinate, outlining a proposal to a superior, or transmitting routine information.[13] Memo format is also appropriate for requesting information from someone who routinely provides that information as part of his or her job. For example, write a memo to request new office equipment from your office manager, account information from a bank officer, or an explanation from the IRS. Finally, use memo format to document information for the files or to record information several readers must be aware of but not know thoroughly. Because of the volume of information

---

12. "Talk of nothing but business, and dispatch that business quickly." Richard Hatch, *Business Communication: Theory and Technique* 9 (1983) (from a placard on the door of Adine Press, Venice, Italy, established in 1490).

13. Researchers have identified five types of on-the-job messages sent from supervisor to subordinate: job instructions, job rationale, policy and procedure, feed-

back, and indoctrination. Written communication from subordinate to supervisor was used less, and generally was concerned with either personnel information or technical feedback about progress toward an assigned goal. For a useful discussion of this information, *see,* Thomas Tortoriello, Stephen Blatt and Sue DeWine, *Communication in the Organization: An Applied Approach* 52–54 (1978).

in a law practice, readers must skim some information; the memo's subject line, headings, and subheadings facilitate this.

Although the memo format was previously used for in-house correspondence only, that is no longer the case.[14] Memo format is becoming more popular because it is easier to produce. It avoids some time-consuming problems, such as what to put after "Dear" ("Ms. Jones:" "Joan Jones," "Joan Jones:" or "Joan,") and what to put above the signature: ("Sincerely," "Sincerely yours," "Yours very truly," or "Very truly yours,"). After wrestling with these questions, writers sometimes turn to the memo format in despair because it omits those elements altogether. Your choice between memo and letter is better made by considering the occasion causing you to write. Consider the uses of the letter format, described below, and then use the memo format only when it best suits your purpose.

Letters

Letters are appropriate when you are communicating on a topic about which the reader may have some feeling. For example, no writer would send a memo to a friend expressing regret over the death of a spouse, nor would an interviewer send a memo of rejection rather than a letter. These situations call for addressing the reader as an individual, and a letter does that well.

Applying this to subtler situations, choose the letter format when telling a client bad news or when communicating with another individual on behalf of a client. In the latter situation, a letter is useful because receiving mail from an attorney may be alarming, and you may want to use the letter's tone to help the reader calm down. The letter format facilitates a personal tone, and you can use that opportunity to communicate whether your purpose is friendly or not. For example, a letter suggests this tone in the opening sentence.

Dear Mr. Abernathy:

> Your colleague, Heng Yon, has suggested you might be interested in . . . .

The word "colleague" in the first sentence suggests a cordial tone. In contrast, the following opening sends signals that bad news is coming.

Dear Mr. Abernathy:

> At the request of my client, Dr. Heng Yon, I am writing to inform you that . . . .

A memo, which opens with a subject line, would leave no room for such signals of the writer's tone.

A letter may also be the format of choice when you want to communicate deference to the reader. Write a letter to a hiring partner

---

14. A more traditional view is that memos are not used for official business with clients and others outside the organization. Elizabeth Tebeaux, *Design of Busi-* *ness Communications: The Process and the Product* 125 (1990). But in practice attorneys are now sometimes using memos for out-of-house communication.

to apply for a position, to the president of a corporation, or to an elderly person. You might choose this format when writing to any reader who will be more inclined to cooperate if he or she sees you as respectful.

Dear Ms. Marino:

I am writing to apply for a clerking position in . . . .

Finally, a letter is the usual format for writing messages of a social nature, such as thank you or congratulatory notes.

Denise,

Congratulations on the well-deserved praise from Judge Crain!

In summary, all three formats are useful, depending on your working relationship with the reader, the preferences of that reader, your task for this piece of correspondence, and the tone you want to convey.

ADJUSTMENTS FOR VARIOUS READERS

Adjusting your correspondence in light of your specific reader is part of the writing process because the letter's primary purpose is to communicate information to that person.[15] Therefore, a primary step when corresponding is considering what will make the reader more willing to accept information from the writer. Although you may also adapt your letter writing to individual readers,[16] you will generally have different priorities when writing to in-house readers (employers, colleagues, and employees) and out-of-house readers (clients and other lay people, attorneys and judges, and other business persons).[17]

In-House Readers

A common element of in-house writing is a need for efficiency. You want to be concise, whether your tone is cordial or reserved. Communicate your tone only in the briefest ways, and focus on the content. In general, use memo format and the tone established by understood, in-house rules.[18] In-house correspondence usually begins with the main point.[19] For example, a memo from a supervisor to an employee might state a request as follows.

15. For an example list of questions to consider when analyzing an audience, *see* Hatch, *supra* note 12, at 51.

16. For example, one researcher found that flattery will appeal to some people, but not to people who have low opinions of themselves—they will react negatively. Simons, *supra* note 2, at 25. Yet other research shows that obvious flattery does not persuade. Tebeaux, *supra* note 14, at 142.

17. Business communication texts often divide readers into four categories: laypeople, executives, experts, and technicians. Kenneth Houp and Thomas Pearsall, *Reporting Technical Information* 67–69 (2002). For legal writing, these four categories would translate roughly into clients, judges, other attorneys, and paralegals, which does not delineate the most pronounced distinctions between readers of legal correspondence.

18. Language used in a group is influenced greatly by the power structure, more so than by the sex of the reader or writer, the socioeconomic class of the reader or writer, or any other factors. For a discussion of research in intergroup communication, *see* Howard Giles and John Wiemann, *Language, Social Comparison, and Power* in *Handbook of Communication Science* 356–59 (C. Berger and S. Chaffee eds., 1987).

19. "The first step toward making a message efficient is to get right to the point." Hatch, *supra* note 12, at 11.

Please call the Red Cross to see if .... We need to find some verification of Kelsey's claim that he was giving blood at the time of ....

The employee might begin the answering memo as follows.

The Red Cross should have the information we need, but to obtain that information we will have to .... The Red Cross does have a log of all donors, including .... They will not release that information, however, unless ....

With your OK, I will start the paperwork needed to get the ....

In each case, the first line states the point of the memo.

Despite this focus on efficiency, the ongoing relationship between the reader and writer still affects the correspondence. In the previous memo from supervisor to employee, the "please" in the request signals politeness. The sentence explaining the why behind the request suggests that the writer values the reader's understanding of the situation; the reader is helping to accomplish a task. In response, the quick answer at the beginning of the employee's response suggests the employee is focused on the task, valuing the supervisor's goals, and being efficient in meeting the supervisor's request. The concise explanation communicates the employee's competence and efficiency, and the ending communicates the employee's recognition of the boundaries of his or her authority to act. Thus the wording, content, and organization confirm the working relationship. Before writing, clarify in your own mind the working relationship you want with the reader so you communicate it appropriately.

Writing to someone above you on the organizational ladder can be simplified by taking some time to determine what your reader wants. Readers higher on the organizational ladder usually cannot spend much time on any one piece of correspondence. When writing for these readers, state the point in the first sentence and summarize your content in the first paragraph. These readers put a premium on their time, and they will appreciate it if you do, too.

One way to condense information for the reader is to state it in terms of its importance to that reader. For example, if you have secured a maintenance contract for office equipment, you can state that fact, the name of the company, the overall cost, and perhaps how the cost compares with other competing bids. Do not go into the details of how you reached this contract or of what the service will include. Give the reader the information wanted, but do not burden him or her with the details of your job.

When deciding how much detail to include, consider the inclinations of the reader. As discussed in Chapter 9, memo discussion sections, include more detail for supervisors who want to be fully informed; provide a quick summary for supervisors who do not want to deal with technicalities. For many supervisors, the optimum amount of information lies between. For these readers, include a summary of routine information and somewhat more detail when describing any problems that have arisen or may arise in the future. If more support is needed, attach documents the reader might want to see, but summarize the important information in your memo.

Also consider the working relationship you want to communicate through your tone. Again, the personal qualities of your reader will be a major influence. Is she impatient? If so, be concise and worry little about courtesy. Does he emphasize courtesy and respect for the client? If so, make sure your memos to him, although concise, do not omit these courtesies. Often the tone you want is a blend of several qualities. You will write in a conversational-yet-concise tone, a respectful-yet-confident tone, or an efficient-yet-personable tone. Finding the balance of qualities you want may take time, but when you have found it you can use it in all your correspondence with that reader.

When writing for employees whom you supervise or over whom you have some rank, clarity is critical. When achieving this clarity, worry less about conciseness, more about specificity. One common complaint employees have about supervisors is their directions are not clear. Also consider your working relationship with the reader. For example, if writing a memo instructing your secretary about handling rejection letters, focus on content but word your request politely, indicating your appreciation for the work done.

State the information from the reader's point of view. For example, if announcing the company picnic, begin with "You are invited to ...." rather than "The company picnic will be held ...." The former subtly reflects that you are thinking of your reader's interests, and this sense of inclusion helps build goodwill.

When writing to colleagues, avoid treating them like employees or supervisors. So, for example, do not begin simply by stating the request because that would suggest that it is routine for the colleague to grant your requests. Instead you might begin with an acknowledgment that you are asking for something that is within the colleague's discretion to do.

> If you have time, I could use your advice on a particularly troublesome issue in ....

> Joe, could you handle another case right now? I have a client who ....

Yet do not use an overly deferential tone, because you are an equal in this situation. For example, you would not write the following.

> I am requesting your review of the ... because ....

Instead, you would speak less formally, perhaps as follows.

> Could you review a contract I have written for ... ?

Your tone with colleagues is more like informal conversation than correspondence with supervisors or employees.

When writing for in-house readers, focus on your point, state it quickly and clearly, and use the organizations suggested in the task section below. Also consider the particular concerns of the reader. Then you will avoid errors in content or tone that could hamper your communication.

Out-of-House Readers

Adjusting the format for the out-of-house reader will require you to change your approach somewhat in planning, choosing content, and revising your content. Out-of-house readers are more varied. The most common reader is the client, but other common readers of your correspondence include witnesses, experts, interested parties, and other business contacts, such as vendors. You will also write to other attorneys, including the opposition, the general bar, and the bench.

When planning your client correspondence, begin by considering the question in the client's mind, similar to your approach for an in-house reader. This will help you determine what content to include. Also consider whether the client will experience an emotional reaction to the message, and if so choose a letter format. If you are presenting good news, you may use a memo format, unless you want to use a letter to add a personal touch to underscore the news. If you are communicating news that may upset the client, choose the more personal letter format and begin by preparing the client for the bad news, as suggested below. Consider also whether the client is a willing receiver of this news. If so, your task will be informing. If not, the correspondence will involve some persuading.

Whatever choices you make, check during revision for any wording that makes the content difficult for the client, such as a term the client does not understand or a word with an unneeded emotional overtone. For example, you would revise the following.

If you go bankrupt, then, this provision allows you to . . . .

Since Texas is a community property state, your will needs to state that . . . .

Instead, you would write the following.

This provision offers some protection in the event of financial difficulties, such as bankruptcy, by . . . .

Clause 2(b) of this draft of your will is needed to clarify which property belongs to you individually, rather than belonging to you and your husband together. Texas is a community property state, which means that . . . .

When writing for other out-of-house readers, follow the same approach, with one exception. While you do not want to upset your client, you may occasionally want to upset other readers, although without appearing to do so. To do this, omit the preparatory introductions you add to soften the blow. Structure the correspondence as you would if simply informing the reader. The result will be correspondence with a tougher tone.

March 13, 1990

Dear Ms. McKinney:

> On behalf of my client, Geron's Department Store, I am writing to inform you that one week from today I will be presenting a motion to the Circuit Court of Dade County to instruct the Sheriff to repossess.... This action will be required unless you ....

This approach can galvanize the reader into action. Use it only as needed, however, because it seldom pays to make enemies.[20]

When writing to business readers, such as vendors or attorneys who are not representing an opposing party, standard business practice is your best guide, because this will be the tone and style with which the reader is most familiar. When writing to attorneys, you can worry less about using legal terms of art; in fact, you may use them extensively as a convenience.

Dear Margaret,

> Good news! We won the 12(b)(6) motion, and it looks like plaintiffs will not be able to amend their complaint. We were not able to win a dismissal on the other counts, but we should be able to discourage them with a Rule 11 filing on the basis of the 12(b)(6). They told Judge Hertz they wanted expedited discovery, relying on his rocket docket, but he just took it under advisement.

> I think we can get summary judgment on two counts, and we ought to file on all four, before they notice any more depositions. I have filed an application to quash the subpoena duces tecum of Jones, since it is a boxcar demand, but I expect a cross application to compel production. They'll have to work quick, because we're on the calendar Tuesday and I'm going to notice the application for a protective order by FAX Friday at 6 p.m.

> Sincerely,

> Jim

Avoid using legal terms for intimidation. Remember, the other attorney has a law dictionary and may only be irritated or amused by your attempts.

ADJUSTMENTS FOR VARIOUS TASKS

The organization, content, and tone of correspondence are affected not only by the format and the writer's relationship with the reader, but also by the particular task the writing must accomplish. In correspon-

---

20. The reader will treat you as you have treated the reader. Cappella, *supra* note 1, at 213.

dence, this involves some combination of informing or persuading. These tasks are not discrete categories, but instead lie at opposite ends of a continuum.

Informing and persuading create different reasons for the content of the letter. Informing provides the reader with information without advocating any particular use of the information. Examples of informing include the following:

- a cover letter stating that you are delivering a requested document,

- a memo notifying the supervisor that you have completed a request,

- a letter responding to a client that you have made the changes he requested, and

- a memo answering a simple question from your supervisor.

Persuasion, on the other hand, focuses on influencing the reader's use of the information. Although persuading involves presenting information, its purpose is getting the reader to do, think, or believe something. Examples of persuading include the following:

- a letter asking someone to schedule a meeting with you,

- a memo to a law clerk outlining a question you want researched,

- a letter requesting further facts from a client, and

- a letter requesting payment for services rendered.

Much correspondence combines the functions of informing and persuading. Examples of combinations of informing and persuading include the following:

- a letter of retainer that reviews a conversation and asks the client to sign the retainer contract,

- a letter discussing the negotiation of a business deal, and

- a memo answering questions and requesting some follow-up action.

When informing and persuading are both involved, decide which function dominates. For example, sometimes an element of persuasion is needed, but informing is still the dominant task. If you decide that informing is the dominant task, then begin your paragraphs with a balanced statement.

Your choice here will depend on your primary objectives.

Or

This choice will require you to consider several factors.

In contrast, if you place yourself further toward persuading, you might indicate in the beginning that a recommendation is coming.

When deciding how to proceed at this time, your primary consideration should be establishing a solid record to prepare for an eventual lawsuit.

Although either action is possible, negotiation offers some additional advantages.

This beginning sentence leads you to structure the body of your correspondence differently and to include different supporting detail. So if informing, you might write the following.

Although three options are possible, I recommend .... This option is most advantageous because ....

But you might state the following if persuading.

Now that we have the basic terms of your will established, you need take only a few more steps to fulfill your objectives. First, I recommend that you ....

In the paragraphs framing your main message, as with any letter, echo the tone you have established.

The choice made here sometimes reflects your working relationship with the reader. You may find, for example, that some clients or employers prefer that you take a position while others prefer that you do not. Their tastes, however, cannot overshadow your duty to the profession and to yourself. Do not attempt to persuade when you cannot justify the action to yourself or another attorney. Do not simply inform when you have a duty to warn the reader and to recommend an action. Where you place your letter on this continuum is a facet of your professional responsibility.

Informing

If you are informing the reader, your writing task is simpler than persuading, but not simple. You can begin with a summary of your message and then launch into details. You may modify your organization depending on whether the information you are providing is good news or bad.

Communicating Good News or Neutral Information

One way to communicate your message quickly is to write a heading communicating the main point. For example, you might write "Settlement of Contract for Client's Purchase of Whittier Canning." If you are writing a letter, you can insert the heading before the salutation or give the reader this information in the first sentence.

Dear Mr. Aitch:

Here for your review is the version of the contract to purchase Whittier Canning that James Builder has agreed to accept ....

Do not start with a filler sentence; the reader does not want it and the situation does not require it.

In the body of the correspondence, elaborate or explain as needed. If you are explaining options to the reader, use "you may" to underscore that the reader is in charge. Also set out the options so the reader can see them easily. One useful way to do this is with a tabulated list. The following letter, for example, gives the various choices the reader could make.

> **Now that we have the signed confession of judgment, you have three actions you may take:**
>
> (a) **you may have us retain the confession of judgment in your files at our office, so that it will be available if you choose to take action on it in the future;**
>
> (b) **you may have us record the judgment in Bernalillo County, so that it is recorded although no further action is taken; or**
>
> (c) **you may have us both record the judgment in Bernalillo County and ask the Sheriff to act upon it.**

The signals of structure and wording here make the content much clearer than the more abstract below one would have been.

> We have the following options for developing the file documentation of this default: the confession of judgment retained in our office files, the confession of judgment recorded in the appropriate county, or the confession filed in the county and with the county sheriff for execution.

Adjust the degree of detail to suit the reader. For example, if the reader of the letter above needed more guidance, you could include three paragraphs after the list, each one beginning as follows.

> Choosing the first option of ... would mean that ....
>
> Choosing the second option, or ... , would mean that ....
>
> Finally, choosing the third option ....

If possible, arrange questions in the order in which the reader will need to retrieve the information. For example, if you are asking a client for information about creating an estate plan, group the questions so you ask all questions from one set of documents at once and label the group.

> Life Insurance Policies
>
> *For each policy*, list the following information:
>
> • name of beneficiary
>
> • name of owner
>
> • face value of policy
>
> • benefit value

If you think your reader will need help complying with the request, give that help in the letter, tell the reader how to find the help needed, or offer to help yourself. For example, you might add the following to the previous request.

Life Insurance Policies

For each policy, list the following information:

- name of beneficiary (this is normally listed on the first page of the policy)

- name of owner (this is also usually listed on the first page, and may be a person different from the beneficiary or the insured)

- face value of policy

- benefit value (this information may be stated in a table in your policy, with the benefits increasing with the years you hold the policy. If so, use the number . . . .)

Make sure your requests are no more extensive than needed and are clearly worded.

Consider setting out your list in fill-in-the-blank form, if that would be easier for your reader. Rather than drafting a separate document to respond, readers often prefer to write a response on the original and return it to the writer. Anything you do to make it easier for the reader to comply increases the chance of a timely and complete response and augments goodwill.

Make sure that your request is unambiguous and that you have stated any deadline for fulfilling this request. If the request is for something to be done "when you have the time," say so, but realize this statement moves the request to the bottom of the priority list and the request may never be answered.

Close your correspondence politely by offering assistance, telling how to obtain more information, or thanking the reader for cooperation. When thanking the reader, watch for the occasional situation when saying thank you seems somewhat sarcastic. In sum, take pains with each section to increase the chance of a successful response.

Communicating Bad News

When communicating bad news, consider calling or meeting instead of writing a letter. You probably do not want to communicate stand-offishness or rejection, and a written communication of bad news is likely to create that impression. Facing someone with bad news may be difficult, but it may be more effective for maintaining your working relationship. A need for documenting the event might be the only reason to write a letter here, and you could do this after the meeting.

Dear Jane Eyre:

As I stated in our conversation on June 9, I regret having to release you from employment as governess for my daughter. Nevertheless, I must do so because . . . .

When you need to communicate bad news in writing, you must communicate the point clearly, no matter how much you want to soften the blow. In general, state the point in one clear sentence. This is important because readers are more likely to misunderstand bad news than good.[21]

Often, you can soften the blow by adding a sentence or two before stating the point. This preliminary text allows you to establish a relationship with your reader before the bad news appears, so you can separate the relationship from the bad news.[22] For example, if you had to tell a client you could not take a case because of a conflict of interest, you might begin as follows.

Dear Ms. Eyre:

> I appreciate the confidence you expressed when you asked me to represent you in your employment discrimination case and was happy to accept your case. Regrettably, I have since discovered that my senior partner has represented Mr. Rochester in other matters. Therefore it would be inappropriate for me to represent you in this case because of the potential conflict of interest.

In your concern for softening the blow, do not neglect to deliver the information. Make sure you deliver the summary of that information at least by the beginning of the second paragraph.

Dear Ms. Eyre:

> I appreciate the confidence you expressed when you asked me to represent you in your employment discrimination case and was happy to accept your case. I was happy to be of service to you when you prepared your will and established a trust fund for the . . . . With respect to those legal matters, I can still represent you as needed.
>
> In regard to the employment discrimination case, however, I am unable to represent you effectively because of a potential conflict of interest. After talking with you, I discovered that my senior partner has represented . . . .

Delaying further may mislead the reader into thinking the news will be good, may make the reader impatient, or may make you seem tentative. None of these are useful effects for you.

In the body of the correspondence, elaborate as needed, as when giving good news. Often, bad news will require more detail than good, because the reader will want to know more of the how and why. If needed, you may attach explanatory documents. You want to avoid two extremes here: you do not want to look as if you are covering up by being too brief, nor do you want to look as if you are being defensive by going

---

21. "When someone doesn't want to recognize something, he or she may honestly miss implications that would be entirely apparent otherwise." Hatch, *supra* note 12, at 255.

22. Richard Hatch describes this as the strategic aim of reducing the reader's anger at you, although you probably cannot reduce the reader's disappointment. *Id.* at 243.

on too long. Aim for balance, in light of what you know about your reader. When giving bad news, always look for options. Is there any silver lining here? May things get better in the future? Do not make up good news, but report any if you can.

If your news is somewhat good and somewhat bad, you can start with the good news but hint about the bad news to come so it will not jar the reader when it appears later.

> You may benefit at this point by doing nothing until the Weber situation is resolved. Although we could proceed with the suit now,
>
> . . . .

If the good news is much less significant than the bad, it may be better placed at the end of the statement.

> The statutes in Wisconsin will not allow you to disinherit your spouse completely in your will. Instead, to protect your estate you would have to . . . .

In any case, close the letter with a few sentences reiterating the tone you established in the opening paragraph. This will unify your letter, which will make you sound more sincere. It may also soften the blow of the bad news by leaving the reader with a touch of consolation.

> Thus, although you cannot pursue the estate plan you had originally envisioned, you may be able to achieve the same result using a different approach. If you wish to pursue this further, please
>
> . . . .

Or

> Although we have not been able to recover the funds lost through Mr. Gaither's mismanagement of your company, we have at least . . . .

Giving bad news requires a delicate balance between clarity and tact. To achieve the balance, let this letter sit overnight before mailing.[23] If that is not possible, read the letter before mailing with an eye toward any word or phrase that will sting; see if you have worded the letter kindly but clearly. Communicating bad news does not mean piling on language; it means thinking about the reader's needs and addressing them.

Persuading

As you move toward advocating for a particular position, you will begin to incorporate persuasive techniques. The first step in using these techniques is determining when and to what degree it is appropriate to use them. For example, when you request action or information, you are always persuading the reader to some extent. When the request is routine, you may not spend much time explaining the request. But you may write a letter instead of a memo to suggest that the reader's cooperation is not being taken for granted.

23. Anne Eisenberg, *Effective Technical Communication* 301 (1992).

If you decide more persuasion is needed, add it by stating concisely how the action requested will help the reader. For example, if a request entails a substantial commitment of money or time from the reader, take time to list the benefits to the reader.

When the challenge of the correspondence is more to motivate the reader than to explain the desired action clearly, your primary task is persuasion. Persuading is a challenging task, in part because individual responses are difficult to predict.[24] Additionally, persuading is difficult because the reader has many ways to resist persuasion.[25] Finally, persuasion is difficult because it is sensitive to many complex variables. For example, readers are generally more readily persuaded when they do not perceive that the writer is trying to persuade.[26] They are more readily persuaded by someone who is somewhat like them, yet different in ways significant to the topic of the persuasion.[27] Furthermore, each time the writer tries to persuade the reader to change an opinion, that writer risks reducing his or her credibility in the reader's eyes.[28] Persuasive correspondence is complex and occurs within a larger framework.

In persuasive correspondence, the structure may or may not vary from a routine request. One thing that does vary is the weight you give to each part as you are writing. The request for action itself is not likely to change, but the motivation to comply receives more attention.

In short correspondence, this motivation may require only a little more content. For example, you may add a phrase explaining the way the reader will benefit from this action.

> Although finding this information will be somewhat time-consuming, it should enable you to save time later when . . . .

This small persuasion may help you gain substantial cooperation.

Often, however, the persuasion will require fuller development. Then apply the general techniques for persuasion discussed in Chapter 8 on persuasive facts and Chapter 10 on argument sections. Apply these techniques, using one of several broader persuasive strategies, because the range of possible reader responses has broadened in correspondence. Before you were convincing a judge who had to make a decision within

---

24. William B. Gucykunst, *Cross-Cultural Comparisons* in *Handbook of Communication Science* 858 (C. Berger and S. Chaffee, eds., 1987).

25. For example, under cognitive dissonance theory, the reader may "(1) derogate the source; (2) decide that [the] disagreement is not very important, or rationalize it in some other way; (3) seek social support or supportive evidence for [his or her] own viewpoint (4) misperceive the source's position; (5) compartmentalize (ignore or forget that the cognitions are discrepant); (6) attempt to convince the source (if available) of his or her error; [or finally] (7) modify [his or her] own attitudes." Simons, *supra* note 2, at 61.

26. Sandell, *supra* note 5, at 297.

27. A persuader is likely to be most effective when similar to the audience in values and background, but different in ways that increase credibility (experience, etc.) so the persuader is a "super-representative" of the group. Simons, *supra* note 2, at 135.

28. One example Herbert Simons gives is that if you see Bill Cosby saying that Jello is great and you like Bill Cosby but do not like jello, you will subsequently like jello somewhat more but also like Cosby somewhat less. *Id.* at 58–62.

the context of the law. Here you may be writing to a reader who has the option to take no action, to make no decision, and to base that decision on factors having nothing to do with the law.

Deciding what persuasion strategy to use is a major part of your task when writing this correspondence. Possible strategies include persuading based on common goals, solving problems, seizing opportunities, and warnings. To help you make this choice, this section discusses each of these strategies separately.

Persuading by Common Goals

Generally the most effective way to persuade a reader is to show the reader that doing what you suggest will accomplish something the reader wants to accomplish. You and your reader can cooperate rather than compete. This approach is useful in much of your out-of-house correspondence. For example, when writing to negotiate with an opposing attorney, you might explain how a particular settlement can benefit both parties. When writing to a nonlawyer, this explanation of a common goal can also add reassurance.

As you present your reasoning, be straightforward. The reader may be suspicious or nervous; allay those fears by helping the reader see your reasoning and its merit. Reassure the reader that the action you request will not hurt him or her, if possible. State the needed action clearly and make it as easy as possible for the reader to comply. As with other requests, enclose a self-addressed envelope, use a fill-in-the-blank form, and request only the action or information needed. In your closing, you can let the reader know you are available to help or answer questions.

Because this common goal approach is effective, sometimes the most persuasive letter may not seem persuasive in the usual sense, and it may be persuasive in part for that very reason. For example, the attorney who wrote the following letter represented a client who did not want to initiate a lawsuit for religious reasons, but who did want compensation for his injuries. The client felt he was partly at fault and, under his religious convictions, he could not accuse another. The attorney, knowing he could not take the case to court, wrote the following successful letter.

Mr. Alfred W. Hitchcock

Insurance Claims Service

Box 123

Prairie View, Kansas

Dear Mr. Hitchcock:

This letter follows our earlier conference with you concerning Hans Anderson's settlement demand for $1,200,000 for injuries suffered when he was hit by a truck whose driver is insured by your company. When we conferred, your company was unwilling to agree to settlement.

When our firm presented Mr. Anderson's demand, we did so only after reviewing recent cases involving monetary awards for injuries such as loss of a kidney. Because we think that this case can be settled without costly and time-consuming court procedures, we have decided to spell out in detail why we believe Mr. Anderson's demand is justified.

. . . .

On the basis of what we have set out in this letter, we think that this case merits the claim we have made. We welcome your serious consideration of our demand.

Very truly yours,

Timothy Huebner

One final touch that may increase your success is to reiterate that the decision is a good one after it has been made, when the reader is most likely to have second thoughts.[29]

Persuading Through a Problem–Solution Approach

The problem-solution structure is a traditional form that many clients may easily understand. This logical pattern is well suited to memo format, lending itself to division into subsections. In this structure, begin by describing the problem; in later paragraphs describe your solution, persuading the reader to accept it.

Explain the problem as concisely and clearly as possible.

In the past six months, several attorneys have found it difficult to retrieve accounting information quickly. The accounting system

. . . .

This preliminary step is logically necessary to convince your reader that the problem requires action. If you do not succeed on this point, the reader has no reason to accept the solution you present later in your letter.

After convincing the reader that a problem exists, explain your solution, including why it is feasible and worth its cost. At this point, think particularly about benefits the reader will see. These might be different from the benefits seen by you or your client, so focus on benefits that will persuade your reader.

This change in our accounting system should . . . .

When using this approach with legal readers, do not leave unanswered questions. Yet avoid letting the memo get too lengthy or delaying too long before getting to your point. For these reasons, the problem-solution approach may not be the best choice for writing to a senior partner or lawyer out-of-house.

---

29. Research has shown that one of the vulnerable moments in the persuasion process is after the decision has been made. O'Keefe, *supra* note 6, at 80–81. At this point, the arguments against the position taken seem to have more force with the decider. If, however, the persuader follows up with some communication about the desirability of the decision made, this regret is reduced. *Id.* at 84.

Persuading with Opportunities

An opportunity-benefit structure is useful when you are persuading the reader to take action but you do not want to label the need for action as a problem. It is well-suited to situations where you initiate the correspondence because it provides a positive framework. In this structure, explain first that an opportunity exists.

> The closing of the local branch of Carson, Carson, Englemeier, and Schneiderman makes available the seventh floor of the First Federal Building. Thus we have an opportunity at this time to expand our offices up one floor and gain space currently needed for our new computers and for record storage. It would also provide space we could use to expand ....

Explain that the benefit is substantial and worth pursuing, getting the reader to agree with you on this common goal.

After convincing the reader of the opportunity, explain your proposal for taking advantage of it. This part focuses on how your proposal is feasible.

> Although leasing the seventh floor would double our office space, it would only increase our costs by 60%. Thus our cost per square foot would decrease ....

> To cover this increase in fixed costs, we would need to increase income by only ....

The final step moves the reader to a position in which your proposal seems logical and the best solution for the reader, as well as for your client.

Persuading Through Warnings

Warning involves notifying the reader that some undesirable consequence will result if he or she does not take or refrain from a certain action. A warning's persuasiveness depends on the reader's motivation to avoid something. Using warnings is similar to the opportunity-benefit approach because, just as that approach creates a positive framework, the warning strategy creates a negative one.[30] The overall negative tone leads the reader to think about avoiding the negative consequences, rather than achieving some other benefit.

To use a warning strategy, use the organization of the problem-solution approach, stating the problem and then explaining the warning clearly but unemotionally.

> Our client, Mr. Ibani, has not yet received the $10,000 payment agreed upon as settlement of his claim against your company, even though this payment was promised over six weeks ago. If Mr. Ibani does not receive a certified check for this amount within ten working days, we will need to start legal proceedings to recover the amount.

---

30. For a discussion of the complex effects of fear appeals, *see* O'Keefe, *supra*   note 6, at 224–29.

To avoid this unnecessary expense and publicity, please send payment immediately.

This approach can be particularly useful because you are not working completely against the reader's interests, so it incorporates some aspects of more positive motivations. Nevertheless, if the warning does not work, your available alternatives are usually expensive. Thus, before resorting to a warning or threat, ask yourself the following questions.

1. Have I tried all the cooperative approaches available?

   Once you have begun to threaten, it will be difficult to return to a cooperative relationship.

2. Is there anything I can actually do, and therefore, can use as a warning or threat?

   Idle threats have a low chance of succeeding, especially if the reader has a lawyer, and they often only undercut credibility.

3. Are the reader's options limited to things the reader will not want to do, so that taking the action you want is the most likely response?

   Avoid a threat that provides an option that is either undesirable to you or not awful for the reader, because the likelihood of success is too small.

4. Would a neutral reader see the threat as fair and appropriate?

   Avoid creating a paper trail that could create sympathy for the other side, in case you cannot resolve the matter without bringing in the court or another legal entity.

If cooperative persuasion has not worked, you may have no other viable strategy. You may have to "back the hearse up to the door," as advertising copywriters put it.[31]

If you decide a warning is appropriate, then make sure you do the following to maximize your chance of success: (1) present the warning unemotionally and unambiguously, (2) clarify the reader's options, (3) clarify the time frame for the decision, and (4) avoid bluffing. Most people fear lawyers, but their fear may only move them to call lawyers of their own.

The persuasive strategy you choose depends mainly on the consequences you can present to the reader. When positive consequences exist, present those first. They may persuade the reader and will not cost your goodwill. When you must resort to using negative consequences to persuade the reader, let the consequences themselves do the persuading, rather than depending on emotional writing.

31. Thomas Pearsall and Donald Cunningham, *How to Write for the World of*   *Work* 60 (1994).

ADJUSTMENTS FOR TONE

Although your tone will shift depending on your relationship with the reader and your task, that tone should remain businesslike in all correspondence. Even in a tough letter where your tone may be one of impersonal firmness, you will be more effective if you maintain a businesslike image that does not communicate loss of emotional control. Similarly, no matter how friendly your relationship with the client is, focus your correspondence on the matter at hand. The client wants to know you are getting the job done. In all your correspondence, be courteous. Treat each reader as someone whose goodwill it will be advantageous to have, if at all possible.[32]

Three things to avoid are condescension, impatience, and irritation. Although you may experience these feelings in your work, communicating them in out-of-house correspondence generally does not positively influence the reader.[33] With in-house correspondence, your feelings may influence your reader but they are often ineffective for obtaining the results you want. For example, if you complain to a supervisor about your unhappiness at work, the reader might respond emotionally. But what you probably wanted was a particular action, not an emotional response, and the correspondence probably did not lead to that result.

Do not communicate condescension, either through sarcasm or a demanding tone,[34] because it will not inspire cooperation. Even if you do get a person to comply through such tactics, it will be resentful compliance, which can lead to that person creating obstacles or rebelling at some future request. Similarly, communicating impatience is usually not effective. If the out-of-house reader does not like you or your client and wants to frustrate your plan, communicating irritation will signal that the reader is successful and will encourage him or her to continue. If the in-house reader is moving slowly, communicating irritation may make that reader feel bad but is not likely to cause him or her to be more efficient. Finally, irritation can imply you are feeling that you may fail in your task, which could be good news for the adversarial reader. If not, it will only irritate the reader.

Effective tone results from blending several different dimensions, which together communicate the writer's style of communication and attitude toward the situation. These dimensions include

- unemotional or emotional regarding the subject
- impersonal or personal regarding relationship to the reader

32. This is not only a good ideal, but a pragmatic goal. Research indicates that weak ties, such as with acquaintances and people with whom you have infrequent contact, are more likely sources of some useful information, such as information from new areas of knowledge. For example, "people were nearly twice as likely to hear about new jobs through weak ties than strong ties." Peter Monge, *The Network Level of Analysis* in *Handbook of Communication Science* 251 (C. Berger and S. Chaffee, eds. 1987).

33. One exception here might be a vendor, because the vendor is hired by you and thus benefits from your goodwill.

34. Especially when trying to be clear, you must watch for the possibility of creating a demanding tone. Tebeaux, *supra* note 14, at 130.

• formal or informal stance toward the reader

As with informing and persuading, these three dimensions each represent a continuum rather than a set of discrete categories. Some of these dimensions are correlated; as a document becomes more personal, it generally becomes more emotional and more informal. For example, a congratulatory note to a colleague is often more emotional as well as more informal. Some are closely related to particular tasks. A persuasive letter on behalf of a client to another party is likely to be unemotional and impersonal. Because the interaction of these dimensions is complex, each is discussed separately.

Unemotional or Emotional Regarding the Subject

Your legal correspondence will usually lean toward the unemotional. Although the content of the correspondence may stir emotions, the delivery should not. An unemotional tone is effective, especially when the reader is frustrated.[35] For example, if you are trying to convince your employer to give you a raise, you want to sound reasoned, not emotional.

I base this request for a salary increase on my length of service with Carer's Insurance, the strength of my career reviews, and my success in securing several new corporate clients.

But not the following.

> I feel that I deserve a salary increase for several reasons. First, my length of service with Carer's Insurance clearly entitles me to a salary review. Second, my career reviews have been, I believe, excellent and I am proud to provide this record for your review. Finally, ...

If you are writing a collection letter, do not distract from that message by showing that you or your client are getting emotional. You might write the following.

If you do not contact us within seven days to arrange payment of the balance due, we will, on behalf of our client, file

. . . .

But would not write the following.

> If you continue to avoid our attempts to contact you about this bill, we will be glad to talk to you in front of a judge.

You can reduce emotion by avoiding modifiers that express judgment. For example, the request for a salary increase was more effective without the writer's judgments of "excellent" or personal statements of "I am proud."

A somewhat more emotional tone is appropriate and desirable when you are celebrating or commiserating with the reader. For example, some emotion is needed to make a congratulatory note believable.

---

35. Sandell, *supra* note 5, at 79.

> **Just wanted to let you know how much I enjoyed your presentation last week at the Bar luncheon. Congratulations on a tough job well done; your remarks really stirred the crowd, even after a big meal.**

An unemotional tone would be inappropriate and might sound reluctant.

> Your speech before the Bar last Wednesday has caused several members to ask about ways to improve our referral service, and thus you communicated effectively.

Impersonal or Personal Regarding Relationship to the Reader

This dimension is related to emotion, because more emotional text becomes more personal. But you can be personal without being too emotional. Legal correspondence at its most effective does not reach extremes on this continuum. Extremely impersonal language is ineffective because it can sound defensive and is usually hard to read.

> In response to the request for an explanation of the definitions included in the draft of the contract received by your office for review, the explanations of these definitions have been included in the attached . . . .

Very personal language is easier to read, but often sounds unprofessional.

> Well, since you were wondering what I meant by "force majeure" in the draft you got, I thought I'd send over . . . .

The middle ground is more appropriate.

> **In response to your question about the significance of Clause 12, the reason for this "act of God" clause is to prevent either party from being able to sue the other when**
> . . . .

It is wise to proofread your letters routinely for extremes in this area. Revise as needed to make the text return to the safer middle ground.

Formal or Informal Stance Toward the Reader

The choices are generally subtle on this dimension. For example, avoid both of the following because they are too extreme.

> It would be appreciated if you would sign the enclosed copy and return it to me in the envelope enclosed herewithin. Your assistance in this matter is appreciated.

> Just sign it, stuff it, and send it back. See ya!

But you might use either of the following.

> **Please sign the enclosed copy of this agreement and return it in the enclosed envelope. I appreciate your assistance in this matter.**

> **Just sign the copy and return it to me in the enclosed envelope. Thank you for your help.**

Your choice here depends on your personal image. If you always wear a suit to the office, prefer speakers with more formal styles, and prefer more reserved greetings from people, you will probably choose a more formal writing style for your correspondence. If you hate dressing up and do it only for a day in court, if you like a down-to-earth speaking style, and greet your friends without reserve, you may choose a more informal style.

Whichever style you pick, watch for two common problems: inconsistency and inappropriateness. For example, if you use an informal style, write the following.

> **If you agree, please sign this form and return it to me as soon as you can.**

But not the following.

> If you agree, please sign the enclosed form and forward it to my office expeditiously.

The latter can seem insincere or unprofessional because it is inconsistent. Similarly, if you choose a formal style, write the following.

> **If you find this alternative acceptable, please sign the enclosed release form and return it to our offices so that we may proceed.**

But do not write the following.

> If you find this alternative acceptable, please sign the enclosed release form and bring it back right away.·

Here inconsistency is likely to make the writer look like he or she is trying to be impressive—a pitfall that catches many formal writers. Also avoid extremes. No matter how much you like an informal style, avoid emotion-laden slang in your legal correspondence.

> I know this whole situation has been a real bummer for you.

Instead write with conversational-but-standard words.

> **I know this situation has been discouraging for you.**

No matter how much you love elegant language, do not drive your reader to the dictionary unnecessarily.

> This situation, I know, leaves you discombobulated and wishing for legerdemain rather than legal processes.

Instead, write the following.

> **This situation, I know, leaves you frustrated and wishing for some magic rather than the slow legal process.**

As with the previous continuum, almost all legal correspondence avoids the extremely formal or informal. Extremely formal language is inappropriate in correspondence generally, and informal language does not create the aura of an educated writer that most lawyers want.

Express your own professional style in correspondence, but be consistent so the reader knows who you are and appropriate so you always seem professional.

CONCLUSION

Writing effective correspondence requires you to call into play your skills as a writer, your understanding of persuasion, and your common sense about people. It involves many variables whose interactions are understandable, but infinitely varied and complex. Because writing correspondence means blending many concerns into one unit, it is hard to keep all those concerns in mind when writing. Mastering the blend takes practice.

Exercise 1

You are the attorney representing Barbara Brown Deer, who wants to recover for damage to her property. Barbara was living in a rented flat in an older house when a garbage truck driver lost control and drove through the wall of her flat. The truck ended up in the middle of her living room. The accident also caused a water line to rupture, and the resulting flood damaged Barbara's furniture, book collection, and other belongings. (Barbara was not at home at the time of the accident.)

Write a letter to Barbara asking her to list all the items damaged or destroyed by the accident. You also need to have her describe the amount of damage and the approximate value of each item. You need to describe clearly what she must do, but you also need to write with sensitivity to her situation.

This task is going to be time-consuming for Barbara, who is a busy graduate student. Barbara has been studying for her preliminary examination in American literature, and this accident has made it hard for her to focus. She may have to delay taking her preliminary exams for a semester. Furthermore, Barbara was quite upset about the damage to her belongings, and she still breaks into tears whenever she talks about the damage done to her small collection of first-edition American novels. Her early edition copy of *The Adventures of Huckleberry Finn* suffered serious water damage, and this particularly bothers her. Nevertheless, doing the inventory herself will be to her long-term advantage. It will save her quite a bit of money now, because hiring a professional appraiser would be expensive. You are hoping to negotiate a settlement for Barbara rather than having to take the case to court, and you believe that a formal appraisal may not be needed.

Exercise 2

You have worked for a large law firm for several years, and you have earned a reputation as an outstanding writer. The firm's senior partners are now asking you to revise their form retainer letter to make it clearer and to improve the tone. You may assume the content is correct. Your task is to cover this content more clearly and concisely, and to revise the letter to explain the content in terms of the reader's interests, rather than the firm's.

Form Letter to be Revised

[Date]

Re: _____

Dear _____:

This letter confirms our meeting on [insert month, day, and year] during which we agreed to represent you regarding [insert description of legal matter]. Because our firm has found that it is important for there to be a clear understanding of our financial arrangements, it has become our practice to send our clients a letter confirming those arrangements shortly after beginning representation.

Our fees for legal services will be based on the hourly rate for the attorney providing the services. This rate may vary depending on the experience of the attorney and may also change over time, although we do not anticipate any changes before July 1. When any member of our firm performs services on your matter, we will record the time spent, the nature of the services performed, and the hourly rate. Services may include, but need not be limited to, office conferences, phone conferences, court time, travel time, review of documents, and legal research. If you ever have any questions about the services we are providing or the charges for those services, feel free to contact the attorney who has been assigned to oversee your case.

You will also be charged for out-of-pocket expenses, including such items as long distance telephone calls, photocopies, faxes, computer aided research and document drafting, court costs, and fees for filings, recordings, court reporters, witnesses, or service of process. When appropriate, we will forward invoices for expenses which exceed $100.00 to you for direct payment. Any expenses paid by us and charged to you will be itemized on our monthly statements.

Our complete itemized statements will be sent to you each month. The full balance due should be paid within 30 days of receipt. If you ever have any questions about the charges for services we are providing or the services themselves, feel free to contact our offices.

When we are initially retained by a client who does not have an established relationship with our firm, we generally require an advance of $_____. Please forward this advance payment to us. It will be applied against your final statement for services and disbursements or against any delinquencies in your account. We may require additional advances, if necessary, to cover anticipated fees or expenses.

When our representation ends, we will, at your request, make available any papers, property, and file materials to which you are entitled. We may retain our internal notes and memoranda, our work product, and any duplicate materials.

Please confirm that this is an acceptable arrangement by signing both copies of the letter and returning one copy to me along with the requested advance. A self-addressed, stamped envelope is enclosed for your convenience. If we do not receive a signed copy of this letter and the advance within ten days, we will conclude that you are no longer interested in having us represent you and will close your file. You will remain responsible for any charges incurred up to that date.

We hope that our relationship will be founded on mutual confidence and respect. Therefore, we encourage you to discuss with us the progress of work performed for you, our billing policies, and the details of our statements.

We are pleased to represent you and look forward to working with you.

Sincerely,

[Attorney]

Enclosures

The fee arrangements described in this letter are agreed to:

Dated:

Exercise 3

The following series of letters is a realistic exchange of correspondence regarding a dispute over a bill. The appraiser is asking to be paid the final portion of his fee, but the City refuses because of errors in the appraiser's work, errors which resulted in a loss of revenue for the City.

Read each letter and think about how you would respond if you received the letter. Discuss how it is effectively or ineffectively written. In each example, you will find many things that need to be improved, but you may also find some good ideas that could be implemented more effectively.

When you have finished your discussion, write a response to the appraiser's original letter, writing to settle the matter quickly and to avoid the pitfalls that caught the writers of the original letters.

Initial Letter from the Appraiser to the City, Requesting Payment

WILLIAM WILSON REAL ESTATE APPRAISAL
CONSULTANTS, INC.

EXECUTIVE OFFICES . P.O. BOX 2, Othertown, Mass.

August 4, 20__

Ann Burns, Clerk

City of Goodville

Goodville, Massachusetts

I am sorry that it has taken me so long to respond to your June 23, 20— letter, which was a reply to our request for payment for services rendered.

Since the law clearly states that the Clerk and the Board of Review, as part of their duties, are to review the roll for errors, omissions and duplications of assessments, it would seem inappropriate for us to assume that responsibility.

Also, if you remember, prior to the values being put on the roll, you reviewed with Arlene Haunschild a list of all the Personal Property Assessments, prior to their being entered.

We would appreciate a prompt and reasonable settlement of this account.

Respectfully yours,

William Wilson

President

First Response from the City Attorney

CC: City Attorney Mary Wright

CITY OF GOODVILLE

Goodville, Massachusetts

August 10, 20—

WILLIAM WILSON Real Estate Appraisal Consultants

WILLIAM WILSON, President

1111 W. Main St.

P.O. Box 2

Othertown, Mass.

Dear Mr. Wilson:

Bill Willing, City Clerk for the City of Goodville, has given me a copy of your dunning letter of August 4, 20—, and I've re-read the City's letter of June 23, 20—, which was addressed to you. That caused me to take more notice of your letter, and that in turn raised a question only you can answer.

Specifically, your letter appears to say that your firm takes no responsibility for errors in the assessments your firm undertakes, and that when errors occur through faulty mathematics and substandard investigations done by your firm that it's the City clerk's fault for not having done an independent assessment of his own with which to check your work. Is this the position you're taking when you say "it would seem inappropriate for us to assume the responsibility" for errors, omissions and duplications of assessments?

I would appreciate a reply at your earliest convenience. The assessment you did resulted in a $5,749.08 expense for the City, and as you know the City Council has refused to pay the last $500.00 of the $7,200.00 bill for your services, at least partially because of the lack of an explanation of why your firm should be paid for a late and erroneous assessment. I'm sure you would be welcome at a meeting of the City Council to answer the Council members' questions and speak in favor of reversing the resolution denying your payment of your bill. The Council meets on the first and third Tuesdays of each month at 7:30 P.M. in the City Hall. Please give us some advance notice if you intend to come to a meeting so that a line can be placed on the agenda that must be delivered to the media to comply with the Massachusetts Open Meeting Law.

Sincerely yours,

City of Goodville

Mary Wright

City Attorney

Second Letter from Appraiser, Responding to the Attorney

WILLIAM WILSON REAL ESTATE APPRAISAL CONSULTANTS, INC.

EXECUTIVE OFFICES . P.O. BOX 2, Othertown, Mass.

August 21, 20__

Mary Wright

City Attorney

City of Goodville

Goodville, Mass.

Dear Ms. Wright:

I am replying to your letter of August 10, 20__ which was in response to my earlier communications. I suppose that we could continue exchanging self-serving letters forever but it would not solve the problem of your owing me $500.00 which is your contractual obligation.

There are of course, many statutes in Massachusetts which allow any community the ability to recap its money regarding errors, omissions and duplications.

If a reasonable settlement could be reached, I would be more than happy to discuss it with you, for litigation would only result in a fee for yourself and our legal counsel.

I would appreciate a prompt response.

Respectfully yours,

William Wilson

President

CC: Dudley Domore, Mayor

Second Letter from the City Attorney

CITY OF GOODVILLE

Goodville, Massachusetts

August 25, 20__

William Wilson

P.O. Box 2

Othertown, Massachusetts

Dear Mr. Wilson:

I am afraid I didn't explain the constraints on my powers to you clearly enough in my previous letter to you, as you apparently see a lawsuit as the only response open to you if I don't send you a check. This is not the situation. I think a thumbnail sketch will do it.

The City Council got a copy of your bill, and in the course of dealing with the general claims brought it up for action. There was a consensus of opinion that the City had been substantially damaged by what appears to have been negligence on the part of your firm, that the bill was adding insult to injury, and that there was no reason to pay for work that was for practical purposes not done because it was done so negligently. The Council determined that you would not be paid, but neither would you be asked to reimburse the City for damages caused by your faulty assessment. Considering that you had already been paid the greatest portion of your demands, the City Council felt that you would see the reasonableness and justice of the City's position.

It is becoming swiftly apparent that you do not see the reason in not paying you the last portion of your demands and in effect using the money to defray approximately 10% of the damage the City suffered by your firm. This is most unfortunate for both of us—for you because you apparently feel put upon, and for me because I must respond to your letters without being able to do anything to salve your indignation. As I tried to point out in my last letter, the bills must be paid by the City Council. I cannot bind the City to any disbursements.

Therefore, you have three options: you can come before the Council and present your side, being prepared to answer why you should be paid for doing damage to your client; you can sue and prepare to tell a jury why you should be paid your demands in full and not be asked to pay for even 10% of the damage your negligence caused; or you can forget it and be glad that you had been paid so much before your negligence was brought to your client's attention.

Sincerely,

CITY OF GOODVILLE

Mary Wright

City Attorney

Note: *There was no further correspondence from the Appraiser.*

Assignment 1

You are the attorney who represented Jamie Blottner successfully in his suit; for background information, you may find the details of Jamie's situation in Assignment 1 in Chapter 6. On August 30 of this year, he asked you to draft a will for him, since he now has some assets because of your previous success. Write a letter confirming that you will represent him in this matter. You do not need to address any details of the will itself in this letter; focus only on what services you will provide, the fee arrangement, and other such matters.

Since the previous work was performed on a contingency basis and this work will be done on a fee basis, you need to explain your fee structure to him. You have a copy of the following retainer letter from a big firm to help you determine the content you need, but you do not want to copy the stuffy tone of the letter, especially with a client with whom you have worked extensively. You also notice that the letter is poorly organized, so you want to regroup the content. Additionally, some of the information included does not fit your situation and you can omit it. Finally, you want your letter to be more concise and clear, so you should plan to revise any of the language you do use from the letter.

Sample Formi Letter from Another Firm

Dear [name of client]:

This letter will confirm our discussion of [day, date].

You have requested that we represent you in the above-captioned matter. Our representation will be limited to _____

The scope of our representation will not be expanded unless agreed in writing by our firm. We have agreed to represent you and will [choose one of the following two phrases.] [begin the representation once you have returned to us the items outlined in this letter.]or [continue the work begun since our discussion according to the terms outlined in this letter.]

My legal services will be provided to you at the rate of $_____ per hour. Any time spent by another attorney in our office will be billed at that attorney's normal hourly rate. These rates may be modified over time, although at this moment we do not anticipate changes until July 1st. We do not ordinarily notify clients of rate changes. Services may include, but need not be limited to, office conferences, phone conferences

(0.2 hour minimum), court time, travel time, review of file materials, and legal research and other investigation.

My basic hourly rate for services rendered is $_____ and this will be an important factor in determining our total fee in this matter. Rates of other attorneys in our firm vary depending upon experience, years of practice, and other factors. In establishing our fees, we will consider all relevant circumstances, including our experiences and ability in a particular area, the responsibility involved, the results obtained, and the nature of the employment such as unusual work hours and extraordinary time pressures, all as specified in the ABA Code of Professional Responsibility EC2–18 and DR 2–106.

[Choose one of the following two paragraphs.]

[Because of the nature of this matter, currently it is not possible to provide an accurate estimate of our total fee. However, we will attempt to provide such an estimate in the future, if possible, upon your request. In any event, we will attempt to make efficient use of our resources. Further, we shall reserve the right to associate with other counsel on your behalf whenever we deem it necessary or desirable upon notifying you. Such representation shall be at that attorney's normal hourly rate, if acceptable to you.]

[Or]

[Our present estimate of total fees in this matter is [choose one of the following.] [$_____] or [in the range of $_____ to $_____.] However, unanticipated complications or additional incidental services that you may request could result in a higher total fee. Consequently, this should be considered as a good faith, though non-binding, estimate. In any event, we will attempt to make efficient use of our resources. Further, we shall reserve the right to associate with other counsel on your behalf whenever we deem it necessary or desirable upon notifying you. Such representation shall be at that attorney's normal hourly rate, if acceptable to you.]

In addition to our legal fees, we may incur and consequently will be reimbursed by you for various out-of-pocket costs, such as recording or filing fees, sheriff's fees, deposition costs, mileage charges, photocopies, telecopier charges, and long-distance telephone calls.

It is expressly understood that we have made no promises, assurances or guarantees as to the outcome of this matter. Payment of our bills is not contingent upon the outcome of this matter.

You shall at all times have the right to terminate our services upon written notice. If you choose to terminate our services, it is understood that we will be paid in full or that arrangements will be made for payment before the file is released. We shall at all times have the right to terminate our services upon written notice in the event that you either fail to cooperate with us in any reasonable request, to timely pay the periodic statements, if any, in full as submitted, or not replenish any retainer, or in the event we determine in our reasonable discretion that to continue our services to you would be unethical or impractical.

Until all fees and costs are paid in full, we shall retain a lien on your file. If the file is released to you, we shall have the right to make copies of any portion thereof and to withhold internal office memorandum and personal notes.

[Choose one of the following two paragraphs.]

[Payment of our bills, including requested retainers or prepayments, will be due within 30 days of their dates. We cannot overemphasize the importance of timely attention to these payments. If full payment cannot be made within that time period, arrangements must be made with us by the end of that 30 days for an alternative payment plan.]

[Or]

[Although our practice is to require full payment within 30 days, in your case, we have already discussed and agreed to an alternative payment plan. This plan will take effect if your monthly bill exceeds $_____ and, despite your good faith effort to do so, you are unable to pay it in full. Given those circumstances, we will accept a $_____ payment and will carry the remaining balance forward. We reserve the right to renegotiate this alternative payment plan during the course of our representation.]

[Insert the following if needed.] [All bills not paid at the end of 30 days shall have interest charged against them at 12% per annum, which shall be computed on a monthly basis.]

By this letter, we acknowledge receipt of your payment of $_____ as a non-refundable retainer to be applied against our fees and against out-of-pocket costs incurred by us. We reserve the right to request an additional amount in the future as this case progresses.

If this letter properly sets forth our understanding or is an acceptable arrangement for you, please sign and return the enclosed copy of this letter

[Insert the following if needed.][Along with a check in the amount of $_____ as a non-refundable retainer to be applied against our fees and against out-of-pocket costs incurred by us.]

A self-addressed, stamped envelope is enclosed for your convenience. If we do not receive this within 10 days from the date of this letter, we will assume that you have obtained other counsel and will mark our file "closed" and do nothing further. We will furnish a bill for services rendered to the day we closed our file.

If this does not properly set forth our understanding or is not an acceptable arrangement for you, please contact me within 5 days from the date of this letter. At such time, we will stop working on this matter and will incur no additional legal expense for you until the misunderstanding has been resolved or until an acceptable arrangement has been established.

If you have any questions concerning the items covered in this letter, please do not hesitate to contact me.

Sincerely yours,

[Attorney]

The above is understood and agreed to.

Client's signature   Today's date

Assignment 2

You are an attorney working for the firm that has represented the Putnams through their various legal concerns. Most recently, you have received an offer via a phone call from the Hospital's attorney to settle the claim for $50,000 in return for a promise not to sue under any claims for the death of their daughter. You do not recommend that they accept this offer, but you need to explain the offer to them. Write the letter to the Putnams. For background facts and law, see Assignment 2 in Chapter 4.

BIBLIOGRAPHY

Ackerman, John M., *Reading, Writing and Knowing: The Role of Disciplinary Knowledge in Comprehension and Composing,* 25 (2) Research in the Teaching of English 133 (May 1991).

Andrews, Deborah C. and Margaret B. Blickle, *Teaching Writing Principles and Forms.* New York: MacMillan Publishing Co., Inc., 2d ed. 1978.

Berger, Charles R. and Steven H. Chaffee, eds., *Handbook of Communication Science.* Newbury Park, CA: Sage Publications, 1987.

Brannon, Lil, Melinda Knight, and Vara Neverow–Turk, *Writers Writing.* Montclair, NJ: Boynton/Cook Publishers, Inc., 1982.

Eisenberg, Anne, *Effective Technical Communication.* New York: McGraw–Hill Co., 2d ed. 1992.

Fowler, Roger, ed., *Essays on Style and Language: Linguistic and Critical Approaches to Literary Style.* London: Routledge and Kegan Paul, 1970.

Hatch, Richard, *Business Communication: Theory and Technique.* Chicago: Science Research Associates, Inc., 1983.

Houp, Kenneth W. and Thomas E. Pearsall, *Reporting Technical Information.* New York: Oxford University Press, 2002.

Jacobi, Ernst, *Writing at Work: Dos, Don'ts and How Tos.* Rochelle Park, NJ: Hayden Book Co., 1976.

Kirsch, Gesa, *Writing Up and Down the Social Ladder: A Study of Experienced Writers Composing or Contrasting Audiences*, 25 (1) Research in Teaching of English 33 (Feb. 1991).

Mansfield, Carmella E. and Margaret Hilton Bahnick, *Writing Business Letters and Reports*. Indianapolis: Bobbs–Merrill Educational Publishing, 1981.

McDonald, Daniel, *The Language of Argument*. New York: Harper and Row, 3d ed. 1989.

Murphy, James J., ed., *A Short History of Writing Instruction*. Mahwah, NJ: Lawrence Erlbaum Associates, 2d ed. 2001.

Novello, Don, *The Lazlo Letters*. New York: Workman Publishing Co., 1977.

O'Keefe, Daniel J., *Persuasion: Theory and Research*. Thousand Oaks, CA: Sage Publications, 2d ed. 2002.

Pearsall, Thomas E., and Donald H. Cunningham, *How to Write for the World of Work*. Ft. Worth: Harcourt Brace College Publishers, 5th ed. 1994.

Sandell, Rolf, *Linguistic Style and Persuasion*. San Francisco: Academic Press, 1977.

Schauble, Leona and Robert Glaser, eds., *Innovations in Learning: New Environments for Education*. Mahwah, NJ: Lawrence Erlbaum Associates, 1996.

Simons, Herbert G., *Persuasion: Understanding, Practice, and Analysis*. New York: Random House, 2d ed. 1986.

Smagorinsky, Peter, *The Writer's Knowledge and the Writing Process: A Protocol Analysis,* 25 (3) Research in the Teaching of English 339 (Oct. 1991).

Tebeaux, Elizabeth, *Design of Business Communications: The Process and the Product*. New York: MacMillan Publishing Co., Inc., 1990.

Tortoriello, Thomas R., Stephen J. Blatt, and Sue DeWine, *Communication in the Organization: An Applied Approach*. New York: McGraw–Hill Book Co., 1978.

Chapter 15

OPINION LETTERS

Opinion letters do not involve the wide range of variables present in general correspondence; their primary readers are clients and their primary task is to answer clients' questions. They do, however, blend the writer's concerns with those of a legal researcher. Writing opinion letters therefore allows you to synthesize much of what you have learned while working on writing tasks discussed in earlier chapters.

The usual purpose of the opinion letter is to give the client the answer to a legal question or to give legal advice. An opinion letter attempts to state how the law will apply to a particular set of facts, based on the expectation that "the courts will proceed in an orderly manner in the direction indicated by prior decisions."[1] You write this correspondence to inform, rather than to persuade. So you use the general tone and focus for informing clients discussed in the correspondence chapter. When providing legal services to clients, lawyers frequently are also asked to analyze issues of fact or law and to provide that analysis to third parties, in an effort to help the client obtain a loan commitment, purchase property, or negotiate a deal. In these cases, "the client's interest is advanced by making it possible for the third person to proceed with the transaction on the basis of the evaluation."[2] Even though the client may use the letter to help persuade others, your primary purpose as you write the letter is to answer the client's question, and your letter needs to be phrased to do so.

When you have to give bad news, the techniques in the correspondence chapter will be helpful. Although you may need to say no, be sensitive to your client's hopes, wishes, and fears.[3] For example, instead of saying "Claims like yours have been flatly rejected by the Nebraska courts," rephrase your statement to be less harsh: "This claim has been unsuccessful in other cases" or "is unlikely to prevail." But your client

---

1. Mortimer Levitan, *Dissertation on Writing Legal Opinions*, 1960 Wis.L.Rev. 22, 23.

2. *Restatement (Third) of the Law Governing Lawyers* § 95 cmt.b (2000).

3. Raymond Ocampo, Jr., *The Opinion Letter*, 3 Cal.L.Rev. 28, 28 (1983).

needs to understand your answer, even when your answer is not the one he or she had wanted. You can be sensitive to your client's wishes and still honestly state your opinion on the likelihood of their success.

Unlike general correspondence but like research memos, opinion letters contain more complex content and provide the reasoning to support any conclusions. The depth of this research depends on the needs of your reader. To handle this complexity, opinion letters need a more elaborate structure than general correspondence. Opinion letters commonly have the following sections:

- the date and addressee of the letter,

- an opening, which includes a reference to the question and the client's request for an opinion, among other things;

- a fact section, which recounts the facts upon which your opinion is based;

- an answer to the question, which is often labeled the conclusion;

- an explanation of the reasoning behind that conclusion, which may be called a discussion; and

- a concluding section, which includes a polite closing and may include advice about how to proceed.

This chapter discusses these sections and provides guidance for drafting each.

Before writing the letter, however, you must look at several general considerations. With regard to content, opinion letters should always address the client's question, answer it clearly, objectively explain the legal reasoning that supports the answer, and inform the client of any necessary details, such as a statute of limitations deadline. Throughout, the letter should maintain a respectful and professional tone. Within this structure, however, there is still quite a bit of latitude. For example, the tone may be formal or conversational, but always within the bounds of professionalism. The reasoning may be technical and in-depth or may only summarize the information. The opinion may or may not include formal citations. When making these choices, the major factors you should consider are your reader's needs and your professional obligations to your client. These considerations are the subject of the next section.

GENERAL CONSIDERATIONS

Your opinion letter, no matter how formal or complex, should:

- answer the client's question;

- be understandable by the client or other reader;

- clarify the opinion's limitations, including that the letter itself does not guarantee that any court will reach a particular result and does not give an answer that will remain unchanged over time, facts, or jurisdiction; and

- fulfill the professional responsibility you owe your client.

Answering the Client's Question

In your opinion letter, address the specific question asked rather than discussing the law in general. There are several ways to do this. You can begin the letter with a reference to your conversation with the client and the client's question.

> At our meeting last week, you asked for my opinion as to the possibility of successfully suing Dr. G.W. Haverford for malpractice based on the following facts.

You can also refer to the question in a subject line.

> RE: Possibility of suing Dr. G.W. Haverford for failure to warn of risks associated with transplants

When you state your conclusion later in your opinion letter, you can state it using the terms of the reader's question.

> You can sue Dr. Haverford with a reasonable probability of success.

If the client worded the question more informally and if you need to introduce the client to the more specific legal question, you can accomplish that in your opening sentences.

> When we met in my office last week, you asked me to determine whether you could legally require Dr. Haverford to pay for the medical costs you have incurred as a result of the complications you suffered after he performed surgery. To do this, as we discussed, you would need to bring a lawsuit against Dr. Haverford for medical malpractice. Accordingly, I have researched this question for you.

The purpose of each of these techniques is to keep the letter focused on the specific question you are answering. This is necessary because you want to ensure that your client or any other reader does not broaden the answer to apply to other questions. That broadening would be inaccurate because, without additional facts and research, you cannot provide advice on those questions. You also want to keep the question specific because that is the question you were hired to answer.

Making the Answer Understandable to the Client

Often you are writing for one particular reader and can tailor your explanation to that person. For example, if the reader is a business-woman with extensive experience in the subject relevant to the question, you may use technical business terms and may state the pros and cons of the alternatives in specific, no-nonsense terms. If, in contrast, your client is someone who has trouble remembering details, you may want to state your point more simply and without technical words. You may also focus on explicitly stating the potential outcomes rather than the complicated reasons behind those outcomes and summarize them, so your reader can see how it all fits together. If your reader is a person with no experience in the area your opinion addresses, then you may introduce needed technical language, but you should include definitions.

Additionally, you may adjust the formality, technicality, and amount of explanation in your letter based on your reader's preferences. Some readers, just like some supervisors, want quick, concise answers, unencumbered with legalese or extra words. Others may want more formal documentation with legal citations and explanations of the law behind the answers. For example, if you are writing to a corporate executive who values time highly and does not like to bother with details, you may state your opinion in a short letter and then include a separate attachment, summarizing the reasoning. Then the executive can read and file the letter without reading the attachment, even though that reasoning must be included. If you are addressing a particularly uncertain issue, one whose ramifications could be profound for your client, you may need to include all the reasoning supporting your conclusion. Subdivide your explanation section to detail your reasoning systematically, stating each main point the reader should note in a subheading. Within the text under each heading, you can state each reservation in a tactful or matter-of-fact tone, but state it specifically so the record is clear.

Clarifying the Opinion's Limits

One important portion of an opinion letter is the opinion letter's limitations. These limitations include ones based on time, jurisdiction, and facts, ones stating the letter cannot guarantee legal results, and ones needed when third parties will be relying on your opinion letter.

Your opinion will be limited by time because the law is constantly changing. Thus your opinion must clearly state that it is limited to the legal consequences of the stated facts for this particular moment in time. The opinion's recipient must understand that your answer cannot include an obligation to keep the law up to date and cannot anticipate subsequent factual or legal developments.[4] You might state:

> I have based this opinion on the facts as set out below, the current Montana statute regarding restrictive covenants in employment contracts, and the pertinent Montana case law as of today's date.

or

> Because the law may change over time, the validity of this opinion is limited to the law as it currently stands.

Additionally, you must indicate that your opinion is limited to the jurisdiction in which you practice.[5] As an attorney licensed in one state, you are not qualified to practice in other jurisdictions, and your client

---

4. Committee on Legal Opinions, *Legal Opinions Principles*, 53 Bus.Law. 831, 833 (1998).

5. Most lawyers also are qualified to give an opinion based on federal law. If your client needs an opinion based on state law outside your jurisdiction or if your client needs the opinion of a specialist, you have many options. You can hire local counsel to research the matter and provide an opinion letter which you will incorporate into your own letter. Or you can have local counsel provide a separate opinion letter directly to the client. You should discuss this matter with your client. Remember, if you incorporate the local counsel's or specialist's opinion into your own, you will become liable for that opinion.

needs to understand that he or she cannot use your opinion rendered in one state to resolve a problem that occurs in another state.

> This opinion, which is based on New York law, is valid only within the State of New York. We are not admitted to practice law in any state other than the State of New York and thus are not experts in the law of any state other than the State of New York.

More generally, remind the client that the opinion should not be broadened beyond the jurisdiction for which it was written.

> This opinion should not be relied on for any other purpose because any change in law, facts, jurisdiction, or other factors could affect the opinion's validity.

You must also indicate that your opinion is based on the facts you have included in your letter and any change in the facts noted may result in a change in the opinion reached.

> The facts upon which the opinion is based are set out below. Because any change in these facts might alter my opinion, please contact me if any facts are incorrect or omitted.

or

> Please review the facts I have included and contact me if any facts are misstated or if you have any additional information.

The following sections on interviewing the client and drafting the facts provide suggestions for helping you obtain the facts and write them.

> Be sure your client realizes that your opinion letter does not guarantee any legal result. In order to convey this to your client, you must realize it for yourself.[6] You must also indicate this limitation to your client.

> This opinion states my legal opinion. It cannot, however, create any legal rights.

or

> Please understand that this opinion expresses my professional judgment on this matter, but cannot guarantee that a court will reach any particular legal result.[7]

These limitations will be present in virtually all opinion letters. Additional limitations may arise in some situations. For example, business transactions are often based on one side's attorney providing an opinion letter on matters at issue between the parties or on problems that must be resolved before the transaction can be completed.[8]

---

6. Some attorneys mislead others into believing that their opinions have the force of law, when, in fact, they confer no genuine protection at all. Levitan, *supra* note 1, at 32.

7. Committee on Legal Opinions, *supra* note 4, at 832.

8. John P. Freeman, *Legal Opinion Liability* in *Drafting Legal Opinion Letters* § 12.1 (John M. Sterba, Jr., ed., 2d ed. 1992).

The rendition of legal opinions has been called, accurately, 'the quintessence of a business lawyer's practice.' These opinions play a significant role in the economy: No major corporate or commercial transaction is complete unless as a condition of the closing, the participating lawyers deliver opinions on relevant legal matters.[9]

In recent years, the issue of third party opinion letters has been widely discussed by the practicing bar.[10] These third party opinion letters may subject a lawyer to an increased risk of financial liability and lawyers have been grappling with ways to limit their liability.[11] Initially few resources addressed these issues. Then, in 1998, the American Law Institute approved the *Restatement (Third) of the Law Governing Lawyers*, the American Bar Association Business Law Section issued its *Legal Opinion Principles*, and the TriBar Opinion Committee completed a new report on *Third Party "Closing" Opinions*.[12] These documents considered together provide a comprehensive description of legal opinion practice today.

Third party opinion letters are frequently subject to negotiations about the limitations or qualifications placed on the letter. When negotiating with another attorney to receive an opinion letter, do not ask your opponent to provide an opinion letter without limitations if you know you would be unable to provide such a letter.[13] Recognize the limitations that must exist, and then attempt to obtain a letter with no more than those necessary limitations.

Significant among the developments in this area is the idea that custom and practice, rather than pages of limitations and disclaimers, should determine the scope of diligence, the limitations on the factual basis of the letter, and the qualifications, limitations, and disclaimers needed to be included in the letter.

> Customary practice establishes the ground rules for rendering and receiving opinions and thus allows the communication of ideas between the opinion giver and counsel for the opinion recipient without lengthy descriptions of the diligence process, detailed definitions of the terms used and laborious recitals of standard, often unstated, assumptions and exceptions. Thus, in opinion practice, customary practice is an important professional tool.[14]

9. *Id.*

10. Those interested in this discussion should read Donald W. Glazer, *It's Time to Streamline Opinion Letters: The Chair of a BLS Committee Speaks Out*, Bus. Law Today, Nov–Dec. 1999, at 32.

11. Koley Jessen, P.C. Legal Opinion Committee, *Third-Party Legal Opinions: An Introduction to "Customary Practice,"* 35 Creighton L.Rev. 153 (2001).

12. *See* Restatement (Third), *supra* note 2, at § 95; Committee on Legal Opinions, *Legal Opinion Principles*, *supra* note 4, at 831; and TriBar Opinion Committee,

"Third Party 'Closing Opinions,'" 53 Bus. Law 591 (1998).

13. John M. Sterba, Jr., *Elements of Opinion Letters* in *Drafting Legal Opinion Letters* § 1.5 (John M. Sterba, Jr., 2d. ed., 1992).

14. Arthur Norman Field and Donald W. Glazer, *Legal Opinions: The Impact of the Tribar Committee's New Report on Legal Opinion Practice* 24–25 (1998)(citing the pre-publication draft of the TriBar Opinion Committee Report).

The consistent reference in these resources to custom and practice has led many law firms to adopt these principles in their own practices, and to move away from the increasingly lengthy opinion letters of prior years that included pages of limitations and disclaimers.[15] Since the use of opinion letters by non-clients has become routine in most lawyers' practices, it is important to become aware of custom and practice in this area and to conform your letters accordingly.

Fulfilling Your Professional Responsibility

When writing an opinion letter, remember this task is just as serious as writing other documents that may be longer or more complex. Rendering opinion letters is one of the riskiest aspects of law practice. You can open yourself to many possible malpractice allegations if the opinion you present does not meet established standards.

> Depending on the circumstances, an improvidently rendered opinion may lead to disciplinary action by state or federal authorities, a negligent malpractice or negligent misrepresentation action, a common law fraud action, claims under the federal and state securities laws, penalties under the Internal Revenue Code, prosecution and civil actions under the RICO statute, an action alleging an unfair trade practice, a demand for punitive damages and criminal prosecution under the securities laws and the mail fraud, wire fraud, and false statement statutes.... In truth, the analysis of lawyers' opinion letter liability is really a particularized study of the body of legal malpractice law, itself a large and growing field.[16]

The standard of care that attorneys are held to in rendering opinion letters is "to use such skill, prudence, and diligence as lawyers of ordinary skill and capacity commonly possess and exercise in the performance of the tasks which they undertake."[17] It is difficult to criticize a lawyer's performance in anticipating the actual outcome of any single case.[18] Malpractice does not usually result from the failure to prognosticate clearly. Instead, malpractice liability usually flows from not providing competent representation. Your reputation as a lawyer will be tied to your opinions, and you must exercise competence, care, and skill in drafting your opinion letters.

15. Koley Jessen, *supra* note 11, at 166–168.

16. Freeman, *supra* note 8, at § 12.1. (See omitted citations in 2d edition and 2000 Supplement for cases finding lawyers liable due to their opinion letters.)

17. *Id.* at § 12.2. The source of these standards, which is the duty to provide competent representation to a client, comes from the ABA Model Code of Professional Responsibility and its Model Rules of Professional Conduct. *Id.* at § 12.4. Disciplinary rule 6–101 indicates that actionable malpractice may be punished as ethical misconduct when it is based on inadequate preparation, neglect, or practice in an area in which the lawyer lacks skill. Model Rule 1.1 requires competent representation of a client which requires "the legal knowledge, skill, thoroughness and preparation reasonably necessary for the representation." *Id. See also, Restatement (Third), supra* note 2, at §§ 50–52.

18. Detlev Vagts, *Legal Opinions in Quantitative Terms: The Lawyer as Haruspex or Bookie?*, 34 Bus.Law. 421, 428 (1979).

Nonspecialists will be held to the specialist's higher standard of care if they hold themselves out as specialists and then fail to exercise a specialist's skill and knowledge.[19] When presented with a matter outside your area of specialty: "(1) be competent, (2) become competent, (3) get help, or (4) get out."[20]

PREPARING THE OPINION

The first step in preparing an opinion letter is meeting with the client. Your client often will have expert knowledge, experience, and understanding of his or her particular field, which will give you essential background knowledge before you research the legal implications of the question.[21] After you obtain this background information, ask your client questions about the facts. As with pleadings, make sure to ask the hard questions now, because your answer to the client's question will be based on these facts. Clients often want to present a situation in the light most favorable to themselves, so you will probably need to probe to get a more realistic picture of the situation.

In your meeting with your client, also clarify the particular question the client wants answered. A client may not yet quite know what he or she wants; you may provide a significant service to that client just by helping define the question. Additionally, you will be helping yourself by framing the question, so you can research more efficiently.

The second step is clarifying the facts. Verify as many facts as possible yourself, when doing so will not cause unnecessary expense or too much effort.[22] This is especially true when you are uneasy about the accuracy of the facts. If the facts you uncover are not complete or are not yet clear to you, consider drafting the facts section of the opinion and submitting those facts separately for the client's approval before you complete the rest of the opinion. As mentioned earlier, be sure to include a statement that your opinion will be based on these facts and that your client should inform you of any additional facts because they would probably alter the answer. By making sure your client realizes the impact of withholding any legally significant facts, you may prompt the client to provide them to you. Verifying the facts early may help you avoid having to redraft the letter to respond to new facts.

The final step is deciding how to provide the answer. When you have completed your research and determined your answer, your first drafting question will be whether to put your opinion on paper, where it may be discoverable.[23] It may be that your opinion would best be presented orally. Because malpractice liability and professional embarrassment can attach to an incorrect opinion, many attorneys prefer to provide oral

19. Freeman, *supra* note 8, at § 12.9.

20. *Id.*

21. Levitan, *supra* note 1, at 28.

22. Harold Segall and Jeffrey Arouh, *How to Prepare Legal Opinions: Boldness* *and Caution,* 25 Prac.Law 29, 32 (June 1979).

23. See the discussion of this concern in the format section of the correspondence chapter.

advice instead of written opinion letters.[24] In an oral presentation, you can also alter your presentation to the client's response, which helps assure that the client understands your opinion and does not have an inappropriate response to the answer.

Assuming you do need a written opinion, your next step will probably be to organize the information within each section. Here the principles discussed in the chapters on objective issues, objective facts, and memorandum discussion sections should help you.[25]

Date and Addressee

Even the routine details of the date and the addressee of the letter require some care. The date on the letter indicates when the legal conclusions contained in the letter take effect. Sometimes you provide an opinion letter in connection with a business transaction and date it for the day the transaction closes. If your opinion requires you to update public records after the letter is provided, you may want to indicate that reservation in the letter.

An opinion letter is usually intended to be received by the addressee, who is the client. Sometimes, however, the letter is addressed to a third party or the third party's attorney. When drafting these letters, be sure to consider whether you are waiving the attorney-client privilege between you and your client by providing your opinion to third parties.[26] Because you may be liable to third parties, you should also consider who may foreseeably rely on the opinion and whether you should not issue the opinion at all or should qualify it in some way.[27] The basic rule has been that a lawyer has no duty to persons beyond those addressed, in the absence of fraud, collusion, or recklessness from which fraud can be inferred, or special circumstances indicating that a duty to a third party has been accepted.[28] But the lawyer owes a duty of care to specific persons or limited classes whom the lawyer knows will receive the letter and rely on it.[29] Given the potential liability that attaches when drafting opinion letters, you may want to include language to prevent reliance on the opinion by third parties.

> We are providing this opinion as counsel for XYZ Corporation and provide it solely for our client's benefit.

or

> This letter may not to be used, quoted, or circulated for any other purpose.

---

24. Sterba, *supra* note 13, at § 1.3.

25. See Chapter 6, Objective and Persuasive Issues; Chapter 7, Objective Facts, and Chapter 9, Discussion Sections.

26. Sterba, *supra* note 13, at § 2.3.

27. *Id.*

28. James J. Fuld, *Lawyers' Standards and Responsibilities in Rendering Opinions*, 33 Bus.Law. 1295, 1309 (March 1978). See

also, *National Savings Bank v. Ward*, 100 U.S. 195 (1879); *Ultramares Corp. v. Touche*, 255 N.Y. 170 (1931).

29. Freeman, *supra* note 8, at § 12.14 and cases cited in 1992 2d edition and 2000 Supplement. For a detailed discussion of liability to third parties, see *Symposium: The Lawyer's Duties and Liabilities to Third Parties*, 37 S.Tex.L.Rev. 957 (1996).

While this language may not completely preclude third party reliance, it does indicate that you did not intend for anyone other than the address-ee to rely on the opinion.

The Opening

The opening provides the context for the opinion letter and states the question you will be answering. Often the opening refers to the meeting or phone conversation in which your client first requested the opinion.

> Last Thursday, we met in my office to discuss your concerns about the offer to purchase you submitted for the house at 2010 Main Street.

or

> In response to your request during our conversation last Thursday, I am enclosing my opinion regarding the validity of your offer to purchase the property at 2010 Main Street.

When you start your letter by reminding your client of the letter's context, it helps to clarify the letter's focus. This organization allows the client to determine immediately whether you understood the question asked or the nature of the advice sought.[30] It also can be worded to clarify that the client asked for a written opinion, if that is the case. Since the client must pay for the opinion, it is best to remind him or her that you are writing it at his or her request. It also sets the tone and establishes the working relationship in this letter.

> When we met in my office last Thursday, we discussed your questions about your offer to purchase the property at 2010 Main Street. At that time, you requested a written opinion on the question of .... In response to that request, I have prepared this answer to your question.

The opening paragraph can also indicate the question presented. As the examples above show, the client wanted to know whether the offer to purchase was valid, and the letter's opening provided both the context and the question asked. If the matter is somewhat more complex and you need to state the question asked more explicitly, then follow the opening sentence with a statement of the question.

> You have requested my opinion regarding the likelihood that the Federal Trade Commission or the Justice Department's Antitrust Division would attack an acquisition of Center Corporation's stock by First Corporation as a violation of Section 7 of the Clayton Act.

After you have clarified the context of the letter and the client's question, you can explain the limitations on the answer. It is logical to place that in the letter at this point. The trick, however, is in doing this without sounding defensive or timid. For example, the following opening can have the reader wondering what the opinion can do.

30. Segall and Arouh, *supra* note 22, at 31.

In response to your request for my opinion about the validity of the covenant not to compete included in your employment contract, I have prepared the enclosed opinion. This opinion does not establish any legal rights. It is limited to Montana law as of the date of this letter and may not be used for any other purpose. This is opinion is for your use only, and its validity is limited to the facts stated below.

In contrast, the following opening handles the same concerns with grace and professionalism.

When we met in my office two weeks ago, you requested my written opinion on a question about your employment contract. Specifically, you asked whether the covenant not to compete was valid. This letter explains my opinion on this question. It is a legal opinion, however, for your use only. It cannot guarantee any particular outcome.

The answer is based on Montana law as of the date of this letter. Therefore the answer could not be relied on in any other jurisdiction. Since the law can change over time, the answer also should not be relied upon at any future date. Finally, the answer is based on the facts as stated below. Any change in the facts could change the opinion. For this reason, please review the following facts carefully and inform me of any changes that need to be considered.

Use the opening of your letter to provide the context and state the question your letter will answer. Because the tone at the beginning of the letter is important, be careful when stating any limitations or restrictions on the letter so that the tone remains professional and respectful.

The Facts

When writing the facts, use the techniques discussed in the chapter on writing objective facts. Make sure you have included all the legally significant facts, the ones that will alter the result of your opinion. Consider including notations indicating the source of the facts, such as who supplied them or how they were otherwise obtained.[31] Many facts are based on documents; thus, you should review them also before stating your opinion.

The Conclusion

When writing your conclusion, begin with your answer to the question you state in the letter's opening.

Based on the facts stated above, you can sue Dr. Haverford with a reasonable probability of success. The most likely theory . . . .

Then add any needed specifics.

---

31. *Id.* at 32.

> The most likely theory to sue under would be negligence, claiming that Dr. Haverford was negligent in not informing you of the risks involved in the course of treatment she recommended.

Also you may refer here to major limitations you will discuss later.

> Success in this case, however, will depend on whether we can convince the jury that these risks are not common knowledge, so you could not reasonably have known of and assumed those risks without the doctor's specific discussion of them.

Although you want to keep this section short, you do want to state your answer fully enough to be accurate. Note major points here but do not go into the supporting reasons. State your answer firmly. Do not provide your client with a nebulous or tentative conclusion but do indicate any qualifications that limit your opinion.

In some opinion letters, the lawyer, after applying the law to the facts, reaches a conclusion substantially free of doubt.[32] For example, "The shares have been authorized and validly issued, and are fully paid and nonassessable" is an opinion that is free of doubt.[33] You are able to apply a given legal rule to particular facts and determine the legal conclusion.

More frequently, the lawyer needs to write what is known as a reasoned opinion letter, where the reasoning is explained.[34] Reasoned opinions are needed when the law is unclear, when the facts are not straightforward, or when reasonable arguments might lead to differing legal interpretations.[35] These letters need longer explanations, and often contain citations to relevant case law or statutes, present different sides of the issues when these are needed by the reader, and provide a qualified answer.

Even though you must qualify your answer in a reasoned opinion letter, remember that your client does expect an answer. Do not include so many reservations that your client has no answer to the question asked. If there are alternatives, discuss them and their relative merits later in the explanation section. In the conclusion, however, try not to hedge with general terms like "probably" or "likely," but instead state the qualifications of your opinion as specifically as you can. You may need to indicate these reservations with phrases such as

> although similar cases have reached different results, so that the law is not settled here
>
> although courts have differed on this issue, the most recent case
>
> while no controlling authority exists on this matter

Thus, your answer can be clear and unambiguous, even though it may not be simple.

---

32. John M. Sterba, Jr., *Introduction* in *Drafting Legal Opinion Letters* § 1.4 (John Sterba, Jr., ed., 2d. ed. 1992).

33. *Id.*

34. *Id.*

35. *Id.*

Explanation Section

The organization of this section should grow out of your analysis of the law. The value of the opinion letter is based on its accuracy in predicting what the legal consequences of the relevant facts are within a given question. Thus, "the cardinal rule in writing opinions is that the reasoning must dictate the result, the result must not dictate the reasoning."[36] Careful reasoning is imperative. Lead your reader step by step through your reasoning, if necessary, to ensure that he or she understands the limitations inherent in that reasoning.

Try to limit your letter to resolving two or three issues. More than that may be difficult for the reader to remember and may be impossible for you to address thoroughly in a letter. If you need to discuss more than a few issues, consider writing a memorandum to your client instead. The organization of the explanation section should follow the same organization as the issues. Develop your letter sufficiently to show the client that you understand the problem and you have provided the information necessary to answer the question.[37] It should include "references to the major legal principles, the trend of decisions in the jurisdiction, the application of legal rules to the present facts, possible arguments which may be raised by both sides, and the probable result if the legal problem is litigated."[38]

The opening paragraph of the explanation section should approach the law from the reader's point of view. The reader may respond with chagrin to a bare explanation of the governing law, such as "Rule 12(b)(6) states that . . . . " But the reader will quickly become motivated to read a paragraph that begins "When deciding whether . . . . a Texas court will . . . ."

As you organize each subsequent paragraph, begin with a topic sentence that approaches the point from the reader's point of view. For example, a paragraph in an opinion letter might begin with the following phrase.

When they have evaluated similar cases, Texas courts have . . . .

In contrast, a research memo to a senior partner might begin as follows

In *Jones v. Smith*, the Texas Court of Appeals held . . . .

While you do not want to bury the reader in legal details, you do want to include enough to explain the reasoning behind your answer. It is particularly important to discuss those arguments helpful to your client's position. Although your letter should be a neutral assessment of the issues, your client wants and will appreciate your special attention to his or her side of the case.[39] The client will be most interested in how the law resolves his or her problem, rather than in the law itself. Therefore, avoid abstract explanations of the law. Where explanations are needed,

---

36. Levitan, *supra* note 1, at 34.

37. Ocampo, *supra* note 3, at 28.

38. *Id.* at 57.

39. *Id.*

let the reader know why this information is necessary to understanding your answer.

> The jury's decision on whether the risk is common knowledge is critical here because Dr. Haverford will be excused from liability for your injury if . . . .

Depending on your client's needs, you may need to provide a more in-depth analysis of the law controlling the situation. If you include summaries of the cases controlling the outcome and present each court's reasoning, be sure to include citations. If your opinion is based on interpreting statutes, you may want to include the relevant portions of the statute either in the text or as attachments.[40] Do not skimp on support simply because this document is a letter, rather than a brief or an office memo. While you will not include the kind of support and full-blown analysis that you might include in a brief or a memo, you will include the highlights of that information, depending on the complexity of the question(s) you are answering and the needs of your client.

When you can explain the law without teaching the reader new terms, do so. If you must use a legal term with which your reader will not be familiar, define it. You can do this gracefully by adding an explanatory note to inform the reader without insulting his or her intelligence. To avoid overemphasizing the definition, put it in a dependent phrase. For example, you may insert a parenthetical.

> This assumption of risk (a plaintiff may not recover for an injury when she voluntarily exposes herself to a known danger) can be
> . . . .

You may add the explanation as a phrase at the end of the sentence.

> This is called an assumption of risk, or . . . .

Or, if the explanation is long, you may add it in a sentence following the sentence in which the term was introduced.

> This is called an assumption of risk. Under Arkansas law, assumption of risk means . . . .

The Closing

In the letter's closing, summarize any action that your client needs to take or decisions he or she needs to make. Also communicate that you stand ready to be of service without sounding like you are attempting to generate more legal fees. The closing, like the opening, requires careful attention to tone.

> Please do not hesitate to call if you have any questions about this opinion or any other matter.

or

---

40. There are two advantages to including the relevant statutory sections: "(1) the writer of the opinion can't quote the pertinent portions of the statute without reading the statute very carefully to ascertain which portions are really pertinent; (2) the reader of the opinion can read the opinion with understanding without referring to unavailable statute books." Levitan, *supra* note 1, at 34.

I hope this letter answers your question fully. I am glad that this issue can be resolved so easily for you. If you have any questions in the future, feel free to call.

Due to the high standards you must meet when providing an opinion letter, many firms restrict the signing of these letters to certain people. These people review all opinion letters leaving the office to consider the impact that expressing a particular legal opinion in one case will have on other cases within the firm.[41] Firms may also establish internal peer review procedures in order to obtain an independent review of the opinion letter before it leaves the office.[42] Peer review often helps the attorney negotiate the limitations placed on the letter so as to avoid providing an unreasonably broad opinion.[43]

After you have the content and organization in place, revise your opinion for readability, using the techniques discussed in the chapter on jury instructions as a general guide. Then revise with an eye for tone, especially remembering to maintain clarity while being tactful. As in general correspondence, this will be particularly important in the opening and closing paragraphs. Finally, reread for polish; you want to avoid any grammatical, spelling, or other errors that could detract from your professional credibility with your reader. This attention to detail will increase the reader's confidence in your work.

CONCLUSION

An opinion letter begins and ends with the form and writing concerns of any other business correspondence, but the middle takes on the form of a research memo. The letter should demonstrate both your objectivity and your sensitivity to the client's needs. You should not distort the answer to please your client, nor should you appear to judge or condemn your client's conduct.[44] Finally, you are providing an opinion on a legal matter, not a guarantee, and your letter must reflect this inherent limitation.

Exercise 1

You have just started your position as an associate with the firm of Sauls, Orsatti, and Demenski. One of your first assignments is to write an opinion letter to one of Ms. Sauls' major clients. In the firm's files, you find the following introductory paragraph that is frequently used in the firm's opinion letters. Based on the techniques discussed in this chapter, revise this opening paragraph so that you can use it as a standard opening paragraph in your future opinion letters.

> This letter is furnished by us as counsel for .... You are authorized to deliver copies of this letter to counsel for ... but only

---

41. Sterba, *supra* note 13, at § 1.6. This may have also occurred earlier in the process, especially if providing one opinion will preclude taking on other possible clients or cases.

42. *Id.* For survey results of law firm opinions procedures, *see id.*

43. *Id.*

44. Ocampo, *supra* note 3, at 57.

as to North Carolina law and to no others. You asked us for our opinion on .... Based upon, and subject to, the foregoing, and on such examination of law and authority and on review of such other matters as we consider necessary for the purposes of this opinion, it is our opinion that, as of the date of this opinion, insofar as the laws of the United States of America and the State of North Carolina are concerned, and subject to the qualifications and assumptions set forth below, ... This opinion has been furnished to you pursuant to your request therefor and has been rendered to you on the condition that the opinions expressed herein may not be published or otherwise communicated by you to any other party without our specific prior written approval in each instance. We have examined such documents and made such investigations as we have deemed necessary in connection with the following opinions. [Or insert: We have relied, with your approval, solely upon of our examination of the foregoing documents and have made no independent verification or investigation of the facts contained in such documents.]

Exercise 2

The senior partner in your firm has given you the following memo, which was written by one of the firm's law clerks, to revise into an opinion letter. The client, Andrea Warren, is an older woman who is friends with the senior partner. She is very concerned about this issue and needs a clear answer to her question and a calming tone to the letter.

To: Senior Partner

From: Law Clerk

Re: Currie v. Warren

FACTS

Our client, Andrea Warren, an elderly woman confined to a wheelchair, wanted to give an expensive antique tea set to her niece, Becky Currie. She asked her neighbor to carry the set down to her basement, where Ms. Warren would keep it until Becky moved into her new home. Ms. Warren clearly marked the crate containing the tea set with Becky's name. Ms. Warren later changed her mind about giving Becky the set after Becky was rude to her on the phone. Becky, however, learned about Ms. Warren's original intention to give her the set and she now contends Ms. Warren made a gift of the set to her. Becky is threatening to sue for possession of the set. Ms. Warren feels she should be able to keep the tea set.

QUESTION PRESENTED

Under Iowa law, has delivery occurred and a gift been completed when one has a neighbor put an item in one's own basement in a marked crate with the intent of eventually giving it to a third party?

SHORT ANSWER

Probably not. Delivery requires relinquishing dominion and control over the item to be given. Here, Ms. Warren kept the tea set in her own house and therefore retained enough dominion and control over it to defeat Ms. Currie's claim that Warren gave it to her.

DISCUSSION

A gift is delivered when a person surrenders all rights and control over the item to be given, even though the person may not yet have physically delivered the gift to the intended recipients. *Kintzinger v. Millin*, 117 N.W.2d 68, 70 (Iowa 1962). In *Kintzinger*, the Iowa Supreme Court considered whether, before he died, Frank Giloon made a valid intervivos gift of stock to his son. Specifically at issue was whether Giloon effectively "delivered" the stock.

Beneficiaries under Giloon's will asserted that they were entitled to certain stock shares that Giloon had owned during his life. Giloon's son, however, contended that Giloon made a valid gift of the stock to him. The evidence showed that Giloon took the shares of stock to a local bank, told the bank officer that he intended to give the stock to his son, and asked the bank officer to mail the stock to an out-of-state corporate transfer office where title would be changed from Giloon to his son. Moreover, Giloon signed stock transfer forms and asked the bank officer to guarantee his signature.

The Iowa Court of Appeals found that Giloon made a valid gift to his son. The court reasoned that, even though Giloon never physically gave the stock to his son, he had surrendered control over the stock when he gave it to the bank officer and signed forms transferring away his rights in it. Once Giloon gave the stock to the bank officer, he no longer had access to it. These actions amounted to delivery. *Id.* at 71.

Using *Kintzinger*, the court will reject Currie's claim to the tea service. Delivery of a gift requires an action relinquishing control over the item to be given. Warren never surrendered control over the tea service. In *Kintzinger*, Giloon relinquished control by giving the stock to the bank officer and signing forms transferring his rights in the stock to his son. Moreover, the bank officer took control of the certificates and mailed them out of state, where they unquestionably were out of Giloon's control. In contrast, Warren merely asked her neighbor to put the tea service into her own basement. She could have retrieved it from the basement anytime; therefore, she retained control over it.

Currie will argue that she relinquished control because, like Giloon, Warren gave the tea set to a third party. However, in *Kintzinger*, the third party bank officer was an independent party, whereas Warren's neighbor was her agent, doing her bidding. Currie will further argue that because Warren was confined to a wheelchair, she physically relinquished dominion and control over the tea service. However, Warren could have asked another friend to bring the service upstairs to her or carry her down to get it. It was still within her house so she continued to exercise physical dominion and control over it.

Currie may additionally argue that Warren's marking the crate with Currie's name is similar to Giloon signing the stock transfer forms. However, *Kintzinger* did not turn upon Giloon's signing the forms, but on his physically handing over the stock to the bank officer and putting it out of Giloon's reach.

CONCLUSION

The court will probably find that Warren did not make a gift to Currie of the tea service. Warren kept the tea service in her house and therefore never put it outside of her dominion and control. The third party to whom she gave the crate was her agent, not an independent party. And her signing the crate does not bear on the issue of control. Therefore, she did not deliver the gift and she may keep the tea service.

Assignment 1

John Smith has come to you for advice on handling a problem with a former employee, Jennifer Huffmeyer. John has recently learned from another employee that Jennifer plans to open her own clothing store in Sun Prairie, WI, in about six months. John wants to know if he can sue Jennifer for violating a non-competition clause in her employment contract, but also wants to know in general how you recommend that he handle the situation.

John owns Claire's Boutique, located in East Towne Mall, a shopping center in Madison, WI. In fact, you drafted the contract for the purchase of the store three months ago. When John bought Claire's Boutique from Clara Ludlow, Jennifer was employed as Clara's buyer for the Boutique. John continued Jennifer's employment, so she has been a buyer for the store since it opened five years ago. Jennifer's employment contract includes the following clause, which was also in her previous contract with Clara Ludlow. (You did not draft this contract. John simply used the same form Clara had used previously.)

> If the employee chooses to terminate his or her employment with the Business [Claire's Boutique], then the employee agrees to refrain from engaging in competition with the Business for two (2) years from the date that his or her employment ends. Competition includes, but is not limited to
>
> - starting another similar business within fifty (50) miles of the Business,
>
> - revealing business secrets to another company within one hundred (100) miles of the Business,
>
> - contacting customers or wholesale dealers related to the Business, or
>
> - advertising the employee's former affiliation with the Business.

Last month, Jennifer gave notice that she would be leaving in two weeks, saying that she wanted to find a job closer to her home in Sun Prairie. Claire's Boutique is 6 miles from downtown Sun Prairie. John now has learned that Jennifer plans to open a new women's clothing store in Sun Prairie.

John is angry about Jennifer's behavior and is concerned about her stealing some customers and reducing his profit, although he is not sure she will attract enough customers to seriously jeopardize the Boutique's business. Claire's Boutique draws customers regularly from a 20 mile radius, and about 8% of the names on its customer mailing list are from Sun Prairie. During some times of the year, such as during the state high school basketball tournament and during the Christmas buying season, Claire's Boutique attracts customers from all over the state.

John has asked you to write an opinion letter advising him about whether the covenant in the contract is enforceable. He wants to prevent her from opening the store in Sun Prairie if he can. You have researched the issue and found the following relevant sources. Assume this law is all current.

Lakeside Oil Co. v. Slutsky, 98 N.W.2d 415 (Wis. 1959).

Sec. 103.465 Stats., (2002) (You can find this quoted in the following two cases.)

Behnke v. Hertz Corp, 235 N.W. 2d 690 (Wis. 1975).

Chuck Wagon Catering, Inc. v. Raduege, 277 N.W.2d 787 (Wis. 1979).

Pollack v. Calimag d/b/a Pain Relief Clinic of Racine, 458 N.W.2d 591 (Wis.Ct.App. 1990).

Some options you may want to consider in your final "what's next" section are writing a letter to Jennifer, waiting until she opens the store to see if her store has an impact on the business at Claire's Boutique, or suing for enforcement of the covenant (an injunction). You do not need to research the law on injunctions.

Assignment 2

Your supervising attorney has reviewed your research in Cliff Claussen's situation and has determined that Cliff does not have a viable case against Eco–Getaways, the tour company he wanted to sue. He has asked you to draft an opinion letter to Cliff explaining this to him. For the law and facts of the situation, see Assignment 2 in Chapter 6. Below is the memo you just received from your supervising attorney.

TO: Associate Andre Delavan

FROM: Kok Peng Yu, Senior Partner

DATE: February 25, 20__

RE: Cliff Claussen's injury on Eco–Getaways

I have looked over the research Simon did on the Cliff Clausen matter, such as it was, and I have decided that, given the limited potential to recover damages, an action against the Eco–Getaways company would not likely be successful.

I would like you to go ahead and draft an opinion letter to Cliff outlining why we believe that the suit would not be worth his time. Cliff will be disappointed, so explain your reasoning fully. In the letter, please encourage Cliff not to pursue this suit—he'd end up losing and blaming us if he persists.

You can explain to Cliff all of the areas where you think we might have trouble pursuing a claim—admiralty jurisdiction (this area of law is very complex and will make the case more expensive to pursue), breach of duty (his accident wasn't foreseeable by Eco–Getaways), assumption of risk (we know they are going to argue this, and they could win on that alone), and proving damages. Since the damages for the sprained ankle would be minimal, Cliff's only theory for substantial recovery would be negligent infliction of emotional distress. He does have an accompanying physical injury required for that tort, so that hurdle is behind us, but there are definite problems showing the damages and cause. For one thing, Cliff did see a psychiatrist after the incident, but he has seen therapists off and on over the years for various things. Additionally, Cliff was worried about whether he would be able to do a spring show, but the show did come off and there's no way to prove he lost money because of his injury; his sales may not have been as successful as some other years' shows, but there are too many factors, especially given the economy and events of this year, to pin any money loss specifically on his mental state.

Please include all of the pieces you would normally put into an opinion letter, and remember that Cliff is a very important client of this firm; don't lose him as a client. See if you can figure out something we can suggest as an alternative to suit—maybe that will help him get over this and get on with his lucrative—for all of us—business.

And, by the way, feel free to move into Simon's office if you prefer it to your current one. I believe it is has a little more square footage.

BIBLIOGRAPHY

Committee on Legal Opinions, *Legal Opinions Principles*, 53 Bus.Law. 831 (1998).

Field, Arthur Norman and Donald W. Glazer, *Legal Opinions: The Impact of the Tribar Committee's New Report on Legal Opinion Practice.* New York: Practising Law Institute, 1998.

Freeman, John P., *Legal Opinion Liability* in *Drafting Legal Opinion Letters.* New York: Wiley Law Publications, John M. Sterba, Jr., ed., 2d ed. 1992 and 2000 Supplement.

Fuld, James J., *Lawyers' Standards and Responsibilities in Rendering Opinions*, 33 Bus.Law. 1295 (March 1978).

Glazer, Donald. W., *It's Time to Streamline Opinion Letters: The Chair of a BLS Committee Speaks Out*, Bus. Law Today, Nov.-Dec. 1999, at 32.

Jessen, Koley, P.C., Legal Opinion Committee, *Third-Party Legal Opinions: An Introduction to "Customary Practice,"* 35 Creighton L.Rev. 153 (2001).

Levitan, Mortimer, *Dissertation on Writing Legal Opinions,* 1960 Wis. L.Rev. 22.

Ocampo, Raymond L., Jr., *The Opinion Letter,* 3 Cal.Law. 28 (January 1983).

Restatement (Third) of the Law Governing Lawyers. St. Paul: American Law Institute, 2000.

Segall, Harold A., and Jeffrey A. Arouh, *How to Prepare Legal Opinions: Boldness and Caution,* 25 Prac.Law. 29 (June 1979).

Sterba, John M. Jr., *Introduction* and *Elements of Opinion Letters* in *Drafting Legal Opinion Letters.* New York: Wiley Law Publications, John M. Sterba, Jr., ed., 2d. ed. 1992 and 2000 Supplement.

Symposium: The Lawyer's Duties and Liabilities to Third Parties, 37 S.Tex.L.Rev. 957 (1996).

Tribar Opinion Committee, *"Third Party 'Closing Opinions,' "* 53 Bus. Law. 591 (1998).

Vagts, Detlev F., *Legal Opinions in Quantitative Terms: The Lawyer as Haruspex or Bookie?,* 34 Bus.Law. 421 (1979).

Wells, Christopher D., *Engagement Letters in Transactional Practice: A Reporter's Reflections,* 51 Mercer L. Rev. 41 (1999).

Chapter 16

WILLS AND TRUSTS

This chapter reviews the drafting principles associated with writing a contract but applies them to the task of writing wills and trusts. As with contracts, with these documents you must determine the clauses you need, find examples of those clauses, and revise them to fit your client's needs. Unlike contracts, wills and trusts do not require you to work out compromises between the parties. The testator's desires are supreme.[1] Your job is to ensure that those wishes are effectuated after his or her death. If the document's language is unclear or ambiguous, however, the court may have to judicially construe or modify the terms of a will or trust.[2] Thus, accuracy and readability are the two most important concerns when drafting these documents.

Wills are the central instruments in most people's estate plans, and at the heart of many wills is the testamentary trust.[3] The essential feature of a testamentary trust is that property is held by an individual or corporation for the benefit of another person or persons.[4] The trustee

---

1. A person who leaves a will disposing of his or her property upon death dies testate and is known as the testator; a person who does not leave a will dies intestate and the statutes of his or her state control disposition of the property. William McGovern Jr., Sheldon Kurtz, and Jan Rein, *Wills, Trusts, and Estates including Taxation and Future Interests* § 1.1 (2d ed. 2001). When a person dies testate, the will must be admitted to probate, through the probate courts, before it has any legal effect. Frederick K. Hoops, *Family Estate Planning Guide* § 14.1 (1982). When the will is admitted to probate, the court appoints an executor to administer the testator's estate and to oversee disposition of the property. *Id.* at § 14.2.

2. David A. Baker & Kathleen O'Hagen Scallan, *Construction, Reformation, Revocation and Modification of Wills and Trusts*, in *Ill. Inst. CLE Handbook on Estate, Trust and Guardianship Litigation* 12.1—12.5

(Dec. 2001). Although the most common reason for judicially construing a will is ambiguity, courts remain very reluctant to reform poorly drafted wills, which leaves malpractice suits by intended beneficiaries as the only remedy. Michael John Byrne, *Note: Let Truth Be Their Devise*, 73 N.C.L.Rev. 2209, 2238–39 (1995). Conversely, reformation of trusts occurs more frequently on grounds of mistake. *See* note 21, *infra*.

3. Hoops, *supra* note 1, at § 31. An inter vivos trust can take effect during the settlor's lifetime, can also be used to control disposition of property, and can be either revocable or irrevocable. Revocable inter vivos trusts increasingly are replacing wills and testamentary trusts as the central estate planning instrument.

4. Trusts often provide professional management of property for the beneficiary who has never managed property or when

has a legal obligation to hold and manage the property for the beneficiaries, and the beneficiaries have legal rights enforceable against the trustee.

Drafting a will, with or without a trust, involves three stages:

- interviewing your client to determine his or her desires,
- determining the substantive and procedural law that controls the transfer of property at death,[5] and
- drafting the will so it accurately portrays your client's desires and is readable by those who will turn to it for guidance.

INTERVIEWING YOUR CLIENT

The possibility of strong emotions pervades this interview. Some clients may be facing imminent death. Other clients, even those not immediately facing death, may feel intense emotion as they prepare their wills. Still other clients' emotions may be related to the deaths of others close to them. By recognizing that your clients may have these emotions, you will be better able to fulfill your role as counselor and to obtain the information needed to draft these testamentary documents.

You may also need to address your own feelings about death. For example, if you are uncomfortable talking about death, you may be distracted or unresponsive when your client has trouble discussing how to structure his or her will. Although drafting wills does not require extensive reflection on your own attitude toward death, you do want to ensure that your feelings and thoughts are not adversely affecting your client.[6]

To reduce the problems that may occur in this emotionally charged atmosphere, structure your interview to proceed step by step so you can obtain all the information you need. This structure is not intended to force your client to answer questions when he or she is caught up in emotional feelings. Instead, it allows you to pause when these emotions may arise, to note where you stopped, and to return to that point without skipping any aspects of the interview.

You can provide this structure by preparing an in-depth interview questionnaire and then proceeding through the questionnaire in every interview. This questionnaire will also help you remember to ask all the questions needed to obtain the details for drafting documents that fulfill

---

age or other factors impair the beneficiary's ability to do so. *Id.* at § 32. Trusts can also be used to give lifetime use of property to a person or persons while ensuring that eventually other persons will receive the property, such as when the grantor provides the surviving spouse with a lifetime interest in a trust, with the remainder passing to the grantor's children.

5. Actually, you will need to have a significant understanding of the substantive and procedural law controlling this area of the law, including complex tax and property issues, before accepting any clients for work in this area.

6. Thomas L. Shaffer, Carol Ann Mooney, and Mary Jo Boettcher, *The Planning and Drafting of Wills and Trusts* 9–17 (4th ed. 2001). This section on "Feelings about Death" incorporates numerous exercises on addressing these feelings in the classroom, the law office, and the courts.

each client's wishes. The questionnaire should contain at least four categories of information: (1) domicile, (2) property, (3) beneficiaries, and (4) the individual's objectives.[7] When composing the questionnaire, be specific.[8] It is better to have a long interview that will elicit most, if not all, of the information you need to begin drafting than to have to schedule follow-up interviews or place numerous phone calls to close gaps that you left during the initial interview.

To save yourself time and the client money, be sure to give your client specific instructions concerning the documents to bring to the interview. Better yet, consider sending your questionnaire or portions of it to your client when scheduling the interview. This allows the client to prepare beforehand by gathering the documents and information needed at the interview. It also allows your client to prepare at home where the information is more readily available and where the client does not have to pay for your time. Then the client can come to the interview prepared to provide the specific information you need.

In the interview, question your client closely to determine how he or she wants to dispose of property. Even after gathering documents or answering the questionnaire, your client may still be unclear about this decision. Your questions, based on the substantive and procedural requirements of your jurisdiction, may lead the client to decide on an estate plan that varies from the one originally envisioned.

Try to puzzle out exactly what your client wants. For example, if a client wants to leave his stamp collection to Uncle Jack, has he considered what he wants to happen if Uncle Jack dies before him? Does he want Uncle Jack's heirs to receive the collection or does he want it to revert to the residuary of the estate? You may have to help your client face the possibility that Uncle Jack will die before he does. Some other questions that your client may not have considered but that you should raise include avoiding tax consequences when possible, planning so that the documents will survive any challenges to them, and anticipating problems that arise when the document is drafted in one state and probated in another.

Also question your client closely about assets. This may be somewhat touchy, because most people are uncomfortable sharing the specific details of how much property they own, how they hold title to that property, and other private information. Take time to establish a rapport with your client so he or she will become comfortable enough to share this information. Emphasize to your client that you will be unable to make intelligent recommendations without all the facts. Additionally, many clients tend to estimate incorrectly the value of their assets and often do not understand the consequences that can result depending on

---

7. Hoops, *supra* note 1, at § 19.

8. For sample will questionnaires, *see* Hoops, *supra* note 1, at § 310; Robert P. Wilkins, *Drafting Wills and Trust Agree-* *ments* 2–1–25 (3d ed. 2001); L. Rush Hunt, *A Lawyer's Guide to Estate Planning: Fundamentals for the Legal Practitioner* 4–13 (2d ed. 1998).

the manner in which title to property is held.[9] For example, many married couples own property as joint tenants with right of survivorship, which is not subject to the terms of the will.[10] The location of the property is important as well. While all personal property and in-state real property will be distributed during the local probate, out-of-state property will require an ancillary probate in the state where the property is located.[11]

When working with a married couple, you should also consider holding separate interviews with each spouse.[12] An attorney representing both spouses must address the potential conflicts of interest that can arise in this situation.[13] For example, whether property is characterized as community property or separate property can have conflicting results for each spouse. You should inform each client of the potential conflicts of interest so he or she can decide whether to allow you to continue to represent them both. If you do continue to represent both spouses, have them sign letters to indicate that they understand the conflicts of interest that may arise from the potential adversarial nature of estate planning and that they agree to have you represent them both.[14]

The client interview and the analysis of the information obtained during it are both time-consuming and vital to accurate estate planning. Unfortunately, many attorneys handling estate work view it as an opportunity to obtain business in the future. Because of this, they frequently do not bill sufficiently to cover the time necessary to prepare a will or trust carefully.[15] This practice forces them to rush through the job. The best way to avoid this problem is to impose realistic time demands on yourself and bill for estate planning just as for other work.

---

9. California Continuing Education of the Bar, *How to Draft Wills* 7 (June 1985) (hereafter C.E.B.). The best way to verify this information is to examine the documents involved. *Id.*

10. The property doctrines section of this chapter, *infra*, discusses these and other issues concerning title to property. Other contracts, such as life insurance policies, retirement plans, and multiple-party bank accounts, may also pass to named beneficiaries outside the control of the testamentary documents.

11. McGovern, *supra* note 1, at § 14.1. These ancillary probates can be costly and often require retaining local counsel. Consequently, placing this property in an inter vivos trust, instead of disposing of it under a will, is a common practice.

12. If you are drafting wills or trusts for two domestic partners, similar concerns may arise even though some laws governing ownership or taxation may not apply. For ease of reference, whenever this chapter refers to "spouses," consider whether the same or a related issue would arise with

domestic partners. For additional information, *see* Diane Hastings Temple, *Estate Planning for the Non–Traditional Family* in *31st Annual Estate Planning Institute* 1145 (2000).

13. Randall W. Roth, *Current Ethical Problems in Estate Planning*, 6 ALI–ABA Estate Planning Course Materials Journal 33, 49–50 (2000); Charles J. Groppe, *Ethical Considerations* in *Basic Will Drafting* 141, 160–63 (2001).

14. *Id.* at 164–68.

15. Gerald P. Johnston, *Legal Malpractice in Estate Planning and General Practice*, 17 Memp.S.U.L.Rev. 521, 528 (1987); *but see*, Manuel R. Ramos, *Legal Malpractice: The Profession's Dirty Little Secret*, 47 Vand.L.Rev. 1657, 1718 n.378 (1994) (arguing that general practitioners usually will not refer estate planning work because they may then lose future work to that attorney in areas they previously handled for that client).

Having completed the interview, recognize that procrastination can also be a serious problem in doing estate planning work. Unlike litigation, where outside factors impose deadlines on you, estate planning, like other transactional work, does not have similar external deadlines. You must impose them on yourself to avoid the unhappy circumstance that results when several months pass following the client interview and the client suddenly dies before executing the testamentary documents. The beneficiaries-apparent would have a valid malpractice claim against you if you unreasonably delayed execution of the documents.[16] After finishing the client interview, set deadlines for yourself to draft the documents and have them executed.

DETERMINING THE SUBSTANTIVE AND PROCEDURAL LAW

After gathering the estate planning information and documents, go to the library. The transfer of property at death is complicated by statutory requirements for probating the will, tax consequences, and property doctrines. Researching these areas of law will allow you to understand the impact that these and other considerations play in developing an estate plan. While this chapter cannot touch on all the factors that you must research and consider before drafting, it will review several of these statutory requirements, tax consequences, and property doctrines. Remember, no amount of graceful English will save the will drafter who lacks an understanding of the substantive law controlling these documents.[17]

Statutory Requirements

The law controlling wills and trusts is essentially statutory, although countless cases exist interpreting those statutes. These statutory requisites are quite specific in each state, and you must strictly adhere to them. For example, one court held that a will was not executed correctly because it had not been attested to by two or more witnesses "in the presence of the testator" as the statute required.[18] One of the witnesses was not in the room with the testator when he signed the will. Although the witness checked with the testator over the phone to verify that the document was his will and that he had signed it, the court ruled that the statutory requirement of presence meant "physical presence" when the will was signed.[19]

Some of the statutory details that you must know and understand to probate a valid will can be seen by reviewing malpractice cases. For example, cases have been won for not using the required number of witnesses, using a person named in the will as a witness, omitting an essential clause from the will, or inaccurately drafting an essential provision.[20] The great weight of authority remains opposed to reforming a will's terms to correct inadvertent mistakes, regardless of the testator's

---

16. Roth, *supra* note 13, at 43.

17. Shaffer, *supra* note 6, at 157.

18. *Matter of Jefferson's Will*, 349 So.2d 1032, 1032 (Miss.1977).

19. *Id.*

20. Johnston, *supra* note 15, at 522.

intent.[21] Knowing these details will allow you to effectuate your client's wishes and prevent malpractice claims against you by unhappy beneficiaries.[22]

You must also consider the potential problem of drafting a will in one jurisdiction and having it probated in another. You can resolve some of these problems by looking beyond the law of your jurisdiction when drafting your documents so the will can meet the requirements of those states, too.[23] For example, your jurisdiction may require only two witnesses to the will, but some others require three. Cautious drafters recommend having three witnesses to better ensure that the will be recognized as valid in other jurisdictions.[24]

If the testator owns property in more than one state, there may be questions about which state is entitled to tax the property upon the testator's death, whether the property will be considered to be community or individual property, which state's rule against perpetuities controls when inter vivos trusts are established, or what powers of appointment the executor or trustee may exercise.[25] Consider retaining local counsel to handle probating out-of-state assets, at least in those states where you are not licensed to practice.[26]

Tax Consequences

One of the most significant aspects of estate planning practice is understanding the tax consequences of the transfer of property at death. These tax consequences often lead general practitioners to shy away from preparing any but the simplest testamentary documents, and with good cause. The tax laws change frequently and the decisions interpreting tax regulations must be continuously updated.[27]

---

21. *Id.* at 523. The *Restatement (Second) of Property, Donative Transfers* § 34.7 cmt.d (1990) and the Uniform Trust Code § 415 (2000) adopt a more liberal position permitting the use of extrinsic evidence to reform a will or a trust to conform to the testator's or settler's intent.

22. Although lack of privity of contract historically precluded beneficiaries from bringing malpractice suits against attorneys, this rule has been relaxed to permit these suits in many states. Most states today have overturned the strict privity barrier to malpractice suits although some states continue to prohibit suits by beneficiaries against the drafting attorney. Bradley E.S. Fogel, *Attorney v. Client: Privity, Malpractice, and the Lack of Respect for the Primacy of the Attorney–Client Relationship in Estate Planning*, 68 Tenn.L.Rev. 261, 262–64 (2001).

23. Commonly, each law firm or attorney will develop a will execution form that satisfies all possible jurisdictional requirements for probating the will.

24. Most states, as well as the Uniform Probate Code, require only two witnesses but the *Restatement (Second), supra* note 21, at § 33.1, cmt.c, recommends using three. McGovern, *supra* note 1, at § 4.3 at 176.

25. *See,* Hoops, *supra* note 1, at §§ 361–78, for a further discussion of these and other conflict of laws issues that arise with multi-state estates.

26. This practice coincides with the limitation noted in opinion letters that restricts their validity to the state in which the opining lawyer practices. See Chapter 15, Opinion Letters.

27. In fact, Congress drastically changed the estate tax system in June 2001, including its repeal for deaths occurring after 2009. The tax, however, rises from the dead in 2010 absent additional Congressional action. M.C. Mirow and Burce A. McGovern, *An Obituary of the Federal Estate Tax*, 43 Ariz.L.Rev. 625, 625 n.1 (2001). For a discussion of changes resulting from this revision, see Jerold I. Horn, *Estate Plan-*

Do not proceed into this area of law unless you have or can obtain the training to become qualified in its complexity. The tax consequences surrounding your client's death require an awareness of estate, inheritance, gift, and income tax ramifications of the estate plan and how federal and state tax laws interrelate. A simplified example shows how knowledge of the tax laws, how they coordinate, and how they can be used in establishing your client's estate plan is vital to protect your client's interests. For example, at the time of this writing, federal law allows each individual to transfer up to $1 million free from transfer tax[28] and, additionally, allows each spouse a marital deduction to transfer any amount of property at any time from one spouse to another tax-free.[29] When the spouses' total estate exceeds $1 million, passing the entire estate to the surviving spouse may result in unnecessary taxes being owed at the survivor's death because the deceased spouse's unified credit would have been wasted. Instead, you can use the deceased spouse's unified credit, in combination with the marital deduction, to obtain substantial tax savings in the surviving spouse's estate.[30] This is accomplished by (1) transferring property worth $1 million either to persons other than the surviving spouse or to a "credit shelter trust" for the surviving spouse,[31] and (2) transferring property exceeding $1 million to the surviving spouse in those forms qualifying for the marital deduction, thus avoiding tax on that property. The details of these tax consequences are beyond the scope of this chapter. We can only remind you to consider them when drafting testamentary documents.

Property Doctrines

In addition to the statutory requirements and the tax consequences, also consider the applicable property doctrines. These come into play because the will or trust you are drafting is intended to change the ownership of the testator's property from the testator to those people or organizations named as beneficiaries. How title to property is held for each of your client's assets will control whether your client can dispose of the property under his or her will or trust; it also will control whether the will or trust is needed to transfer title. For example, if your client

---

ning and Drafting for the Economic Growth and Tax Relief Reconciliation Act of 2001, 7 ALI–ABA Estate Planning Course Material Journal 33 (Dec. 2001); and Howard M. Zaritsky, *How Estate Tax "Repeal" Will Affect Your Estate Planning Practice*, 7 ALI–ABA Estate Planning Course Materials Journal 5, 23 (Oct. 2001).

28. *Id.*

29. Hunt, *supra* note 8, at 57. To meet this requirement, the property cannot be transferred as a life estate or other terminable interest unless specific requirements are met. *Id.* at 58. This is one example of how legal spouses are treated significantly differently from domestic partners, who cannot transfer property between themselves tax free.

30. *Id.* at 61–62. The marital deduction was established in 1948 to equalize the tax treatment of persons living in community property and common law states. In simplest terms, the marital deduction allows a deduction from the decedent's gross estate equal in value to any interest in deductible property passing to his or her surviving spouse. *Id.* at 57.

31. *Id.* at 61–62. To prevent the surviving spouse's estate from having large taxes assessed, you can establish a trust in which to place the decedent's $1,000,000 for the surviving spouse's lifetime benefit. This allows the spouse to receive income and principal from the trust, while not "owning" it for tax purposes upon his or her death. *Id.*

owns property in joint tenancy, it will not be controlled by your client's will or trust, but instead will transfer at your client's death to the surviving joint tenant.[32] In contrast, if the property is owned as a tenancy in common, a right of survivorship does not exist for the other tenant(s) in common, and your client may transfer his or her interest through the will or trust.[33] Concurrent estates can also exist in personal property such as cars, bank accounts, and securities. You must determine how title is held and then discuss with your client whether he or she is content with the title controlling the disposition or wants to change the way title is held to reach a different result.

If your client is married, you must consider whether the state in which your client is domiciled is a community property or common law property state. This will affect what property the testator may dispose of in the will. In a community property state, your client can dispose of all of his or her separate property under the will or trust, but can only dispose of his or her share of community property.[34] Whether property is separate or community may also affect other areas, such as the tax consequences at the time of death.

Equally important to knowing the law before drafting these documents is knowing when you should refer the matter to a specialist.[35] Estate planning is a complicated area that requires extensive knowledge in tax and future interests law for drafting anything more than the most basic will. Failure to make the referral can result in a malpractice action being pursued against you.[36] For example, if you usually do not handle estates substantial enough to warrant using a "credit shelter trust" in combination with the marital deduction, you may want to refer that client to a specialist. Otherwise, if you incorrectly draft the will for a client entitled to this deduction, you could lose that important benefit for your client.

---

32. Joint tenancy's outstanding feature is the right of survivorship inherent in it, which means that each joint tenant owns the whole property, subject to the equal rights of the other joint tenant(s). Thus, your client's title to the property does not "pass" to the survivor as in testate or intestate succession. Instead, a joint tenant's interest in the property ends at death and cannot be devised or descend through intestate succession. John D. Spankling, *Understanding Property Law* 118–19 (2000). *See also,* Stephen S. Case, *What You Need to Know about Joint Tenancy,* 3 ALI–ABA Estate Planning Course Materials Journal 29 (June 1997).

33. Spankling, *supra* note 32, at 117.

34. Additional questions arise when couples move from a separate property state to a community property state, or vice-versa, about how their property will be treated at death. These problems of choice of law between jurisdictions can have signif-

icant impact on what property is included in the decedent's estate and on what property his or her spouse is entitled. McGovern, *supra* note 1, at § 3.8.

35. As noted in the chapter on drafting opinion letters, be competent, become competent, get help, or get out. *See, supra,* Chapter 15, note 20.

36. *See, Horne v. Peckham,* 158 Cal. Rptr. 714 (Cal.Ct.App.1979), where the court held that a general practitioner was liable for malpractice for not referring a complicated estate matter to a specialist in the area. The court used the standard that a general practitioner has a duty to refer to a specialist if a reasonable generalist would have referred the case under similar circumstances. *Id.* at 720. The court also held that if a general practitioner does work usually performed by a specialist, the generalist will be held to the higher standard of care imposed on the specialist if errors occur. *Id.*

DRAFTING CONSIDERATIONS

This section discusses the drafting considerations for wills and trusts. The first section discusses the primary drafting principles for these documents: accuracy and readability. The second discusses organization. The third section discusses how to draft standard clauses for wills and trusts, and the fourth covers ways to prevent challenges to the will. By reviewing these sections after having interviewed your client and researched the procedural and substantive law, you will be prepared to draft testamentary documents that accurately portray your clients' desires while remaining readable for all who use them.

Accuracy and Readability

The primary need when drafting wills and trusts is for accuracy. The document must portray the client's wishes accurately because your client will be unavailable to explain any clauses that are ambiguous. Inaccuracies or ambiguities in these documents could require judicial interpretation. This interpretation could frustrate the client's wishes because the court's reconstruction of the client's intention may not coincide with his or her desires and will cause delay, expense, and inconvenience.[37] Frequently, this need for accuracy will require a longer document. "[P]roperty dispostions cannot be made short and simple without inviting litigation and trouble. Real simplicity has always come through completeness of statement."[38]

A secondary need is for readability. Readability is important so the client can, when reading the documents, determine whether the documents actually say what the client wants. While your client may not be able to understand some of the technical language required to effectuate the estate plan, he or she should be able to understand why it has been inserted and what its purpose is. For example, you may decide to use the phrase "descendants per stirpes" to specify how the residuary estate will be divided. You may need to explain to your client what this means: if one of the beneficiaries named in the will has died, then that beneficiary's share of the estate goes to his or her descendants.[39] Explain that clearly so your client will understand the reason for the clause.

Always be prepared to explain any clause, phrase, or word that you use to your client.[40] One attorney told us of including a clause in a will that she took from an in-house form will because all the form wills contained that clause. She did not take the time to understand it exactly, but included it in case it was important. It was important, because it was the one clause about which her client questioned her. She found herself in the unfortunate situation of having to inform her client that she did

37. William Schwartz, *Sins of Omission and Commission in the Drafting of Wills and Trusts*, 11 Inst. of Est. Plan. § 1100 (1979).

38. Shaffer, *supra* note 6, at 155.

39. Hoops, *supra* note 1, at § 32. *See, Lombardi v. Blois*, 40 Cal.Rptr. 899 (Cal.Ct. App.1964).

40. H.M. Grether, *The Little Horribles of a Scrivener*, 39 Neb.L.R. 296, 301 (1960).

not understand the clause either. Avoid putting yourself in this situation.

Also consider readability for the additional people who will use the testamentary document. For example, the beneficiaries will scan it to determine what they will be receiving, the executor or personal representative will read it carefully to determine what powers have been granted by the testator, the trustee will read it to determine what his or her role is, and the court will read it to determine the client's intent if the will is challenged. For all of these audiences, you must draft a will that remains readable while resolving complex and often competing considerations.

One easy way to increase readability is not to capitalize words needlessly such as "will," "codicil," "guardian," and "executor." In everyday language, those words would be in lower case.[41] Using traditional capitalization will enhance the readability of these documents. Other ways to make the will more readable include dividing content into shorter sentences, using clear transitions, omitting unneeded words, and using familiar words. If more clarification is needed, consider using flowcharts to help your client and his or her family or friends understand how the will works in practice.[42]

Some attorneys worry that revising will language to make it more readable will make it impossible to retain the information necessary to probate a will successfully.[43] But readability can be achieved without sacrificing accuracy. The success of plain English in such complicated situations as insurance contracts shows that this concern is unfounded.[44] Additionally, lawyers sometimes resort to legalese to round out passages that have little substance; watch for these phrases as warnings that you may be using poor or unhelpful language.[45]

Some attorneys feel that clients want or need ornate language to believe the will is official. Although we have never met any client who voiced this concern, the concern is easily addressed if it arises. If your client feels uneasy, try explaining your purpose: the will is drafted to be more readable for everyone and more accurate in stating the client's desires. You may also find that using graphic techniques, such as bold, italics, and different font sizes for headings, may help your client feel that the will looks sufficiently official. Alternatively, you could try

---

41. Leon Feldman, *"Simple Will" Can Be Simplified Further to Produce a More Concise But Effective Document,* 10 Est. Plan. 290, 293 (Sept. 1983).

42. Wilkins, *supra* note 8, at 6–1–9. This author has found that flowcharts provide clients with a better understanding of their wills, both when describing the proposed plan during interviews as well as in the final documents.

43. Lawrence Cusack described his experience with this problem when, after reviewing several form books, he pulled together a will that used "plain English" throughout. Lawrence Cusack, *The Blue-*

Pencilled Will: What's Wrong with a Will in Plain English?, 118 Trusts & Estates 33 (Aug. 1979). He provided the will to six reviewers and five of them agreed that the edited version was more readable and might better please a client. The sixth reviewer felt that nothing would be gained by "word-plucking" through standard testamentary language because most clients did not care about the language and the time saved in typing would be insignificant. *Id.*

44. *Id.*

45. *Id.*

including some resonating language in the opening and closing of the will to set the tone your client wants, leaving the substance of it clearly stated. But avoid adding this language routinely, based on a rumor about what clients want. While we have never heard a client complain that a will, or any legal document, was too clearly worded, we have frequently heard the opposite complaint.

Organization of Wills and Trusts

Having considered the principles inherent in drafting wills and trusts, next consider the organization of these documents. Many lawyers simply follow the organization included in form books when drafting, even though it may not enhance accuracy or readability. The document will be more readable for your client, however, if you organize it to proceed from what is most important to the client to what is least important or least understandable. Rather than starting your wills with a clause calling for payment of "just debts" as do most form wills, begin with those clauses that most concern the client, the disposition of his or her estate to the named beneficiaries.[46] Place technical provisions at the end, where they do not distract as much from the document's readability.[47]

One way to simplify both the organization and the language of your documents is to use everyday language in the clauses and to include a definition section that explains the use of any terms with a particular meaning. This allows you to state the information that is most important to the client in the document's body and relegate technical language that may be confusing to the definition section. For example, you could draft the following clause.

Tangible Personal Property. I give all my tangible personal property:

(a) to my wife, Jane Smith ("my wife"),

(b) if my wife does not survive me, to my descendants,

(c) if none of these persons survives me, to my heirs.

Then you can use the definitions section to define tangible personal property,[48] survival requirements (usually requiring thirty to sixty days' survival after the testator's death for a beneficiary to inherit under the will), descendants, heirs, and how distributions are to be made between them. This format allows the will to be straightforward and readable

---

46. Stanley M. Johanson, *The Orphan's Deduction: How to Handle a Troublesome Drafting Problem*, 14 Inst. on Est.Plan. 26 (1980).

47. *Id.*

48. Trying to write a definition of tangible personal property so that it covers all possible items creates the risk that you will omit something. One will left "all of my personal property, consisting of furniture, carpets, curtains, china, linen, miscellane-ous prints and pictures, antique chandeliers, Louis XVI mantel, mirror and fireback installed in drawing room in my residence, and miscellaneous bric-a-brac...." The court held that the bequest did not dispose of the testator's rare book collection. The court also held that if the phrase "consisting of" had been replaced with "including," it could have construed the clause to include the collection. *Matter of Jones' Estate,* 341 N.E.2d 565 (N.Y. 1975).

without excluding the details necessary to effectuate the testator's wishes.

Some people may object to this format because they find it inconvenient to have to turn to the definition section while reading the document. If you or your client object to this format, develop another that allows for clear organization and readable clauses. One alternative is to reserve definitions for particularly complex terms, thus reducing the amount of cross-referencing necessary. Another is to put the most important, and usually least confusing, clauses on distribution of property at the beginning of the document and place the more complex, confusing clauses at the end. If you use a definition section, do not use it to reinsert your anxieties about drafting a will in plain English. For example, most lawyers agree that it is unnecessary to have the client "hereby give, devise, leave and bequeath" his or her property.[49] Either "give" or "leave" would be sufficient. Having eliminated these unnecessary words from the body of the document, do not reinsert them in the definition section, as the following definition does.

Whenever the term "give" is used in this will it shall include the terms "devise," "bequeath," "leave," or "devise and bequeath."

When deciding what terms to define, remember that overusing definitions will make the document difficult to read. Virtually every term in a will could be defined to clarify its meaning, but doing so would make it unreadable. Also, defining accurately requires care and should not be undertaken lightly. Poorly defined terms have led to much litigation. For example, when defining a term as seemingly straightforward as "children" or "issue," you must consider the questions that may arise when using these terms. Some of these include the following.

- Is the term "children" to be limited to immediate offspring?
- Is the term "issue" intended to include remote descendants beyond the immediate offspring?
- Are the offspring of several different marriages to be included?
- Are adopted children to be included?
- Are adopted children to be considered the children of their natural parents so as to be included in a gift to the children by the natural parent?
- Are children born outside marriage to be included?
- Are stepchildren to be included?[50]

Thus, even when using everyday terms, you must be careful to have discussed these questions with your client and make sure that your

---

49. An historical reason is at the base for many of these ingrained redundancies. At various times, English common law had two languages to choose from—between Celtic and Anglo Saxon, between English and Latin, between English and French. Given these choices, lawyers began to pick one word from each language. Once these were all translated to English, the usage remained. Thomas Word, Jr., *A Brief for Plain English Wills and Trusts,* 14 U.Rich. L.Rev. 471, 473 (1980).

50. Schwartz, *supra* note 37, at § 1110.5.

definition of the term fits his or her desires. Use definitions when they are needed for accuracy or readability.

To ensure that you ask your client how to define these important terms, prepare a section of your interview questionnaire or checklist that includes definitions so that you will be sure to ask your client the questions necessary to incorporate these definitions in the documents.

Another way to clarify organization is to use headings and number clauses.[51] Headings can enhance readability when they serve as signposts telling each section's contents and clarifying the document's organization. Because their value will be lost if they add confusion, the language of these headings should be as clear and simple as possible. For example, do not use "Article First, Article Second, Article Third" because this uncommon phrasing would jar most people. Instead, use headings such as these for easy understanding.

Article I.   Distribution of My Estate.

Article II.   Payment of Charges Against My Estate.

Article III.   Directions for Division of My Residuary Estate into the Marital Trust and the Residuary Trust.

Article IV.   Miscellaneous and Technical Provisions.

Article V.   Executors and Trustees and Their Authority.

Numbering clauses is also useful because it allows for easy cross-reference from one point to another. When numbering clauses, use either letters or whole numbers, rather than decimals. While decimals may be useful in a long contract or a particularly complex will or trust, the simple will with few subparagraphs will be more understandable if you use traditional outline format with whole numbers.[52] Thus, your sections could be A, B, C, and D and the clauses under each would be 1, 2, 3, and 4, instead of 1.1, 1.2, 1.3, and 1.4.

Making your organization clear and straightforward will enhance both the accuracy and readability of your documents. Accuracy is enhanced because your client will be able to check whether the document expresses his or her wishes more easily. Readability is enhanced because the organization combines with clear language in each clause to allow the client to understand the document. Now you must draft your clauses.

Standard Will Clauses

Because the subject matter of most wills is similar, they often include standard clauses. Many attorneys simply repeat these clauses from sample wills or form books for each client.[53] Whenever using standard clauses, however, make sure that you check and revise them, just as you did when drafting contracts. Revise in two ways. First, revise for accuracy, making sure that the clause is appropriate to your client's

---

51. See Chapter 5, Contracts.

52. Schwartz, *supra* note 37, at § 1110.5.

53. For a list of standard provisions for both simple and long will trusts, *see* Wilkins, supra note 8.

situation. Second, revise for readability, making sure that you are not using language that is difficult to read or unnecessary to achieve the purpose of the clause. For example, the following clause is one that adds nothing but verbosity and confusion to the will.

> In the name of God, Amen: Know all men by these presents: That I, _____, of the City of _____, County of _____, and State of _____, being in good bodily health and of sound and disposing mind and memory and not acting under duress, menace, fraud or undue influence of any person whomsoever, calling to mind the frailty of human life, and being desirous of disposing of my worldly estate with which it has pleased God to bless me, while I have strength and capacity so to do, do make, publish and declare this my Last Will and Testament, hereby revoking all other wills, legacies, bequests, or codicils by me heretofore made, in the manner and form following:[54]

This clause could be easily revised.

I, _____, make this will, being in good bodily health, of sound mind, and not acting under duress or undue influence of any person.

The simpler clause achieves the same result as the previous one while indicating from the start that the will is straightforward and understandable. Continue this trend of revising standard clauses to increase accuracy and readability throughout the will and the trust. Avoid "vague notions that will-drafting is a form of magic—that the instrument certainly will fail if the testator says 'I give' instead of 'I give, devise, and bequeath in fee simple absolute,' just as the cave door would not open until Ali Baba said 'open sesame.' "[55]

Payments of Debts and Funeral Expenses

Most wills move from the opening paragraph to a clause ordering the payment of "just debts" and funeral expenses. Many attorneys include a "just debts" clause because they believe the client expects to find this clause in his or her will and will be content only if it is included.[56] But the clause is not needed legally because all jurisdictions require the testator's fiduciary to pay all debts and funeral expenses.[57] You may decide to eliminate it because it may cause more problems than it solves. For example, it may not be desirable to pay off all debts immediately upon the testator's death. Your client may not want to force his or her spouse to pay off a mortgage with a favorable interest rate just because of his or her death.[58] Additionally, although the form books often use the language "just debts," this clause is not clear to most people,

---

54. Frank E. Cooper, *Writing in Law Practice* 338 (2d ed.1963).

55. Shaffer, *supra* note 6, at 159.

56. Cooper, *supra* note 54, at 339.

57. Hoops, *supra* note 1, at § 313.

58. *Id.* If you choose to include this clause, consider writing ones that leaves the residence subject to a mortgage or that permits refinancing by the executor, such as those included in Wilkins, *supra* note 8, at 25–28–29.

and the personal representative may pay bills he or she should not pay. The clause may also legally require the client's estate to pay bills it may not otherwise be required to pay, such as when the client has filed for bankruptcy or when a creditor has missed the deadline for filing debts with the estate.

If you choose to include this clause, clarify which debts are to be paid and who is to bear the burden of paying these debts. For example, suppose the testator borrowed $25,000 from a bank and assigned his life insurance policy as collateral for the loan. The policy's beneficiary was the testator's daughter. The will directs all debts to be paid and the bank collects the insurance proceeds to satisfy the debt. Must the estate reimburse the daughter for payment of the debt?[59] What would the testator have intended? Make sure you know what your client wants when revising this clause, and realize his or her debts will change over time, so prepare for future problems.

Additionally, your client may want to use a clause directing the payment of funeral expenses, while excluding language on the payment of other debts. You could include the following clause, which may satisfy your client's concerns without causing the problems noted above.

> I direct my executor to pay the expenses of my last illness, funeral expenses, and expenses of administration from the residue of my estate, whether or not those expenses are attributable to property included in my probate estate.

Bequests

If you organize the will around the main concerns of your client, rather than starting with the clause on payments and funeral expenses, you will start with the clauses that cover your client's distribution of his or her property to named beneficiaries. These clauses usually include special bequests of particular property to certain individuals or organizations and a residuary clause that disposes of the remaining portion of the estate. When your client wants to make special bequests, draft them as specifically as possible when naming both the recipient and the bequest. For example, write

> **I bequeath to Sylvia Smith, Route #1, Box 470, Ashland, Missouri, my wedding rings, my inlaid turquoise ring, my turquoise pendant, and any artwork or handmade items created by me and in my possession at the time of my death.**

rather than

> I bequeath to Sylvia Smith all my jewelry and artwork or handmade items in my possession at the time of my death.

Providing an address assists the executor of the will in contacting the beneficiaries. Even if a beneficiary subsequently moves, the former address will help in locating that person.

59. Schwartz, *supra* note 37, at § 1102.

Additionally, the first example specifies the items that Sylvia Smith is to receive upon the testator's death. The second example does not specify which jewelry is bequeathed and does not specify that the artwork and handmade items bequeathed are only those that were made by the testator. This lack of specificity may cause problems for the executor when distributing the client's property. If you include specific items in the will, consider taking pictures of the items and incorporating them into the will to clarify their identification.

The bequest would be even clearer if the testator specified the artwork and handmade items that were bequeathed. Sometimes, this specificity is impossible because the testator wants to leave a category of items to the beneficiary and may not be certain that any specific items will be in her possession at the time of his or her death. One way to increase flexibility is to refer in the will to a list extrinsic to the will that includes bequests that may change over time.

When making special bequests, it is often helpful to state an alternative recipient or to clarify that the items become part of the residue of the estate in case the intended recipient does not survive the testator. When a recipient dies before the testator, the bequest will lapse, meaning that it becomes part of the residue unless the testator indicates a contrary intent or a controlling statute produces a different result.[60] Because these statutes may lead to results that conflict with your client's choices, you should always ask your client what his or her wishes are and carefully draft the appropriate clauses to effectuate those desires. Also be sure to ask what your client wants to have happen if the property contained in the bequest is sold prior to his or her death. Should the recipient receive money or other property equal to the value of the original bequest or should he or she receive nothing?

> I leave my Van Gogh painting to my niece Louise Howard if she survives me; if I no longer own the Van Gogh painting when I die, I leave Louise Howard $500,000. If my niece Louise Howard does not survive me, I leave my Van Gogh painting or the sum of $500,000 to my nephew Bill Howard if he survives me. If both my niece Louise Howard and my nephew Bill Howard do not survive me, my Van Gogh painting will become part of my residuary estate.

If your client makes several special bequests, you may want to include a general lapse clause in the will so that you would not have to repeat the last sentence in the example above for every bequest. The following clause handles all bequests and ensures that a beneficiary's heirs will not receive property that your client would prefer to have remain in his or her residuary estate.

---

60. Shaffer, *supra* note 6, at 91–92 and 185–86. Most anti-lapse statutes limit the alternate takers to the issue of the deceased beneficiary, although some are broader. Robert L. Mennell, *Wills and Trusts in a Nutshell* 123 (2d ed. 1994). For example, Maryland's statute substitutes the testate or intestate takers of the deceased beneficiary. These anti-lapse statutes come into play only if the testator does not specify his or her intention on what should happen if any bequest should lapse. *Id.* at 122.

If all the beneficiaries of any special bequest do not survive me, that bequest will become part of my residuary estate and be disposed of as stated in that clause.

Similarly, you must clarify how to distribute property to beneficiaries in a named class. For example, suppose your client wants to leave a piece of property to his brother Adam and his sister Betty's three children. Do Adam and Betty's children take the property on a per capita basis, where each receives one-fourth of the property, or on a per stirpes basis, where Adam receives half and Betty's children receive the other half in equal shares?[61] Be sure to recognize these questions and ambiguities when they arise, ask your client about his or her wishes, and resolve them when drafting.

Residuary clauses distribute the residue of the testator's estate, which is everything remaining in the estate after payment of all bequests, debts, expenses, and taxes.[62] Often residuary clauses contain a large amount of legalese and other unnecessary language.

> All the rest, residue and remainder of my estate, of whatsoever kind and nature, and wheresoever situate, of which I may be seized or possessed or to which I may be entitled at the time of my death, not hereby otherwise effectually disposed of, I give, devise, and bequeath absolutely and in fee simple, to my wife, _____. If my said wife _____ shall predecease me or if we shall die simultaneously, then and in that event, all the rest, residue, and remainder of my property, real and personal, and wheresoever situated, including all property over which I shall have a power of appointment, I give, devise, and bequeath absolutely and in fee simple, to my son, _____.

This clause could be rewritten to be more concise and clear while achieving the same result.

> **I give the rest of my estate to my wife, _____. If she dies first or simultaneously, I give the rest of my estate to my son, _____.**

It is unnecessary to list the property left in the estate, especially when the description is as broad as the one above. If your client wants to leave everything remaining in his or her estate to one or two people, that clause can be simple and straightforward, which will make it less susceptible to questions about its interpretation.

Disinheritance

If your client decides to disinherit an expected beneficiary, draft the disinheritance clause with special care. Disinheritance is an emotional issue and frequently results in challenges to the will. These challenges

---

61. Always check within your jurisdiction for how these terms of art are defined. Different states may define the terms differently and, even within one state, the definition may change depending on certain factual circumstances. Robert J. Lynn, *Introduction to Estate Planning in a Nutshell* § 2.17 (4th ed. 1992).

62. Hoops, *supra* note 1, at § 327.

are often based on the belief that disinheritance is ineffective unless the person disinherited receives $1 or other nominal consideration.[63] Except for the rights given to a surviving spouse, however, a testator may dispose of his or her property in any manner chosen.[64] Consider discussing any disinheritance carefully with your client; you may want to advise your client to avoid being cruel to his or her children, or other family members.[65]

If your client decides to proceed with the disinheritance, the best practice is to disinherit the person specifically by naming him or her in the will, rather than simply leaving the person out of the will completely. Otherwise, the person excluded may challenge the will, not believing that the testator would have intentionally excluded him or her. A specific clause clarifies the testator's intention, which can prevent the courts from resolving any ambiguity by including the individual due to judicial reluctance to uphold the disinheritance.[66]

Many testators also prefer to state the reasons for the disinheritance, perhaps hoping to soften the emotional feelings that may result. Rather than saying "I leave nothing to my sister Monica," the testator may want to say

Having made several gifts to my sister Monica during my lifetime, I make no provision for her in my will.

When stating the reason for disinheriting, be careful not to include reasons that may no longer exist at the time of the testator's death, for these may open the door for a challenge to the will.

I have made no provision under this Will for my husband, _____, because he is adequately provided for financially and is a joint tenant with me on our home and other assets.

If the husband loses his financial well-being between the time the will is executed and the wife dies, that could be cause to challenge the will. If the property that the spouses held in joint tenancy no longer exists, the husband would have reason to challenge the will and could be successful. He could easily argue that his wife's intent was to disinherit him only if those conditions remained true and, because they were no longer true, his wife could not have meant to disinherit him. In drafting these clauses, try to clarify what should happen if any of the conditions change.

As with contracts, jury instructions, and other documents, be careful not to copy clauses straight from form books, because most will undoubt-

---

63. *Id.* at § 318.

64. Most states impose restrictions on a spouse's ability to dispose of his or her property, and many require a statutory minimum to be granted to the surviving spouse. Shaffer, *supra* note 6, at 73–78. Community property states provide half of the community property of the couple to the surviving spouse, which is often more

generous than most states' elective shares. McGovern, *supra* note 1, at § 3.8. You must examine these statutes carefully to determine whether and to what extent your client may disinherit his or her spouse.

65. Shaffer, *supra* note 6, at 157.

66. Hoops, *supra* note 1, at § 318.

edly contain the legalese you are attempting to remove from your documents.

> I have in mind, but make no provision for my son, James, not because of any lack of affection for my said son, but because it is my belief that his welfare will be best served by the disposition herein made of my estate.[67]

Rewrite this clause as follows before including it in the will.

> **I have made no provision for my son James, not because of any lack of affection for him, but because his welfare is best served by this distribution of my estate.**

Some attorneys prefer to place the reasons for disinheritance in a collateral document outside the will, in the testator's own language and handwriting, so that no question arises about whether the intent and reasons for the disinheritance were the testator's, not the attorney's. This can be especially useful depending on the reason for the disinheritance, because a probated will is a matter of public record.

Guardianship

For clients with minor children, selecting guardians for their children in case both parents die is often the most important aspect of estate planning. Be sure to determine what your clients want to do with this important clause. While it may be fairly obvious to everyone that the surviving parent will be the children's guardian upon the testator's death, it is important that the client also name a successor guardian. Help your client think through this point carefully. Many may initially want to name the children's grandparents as successor guardians, but this may not be a wise choice. If the grandparents do not survive the testator, then the choice of successor will be fruitless. If they do survive but are elderly, then it is likely that they may die before the children reach maturity, which would force the children to cope with the loss of their caretakers once again.[68]

If feasible, have the testator name alternative guardians, in case the first choice cannot serve. Often people list multiple possible beneficiaries, multiple executors and trustees, and yet fail to provide a back-up plan for the care of their children. Especially if the testators have young children or children with special needs, a back-up plan is advisable. Also consider whether the guardian should be a different person than the trustee of any trust for the children. Often the person who would be the best choice for raising children differs from the person who would be best at managing the estate. Other questions about guardianship that you must resolve include how the guardianship should work, whether the guardian must post a bond, whether the guardian is also a trustee of funds for the children, and whether compensation should be provided.

---

67. *Id.*   **68.** *Id.* at § 330.

Again, avoid copying clauses appointing guardians directly from form books because they will rarely be worded as clearly as they could be.

> I hereby appoint my beloved wife, _____, guardian of the person and estate of my infant son, _____. In the event that my wife shall predecease me, or shall fail to qualify, shall resign or be removed, I appoint my friend, _____, guardian of the person and estate of my infant son, _____. It is my will and I direct that neither my said wife nor the aforesaid _____ shall be required to furnish any bond for the faithful performance of their offices as such guardian, any provision of law to contrary notwithstanding.[69]

Rewrite this clause to make it more readable by eliminating the legalese.

> **I appoint my wife, _____, as guardian of our son, _____. If she predeceases me or cannot serve, I appoint _____ as guardian. I direct that the guardian not be required to furnish any bond.**

It would also be wise to rewrite the clause to exclude naming the child needing guardianship. Adding the names simply raises problems if other children also survive the testator or if other children survive but the named child does not. It would be better practice to name the guardian of all surviving minor children and include a definition of children in the will. Some testators choose to handle guardianship matters in a separate letter incorporated into the will so they can change the letter without having to revise the will.

Wills With Trusts

Many clients want to establish a testamentary trust as part of their will, and some may request that you establish an *inter vivos* trust while they are still alive. Theoretically, trust documents are rather straightforward. They have two main purposes: they state the duties of the trustee, who is the person managing and controlling the trust's assets, and they state how the trustee is to distribute the assets or income from the assets to the named beneficiaries. They also identify the beneficiaries of the trust and the property that is included in the trust.

A trust is created when the owner of property separates the title of the property from the benefits of the property. Trusts are often developed to avoid some tax consequences at the testator's death or to allow for someone to control the assets when the testator considers the beneficiaries incapable of doing so. The trustee holds legal title to the assets in the trust, but has a fiduciary duty to control those assets and distribute them on behalf of the beneficiaries.

When writing a trust, first determine what property will be held in trust. All trusts must have a *res* or property that is placed in the trust, and you should describe this property specifically. Usually any interest in

69. *Id.*

property that is real or personal, legal or equitable, can be held in trust.[70] For pour-over trusts, which are created when testamentary transfers are made to an existing *inter vivos* trust, using the language "the residuary of my estate" is sufficient to define the *res*.[71]

Then name the trustee, state the trustee's powers, and explain the distribution of the trust. Although failure to name a trustee will not usually result in the trust failing, the testator probably wants to decide who has this important duty, rather than having the court appoint someone.[72] Besides naming the trustee, the trust should also name alternate and successor trustees. It is usually wise to have one of these be an institution, so you can be sure that a trustee will be named according to the client's wishes if the individual trustees do not serve.

As you focused on accuracy and readability when drafting your client's will, continue that focus when drafting a trust document. One way to make trust documents easier to understand is to write them in the first person, rather than in the traditional third person. When written in third person, the client often becomes confused over who is the grantor and who is the trustee.[73] You can increase both accuracy and readability by drafting the trust in the first person. For example, the agreement would begin as follows.

I, Rita Black, desire to create a trust and agree with the First National Bank of Homeville (my trustee) to the following.

Then write the remainder of the trust agreement with the client stating her directions directly to the trustee. Not only does this increase readability and accuracy for the client, it also provides consistency between the form of the will and that of the trust.[74]

Appointing the Executor and Trustee

In addition to appointing guardians, most wills also nominate executors, and all trusts appoint trustees. This appointment is equally as important as appointing a guardian for minor children. Although the executor's duties are broad, including administering the estate and distributing the assets to the beneficiaries, the trustee's duties are even more extensive and usually require significant discretion. Two provisions are needed when appointing executors and trustees: the first nominates the individuals or corporations to serve in those capacities and the second describes the fiduciary powers they have.

When naming the executor, many testators want to name a family member or friend without considering the person's ability to fulfill the fiduciary duties required of the position. You may need to raise this

70. *Id.* A simple expectancy, however, cannot be held in trust, and property sometimes cannot be transferred by the testator due to the manner in which title is held in the property. For example, property held in joint tenancy passes to the survivor and cannot be transferred by one joint tenant to a trust. *Id.*

71. *Id.*

72. *Id.*

73. Word Jr., *supra* note 49, at 480.

74. *Id.*

concern, tactfully, with your client. If your client is concerned about an individual's ability to perform but is also concerned that failure to name this individual will cause hard feelings, you may want to suggest naming co-executors or co-trustees, with a corporation nominated as the other fiduciary. This allows the individual, usually the surviving spouse or child(ren) to serve, while ensuring that someone with experience will be available to assist.[75]

It is also wise to name alternate executors or trustees, in case one or more of those named cannot serve. Frequently the alternate appointment is a corporation (which is usually limited by state law to banks and trust companies). This usually ensures that one of those named in the will or trust will, in fact, survive the testator. When appointing a corporation, the testator should realize that the individuals whom he or she believes will handle the estate or trust may no longer be working in that capacity when the will or trust come into effect. Thus, the testator should focus on the qualifications of the institution in making the choice, not on the individual who may currently be serving that function. Whenever choosing trustees, you need to make sure that your jurisdiction allows them to serve. Some states may restrict executors or trustees to persons domiciled or corporations doing business in that state.[76]

Be careful about placing any one person in two different roles. For example, a testator's desire to protect a beneficiary from wasting his or her inheritance will be defeated if that person is also named the trustee. A guardian of minor children has greater opportunity to misuse the children's funds if that person is also the trustee. In a contentious family, the beneficiary who is also personal representative may be maligned by disgruntled beneficiaries for the way he or she executes the estate. This is not to say you must never place a person in multiple roles, but to ensure that you do so carefully.

Form clauses appointing executors and trustees are usually filled with legalese, so they need to be redrafted to increase readability.

> I hereby nominate, constitute and appoint as Executors and Trustees of this, my last Will, my beloved husband _____. In the event that my husband shall decline to act, or shall predecease me, or for any cause whatever shall cease or fail to act, then I nominate, constitute and appoint the Fiduciary Trust Company, New York, New York, as Executor and Trustee of my said will, in the place and stead of any one of the persons first named herein. It is my will and I direct that my Executors and Trustees, and their successors, shall not be required to furnish a bond for the faithful performance of their duties in any jurisdiction, any provision of law to the contrary notwithstanding.

The following clause is shorter and much easier to understand than the first, while providing the same direction to those probating the will and trust.

75. Hoops, *supra* note 1, at § 336.   **76.** *Id.*

> I nominate my husband, _____, to serve as my executor and trustee, if living; if he does not so serve, I nominate the Fiduciary Trust Company, New York, New York, as executor and trustee of my will. I request that a bond, as set by law, not be required for any Executor or Trustee named in this will.[77]

The second set of clauses concerning executors and trustees delineates the executor's or trustee's duties. Start by conferring with your client to determine how expansively to grant the powers. Oftentimes, the testator recognizes that the executor or trustee needs flexibility and discretion to make decisions that are most favorable for the estate. The purpose of the extensive powers granted in wills and trusts is to allow for this flexibility. In deciding which powers to grant to the executor or trustee, you should determine which powers are granted under a fiduciaries' powers act in your jurisdiction. In states with statutes delineating the executor's or trustee's powers, you can incorporate the statutory language by reference, thereby giving the executor or trustee all the powers permissible by law. Explicit grants of power will override statutory restrictions, unless the statute or court rule expressly prohibits the specific power granted.[78]

When considering which powers to include, review the testator's assets and determine what decisions and actions will likely need to be made in administering the will or trust. Simple wills may not require an extensive listing of the fiduciaries' powers. In those cases, you will not need to include all the boiler-plate clauses that are found in form or practice books.[79]

When revising to eliminate legalese, also revise these clauses so they accurately describe the powers that are applicable in your client's situation. If your client wants to grant his or her executor or trustee the fullest range of powers, it is possible to eliminate pages of descriptions of powers and to include a clause providing expansive powers.

> I confer upon my trustee the authority to do and perform any act that she determines is in the best interest of my trust, with no limitations.

While many clients may be uncomfortable with granting these unlimited powers, especially in terms of a trustee's duties, many clients are content to grant fairly extensive powers.[80] Take care not to limit the

---

77. Consider discussing with your client whether to require a bond from the corporate executor or trustee, even if he or she does not want to require a bond from the individual.

78. *Id.*

79. For example, Hoops includes 5 pages of clauses describing fiduciaries' duties. *Id.* at § 338. He also provides a checklist that delineates the powers contained in each clause so that you can easily check which clauses to use depending on the powers to be granted. *Id.*

80. Additionally, some attorneys have concerns that a clause this simple may cause objections from institutions with which the executor or trustee must work because they are used to finding an explicit listing of powers.

fiduciary unduly, because he or she was selected due to the testator's trust in his or her judgment.

Testimonium Clause

The testimonium clause threatens to pull legalese and ponderous language back into wills.

> IN WITNESS WHEREOF, I the undersigned testator, have on this 20th day of January 20__, signed and sealed, published, and declared the foregoing instrument as and for, my Last Will.

Even the short "In witness whereof, I have hereunto set my hand this 20th day of January 20__" is unnecessary. Wills are not set aside because the signature is not preceded by this "fairy dust."[81] It is useful to include the date at the end of the will to help ensure which will is the most recent version. Use either "Dated this 20th day of January 20__" or "I sign my name to this will on January 20, 20__" instead of the clause above. Just as you began the will without the legalese usually found in the opening clause, end it in the same way.

Attestation Clause

Following the testimonium clause comes the attestation clause. The attestation clause is not part of the will and is not technically required for its validity, unless required by statute.[82] Once the testator's and witnesses' handwriting are established, most jurisdictions presume that the will was executed in the manner required.[83] The attestation clause, however, states that all the formalities required to admit the will to probate were performed. Thus, the clause may prevent the will's rejection if the witnesses cannot remember whether each formality was performed and has become standard in virtually all wills.[84]

> The foregoing instrument, consisting of twenty (20) pages, was on the 20th day of January 20__, signed and sealed at the end thereof and at the same time published and declared by Herbert Johnson, the above named testator, as and for his Last Will in the presence of each of us, who, this attestation clause having been first read to us, did at the request of the said testator, in his presence and in the presence of each other, sign our names as witnesses thereto.

Eliminate legalese from this clause as well.

This will was signed by Herbert Johnson, who in our presence stated it was his last will. Having read this attestation

---

81.   Cooper, *supra* note 54, at 344 (quoting Arensberg, *The Language of Wills,* 21 Pa.B.A.Q. 116 (1950)).

82.   Hoops, *supra* note 1, at § 341. No state's statute requires the use of an attestation clause. The requirement of due execution can be satisfied by having the witnesses sign below the testator's signature as "witness." An attestation clause is very important, however, because it states a pri-ma facie case that the will was duly executed and may thus be admitted to probate, even though the witnesses predecease the testator or cannot recall the events of execution. Dukeminier and Johnson, *Wills, Trusts, and Estates* 244–45 n.12 (6th ed. 2000).

83.   Hoops, *supra* note 1, at § 341.

84.   McGovern, *supra* note 1, at § 4.3.

clause, we sign as witnesses, at his request, in his presence, and the presence of each other.

The witnesses should sign and print their names and provide their addresses so that they may be easily contacted if needed. When choosing witnesses, it is useful to choose those who are younger than the testator. Additionally, the witnesses should not be beneficiaries under the will, so that no question of undue influence or duress arises.[85] Whenever possible, use three witnesses because some states require that number.[86]

Many attorneys add a self-proving affidavit at the end of the will. These affidavits allow the will to be admitted to probate on the basis of the affidavit without needing to bring the witnesses into court to testify that the requirements for the will to be admitted to probate were met.[87] Some confusion has resulted, however, on whether the witnesses must sign both the attestation clause and the self-proving affidavit. The technically correct form is for the testator to sign the will, the witnesses to sign the attestation clause, and then for all of them to sign the self-proving affidavit, which is then notarized.[88] An example of a self-proving affidavit follows.

I, _____, the testator, being duly sworn, signed this instrument willingly, executed it voluntarily, and am over eighteen years of age, of sound mind, and under no constraint or undue influence.

_____

Testator

We, _____, _____, and _____, the witnesses, being duly sworn, declare that the testator signed this instrument willingly. Each of us, in the presence and hearing of the testator and each other, signed this will as witnesses, and to the best of our knowledge, the testator is over eighteen years of age, of sound mind, and under no constraint or undue influence.

_____

Witness

_____

Witness

_____

Witness

85. Many states have statutes requiring that witnesses be disinterested. Even if not required, using disinterested witnesses will help prevent challenges to the will. Shaffer, *supra* note 6, at 81. Additionally, some cases contain dicta saying that, when the lawyer who drafted the will is a witness to the will, the attorney-client privilege for communications between the testator and the attorney is lost. This provides another reason for attorneys to avoid serving as witnesses. *Id.* at 198.

86. *Id.* at 80–81.

87. McGovern, *supra* note 1, at § 4.3.

88. Shaffer, *supra* note 6, at 41.

When executing wills, it is a good idea to develop a procedure and follow it exactly. This may require you to develop a checklist to ensure that you take each necessary step, and keep a record that these steps were followed.[89] Doing this will allow you to testify in court that you performed all the steps on your checklist, even though you may not recall that particular will execution.

This chapter has outlined many of the standard clauses that are included in most wills. However, other clauses are frequently necessary to address the client's needs and the complexity of his or her estate plan. When drafting those clauses, keep in mind the goals of accuracy and readability. Doing so will ensure that you provide the best possible assistance to your client.

Challenges to the Will

When drafting, you must anticipate the possibility of challenges to the will. For example, suppose your client has a new wife and family and wants to disinherit his children from an earlier marriage. Those children may try to challenge whether your client was incompetent or under duress when making the will. Or suppose your client is a single person who wants to leave her property to her unmarried partner and wants to avoid challenges by her family. In these situations, you need to create a paper trail that will show that the testator was competent and not under duress when making the will.

One way to create this paper trail is to ask the client to write to you before the initial interview, setting out his or her desires and specifying the beneficiaries under the will. Then you can send a letter to the client repeating those desires and setting up the initial interview. After drafting the document, mail it to the client asking whether it states his or her desires. The client can respond by mail. Then when the will is signed, you can ask these questions again. A few weeks or months after the execution, ask the client to write you, thanking you for drafting the will to conform to his or her desires. This will give you a paper trail over several months that establishes that the will does state the desires of your client. This paper trail, when shown to the plaintiffs upon receipt of their initial complaint, will often result in them voluntarily dismissing the complaint. Although this may seem to be considerable work, attorneys in this area realize that litigation means drafting failure and that avoiding litigation is one of the most important of your roles in will drafting. This technique may be useful in any situation when the document does something non-standard, such as disinherit someone.

You may also want to have "an especially stern, *protective* execution" of the will if you anticipate that someone may challenge the will.[90] This may include having a protective will execution conference, where you make sure that all formalities are carefully met and documented,

---

89. For an example of a checklist, *see* Hoops, *supra* note 1, at § 342.

90. Shaffer, *supra* note 6, at 82.

and you may want to have the conference videotaped or use a court reporter.[91]

CONCLUSION

Drafting a will, with or without a trust, calls for your understanding of the interrelationship of statutory law, tax law, and property doctrines. It also requires carefully interviewing your clients and determining their wishes. Having determined those wishes, your job is to draft documents that accurately reflect your clients' wishes while remaining readable by them and others who must use the documents. By focusing on accuracy and readability, you can transform these documents from ones that are confusing and even frightening for your clients into ones that allow them to feel comfortable with the steps they have taken to protect their property's disposition upon their deaths.

Exercise 1

Go to the library and find two examples, in form books, of the following clauses and make copies of those clauses. Then select two to revise according to the techniques suggested in this chapter.

- A specific gift/bequest with a lapse clause (used when the named beneficiary does not survive the testator or accept the gift/bequest);
- Appointment of a personal representative or executor with alternates;
- Appointment of guardians for children with alternates;
- Powers for a personal representative or trustee with alternates;
- A bypass trust (credit shelter trust) for benefit of spouse (if this is lengthy, just select two or three paragraphs to copy and revise);
- A disinheritance clause;
- A spendthrift trust (again if this is lengthy, just select two or three paragraphs); and
- An attestation clause.

Exercise 2

This exercise allows you to practice interviewing a client who wants to have his or her will drafted. Each of you will select one of the two clients below and take turns being both the client and the attorney. After you have collected the necessary information, draft the three clauses that you believe are most important to your client.

Client 1

You are Jared LeBoeff, a drummer in the heavy metal group "Carnage." You are now turning 40 and thought you should have a will. You have a vintage Rolls Royce (which you own outright), a house in Malibu, California (mortgaged), a few mutual funds worth a substantial

---

91. *Id.*

amount (select any amount), and some stock in a recording studio (select the label). You have never been married and have no children (as far as you know). You were using drugs and were pretty wild in your early years with the band, and are not sure whether there are any children. Now that you are sober, you want to provide for any children, but only if they can prove your paternity using DNA tests. If you have no children, then you want to leave your estate to some charity that you like (select one yourself).

Client 2

You are Sandra Martinez, a securities dealer in the Midwest and a single mother. You are concerned how to best provide for your disabled son, Luke, who is autistic. Because of his condition, he will need care and assistance for the rest of his life. You want to make sure that you have the right people selected to be his guardians (select two or three people you want to name). You also are concerned about making sure that you leave your property, which is significant, in trust for your son's guardians to use on his behalf. You are concerned about not placing too many restrictions on the guardian's powers because you know that your son has often achieved a lot of success using numerous different therapies and learning opportunities, and you want to make sure that his guardian can remain flexible in providing for his care. But you also want to prevent excessive use of the resources you have because you know they need to last through all of Luke's life.

Assignment 1

You have just started working for a law firm that is quite successful in Oklahoma. Although the firm's main practice area is business and employment law, a few of the partners in the firm handle estate planning for the firm's clients as well as referrals. The partner you work for has given you the following portions of her standard will and asked you to revise them. (She noticed your resume lists taking this class and is eager to use your writing expertise.) While there are substantive revisions that you may want to make in the will, primarily focus on formatting, organization, and language to make the will more readable by the firm's clients.

LAST WILL AND TESTAMENT

OF

NAME

I, NAME, of CITY, Okmulgee County, Oklahoma, being of sound mind and disposing memory, do hereby make, publish, and declare this to be my Last Will and Testament and do hereby revoke all wills and codicils at anytime heretofore made by me.

ARTICLE I.

DEBTS, FUNERAL EXPENSES, AND TAXES

I direct my Executor to pay from my estate as soon as practicable after my death all of my debts, funeral expenses, and costs of administration; provided, however, that my Executor shall not be hereby required to pay any secured indebtedness on property passing by reason of my death, it being my intention that any successor in title to such property shall take it subject to any liens existing at my death. All transfer, estate, inheritance, succession and other death taxes which shall become payable by reason of my death shall be paid out of that portion of my estate not elected as a marital deduction gift under Article III below as an administration expense, without apportionment, if and to the extent that the same are imposed (a) in respect of property owned by me and passing under this Will, and, if my wife survives me, and (b) in respect of any other property which is included in the computation of such taxes and whose value is allowed as a marital deduction in the federal estate tax proceeding relating to my estate. All such taxes in respect of any other property shall be apportioned against and paid by the persons in possession thereof or benefited thereby, in the manner provided by law.

I direct that any incremental increase in transfer, estate, inheritance, succession and other death taxes which become payable in the estate of my wife, WIFE, (hereinafter sometimes referred to as "my wife"), if she shall survive me, by reason of any election by my Executor of all or any portion of the assets of the Qualified Terminable Interest Trust as a marital deduction gift to my wife shall be paid out of the assets of such trust by my Trustee on the death of my wife to the Executor of the estate of my wife, unless my wife shall direct otherwise in her Will. Further, upon the transfer by my wife of any of the trust assets pursuant to Section 2519 of the Internal Revenue Code, my Trustee shall pay from the principal of such Qualified Terminable Interest Trust all gift taxes occasioned by the application of Section 2519.

ARTICLE II

TANGIBLE PERSONAL PROPERTY

I bequeath in fee simple to my wife, if she shall survive me, all of my tangible personal property and effects which I own at my death. I make no disposition of the furniture, fixtures, and furnishings in our home, as my wife owns all of them. If my wife shall predecease me, then all of my tangible personal property and effects which I own at my death shall pass in fee simple, per stirpes and free of trust, to those of my said issue who shall survive me, or if none of my said issue shall survive me, this bequest shall lapse and the property which would have passed hereunder shall become a part of my residuary estate hereinafter disposed of.

ARTICLE III

RESIDUARY ESTATE

All of the rest, residue, and remainder of the property which I own or have the right to dispose of at my death, whether real, personal or mixed, tangible or intangible, of whatsoever nature and wheresoever situated, including all lapsed legacies and devises and any property over or concerning which I may have any power of appointment, all of which property is herein referred to as my "residuary estate," I give, bequeath, devise, and appoint as follows: if my wife shall survive me, I hereby give, devise, bequeath, and appoint my residuary estate in trust to my trustee as the corpus of a trust (hereinafter called QUALIFIED TERMINABLE INTEREST TRUST) which shall be held, administered, and distributed by trustee upon the trusts, terms, and conditions set forth in this Article; if my wife shall predecease me, then I give, bequeath, devise, and appoint my residuary estate as provided in this Article.

Whenever any payment or distribution is required to be made from my estate or upon the termination of any trust established hereunder pursuant to the provisions of this Article, such payment or distribution shall be made per stirpes and in fee simple (subject to the provisions of this Article) to those of my issue then living.

Whenever any payment hereunder is required to be made from my estate or upon the termination of any trust established hereunder to any issue of any child of mine who is under the age of 21 years at such time, the interest so required to be paid shall be indefeasibly vested in such beneficiary but the Trustee may retain the amount payable until the beneficiary attains 21 or dies, whichever first occurs, and the Trustee may pay the income and corpus to such beneficiary in such amount or amounts and from time to time as it may determine is needed for such beneficiary's support, maintenance, and health, and if such beneficiary lives to attain 21, then when he so attains 21 the Trustee shall pay the then remaining corpus and the undistributed income to him, and if such beneficiary dies before attaining 21, then on such beneficiary's death the Trustee shall pay the then remaining corpus and undistributed income to such beneficiary's estate. During the minority or incapacity of any beneficiary to or from whom income or corpus is authorized or directed to be paid, my Executor or Trustee may pay, transfer, or assign same in any one or more of the following ways: directly to such beneficiary such amount as it may deem advisable as an allowance; to the guardian of the person or of the property of such beneficiary; to a relative of such beneficiary upon the agreement of such relative to expend such income or corpus solely for the benefit of the beneficiary; by expending such income or corpus directly for the education, maintenance or support of such beneficiary. My Executor or Trustee shall have the power in its uncontrolled discretion to determine whether a beneficiary is incapacitated, and its determination shall be conclusive. For all purposes of this Will and the disposition of my estate hereunder, the terms "children," "issue," or "descendants" shall be deemed to include persons adopted prior to attaining 18 years of age.

ARTICLE IV

FIDUCIARIES

I make, nominate and appoint my wife as my Executor and I direct that she shall qualify and serve as such without surety upon her official bond. If my wife shall fail to qualify or cease to serve in such capacity, I make, nominate, and appoint as alternate or successor Executor, as the case may be, ALTERNATE EXECUTOR. I make, nominate and appoint TRUSTEE as Trustee. If he shall fail to qualify or cease to serve in such capacity, I make, nominate, and appoint as alternate or successor Trustee, as the case may be, ALTERNATE TRUSTEE. I direct that all of the above persons shall qualify in the above capacities without surety upon their respective official bonds.

I grant my Executor and Trustee (including any substitute or successor personal representative) the continuing, absolute, discretionary power to deal with any property, real or personal, held in my estate as freely as I might be in the handling of my own affairs. Such power may be exercised independently and without the prior or subsequent approval of any court or judicial authority, and no person dealing with the Executor or Trustee shall be required to inquire into the propriety of any of my Executor's or Trustee's actions.

. . .

Any Trustee of any trust established hereunder may resign at any time by giving sixty (60) days prior written notice of its intention to do so to the beneficiaries then receiving or entitled to receive the income from such trust. If any such beneficiary is then a minor, notice to such beneficiary shall be directed to his statutory guardian, or if a statutory guardian has not been appointed, notice shall be directed to the person or persons then having the care, custody, nurture, and control of such beneficiary. Upon receipt of such notice, the alternate or successor Trustee in the above order of alternation or succession shall qualify as successor Trustee. If the alternate Trustee or Trustees set forth hereinabove shall fail to qualify or cease to serve in such capacities, a majority in beneficial interest of all trust beneficiaries then receiving or entitled to receive the income from the trust to which any resignation is referable may nominate to a court of competent jurisdiction, or, if legally possible, may appoint, as successor Trustee hereunder, any bank or trust company having a capital and surplus of no less than $10,000,000 and authorized to administer trusts. If any such beneficiary is then a minor, he shall act through his statutory guardian, or if a statutory guardian has not been appointed, he shall act through the person or persons then having his care, custody, nurture and control. If my wife shall survive me, then after my death and while she lives, she may at any time and from time to time by prior written notice delivered to the Trustee, remove the Trustee and nominate to a court of competent jurisdiction, or, if legally possible, may appoint as successor Trustee, the successor Trustee as hereinabove set forth, or if such successor Trustee shall fail to qualify or cease to serve in such capacity, any bank or trust company having a capital and surplus of no less than $10,000,000 and authorized to administer trusts. The notice shall state a future date at which time it shall be effective.

ARTICLE V

MISCELLANEOUS

If my wife and I shall die under such circumstances that it is doubtful which of us survived the other, then it shall be presumed that she survived me and my estate shall be accordingly administered.

No beneficiary of any trust established hereunder shall have any right or power to anticipate, pledge, assign, sell, transfer, or alienate (by operation of law, legal process or otherwise) or encumber his or her interest (in income or principal) in any trust, in any way; nor shall any such interest in any manner be liable for or subject to the debts, liabilities or obligations of such beneficiary or claims of any sort against such beneficiary.

Whenever the context hereof so permits or requires, the singular of any word shall include the plural, the plural shall include the singular and any gender shall include all other genders.

IN TESTIMONY WHEREOF, I subscribe my name to this my Last Will and Testament, this ___ day of _____, 20__. _____

NAME

We certify that the foregoing instrument of writing was this day produced before us by NAME who signed it in our presence and declared it to be his Last Will and Testament, and we, in the presence of the testator, and at his request and in the presence of each other, do subscribe our names hereto as attesting witnesses, this ___ day of _____, 20__.

residing at _____

residing at _____

residing at _____

STATE OF OKLAHOMA)
) SCT.
COUNTY OF OKMULGEE)

Before me, the undersigned authority, on this day personally appeared NAME, known to me to be the testator, whose signature appears at the end of the attached instrument dated _____, 20__, and _____, _____ and _____ known to me to be the witnesses whose names are signed to said attached instrument, and all of said persons being by me first duly sworn, NAME, the testator, declared and acknowledged to me and to the witnesses in my presence that said instrument is his last will and that he had willingly executed it as his free and voluntary act for the purposes therein expressed; and said witnesses stated to me, in the presence and hearing of said testator, and in the presence and hearing of each other, that each of them signed said will as witness, and that to the best of their knowledge, at the time of the execution of said will, the testator was eighteen years of age or over, of sound mind, and under no constraint or undue influence.

Testator

Witness

Witness

Witness

Subscribed, sworn to and acknowledged before me by NAME, the testator, and subscribed and sworn to before me by _____, _____, and _____, the witnesses, this ___ day of _____, 20_.

My Commission expires: _____

NOTARY PUBLIC, STATE AT LARGE, OKLAHOMA

Assignment 2

You are the attorney for Jim and Kate Putnam. The lengthy legal proceedings surrounding their daughter's death have now been resolved and they received $15 million dollars from the defendants. They now are concerned about preparing a will. They want you to draft a will for them, without a trust (very unusual for clients with this large an estate but they are tired of legal complexities and want a very simple will). They want to leave everything to two of their three children, who are all over 21, but want to disinherit their other child who was opposed to their lawsuit against the hospital and who criticized them for suing and not just getting on with their lives. They also want to leave $50,000 to Jane Evans, the nurse who cared for their daughter while she was in the hospital and who was very kind to them throughout all their battles with the hospital. You need to name an executor for the will, and draft a testimonium clause and an attestation clause also. When drafting the will, focus on making it as accurate and readable as possible. For background facts and law, see assignment 2 in Chapter 4.

BIBLIOGRAPHY

Baker, David A. and Kathleen O'Hagen Scallan, *Construction, Reformation and Modification of Wills and Trusts*, Ill. Inst. CLE Handbook on Estate, Trust and Guardianship Litigation 12.1–12.5 (Dec. 2001).

Barkhorn, Karin J., *Basic Will Drafting*. New York: Practising Law Institute, 2001.

Bell, Erica, chair, *Basic Estate Planning*. New York: Practising Law Institute, 2001.

Byrne, Michael John, *Note: Let Truth Be Their Devise*, 73 N.C.L.Rev. 2209 (1995).

California Continuing Education of the Bar, *How to Draft Wills*. 1985.

Case, Stephen S., *What You Need to Know about Joint Tenancy*, 3 ALI–ABA Estate Planning Course Materials J. 29 (June 1997).

Cooper, Frank E., *Writing in Law Practice*. Indianapolis: Bobb–Merrill Co., 2d ed.1963.

Cusack, Lawrence X., *The Blue–Pencilled Will: What's Wrong With a Will in Plain English?*, 118 Trusts and Estates 33 (Aug. 1979).

Dukeminier, Jesse and Stanley M. Johanson, *Wills, Trusts, and Estates*. New York: Aspen Law & Business, 6th ed. 2000.

Feldman, Leon, *"Simple Will" Can Be Simplified Further to Produce a More Concise But Effective Document*, 10 Est.Plan. 290 (Sept. 1983).

Fogel, Bradley E.S., *Attorney v. Client: Privity, Malpractice, and the Lack of Respect for the Primacy of the Attorney–Client Relationship in Estate Planning*, 68 Tenn.L.Rev. 261 (2001).

Grether, Henry M., *The Little Horribles of a Scrivener*, 39 Neb.L.R. 296 (1960).

Groppe, Charles J., *Ethical Considerations in Basic Will Drafting*, New York: Practising Law Institute, 2001.

Henry, J. Gordon, *How Not to Draft Wills and Trusts–Common Drafting Errors to Avoid*, 5 Notre Dame Est.Plan. 841 (1980).

Hoops, Frederick K., *Family Estate Planning Guide*. New York: The Lawyers Co–Operative Publishing Co., 3d ed. 1982.

Horn, Jerold I., *Estate Planning and Drafting for the Economic Growth and Tax Relief Reconciliation Act of 2001*, 7 ALI–ABA Estate Planning Course Materials J. 33 (Dec. 2001).

Hunt, L. Rush, *A Lawyer's Guide to Estate Planning, Fundamentals for the Legal Practitioner*. Chicago: American Bar Association, 2d ed. 1998.

Johanson, Stanley M., *The Orphan's Deduction: How to Handle a Troublesome Drafting Problem*, 14 Inst. on Est.Plan. 1505 (1980).

Johnston, Gerald P., *Legal Malpractice in Estate Planning and General Practice*, 17 Memp.S.U.L.Rev. 521 (Summer 1987).

Joslyn, Robert B., *Use of Plain English in Drafting Wills and Trusts*, 63 Mich.Bar J. 612 (July 1984).

Laurino, Louis D., *Avoiding Will Construction Problems*, 11 A.L.I.-A.B.A Estate Planning Course Materials J. 83 (1987).

Lynn, Robert J., *Introduction to Estate Planning in a Nutshell*. St. Paul: West Group, 4th ed. (1992).

Mann, Bruce H., *Self-Proving Affidavits and Formalism in Wills Adjudication*, 63 Wash.U.L.Q. 39 (1985).

McGovern, William M., Jr., Sheldon F. Kurtz, and Jan Ellen Rein, *Wills, Trusts, and Estates Including Taxation and Future Interests*. St. Paul: West Group, 2d ed. 2001.

Mennell, Robert L., *Wills and Trusts in a Nutshell*. St. Paul: West Group, 2d ed. 1994.

Mirow, M.C. and Burce A. McGovern, *An Obituary of the Federal Estate Tax*, 43 Ariz.L.Rev. 625 (2001).

Ramos, Manuel R., *Legal Malpractice: The Profession's Dirty Little Secret*, 47 Vand.L.Rev. 1657 (1994).

Restatement (Second) of Property, Donative Transfers. Philadelphia: American Law Institute, 1990.

Roth, Randall W., *Current Ethical Problems in Estate Planning*, 6 ALI–ABA Estate Planning Course Materials Journal 33 (2000).

Rubenstein, Neil J., *Attorney Malpractice in California: The Liability of a Lawyer Who Drafts an Imprecise Contract or Will*, 24 U.C.L.A.L.Rev. 422 (1976).

Schlesinger, Edward S., *English as a Second Language for Lawyers*, 12 Inst. on Est.Plan. 700 (1978).

Schwartz, William, *Sins of Omission and Commission in the Drafting of Wills and Trusts*, 11 Inst. on Est.Plan. § 1100 (1979).

Shaffer, Thomas L., Carol Ann Mooney, and Mary Jo Boettcher, *The Planning and Drafting of Wills and Trusts.* New York: Foundation Press, 4th ed. 2001.

Spankling, John D., *Understanding Property Law.* New York: Matthew Bender & Co., 2000.

Squires, Lynn B. and Robert S. Mucklestone Inc., *A Simple "Simple" Will*, 57 Wash.L.Rev. 461 (1982).

Temple, Diane Hastings, *Estate Planning for the Non–Traditional Family*, 31st Annual Estate Planning Institute 1145 (2000).

Wilkins, Robert P., *Drafting Wills and Trust Agreements.* St. Paul: West Group, 3d ed. 2001.

Word, Thomas S., Jr., *A Brief for Plain English Wills and Trusts*, 14 U.Rich.L.Rev. 471 (1980).

Zaritsky, Howard M., *How Estate Tax "Repeal" Will Affect Your Estate Planning Practice*, 7 ALI–ABA Estate Planning Course Materials J. 5 (Oct. 2001).

Chapter 17

SCHOLARLY ARTICLES AND OTHER RESEARCH PAPERS

The previous chapters of this book have led you from discovering your writing process through refining, altering, and strengthening that process, as you have learned to draft the various documents discussed in each chapter. This chapter now turns to applying your writing process to a major research paper or scholarly document. In many respects, writing research papers is similar to the other writing tasks you have already learned. The difference that you will be applying not just some, but all, of the writing techniques you have learned.

Research papers take numerous forms. For example, you may write a research paper for a seminar, a note or comment for the law review, a research memorandum for a trial practice course, or a brief for an appellate advocacy course. Once in practice, you may write similar documents, such as an interoffice memorandum deciding whether your firm should pursue a client's case, a memorandum of points and authorities urging a trial court to grant the preliminary motions you made, or an appellate brief urging a court to affirm or reverse the lower court's decision.

Whatever form your document takes, this chapter shows you the writing tasks required to draft an excellent research paper. It addresses these tasks as they arise within the six steps that we have had students complete when drafting their project papers for our advanced legal writing seminar.[1] While you may not write out each step in your own process, you must address all of the tasks to succeed in your writing.

These six steps are

- the initial proposal,

---

1. For a fuller description of this seminar, *see*, Barbara J. Cox and Mary Barnard Ray, *Getting Dorothy Out of Kansas: The Importance of an Advanced Component to Legal Writing Programs*, 40 J. Legal Ed. 351 (1990). For a focused text on scholarly articles, *see*, Elizabeth Fajans.and Mary R. Falk, *Scholarly Writing for Law Students* (2d ed. 2000).

- the progress report,
- the outline or rough draft,
- the complete draft,
- the good draft, and
- the final draft.

Dividing the writing into these steps makes even a large writing project more manageable. It also makes it easier for you to plan ahead and budget your time well.

THE INITIAL PROPOSAL

The initial proposal should state your precise issue, the type of document you plan to draft, and any questions you may have before proceeding. Even if only for your own use, this last element is helpful. If read by your professor or supervisor, the specificity and clarity in this proposal will provide an opportunity for him or her to steer you in a specific direction or to identify problems with the proposal, so you may address them now.

In this proposal, determine the topic and complete the background research needed. In an upper-division seminar, a professor often assigns you a topic. A senior partner may provide you with a memo to the file made after a client interview, stating the relevant facts and presenting issues for you to research. In these cases, you will not be given a choice in selecting your topic but you may need to clarify the topic or narrow its focus.

In other situations, you may be given a list of topics from which to choose or may be told to select any topic corresponding to the relevant course. You may be choosing a topic on which to write a law review article, competition paper, or conference paper. In these cases, your initial proposal encompasses choosing and developing your topic.

Topic selection itself often requires some background research before undertaking further substantive research. At this stage, you are simply doing the preliminary work necessary to decide whether your ideas are feasible. For example, if you are writing a law review article or a competition or conference paper, you want to write a paper that is different from those already published. In these situations, survey the literature to make sure your topic has not been pre-empted. Often you must narrow the issues to find a niche between previous papers. If you are writing an office memo or a brief in support of your client, complete preliminary research to determine how others have handled this issue previously. In either situation, this preliminary research allows you to determine your initial focus for researching and drafting and to become confident in your choice of topics.

If you are writing your initial proposal for another's review, describe your topic explicitly. Obtaining this focus permits you to spend less time doing irrelevant research. If you have a choice, next determine the type of document you will be writing. Having the type of document in mind allows you to be more selective in your research tools. For example, if you are writing an appellate brief to the Montana Supreme Court, you will focus your research on Montana law and, perhaps, law from neighboring states. But if you were writing about the same issues in a law review article, you would have to expand your research to consider how all courts have handled those issues, even if your article will ultimately focus on how you think Montana courts should handle the issue.

Part of planning the research will be recognizing your audience. Different readers have different needs, and one of the jobs of the initial proposal is to determine those needs and alter your focus to meet them.[2] Using the example above, if you were drafting an appellate brief to the Montana Supreme Court, you would focus on presenting the relevant facts and prior precedent, making an argument in support of your client, and addressing policy concerns the court may need to resolve when making its decision. If you were drafting a law review article, you would focus on presenting the issue you are addressing, providing the legal context for the issue, raising the problem you are addressing, and resolving that problem.

THE PROGRESS REPORT

After making your initial proposal, focus the issue further, complete the research, and resolve any problems that arise.[3] The progress report summarizes this process. Even if you do not write a progress report for your reader, you may find it helpful to monitor your progress so you remain focused. Monitoring helps you set and meet interim deadlines so you can meet the final deadline without cutting short the last steps in the process.

A progress report facilitates conversation with your professor or supervisor after you have completed your research and before you begin drafting. When writing a progress report for another reader, explain your progress specifically enough so the reader can help you. State your issue, summarize your research to date, and explain what you plan to do next. Mention any concerns that you have, so the reader can advise you. Even if you do not write a progress report, sketch out the information and then confer with your supervisor. Discussing your ideas with someone after having completed your research and before beginning to draft

---

2. For more on determining your reader's needs, see Chapter 9 on Discussion Sections of Memos.

3. We will not be discussing the various research tools in the law library and how to use them. There are numerous excellent books available that provide this information. *See,* Christopher Wren and Jill Wren, *The Legal Research Manual: A Game Plan for Legal Research And Analysis* (2d ed. 1999); J. Myron Jacobstein, Roy Mersky, and Donald J. Dunn, *Fundamentals of Legal Research* (6th ed. 1994); Christina Kunz, Deborah A. Schmedemann, Matthew P. Downs, and Ann L. Bateson, *The Process of Legal Research: Successful Strategies* (5th ed. 2000). Additionally, these books, as well as others, also provide assistance in developing your research strategies. Two helpful sources are Mary Ray and Jill Ramsfield, *Getting It Right and Getting It Written* 308–16 (3rd ed. 2000) and Helene Shapo, Marilyn Walter, and Elizabeth Fajans, *Writing and Analysis in the Law* 131–143 (4th ed. 1999).

allows you to obtain help in deciding how to proceed. If you discover that the result you had originally intended is not feasible, you can alter your plans before you become resistant to changing them.

As part of this report, revise your issue or thesis. You will have completed the majority of your research by this point, and it is likely that the issue you stated in the initial proposal will have changed. When you draft the initial proposal, you often cannot anticipate the direction your research will lead. While doing your research, remain flexible enough to vary your ideas and make alterations, or you may find you are forcing your research to fulfill your initial ideas, which may limit your objectivity.

Even if you plan to write a persuasive paper, conduct your research as objectively as possible. Many attorneys find it useful to research as though they were trying to reach the result opposite the one planned. This pushes you to consider all the possibilities and challenges your thesis to its fullest extent. Researching objectively also allows you to anticipate the other side's arguments and find its weaknesses, which you can then exploit when you draft your paper.

When you have identified your topic and before starting your research, develop a working list of the major points that you think you will make. In essence, this list of your major points functions as a road map for your research. Thoroughness is needed in developing search words to use when researching, in consulting the sources that may provide information, and in recording the information you obtain.

Developing search words is required in virtually all types of research and for virtually all research sources. Even computerized systems require you to develop queries based on words you think will be found in the needed documents.[4] Thus, your skill at choosing these words is central to your success as a researcher. Do not simply develop a few search words and be content when you find some documents. Developing search words is an attempt to determine how the editors of the research tool you are using have organized the documents. For example, if looking for cases discussing the implied warranty of habitability in rental units, anticipate all the possible places the editors may have located documents pertaining to that issue. Do not stop after looking up "landlord/tenant" or "implied warranty of habitability." Also look under "rental units," "landlord's duties," "unlawful detainer actions," "defenses" to those actions, "implied covenants," "leases," "public policy," "repair and offset," and so forth. Only by checking as many locations as possible can you be assured that you have completely mapped out the issue you are researching and found as many relevant documents as possible.

---

4. If you are starting from a known case or statute, it is possible to Shepardize that case or statute and begin your research that way. If you have a known case, it is possible to obtain the key number from that case, consult the digest, and locate additional cases that way. But if you do not have such a starting point, begin in the indexes of the research tools you consult, which requires developing search words to enter those indexes. Be particularly careful when researching on line; for a discussion of the limitations of on-line research, see Wren and Wren, *supra* note 3.

As you change research tools, continue to use all your search words with each tool and change them, if necessary. Editors organize material in different ways. Avoid overlooking information simply because you did not take the time to develop new search words when the ones you had did not achieve the results you desired. Instead, keep altering and refining your search words as you work through your research.

Consult as many sources as you can within your time constraints. These constraints may include deadlines and your client's ability or willingness to pay for extensive research. If you have a brief to write in one week on a state law issue, you may not be able to consult sources across the country to determine how all jurisdictions have handled the issue. But you can thoroughly consult the sources for your jurisdiction to find how your state's courts have answered the question.[5]

Be creative in considering possible sources for documents. Remember to use tools such as A.L.R. and law review articles. If you can find an A.L.R. annotation or a law review article on the topic you are researching, you will find that much preliminary research has already been completed. This will save you time and your client money. But never rely on these annotations or articles alone. Different factual scenarios or different jurisdictions may lead to different results. Also consider using loose-leafs, bar bulletins, legal history sources, non-legal sources, and other possibilities. Despite time constraints, use your time creatively to obtain information that will help your client. For example, when researching a personal injury case involving the question of whether an avalanche was an obvious and inherent danger in the sport of skiing, one student contacted the U.S. Department of Agriculture, which has regulations on determining when an avalanche is likely. This student was able to use this non-traditional source to make the argument that his client, the ski resort, had not been negligent.

Another aspect of being thorough is updating the documents you find. Because the law is constantly changing, you cannot assume that even recently decided cases are the latest word on a particular issue. Thoroughness here means Shepardizing your information, using computer-assisted research for up-to-the-minute information, and consulting loose-leafs, advance sheets, and pamphlets to ensure that the law you found is current.

Making a decision based on out-dated information is embarrassing. One attorney told us of drafting a decision for a state court of appeals and focusing on the main cases she had learned in law school. After two judges had signed it for release, the chief judge asked her why she had not discussed the U.S. Supreme Court case released the previous week in

---

5. This is one of the times that doing computer-assisted legal research may help you. For example, once you find the important cases in your state, you can take the most relevant digest key numbers and complete a national search using Westlaw's key number system. This search would take you quite some time to complete if you did it by hand searching through the American Digest system and thus you might eliminate it if time or money is a concern. But that same search would be much less time-consuming if performed through computer-assisted research.

her draft. She discovered that the Supreme Court had completely changed the analysis to resolve the issue. Both she and the court had to start over from scratch. And she was lucky; others have been fired for making similar errors.

Update your information periodically throughout the research project so you can alter your paper if anything changes during the process. As you locate useful sources, update them so you can determine whether they are still current. When you have completed the final draft and just before turning in your paper, update one final time to ensure that what you have written is still correct.

Finally, be thorough when taking notes. Keep a research log that records all the sources you checked and the results of that research. It is quite frustrating to have to redo research because you did not record all the information needed to use the points you discovered. Make sure to note all the information needed for your citations. Take notes as precisely as possible so you do not find yourself running back to the source repeatedly.[6] At the same time, avoid copying reams of material straight from the documents. Read the source before taking notes or photocopying so you only include those points important to your issue. Many people photocopy much, if not all, of their research so they have ready access to the actual documents and do not need to spend as much time taking detailed notes. If you proceed this way, mark relevant portions and write annotations on the copies. This helps you avoid having to reread the whole document while drafting.

Collect sufficient information to provide pinpoint citations in our final document. In the document, you should provide pinpoint citations for cases and articles whenever possible, so your reader can go directly to the relevant point and decide whether he or she agrees with your assessment of the document. Omit them only when a specific page reference is unnecessary because the whole document supports the point. A lack of specific page cites frustrates your reader, who does not want to leaf through a sixty-page case to find the language you noted.

Whether you photocopy your documents or take notes, develop a system for organizing the information and recording your research path. Most research papers require extensive research; keeping track of it is daunting. One option is to make a list of the issues and note every document related to each. Another is to keep a running list of all the documents you consulted and rearrange them into coherent groups when your research is complete. If you photocopy your documents, you may also find it helpful to keep a running list of relevant points with page numbers on the document's first page, so you can scan the first page and remember the document's value to your research. Or you may keep track of the different research tools you consult and list all the documents you found in each tool. Even if a source proved fruitless, note that you

---

6. Also be careful to note when you are quoting an author's language and when you are paraphrasing. Many students encounter academic disciplinary problems for plagiarism based on faulty or incomplete note-taking.

checked it and that it was not helpful because, when doing complex research, you can forget why or even whether you considered and rejected a source. Whatever system you use, keep it thorough and efficient.

Like your writing process, your research process is personal to you. There is no one way to do research correctly or efficiently, no one way that works for all people. Your goal is to develop a process that works for you and to use it effectively. Whether you use index cards, copies of documents, yellow pads filled with notes, or a computer file is not important. What is important is that you obtain all the information you need and organize it so you can retrieve it. Depending on your deadlines, you may do your research days or weeks before you sit down to write the paper. Your process must allow you to pick up your notes and use them even when you may have forgotten what you found when you did the research.

THE OUTLINE OR ROUGH DRAFT

Having completed the bulk of your research, you are ready to begin writing. Some people find that they go back and forth from writing to researching to fill in gaps and explore areas that only become clear during the writing process. This movement between writing and research and back again is usual. While you may need to do more research, do not let your desire to research prevent you from writing.

Writing an outline or rough draft involves discerning the points you need to make and providing the large-scale organization for your research paper. Many people choose to outline at this point rather than to write a rough draft because outlining allows them to focus on organization, rather than wording. Outlining requires choosing the ideas that will be the focus of your main sections and grouping them into a large-scale organization. Group and regroup your main points until you find the organization that most clearly leads the reader through your paper. As you do this, keep the wording of your thoughts on each point abbreviated. Save the development and refinement of your ideas for the drafts to come later.

This is the time to determine what points to make and how to organize them. If you catch yourself agonizing about some particular word choice or sentence structure, push yourself to move along, focusing on the big picture. One of the major benefits of doing several drafts of a research paper is knowing that you will return to your paper and can safely ignore small-scale concerns during this step.

This is not to say that if you are struck with ideas for developing some points and feel an urge to write some passages that you should not do so. To avoid losing valuable insights or helpful language, include them in your notes. But once the flash of brilliance has passed, and it will pass, return to developing your major points and sub-points. Resist shifting from organizing to writing in mid-stream. Otherwise, you will not achieve your goal for the outline, which is to develop logical, clear large-scale organization.

Some people find they are unable to organize material effectively using an outline alone. They simply are not comfortable with the less verbal, skeletal process that outlining requires. These people find it more useful to organize their thoughts as they write them. For example, they may write out a specific issue or sub-issue in detail, concentrating on all the concerns that come with writing. In this situation, there is nothing wrong with starting with a rough draft instead of an outline. In fact, if this process works best for you, you will only cause yourself frustration by trying to outline first. But do make sure to check your large-scale organization at some point in the overall process.

If you want to organize before drafting, you may want to try some of the following ideas first before resorting to writing a rough draft to see if they work better for you than traditional outlining. The following steps can help you organize successfully, even if you have never been able to master the more traditional method of organization, outlines.

Organization for Those Who Can't Outline[7]

1. Brainstorm.
2. Group your ideas.
3. Organize the groups.
4. Subdivide further, if needed.
5. Order the groups, points, and subpoints.
6. Write.
7. Check the organization.

In the brainstorming step, list all the points you want to make or might want to make, or just list everything you can think of. Do not worry about order, quality, or anything else at this stage except coming up with ideas. Allow enough time for this stage, so you do not cut it short.

Then, when grouping your ideas, read through all your listed points and see if they fall into any logical groups. Try to group the points several different ways before settling on one way. Often the organization that occurs to you first will be adequate, but not optimal. Alternatively, if your list of points includes six or fewer items, you may already have your logical groups. If so, fill in more supporting points on those items and then check to see if you are still satisfied with those groups.

When you move to the third step, organizing the groups, look at each group and decide which points are the major ones and which ones are subordinate, or supporting, points. At this stage, you may still find some errors in your groupings, but you can revise those groups as

---

7. For a fuller discussion of this concept, see Chapter 9 on Discussion Sections.

needed. You may also find that you have stated the same thing in two different ways, so that you can strike out redundant points.

Next subdivide further, if needed. Divide your arguments, and divide the subpoints made in those arguments. Check each item to make sure that it should not be subdivided further. Remember that you need to make only one point at a time. Even though all your points are inextricably interrelated, divide them into manageable portions for the reader.

After the groups, points, and subpoints are divided, decide how to order them. To determine this order, think about what will be logical to your reader, rather than what seems important to you. To help determine what is logical to the reader, ask yourself the following three questions.

- Is there some point that logically comes first?
- Is one point more significant than the others?
- Is one point stronger than the others?

For example, if your case involved a jurisdiction question, that question would logically come first because the court will not look to any other issues until it has determined that it is the court's job to decide those issues. In contrast, if your case involved clear-cut violations of freedom of speech, that issue would probably be more significant than technical violations of proper notice; you would probably start with the violation of the freedom of speech. The freedom of speech point might convince your reader that justice favors your side, and would probably make more compelling reading. The technical point would then provide a convenient peg upon which to hang the hat of justice. Sometimes the third question will provide you with a clear order, because one point is stronger than the others. For example, if your case involved a clear-cut violation of proper notice but also involved a potential-but-debatable violation of freedom of speech, you might start with the violation of proper notice. This order could enable you to establish some justification for your client's position before you presented more questionable justifications.

At this point, you will have all the information provided by a traditional outline, and you can rewrite it in outline format, if you wish, or go directly to writing your rough draft. If you had started trying to outline by writing a Roman numeral at the top of the page, you would have been expecting yourself to do all of these previous steps in your head, which is why trying to write a traditional outline is futile for many people.

After you have written your rough draft, recheck your organization. In fact, many successful writers write a rough draft first and then outline or go through the organization steps listed above. One way to check your organization is to read the first sentence of each paragraph throughout the document. This should give you a summary of the points of the paper, although it will not document the proof of those points.[8]

We suggest trying these ideas before turning to a rough draft, not because outlining is inherently preferable to writing a rough draft, because it is not. But you need to generate ideas and determine large-scale organization at this step. This involves thrashing through what you are saying at the large-scale level. You cannot work at this level if you are continuously drawn to small-scale concerns. If you try to write without adequately organizing your points, "you find yourself trying to do three things at once: with every detail that presents itself to your mind, you must decide (1) whether or not to include it, (2) if so, how and where to fit it in, and (3) how fully to develop it."[9]

You should organize your paper for your reader's ease, not for your own. Will your reader need a background section in order to understand your paper, or does he or she already know the background and want you to proceed to the focus of the paper? Will your reader be able to understand why you are organizing the paper the way you are or will he or she need to be told the importance of the organization? Will your reader need a thorough overview before you get into the details of the paper or does he or she know where your paper is headed so that a detailed overview is less important?[10] Answer these questions before writing a complete draft of your paper.

THE COMPLETE DRAFT

When writing the complete draft, add the content that supports your organization. This step focuses on letting your creativity flow. Do not rein yourself in or rewrite. Separate this step from the rewriting, revising, and polishing steps that come later. Many people find that writing footnotes or even correcting their spelling interrupts the creative flow and deflects their energy away from the task at hand. "The most common mistake most writers make, one that costs them hours and hours, is to rewrite and write simultaneously. This forces the id of creative thought to work simultaneously with the super-ego of correction, an impossible and insufferable pairing."[11]

Try to write out an entire draft of your paper. What you are attempting to do in this step is to get the thoughts in your head onto paper or into the computer. You have done the research, the brainstorming, and the organizing that are essential preliminary steps to writing. Now write.

Writing a complete draft does not require starting at the first point on your outline and going in linear fashion through each and every subpoint all the way to the end. Many writers find that creative thought

8. Ray and Ramsfield, *supra* note 3, at 234–36.

9. Weihofen, *Legal Writing Style* 139 (2d ed. 1980).

10. We believe, however, that an overview improves most long papers. Remember, you are not writing a mystery or suspense novel; leaving your reader in the dark is not part of your job.

11. Ray and Ramsfield, *supra* note 3, at 317–19.

does not progress in such a nicely structured manner. Do not force your creativity into straight lines or rigid boxes. Instead, allow yourself to write whatever portion of your paper will come at any given point. Do not worry that you will lose your organization and find yourself with a confused mess of ideas. You can always retrieve your organization after you have written the draft.

Otherwise, you may find yourself faced with writer's block. This occurs when you find your creative energy dissipated and you cannot make yourself continue to write. Few things are more frustrating, especially when you have deadlines to meet. One effective way to avoid writer's block is to allow yourself to write what seems easiest. If you are clear about a paragraph or sub-section that will come in the middle of your paper, start your draft with that paragraph or sub-section. Writing often helps you continue to write. You can then move either to the points that logically precede it or follow from it.

Keep writing until all of your thoughts are written out. This is a rough draft; it does not need full documentation or even coherent language but it does need to be completed. Complete this step before starting to rewrite. Finishing the rough draft allows you to see how your thoughts play out. Your draft may be a fraction of the size of the finished paper, but that is not important. You will fill in the documentation, work on the small-scale organization, and add the footnotes later. Or your draft may be much longer than the finished paper, but that is not important either. You will shorten it later as you tighten organization, revise for conciseness, and omit redundancy. What is important is working through all your ideas as completely as possible before going back and rewriting them.

THE GOOD DRAFT

This draft involves moving your energies from the creative forces you just employed to the critical forces you now need. You are moving from being satisfied with getting your thoughts on paper to being concerned with how effectively you communicate your thoughts.

The best way to make this shift from the creative to the critical is to allow the paper to sit for a while before starting this step. Allowing it to sit gives you some perspective on the ideas you have developed and expressed so you are better able to critique them. Always be aware of your ability and willingness to critique your own work. If critiquing comes easily, you will find that you can begin this next step after a short period of time. If critiquing is difficult, you will need more time to distance yourself from the initial draft. Distance allows you to be less impressed with what you already have written and more concerned with taking what often amounts to a rambling, disorganized mess and moving it towards a concise, organized research paper.

Many lawyers believe they do not have the time to gain distance from their drafts due to short deadlines. But often they can do something else between drafts, to clear the head and regain focus. For example, do one or two other tasks between drafts. Complete some pressing correspondence, make a phone call, discuss a different matter with your staff or colleagues, or eat lunch. Try to leave the computer or set aside the writing pad to walk around the block or around the office.

The steps that need to be taken in rewriting will tax your brain and your humor. At this step, revise the draft, concentrating on organization and thoroughness. Take your completed draft, and fit it into your initial organization. Then change the organization if it no longer seems to be the most appropriate; it is too early in the process to be overly attached to that original organization. Rearrange your sections so they logically lead the reader from your introduction to your conclusion and build on the preceding section to reach a clearly understandable conclusion. In addition, write introductory and conclusory paragraphs for your major sections and add clear transitions from point to point and from paragraph to paragraph.

Now focus on thoroughness, filling any gaps. Determine whether any material that would help your reader has been excluded. Often, you may find that you understand where you are headed because you have done all the research, but your reader will probably not have this same understanding. At this stage, you should be nearing the point when all the substance is included.

Concentrate on content, ideas, and organization, making sure that all the components of your paper are included and logically placed.[12] To determine whether you have completed this rewriting stage or need to spend more time here, review the following questions.

CHECKLIST FOR REWRITING

1. Content and ideas
   - Is the law right?
   - Have I included all the relevant issues?
   - Have I included all the relevant research?
   - Have I updated all the research?
   - Have I included all the necessary background information?
   - Have I eliminated those points that I found while doing my research but did not add to the document?

2. Large-scale organization
   - Do I have a logical organization?
   - Have I provided an overview so that the reader can understand how my paper progresses from introduction to conclusion?
   - Have I put threshold issues first?

---

12. *Id.* at 317–19.

- Have I given the answer first and then the explanation?
- If writing persuasively, have I organized the issues in the most persuasive order, putting the strongest first, the second strongest last, and the weakest in the middle, unless logical organization precludes doing this?
- Can any legal reader follow my logic?
- Can the intended reader follow my logic?
- Have I used positions of emphasis well?

When you are satisfied with your answers to these questions, move to the small-scale steps of revising your paper. Making this shift can be difficult. You may find it helpful at this point to step away from your draft again. Many attorneys believe they are finished with the project once their organization is logical and their content is complete. However, this is a major reason why the documents seen most often in the legal arena tend to be poorly written. To attain excellence, you cannot stop here.

What you may find helpful at this stage is doing across-the-board checks, similar to those you did while drafting contracts.[13] These checks allow you to focus on correcting one or two things at a time, rather than trying to do too much in one reading. This also allows you to decide which concerns are most important to your research paper and to focus on these first. Then, if time runs short, you can sacrifice those steps that can be eliminated with less cost to the quality of your paper.

The following list is an example of things to consider when revising. They are prioritized in the list. For example, no amount of readability will compensate for inaccurate information, so check for accuracy first. [14]

CHECKLIST FOR REVISING

1. Accuracy
   - Is the content accurately stated? Could any points be misinterpreted because of ambiguity?
   - Are irrelevant facts or other irrelevant information excluded?
   - Are terms of art used correctly?
   - Are key terms used correctly?
   - Are paraphrases accurate?
   - Are names of parties and their status correct?
   - Are the citations accurate? Are pinpoint cites used for specific propositions, rules, holdings, quotes? Are case names spelled accurately? Are page numbers and years accurate?

---

13. See Chapter 5 on Contracts.

14. Ray and Ramsfield, *supra* note 3, at 315–17.

2. Small–scale Organization

- Are paragraphs internally logical?
- Are there topic sentences that give the overall message of each of the paragraphs, usually at the beginning of the paragraphs?
- Are there clear and precise transitions between paragraphs?
- Are there strong transitions between sentences?

3. Readability

- Are subjects and verbs close together?
- Is there more active voice than passive voice?
- Are sentences free of nominalizations?
- Are unnecessary modifiers eliminated, such as "clearly" and "obviously"?
- Are sentences not overly long?
- Are lists clearly structured?
- Are unnecessary prepositional phrases eliminated?
- Is the text generally concise?

4. Style

- Is style consistently objective or persuasive, depending upon the purpose of the text?
- Is the tone and level of formality appropriate and consistent?

Now show your paper to someone else for review. At this point, you will have taken it about as far as you can without outside assistance. Asking for outside assistance can be scary because the reviewer may think you still have significant work to do before reaching the excellence you desire. Nevertheless, you are trying to reach that goal and this assistance will help you proceed toward it. Excellent writing does not come easy. But it does come to those who persist and have some understanding of the process. You have the choice to reject the criticism at any point. If you believe your reviewer's suggestions will cause problems, do not feel compelled to incorporate them. Feel free to ask for, consider, and then reject some of the criticism you receive. Considering the criticism, whether or not you accept it, allows you to see the paper anew.

THE FINAL DRAFT

Having completely reviewed your paper, revised it, and received outside assistance to improve it, now do the final draft. Unless you have unrelenting time pressures, do not skip this step, even though many of your classmates or colleagues will do so. At this point, your paper is probably quite good. You have taken it through successive steps and worked toward making it excellent. Do not stop just short of excellence, even though you may believe that your paper is as good or better than anything you have written before. Take it through the final step to achieve the excellence that is possible.

This polishing involves removing errors, unclear phrases, and awkward passages. Correct the details that differentiate a good paper from an excellent one. Focus on what you know about yourself as a writer. Develop a checklist to guide you. If spelling is a problem for you, check your spelling throughout. If you overuse passive voice, read through the draft checking each verb and change it as needed.

You do not need to spend a great deal of time doing this. Even an hour or two will make a difference. Remember that the legal reader is focused on details. As a result, when the details of your paper help your reader rather than distract that reader, you will communicate much more effectively.

Having taken your paper through each of these steps, you will now be as sure as possible that you have written your best paper. You can be comfortable in knowing that you have strived for excellence and that you have achieved it.

BIBLIOGRAPHY

Bereiter, Carl, and Marlene Scardamalia, *The Psychology of Written Composition*. Hillsdale, NJ: Lawrence Erlbaum Associates, 1987.

Cox, Barbara J. and Mary Barnard Ray, *Getting Dorothy Out of Kansas: The Importance of an Advanced Component to Legal Writing Programs*, 40 J.Legal Ed. 351 (1990).

Fajans, Elizabeth and Mary R. Falk, *Scholarly Writing for Law Students*. St. Paul: West Group, 2d ed. 2000.

Kunz, Christina L., Deborah A. Schmedemann, Matthew P. Downs, and Ann L. Bateson, *The Process of Legal Research: Successful Strategies*. Gaithersburg, MD: Aspen Law and Business, 5th ed. 2000.

Mersky, Roy M. and Donald J. Dunn, *Fundamentals of Legal Research*. New York: Foundation Press, 8th ed. 2002.

Ray, Mary Barnard, and Jill J. Ramsfield, *Getting It Right and Getting It Written*. St. Paul: West Group, 3d ed. 2000.

Shapo, Helene S., Marilyn R. Walter and Elizabeth Fajans, *Writing and Analysis in the Law*. Westbury, NY: The Foundation Press, Inc., 4th ed. 1999.

Statsky, William P., *Legal Research and Writing: Some Starting Points*. St. Paul: West Group, 4th ed. 1993.

Statsky, William P., and R. John Wernet, Jr., *Case Analysis and Fundamentals of Legal Writing*. St. Paul: West Group, 4th ed. 1995.

Weihoffen, Henry, *Legal Writing Style*. St. Paul: West Group, 2d ed. 1980.

Wren, Christopher G., and Jill Robinson Wren, *The Legal Research Manual: A Game Plan for Legal Research and Analysis*. Madison, WI: Legal Education Pub., 2d ed. 1999.

Index

References are to Pages

†